Virgin Whore

Virgin Whore

Emma Maggie Solberg

Cornell University Press
Ithaca and London

First published 2018 by Cornell University Press

Printed in the United States of America

ISBN 978-1-5017-3033-7 (cloth)
ISBN 978-1-5017-3035-1 (epub/mobi)
ISBN 978-1-5017-3034-4 (pdf)

Librarians: A CIP catalog record for this book is available
from the Library of Congress.

For my mother, who is gone,
and my daughter, who just arrived

Contents

Acknowledgments

First, thanks to John Parker, my *Doktorvater*, for his incisive feedback on so many drafts of this book. No one could ask for a better adviser. My mother always told me to find a better player to practice with or I would never improve. John is that better player, and he has improved my game inestimably. Without him, I would never have found my voice as a medievalist. Before we met, I had no idea that we were allowed to be so wicked.

Thanks to Bruce Holsinger, who, with John, codirected the first draft of this project. Thanks especially for rejecting the first draft of my prospectus and for sending me back to the drawing board with the excellent advice that one should always begin with a close reading.

Thanks to the English Department of the University of Virginia, especially to Elizabeth Fowler, who gave such sage counsel as my third reader, and to Tony Spearing, whose voice I will always hear in my head as the sound of Middle English.

Thanks to Deborah McGrady for setting me straight about Joan of Arc, and for introducing me to Noah Guynn, to whom my heartfelt thanks are also due.

Thanks to the members of the University of Virginia Interdisciplinary Graduate Medieval Colloquium—especially those who rode with me to Kalamazoo in that van: Paul Broyles, Rachel Geer, Gabe Haley, Lise Leet, Ryan McDermott, Will Rhodes, Christine Schott, Chelsea Skalak, Zach Stone, Beth Sutherland, Victoria Valdez, and Ellie Voss. Thanks to the writing group that workshopped the first draft of what is now my final chapter, and especially to Adriana Streifer. Thanks also to Rebecca Strauss for all her help, and for being ever on the lookout for pop-culture references to the Virgin.

Thanks to my colleagues at Bowdoin College, and especially to the English Department (to Aviva Briefel for her daily counsel; to Belinda Kong and Hilary Thompson for asking good questions about unicorns; and to Tess Chakkalakal, Dave Collings, and Marilyn Reizbaum for pressing my thinking on the second chapter) and to the members of the medieval and early modern studies area group who workshopped an earlier draft of the first chapter (Dallas Denery, Ann Kibbie, Aaron Kitch, and Arielle Saiber). Thanks to my invaluable writing group: Margaret Boyle, Sakura Christmas, Jack Gieseking, Barbara Elias Klenner, Samia Rahimtoola, Meghan Roberts, and Peggy Wang. Thanks to Crystal Hall for helping me with Italian, and Jens Elias Klenner for helping me with German. Thanks to all my students, especially Katherine Churchill and Maria Solis Kennedy. And thanks so much to the librarians at the Hawthorne-Longfellow Library, without whom I could not have gotten anything done.

Thanks to my tutors at Saint Hilda's College, who got me interested in the Middle Ages in the first place: Professor Sally Mapstone and Professor Margaret Kean.

Thanks to the colleagues and mentors in the field of early English drama studies who clarified my thinking on these matters at conferences, seminars, and colloquiums—including the International Congress on Medieval Studies at Kalamazoo, the Shakespeare Association of America, the Renaissance Society of America, the Medieval Academy of America, the Harvard Medieval Colloquium, and the Meeting of Medievalists at the University of Southern California. Thanks in particular to Kathy Ashley, Sarah Brazil, Katie Brokaw, Theresa Coletti, Helen Cushman, Carolyn Dinshaw,

Gail McMurray Gibson, Blake Gutt, Carissa Harris, Emma Lipton, Jeanette Patterson, Masha Raskolnikov, Nicole Rice, Matt Sergi, James Simpson, Alicia Spencer-Hall, Claire Waters, and Nicholas Watson. Thanks also to Mary Dzon, Pamela Sheingorn, and Anne Williams for their generous and helpful answers to my e-mail inquiries.

Thanks to the Rare Book School at the University of Virginia; the Folger Shakespeare Library in Washington, DC; the Huntington Library in California; the Fletcher Family Fund; and Bowdoin College for their generous support.

Thanks to my editor, Mahinder Kingra, for all his help and for his faith in this book.

And, finally, thanks to my family—to Mette, Lisbeth, and Lars; to my brother, father, and sister; to my daughter, whose birth has informed so much of the process of writing this book; and, above all, to my husband, Morten, who talked through every sentence with me on long walks all over the world—in Colombo and Yau Ma Tei, Søllerød and Montepulciano, Charlottesville and Brunswick.

Virgin Whore

Introduction

When did the Virgin Mary become so chaste and so fragile?[1] At the turn of the twenty-first century, the Brooklyn Museum of Art exhibited the British Nigerian artist Chris Ofili's painting of a black Madonna ornamented (or "splattered," as the *Daily News* had it) with elephant feces and cutouts of female genitalia clipped from pornographic magazines.[2] Ofili's painting so offended Mayor Rudy Giuliani, a devout Catholic, that he attempted to defund and evict the Brooklyn Museum of Art.[3] Giuliani accused Ofili of having "attacked," "desecrated," and—most tellingly—"defiled" the Madonna.[4] The verb *defile* (which descends from the Latin *fullāre*, meaning "to trample," and from the Old English *fúl*, meaning "foul" or "dirty") suggests the acts of polluting, besmirching, breaking, violating, and deflowering—especially when used in reference to a virgin, or, as in this case, *the* Virgin.[5] To Giuliani's mind, it seems, Ofili's painting registered as a sexual assault. Ofili touched the Virgin's image with pitch, and so she was defiled. Taking this notion further, Giuliani also accused the Brooklyn Museum of having "desecrate[d] the most personal and deeply held views of the people in society," as if faith too were a kind of fragile innocence—once lost, lost forever.[6] According to Giuliani, Ofili and the Brooklyn Museum had deflowered the until-then unblemished purity of the Virgin and so too the innocence of the faithful.[7]

And yet despite this rhetoric of never-before, Ofili was hardly the first to deflower the Virgin, even within recent memory. In 1948, the Italian director Roberto Rossellini released *Il miracolo*, a film starring Anna Magnani (La Lupa, "the she-wolf") as a delusional and destitute innocent whose rape, pregnancy, and persecution mirror the narrative of the virgin birth. When *Il miracolo* premiered in the United States, the Catholic Legion of Decency picketed cinemas (signs read, "This Film Is an Insult to Every Decent Woman and Her Mother"), lobbying for censorship.[8] The Reverend Patrick J. Masterson of the Legion complained that the film had "defamed" the Virgin.[9] "Satan alone," Francis Cardinal Spellman agreed, "would dare make such perversion."[10] Again, in 1998, when the British artist Tania Kovats's *Virgin in a Condom* toured Australia and New Zealand, concerned citizens protested that the encased statuette "libeled" Mary, an offense for which it was protested, attacked, and, in one case, kidnapped.[11] And in 2012, when Pussy Riot sang an obscene song to the Madonna (the chorus: "Shit, shit, the Lord's shit!") from the pulpit of Moscow's Cathedral of Christ the Savior, they were arrested and condemned for the crime, in the judge's words, of "hooliganism motivated by religious hatred."[12]

In each case, Mary's champions claimed that the touch of filth (whether feces, obscenity, contraception, or pornography) had defiled the chastity of the Virgin. Even the opposition agreed with that interpretation—at least with its terms, if not with its values. Across a spectrum of media outlets, Ofili's supporters lauded the artist as an iconoclastic genius whose "new way of seeing old subjects" boldly broke with history and defied tradition.[13] Secular progressives can also see faith as a kind of innocence—like a child's belief in Santa Claus, or like maidenhead—and modernity as its necessary loss. The modern adult, according to this way of thinking, must put aside childish things: virginity, faith, and Mary. In this sense, detractors and defenders alike understood the artist and the museum as the vanguards of the future and Mary and Giuliani as the bulwarks of the past. Like their opponents, Ofili's allies assumed the Madonna's innocence and fragility, thereby reducing her to the vulnerabilities of her epithet. Once torn, the hymen does not grow back.[14] Transferring the qualities of virginity to the Virgin, activists on both sides of the controversy concurred that Ofili had broken the membrane of innocence protecting Mary, Christianity, and tradition from the disenchantment of the present—a violation seen by some as progressive and others as destructive, by some as valiant and others as villainous.[15]

And yet despite this consensus between enemies, the Virgin's vulnerability is hardly fragile, but rather uncannily resilient. History teaches us that although Mary is often deflowered, she remains eternally untouched, always newly ready for the next inevitable attack. Contrary to the pull of empiricist and fundamentalist habits of modern thought, Mary's purity functions in accordance with the laws of magic and metaphor. Unlike a hymen, the construct of her virginity cannot be destroyed. The Virgin Mother, paradoxically, is both innocent and experienced. Her miraculous impenetrability, although so often proved, seems strangely easy to forget. There are those who register every ultimately impotent attack against her integrity as an unprecedented shock and irreparable loss. Not, however, the avant-garde provocateurs—such as Ofili, Rossellini, Kovats, and Pussy Riot—who launched those attacks. Their memories are longer.

Ofili, who was raised Catholic, defended his work on the grounds not of freedom of expression but rather of religious tradition, describing his painting as "merely a hip hop version" of the sacred and yet also "sexually charged" representations of the Madonna at which he had gazed as an altar boy during Mass and as a student of art history in the National Gallery.[16] Likewise, Rossellini (also raised Catholic)—and, for that matter, the Vatican—interpreted *Il miracolo* not as a blasphemous parody but rather as an updated Miracle of the Virgin, a devotional meditation on God's scandalously promiscuous mercy.[17] Likewise, Kovats (also raised Catholic) defended *Virgin in a Condom* as the culmination of her lifelong contemplation of the history of Mariology.[18] Likewise, Pussy Riot represented their political protest not as an attack *against* but rather as a prayer of supplication *to* the Virgin. "Mother of God," they begged, "put Putin away!"[19] Although these artists were taken for iconoclasts, they all identified themselves as iconographers.

These provocateurs did not offend against tradition by being too modern but rather offended against modernity by being too medieval.[20] Strangely, what looks like avant-garde iconoclasm also strikingly resembles the devotional practices of the late medieval cult of the Madonna. Ofili's canvas radiates gold and ultramarine, the deluxe blue made from imported cobalt or lapis lazuli and reserved for the late medieval robes of the Virgin.[21] Like medieval craftsmen, Ofili layers translucent pigments over a wash of gold to create a shimmering effect. And just as medieval artists punched geometric patterns into burnished gilt to create stippled crystalline refractions circling the heads of saints, Ofili layers various golden textures (swirls of paint, drips of glitter, and raised, sequin-like dots) to make Mary's resplendent halo. And yet despite all this radiance, Ofili's critics emphasized and exaggerated his use of black and brown. The polemic written about the painting—reacting against the blackness of Ofili's Madonna as much as against his use of elephant dung—gave the impression that the canvas oozed fecal darkness.

Ofili challenged the ideal of the lily-white and hygienically immaculate Virgin. And yet Mary was not always and is not always so vanilla. From the twelfth through the fifteenth century, European artists habitually represented the Virgin as black—a tradition that continues in the contemporary cult of Our Lady of Guadalupe.[22] In fact, many of medieval England's most visited shrines of Our Lady—including Our Lady of Willesden, Our Lady of Crome, and Our Lady of Muswell—housed statues of Mary that were said to be black.[23] Neither was the Virgin always so inimical to excrement. According to the fourteenth-century *Prickynge of Love* (a Middle English translation of the *Stimulus amoris*), the Madonna handled the filth of human sin as a mother handles the feces of her infant: with love and patience.[24] Mankind may "stynke foule," but Mary "farist with us as a modir with hir owne childe that kisseth hym with her mowthe & with hir handis makith clene his taylende"—she deals with us as a mother with her own child, kissing him with her mouth and with her hands making clean his tail end.[25] To medieval theologians, Mary's earthiness proved (in the words of the twelfth-century Benedictine Odo of Tournai) that "God created all things good," including "viscera and excrement."[26] But to the early modern reformers, her earthiness stank. Roger Hutchinson compared the rankness of Mary's flesh (and her womb) to the "stinking scents" of "carrion and filthy jakes," *jakes* being an early modern term for "toilet."[27] Since then, the Virgin may have been cleaned up and bleached white in the Anglo-American imagination, but Ofili's Madonna remains old-fashioned.

Even the pornographic clippings of buttocks framing labia that surround Ofili's Madonna resonate with the theology and iconography of late medieval Mariology. From a distance, these heart-shaped cutouts resemble the choirs of naked, chubby putti that attend the Virgin. As the art critic Jerry Saltz wrote, "It's only when you get close to the painting that these flickering cherubs turn rude." Ofili's use of genitals in his representation of the Mother of God struck Saltz—and many others—as "irredeemable."[28] Yet as Lady Reason explains in the fourteenth-century *Roman de la Rose*, God made the noble genitals (*les nobles choses*) with his own hands in paradise; they are not shameful, sinful, or unpleasant.[29] Proving this point, the Son of God deigned to descend into Mary's reproductive system, live there for nine months like a monk in a cell, and enter the world through the vaginal gates of her body.[30] According to one interpretive tradition, he endured this awful ordeal just as he endured his ignominious Crucifixion.[31] Yet according to the interpretation that held sway over Christendom from the twelfth through the early sixteenth century, Jesus relished this fleshly intimacy with his bride and mother, prizing it (as one fourteenth-century devotional lyric had it) "above all that was ever His."[32]

It is no wonder, then, that vaginal imagery—split figs and pomegranates, red roses and dripping honeycombs, passageways and aqueducts—ornaments so many late medieval representations of the Virgin.[33] Historians have called this phenomenon by many names: "genital theology," "theological gynecology," "gynotheology."[34] Iconographers depicted Mary's body as a *hortus conclusus deliciarum*, an intimately enclosed garden of delights, the Trinity's playpen.[35] Vermillion, vulva-shaped mandorla encased the medieval Virgin, as they do Our Lady of Guadalupe today.[36] More explicit still are the strange (or rather, strange to us) metallic souvenir badges recently excavated from medieval pilgrimage sites that depict the Virgin as an ambulant, crowned vulva worshiped by walking phalluses with tiny, wagging tails.[37] In this context, Ofili's *Holy Virgin Mary* seems less like a break with the past and more like a continuation of old, if half-forgotten, traditions.

The controversy surrounding Ofili's representation of the Madonna—and Rossellini's, Kovat's, and Pussy Riot's—confused the categories of old and new, making and breaking, iconography and iconoclasm. In perhaps the most illuminating example of these apparent contradictions, one Dennis Heiner—a retired English teacher from Murray Hill and a devout Catholic—desecrated an image of the Virgin in order to protest the desecration of the image of the Virgin. Deeply offended by Ofili's *Holy Virgin Mary*, Heiner resolved to rescue the Madonna from her shame before Christmas (in other words, before her due date).[38] In the December of 1999, he smuggled a bottle of white paint into the Brooklyn Museum and faked a heart attack in order to draw the guard away from his post, at which moment—"with an amazing burst of speed," as a museum spokesperson reported—he darted behind the plexiglass shield protecting the painting and smeared white all over the canvas.[39]

Heiner's wife later explained to reporters that her husband had been "trying to clean the painting."[40] Her phrasing suggests that Heiner did not consider the image itself (or rather herself) to be the problem, but rather some pollution besmirching its surface—some smear that could be wiped off. Yet, surprisingly, Heiner did not target the most flagrant pornographic cutouts located in the margins of the frame, nor any of the three most conspicuous lumps of dung. Instead, he reached for the very focal center—the face of the Virgin. This is not to say that Heiner could have had no reason to attack Mary's face: Ofili has drawn her lips as red labia, layered a palimpsest of clippings of buttocks underneath her cartoonish features, and fixed a tiny ball of dung dotted with two pinpricks of white paint on the pupil of her left eye. Yet these are subtleties, not easy to spot. In his haste, Heiner probably registered only the quickest of impressions: an abstract African face with strange, staring eyes. In a grainy black-and-white photograph captured by one of the museum's security cameras, Heiner (who wore a suit and tie for the occasion) is seen with his right hand reaching above his head, having just smeared the first stroke of white across Mary's eyes—hiding her from us, her from herself, and us from her. An inoffensive image of the Virgin, it seems, is blank.

The iconoclasts of the Protestant Reformation certainly thought so. Sixteenth-century reformers accused the medieval Catholic Church of having turned the chaste, silent, and obedient Mary of the Gospels into a whorish idol—specifically the Whore of Babylon prophesied by the book of Revelation.[41] Iconoclasts made it their mission to rehabilitate this fallen woman. They stripped her of her prayers and powers, burned her statues to ash, and whitewashed her image from the walls of churches.[42] Their chastisement of the Virgin checked the Catholic Church, which effectively capitulated to Protestant critique by reining in and regulating the excesses of the late medieval cult of the Madonna.[43] Strange things had flourished in the autumn of the Middle Ages (to borrow Johan Huizinga's lovely phrase), after Christianity's conquest of Europe but just before its Reformation—things that shocked and disturbed those in the future who looked backward: monstrous obscenities in the margins of manuscripts and cathedrals; corrupt bureaucracies binding sinners on earth to the dead in purgatory and saints in heaven; rampant heterodoxies mingling piety and paganism.[44] Perhaps strangest of all was the fifteenth century's unprecedented and unmatched devotion to the Virgin, who was hailed as the Queen of Heaven, Mother of Mercy, Empress of Hell, Savioress of Mankind, and Recreatrix of the Universe.[45] Reformers had their own name for this devotion: "Mariolatry," the idolatrous elevation of an upstart fertility goddess over the one true God of the Bible.[46]

The protestations of Catholic apologists notwithstanding, this accusation was not unfounded.[47] During the late Middle Ages, the Church tolerated the eccentricities of Mariology with remarkable leniency. In fact, those positioned to police were as guilty as anyone else. Adoration of the Madonna cut across all three estates. Popes, princes, and peasants all preferred to offer their prayers through the merciful Mediatrix rather than directly to God.[48] Minstrels in taverns, troubadours in castles, and Scholastics in their ivory towers venerated Mary's genitals and breasts as devotedly as they did Christ's wounds—if not more.[49] Whereas early modern reformers worshiped a highly jealous deity who reigned over the universe alone, the unreformed Christians of the late Middle Ages believed that the besotted Trinity could not bear to cross their beloved bride and mother, the fourth member of the heavenly "Quaternity" and, in many ways, *omnium potentissima*—the most powerful of all.[50] Medieval theologians, mystics, and artists preached that Mary had seduced God with her sexual charisma, bewitched his better judgment, and remade both the Word and the entire universe in her irresistibly attractive human image.[51] Under her reign, they promised, the strict old rules no longer applied. If God refused to listen, Mary would answer. If he said no, she would say yes. If he condemned, she would forgive. To reformers, this sounded like blasphemy, idolatry, paganism, and devil worship.[52] But before the Reformation, Mary's triumph over the Trinity was taken, by and large, as extraordinarily good news.

But not by all. A certain strain of Christianity (upright, fastidious, prim) has never had any patience for this nonsense—not now and not then. Neither Jerome, nor Thomas Aquinas, nor Jean Gerson could stomach the embarrassing exaggerations and excesses of the medieval cult of the Virgin. (I echo the language of their rather condescendingly tolerant irritation: Mary inspires "excess," "exaggeration," "eccentricity," "levity," "deviancy," and "indiscretion," almost never heresy.)[53] Even at the very zenith of her cult in the High and late Middle Ages, the Queen of Heaven provoked both enthusiasm and embarrassment, sometimes from the same person. While Bernard of Clair-vaux lavished unprecedentedly heady lyricism on Mary's breasts, he also felt the need to sharply chastise those who, as he saw it, let their love of the Madonna carry them beyond the bounds of reason and decorum.[54] And yet despite this resistance, Mary conquered Bernard in the end. Long after his death, a legend arose that Bernard had begged Mary to nurse him like the infant Christ.[55] Late medieval images of this scene tend to depict this grave doctor in a state of helpless ecstasy on his knees before the Virgin, who squirts a stream of milk into his eager mouth.

So much for restraint. Before the Reformation, protestations against Mary's ever-expanding power tended to flounder. When staunchly Christo-centric Dominicans called on the Vatican to discipline the Franciscans whose Mariology transgressed the limits of orthodoxy, the pope refused to act.[56] When Lollardish townspeople complained that their neighbors idolized rather than venerated images of the Virgin, the Inquisition brought in the accusers, and not the accused, for questioning.[57] Heretics burned at the stake for refusing to recant their imputations against, among other things, the cult of Mary. Until the Reformation, her power proved hard to check.

Nowhere more so than in England—"the dower of the Virgin," as it was called—the site of perhaps the most visited Marian pilgrimage destination in late medieval Europe, the shrine of Our Lady of Walsingham in East Anglia, "England's Nazareth."[58] As Gail McMurray Gibson writes, "The Marian fervor that we associate today with Italy or Spain . . . was in the Middle Ages of English renown."[59] It was theologians working in the British Isles (most notably Anselm of Canterbury, Eadmer of Canterbury, Aelred of Rievaulx, Duns Scotus, and William of Ware) who constructed and defended the new theory of the Immaculate Conception of the Virgin, one of the most controversial theological innovations of the late Middle Ages.[60] Englishmen's infatuation with the Madonna provoked Peter of Celle to wonder from his cloister in France whether the soggy British climate had not addled their wits: "Insula enim est circumfusa aqua, unde hujus elementi propria qualitate ejus incolae non immerito afficiuntur, et nimia mobilitate in tenuissimas et subtiles phantasias frequenter transferuntur, somnia sua visionibus comparantes, ne dicam praeferentes. Et quae culpa naturae, si talis est natura terrae?" (England is an island surrounded by water, hence her inhabitants are understandably affected by the property of this element and are often led to odd and unfounded fancies, comparing their dreams with visions. And how can they be blamed for this, if this is the nature of their country?)[61] Here, Peter describes England as a feminine landmass, governed by sluggish water and drossy earth rather than by the masculine elements of air and fire. Suffering from disordered humors, the island's humid brain takes phantasms rising from its womb for truth. Hence, Peter argues, England's light-headed, light-hearted mania for Mary—*Anglica levitas*.

This Madonna mania expressed itself in outpourings of artistry.[62] Appropriately, gifts given to Mary tended to imitate the gifts of Mary herself. When she seduced God with her beauty and incarnated Jesus in her flesh, it was believed, the Virgin had redeemed humanity's capacity for invention.[63] Whereas the sweaty labors of Adam and Eve perpetuated the curse of original sin, Mary's flawless masterpiece saved mankind. In accomplishing this sacred work, she used only the most human tools: her beauty, uterus, and breast milk—her body, in short.[64] Honoring her methods, makers felt it right to celebrate Mary with the handmade fruits of their crafts, however humble, carnal, undignified, or even scandalous.

Medieval Miracles of the Virgin emphasize Mary's love of artists, from cloistered composers of heavenly music to itinerant acrobats juggling in the streets.[65] In an infinite regress on the walls of Winchester Cathedral's Lady Chapel, a painter has painted an image of Mary saving a painter who is painting an image of Mary.[66] Troubadours sang songs about the Virgin favoring troubadours who sang songs about the Virgin.[67] In the enchanting story of *Le jongleur de Notre Dame*, an illiterate jongleur (meaning a minstrel, juggler, or jester) better pleases the Virgin by performing joyful tricks and acrobatic tumbles naked than an abbey of monks in full regalia with their solemn liturgy.[68] Demonstrating her preference, a statue of Mary bends down from her pedestal to wipe the sweat from his brow, much to the astonishment of the learned brethren who had gathered to mock his foolish antics. The Virgin, apparently, deeply respected a good show—and a good laugh.

Her interest in comedy might even be called professional. In the *divina commedia* of medieval Catholicism, Mary plays the part of the trickster, outfoxing both Satan and God the Father at every turn.[69] According to an ancient exegetical tradition, Jesus and Mary performed the comedy of the virgin birth in order to distract the devil from the stealth operation of the Harrowing of Hell.[70] In medieval adaptations of this farce, Mary takes on the fabliau role of the crafty adulteress and Joseph the grouchy old cuckold duped by her wit.[71] For these reasons, jugglers, jesters, buffoons, and players of all stripes laid special claim to Mary's favor. As Carol Symes has demonstrated, the jongleurs of Arras—the pioneers of medieval vernacular drama—made this claim official.[72] According to their origin myth, the Virgin had appeared to their founding fathers, like Gabriel to the shepherds, and bestowed on them ("you who live by jest and acting") a contract of eternal partnership.[73]

But, then, Mary has always been funny. We all know that mothers have a special ability to embarrass their children. As the Theotokos, the Mother of God (and God's only mother among the three desert monotheisms), Mary has been making Christianity look silly since the very beginning.[74] In the Gospels, anonymous hecklers in the crowd mock Christ with innuendos about the suspicious circumstances of his birth.[75] Exacerbating this problem, Mary follows the Messiah around, reminding everyone that the Son of God also had an all-too-human parent. First, she spoils twelve-year-old Jesus's precocious domination of the doctors in the Temple by scolding him in front of everyone for having run away from his parents.[76] Christ retorts, "How is it that ye sought me? Wist ye not that I must be about my Father's business?" (Luke 2:49). But his mother's business continues to intrude. In the early days of his ministry, Jesus finds his sermon to the multitudes rudely interrupted.[77] Your mother is outside, he is informed, and wants to speak with you. Expressing what we might call wishful thinking, Jesus replies that he has no mother. Yet, frustratingly, there she stands, demanding his (and our) attention. Again, at the wedding at Cana, Mary pesters Jesus to turn water into wine. "Woman," he snaps, "what have I to do with thee?" (John 2:4).[78] Far too much, it seems. These comical moments from the life of Christ inspired what is perhaps Monty Python's most celebrated joke: "He's not the Messiah," the Virgin Mandy protests. "He's a very naughty boy!"[79]

By means of the Incarnation, Mary both humanized and humiliated God, pulling him down from heaven to earth—much to his, and mankind's, benefit and delight. Her late medieval devotees compared this transformative seduction to the metamorphoses wrought by the goddess Venus.[80] Love turned Jupiter into a swan and Jehovah into a helpless infant. "The Virgin made God finite, mortal, poor, temporal, palpable, sentient, visible," the fifteenth-century Franciscan "Apostle of Italy" Saint Bernardino of Siena wrote.[81] Imitating and commemorating this ravishing and amusing metamorphosis, late medieval communities cyclically reincarnated the sacred mysteries of Christianity as theater, that most Incarnational of art forms.[82]

Marking the affinity between theater and the body of Christ, the citizens of York and Coventry performed their cycle of biblical pageantry on Corpus Christi Day, and those of Lincoln did so on the Feast of Saint Anne, Mary's mother—because Saint Anne's flesh is Mary's flesh, which is also the flesh of Jesus.[83] Dramatizing this matrilineal genealogy, Dublin's guild of bakers produced the pageantry of Saint Anne (who leavened the dough of Jesus's flesh) and the butchers that of the Virgin (who butchered the bloody sacrifice of the Lamb of God).[84] At these theatrical festivals, actors embodied the text of scripture just as Mary had clothed the Word in her body.[85] Extant play-scripts, therefore, describe the Incarnation in metatheatrical terms, calling Mary's skin and bones a "gyse" (as in "disguise") worn by Jesus on the world stage.[86] Gazing down at Mary from paradise just before the moment of the Annunciation, Jesus says, "I have so grett hast to be man thore / In that mekest and purest virgyne," and puts on the "weed" (or costume) of her body.[87]

Julian of Norwich described the Incarnation as "a mervelous medlur" of the Holy Spirit and the flesh of the Virgin.[88] Mirroring this hypostatic union, sacred drama muddled divinity and humanity, tragedy and comedy, sacred and profane—or, in Erich Auerbach's terms, the high style of the *sermo sublimis* and the low of the *sermo humilis*.[89] The register of medieval playscripts ranges freely between the loftiest Latin and the homeliest vernacular, mingling the sounds of Scholastic disputation and liturgical music with those of dirty jokes and violent children's games.[90] Records of performance indicate that while these productions moved some spectators to weep penitent tears, it inspired others to carouse, brawl, and flirt.[91] While Margery Kempe sobbed at the sight of Christ's Passion, Chaucer's Wife of Bath attended "pleyes of myracles," she tells us, to play, to see, and to be seen by lusty folk.[92] The savants of the Renaissance and Enlightenment found this characteristically Gothic jumble of registers, styles, and affects "grotesque"—*sì goffe e sì ree, e tanto malfatte* (so rude and vile, so misshapen).[93] Until the twentieth century, in fact, medieval drama struck almost all of its readers (including Milton, Voltaire, and Lord Byron) as "undignified," "indelicate," "vulgar," and "very profane."[94]

Even before the Reformation, there were those who decried the blasphemy of sacred drama. The late medieval antitheatrical diatribe "A tretise of miraclis pleyinge" makes the case that play and games should have no place in Christendom.[95] Theater, the text insists, impudently "bourdith" (jokes) with God like an equal when it should "drede to offend" like an underling.[96] Drama, it continues, mocks, scorns, and "bobs" (meaning "to strike," as in a game of blindman's buff) Christ, "as did the Jewis" during his Passion.[97] "Myraclis pleyinge," the treatise concludes, "is of the lustis of the fleyssh and myrthe of the body" (is of the lust of the flesh and mirth of the body) and therefore incompatible with the solemnity and spirituality of Christianity.[98] Speaking as God, the treatise chastises theater for these offenses, warning, "Pley not with me."[99]

And yet, as the playscripts of early English drama emphasize, God chose the Virgin, a mere mortal, to be his consort and "pleynge fere," meaning "playmate."[100] When in early English pageantry Saint Joseph protests to Mary that God could not have fathered her unborn child because God would never "jape so" (meaning "joke," "play," or "have sexual intercourse") with any human woman, he is proved wrong.[101] According to medieval Mariological doctrine, God did play with Mary, and their merriment redeemed the fallen universe. Drama's defenders protested that theater, like the Mother of Mercy, had a special power to save what seemed lost past all hope of recovery.[102] One particularly illustrative Miracle of the Virgin tells the tale of a sinner named Mariken or "Little Mary," the devil's own paramour, who was miraculously converted back to the faith by watching a play about the infinite mercy of the Madonna.[103] The parable concludes with a moral: "A play often tymes were better than a sermant to some folke."[104] In other words, theater, a type of the Virgin, dotes on mankind, its loving bride and mother, irresistible and indulgent, leaving the paternal Church militant to dispense discipline and punishment. Obeying this logic, the founders, leaders, and practitioners of medieval theatrics venerated Mary as the patroness, muse, and diva of their craft.[105]

Often, pageantry dedicated to the glorification of the Virgin—such as the Parisian *Miracles de Nostre Dame par personnages* or Lincoln's festival of Saint Anne—expressed this devotion with luxury craftsmanship, dazzling special effects, and lyrical encomiums to the Madonna's supremacy.[106] While no playtexts from Lincoln survive, city records yield vivid images: Mary wearing a "cremysyng gowne of veluet" (crimson gown of velvet), a walking Tree of Jesse performed by a parade of kings dressed in silks, and a mysterious golden head projecting beams of light from its gigantic mouth.[107] This type of veneration of the Virgin is laudatory, spectacular, and gorgeous—if also (as its naysayers have complained) idolatrous, antinomian, and aggressively, even blasphemously, erotic.[108] But by contrast, the shock value of another medieval mode of veneration of the Virgin registers on a higher order of magnitude.[109]

Sometimes, and especially often in the English tradition, devotional pageantry mocks, insults, and attacks the object of its devotion.[110] These theatrical reenactments of the legendary life of the Virgin repeat and reenergize the ancient polemical accusation that Mary conceived Jesus in sin. They charge her with the crime of adultery and subject her to Inquisitional interrogations, gynecological examinations, and deadly ordeals. Most puzzlingly, these plays seem to play these trials for laughs, as if the practice of abusing the Virgin constituted some kind of exhilarating game—like beating a piñata. This strange laughter has flummoxed (and angered, appalled, and terrified) readers of these texts for quite some time.[111] (Specifically, since the waning of open antipapism in academic discourse over the course of the late nineteenth and early twentieth centuries; before then, there was no mystery: these texts demonstrated the all-too-evident barbarity of the Catholicism of the Dark Ages.)[112] And yet as strange as it might seem to us, this violent and obscene abuse of the Virgin actually harmonizes with the accords of late medieval Mariology.[113]

Legend had it that Mary had robbed God of his reason; bent and broken the rules of precedence, nature, and the Old Testament; and redistributed her infinite treasury of merit among her supplicants, deserving and undeserving alike.[114] Thanks to Mary's irresistible powers of attraction, God punished these crimes with exemptions and rewards. A comedienne through and through, Mary turned the tragedy of Eve into a farce, happy ending guaranteed no matter how rough the slapstick or rude the jokes. It made sense, then, to honor this permissive goddess with laughter, naughtiness, and mischief. What better way to celebrate her lawlessness than by testing and proving the limitless limits of her mercy? When players craved the attention of the Mother of God, they offered her obscenity, violence, and blasphemy—just as supplicants demanding her blessings were known to attack her statues with whips and scorns.[115]

Both modes of theatrical devotion to the Virgin—panegyric and polemical, gentle and rough—are best represented in the N-Town plays, a Middle English compilation of forty-two pageants that dramatize the story of Christianity from Creation to Doomsday.[116] The N-Town plays survive only in one unique manuscript (MS Cotton Vespasian D.8), which was compiled in the late fifteenth or early sixteenth century, just before the Reformation, and then rescued from oblivion by the early modern recusant Robert Hegge.[117] The name N-Town derives from the manuscript itself: in its prefatory banns, *vexillators* (flag bearers) advertise that the play will be performed the following Sunday "in N. town" (527)—meaning, basically, "fill in name here" (with the *n* standing for *nomen*).[118] N-Town is named for nowhere— or anywhere. Unlike the annual Corpus Christi theatrical festival of York, which impressed gargantuan footprints in local parish archives, the N-Town plays left behind no certain records of performance.[119] Scholarly consensus has located N-Town at some ecclesiastical hub within East Anglia, whether the Benedictine abbey of Bury Saint Edmunds or, more likely still, the Cluniac Priory of Saint Mary and College of Saint Mary at Baily End at Thetford—a center of Marian devotion that, intriguingly, sponsored a powerful guild dedicated to the Virgin.[120] This manuscript preserves the traditions of an era and a region rather than one place or production in par- ticular. Specifically, it is a library of East Anglian devotion, an area of England known in the late Middle Ages for its vibrant theatricality, hetero- dox religiosity, and impassioned veneration of the Virgin—the perfect breeding grounds for this remarkable textual artifact.[121]

N-Town's devotion to the Virgin knows no bounds.[122] In N-Town, the Trinity, orders of angels, and all mankind hail the Madonna as the "Qwen of Hefne, Lady of Erth, and Empres of Helle" (11.335). While in the Gospel of Luke, pubescent Jesus sharply rebukes his mother when she interrupts him in the Temple, N-Town does not let this backtalk stand. Mary scolds Jesus:

> Youre Faderys wyl must nedys be wrought.
> It is most wurthy that it so be,
> Yitt on youre modyr have ye sum thought
> And be nevyrmore so longe fro me! (21.265–68)

In a one-hundred-and-eighty-degree reversal of scriptural precedent, N-Town's Jesus responds to his mother's reprimand with humble obedience. He *apologizes*:

> Now for to plese my modyr mylde,
> I shal yow folwe with obedyence.
> I am youre sone and subjecte childe
> And owe to do yow hygh reverence. (21.273–76)

When Jesus submits to the Virgin's maternal authority, God the Father and the Holy Spirit follow suit. Dominus, the three-personed God, tells Mary, "Yow to worchepe, moder, it likyth the hol Trinyte" (41.523). While the other English cycles and compilations of biblical drama (York, Chester, Towneley, Coventry) follow the canonical Gospels by first introducing Mary when Gabriel announces the coming birth of Christ, N-Town precedes the Annunciation with three pageants (each unique in the English tradition) detailing the Virgin's progress from conception to puberty to marriage.[123] She steals the show. In the late Middle Ages, statues called "cupboard Madonnas," *vierge ouvrantes*, or Shrine Madonnas, proliferated across Europe: three-dimensional images of Mary that opened up—or, as Elina Gertsman so vividly puts it in her magisterial study of these fascinating objects, "split open"—to reveal the Trinity contained inside her womb.[124] None from England survived the Reformation.[125] But, like these statues, N-Town encloses its dramatization of the Life of Jesus inside a Marian frame, beginning the New Testament with the Annunciation of the Immaculate Conception of Mary (rather than of the virgin birth of Christ) and ending with Mary's Assumption and Coronation (rather than the Ascension of Jesus).[126] A textual shrine to the Madonna, N-Town sings hymns, explodes pyrotechnics, and chants encomiums in celebration of her perfection and preeminence.[127]

And yet N-Town also expresses its devotion to the Virgin in that *other* way—with violence, obscenity, abuse, and laughter. Outdoing its sources and analogues, N-Town's pageant of the Nativity subjects Mary to two back-to-back, full-frontal, postpartum gynecological examinations in which doubting midwives penetrate and probe the genitals of the Virgin Mother of God, *onstage*, for our entertainment and edification.[128] Losing no opportunity to put Mary to the test, N-Town also contains the only extant dramatization of the apocryphal legend of "The Trial of Mary and Joseph" from all of medieval Europe.[129] N-Town amplifies and extends the polemical charges against the Virgin that it inherits from its sources, repeatedly accusing her of having broken her vows of celibacy with Joseph, Jehovah, the Holy Ghost, Jesus, the archangel Gabriel, and some boy or boys or man or men from the neighborhood. The text gives voice to obscene speculations about the intimate details of these alleged crimes—some fresh young gallant, her neighbors gossip, must have laid his legs to her and shot his bolt into her ticklish tail.[130] N-Town gives detractors free rein to harass the Virgin with slurs (a litany of Middle English synonyms for *whore*, such as "scowte," "quene," and "bold bysmare"), threats (of sexual violence, mutilation of the face, and death by stoning), and violence (by penetration, poison, and battery).[131] All played for laughs. Justifying the jocular tone of her detractors, Mary responds to all this abuse with infinite patience, if not amusement and pleasure. Her trials end happily—or, as N-Town's stage directions instruct, *cum gaudio* (with joy), with the Mother of Mercy bestowing forgiveness, thanks, and blessings on her merry persecutors.[132]

How are we supposed to take this? In his *English Drama from Early Times to the Elizabethans* (1950), Arthur Percival Rossiter tried to describe the confusing mix of feelings that N-Town's trials of the Virgin provoked.[133] He admitted that he found the "bullying" and "shaming" of the Virgin deeply moving and yet—somehow—also quite "funny." In an aside, and with some surprise at his own impression, he remarked that N-Town's version of the Virgin reminded him of no one so much as the stock comic figure of, in his words, "the servant girl who has slipped up"—in other words, as the comic heroine of a B plot: amusing, sexy, and sluttish.

In his seminal *Play Called Corpus Christi* (1966), a book that continues to guide our understanding of early English drama, V. A. Kolve sharply disagreed with Rossiter's reading.[134] Kolve countered that although N-Town's Virgin might "move in a mimetic world which includes the comic, the violent, the noisy, the grotesque," that world "never really touches [her] character."[135] Mary's "sanctity," he wrote, "defies circumstance."[136] In a particularly beautiful passage, Kolve describes N-Town's Virgin as "a green island in a turbulent and dirty sea"—the turbulent and dirty sea being the text itself, from which Mary, miraculously, manages to stand apart.[137] In short, Kolve argued that readers should subordinate the rather perplexing representation of Mary as "a comic character" found in N-Town to the "character and history" of the *real* Madonna "known to us from sources outside the play"—an approach that dominates the interpretation of N-Town's Virgin to this day.[138] And not only N-Town's Virgin. So many of her late medieval sisters demand this same kind of interpretive reformation.

Indeed, these troublesome versions of the Virgin have been vexing antiquarians since the Renaissance. From the sixteenth through the mid-twentieth century, men of letters tut-tutted over the blasphemous impropriety of the late medieval cult of the Virgin—its feverish eroticism, presumptuous curiosity, and raucous laughter. Repeating the talking points of Reformation polemic, these antiquarians all but called the Virgin of medieval Catholicism (and the Virgin as a synecdoche for Catholicism) a whore.[139] Twentieth- and twenty-first-century academics, trying their best to repudiate this polemical tradition, have taken a more clinical (even antiseptic) approach, cataloging and categorizing regional microhistories without making macro judgments.[140] By and large, the overarching pattern of Mary's promiscuity has been taken as offensive and therefore unspeakable, metaphorical and therefore insubstantial, comical and therefore insignificant, ubiquitous and therefore unremarkable, obvious and therefore uninteresting. When, as in N-Town, she cannot be ignored, she has all too often been explained away—as an aberration, a misinterpretation, an unintended side effect (of, say, naturalism or didacticism), or an anachronistic illusion (a trick of hindsight projected by, for example, feminist or psychoanalytical fantasies).[141]

I have taken a different approach. Rather than interpreting N-Town's Mary in the context of "sources outside the play," I have interpreted her as she stands—to return to Kolve's image, not an island apart but rather part of the main. Instead of navigating through the N-Town manuscript under the assumption that it lies at the periphery of the map (or even beyond the edge of the map, among the monsters), I have made it the center and focus of my study. When so aligned, the landscape of late medieval literature and culture (East Anglian, English, and, more broadly, Christian) looks quite different. N-Town's Virgin no longer seems like an aberration or an illusion but rather reveals herself to be part of a surprisingly widespread pattern—a pattern evident in dirty jokes told by Boccaccio and Chaucer, apparent contradictions in the Arthurian romances of Sir Thomas Malory and Gottfried von Strassburg, and the double entendres of the allegory of the Mystic Hunt of the Unicorn. Rather than using preconceptions about Christian doctrine to interpret medieval cultural artifacts, I have used those artifacts to interpret doctrine.[142] When Leo Steinberg took this approach with fifteenth-century icons, he discovered what he called "genital theology": the late medieval veneration of the genitals of Jesus Christ made invisible not only by the Reformation but also by "modern oblivion."[143] Mining the Middle English playscripts of this same rich vein of history, I have uncovered the celebration and veneration of the Virgin Mary not only for her exceptional chastity but also for her merciful promiscuity.[144]

Late medieval theatrical adaptations of Christian history and mythology were collaboratively produced and publicly consumed by local communities—by men, women, and children; knights, clerks, and peasants.

These living bibles provide an invaluable record of the flexibility of late medieval hermeneutics.[145] More unmistakably than any other cultural artifacts from the period, they do not rigidly or exclusively interpret Mary as a virgin, or at least not as we would understand the term. Whereas we tend to think of virginity as a literal and fragile membrane, the medieval preference for allegorical rather than literalist interpretation opens up more expansive and (to use the term employed by Boccaccio to describe the multivalence of Dante) "polysemous" possibilities.[146] Interpreting playfully, medieval biblical drama represents Mary not only as virgin and mother but also as virgin and promiscuous adulteress, dallying with the Trinity, angels, and mankind in kaleidoscopic erotic combinations. In this interpretive vein, Mary's "virginity" signifies invulnerability rather than fragility, redemption rather than renunciation, and merciful license rather than ascetic discipline. Early English biblical drama—and the N-Town manuscript in particular— takes the ancient slander that Mary conceived Jesus in sin as cause for joyful thanks and laughter. Such was Mary's power that she made a virtue of the accusation: she redeemed and even exalted the crime.

This carnival could not last forever. By the end of the sixteenth century, iconoclasts, puritans, and reformers (both Protestant and Catholic) had successfully split the multivalent Virgin of the late Middle Ages into a binary opposition: a true virgin and a false whore.[147] Christianity reformed the virgin and banished the whore. Stripped of her powers and privileges, the unchaste version of the Virgin became a joke, an insult, and a half-remembered nightmare. She survives in anti-Catholic polemic (from John Bale to Jack Chick), gothic horror (from *The Monk* to *The Exorcist*), shock comedy (from Monty Python's *Life of Brian* to *South Park*'s "Bloody Mary"), and, as we have seen, avant-garde art—but not within our understanding of Christian theology, tradition, or devotion.[148] Across academic disciplines, an overwhelming consensus maintains that no viable interpretive alternative to Mary's monolithic virginity has ever flourished except far beyond the reaches of Christianity (within ancient polemic, for example, or modern atheism).[149] When twentieth-century New Yorkers beheld the long-forgotten face of the promiscuous Virgin in Ofili's *Holy Virgin Mary*, they did not recognize her as an icon. Instead, they saw the bleeding edge of a new iconoclastic weapon, designed to destroy the innocence of faith. Likewise, when spectators witnessed the first attempted revival of the N-Town plays in the early twentieth century, they took devotion for desecration.[150] The producer, Nugent Monck, was arrested for violating England's blasphemy laws.[151]

The version of the Virgin that we recognize—the reformed Virgin of modernity—serves limited functions, befitting her humbled station. She suffers and comforts the suffering; she keeps chaste and shames the unchaste.[152] At the end of the nineteenth century, Elizabeth Cady Stanton called this version of the Virgin "a slur" designed to denigrate "natural motherhood"; in the mid-twentieth century, Simone de Beauvoir called her "the supreme masculine victory" over womankind.[153] Today, she stands before us—on pedestals and Christmas cards—pale and serene, generic and mild, modestly veiled in white and blue. She often weeps, and smiles almost imperceptibly, only in the very corner of her mouth.[154] She radiates the conservative virtues of silence, obedience, and—above all else—chastity. While her powers have diminished, her purity has only augmented.[155] In 649, the Vatican declared Mary's perpetual virginity; in 1854, her Immaculate Conception; and in 1950, her bodily Assumption. According to contemporary dogma, Mary was, is, and shall always be perfectly intact and unblemished: exempt from the taint of original sin, the pollutions of intercourse and childbirth, and even the sting of death. Worms never tried that long-preserved virginity. While we tend to narrate history as a progressive loss of innocence, the opposite is true of the progress of the Virgin: she becomes steadily purer with every passing century. We have forgotten that she was not always so fragile and chaste.

Chapter 1

The Many Fathers of Jesus Christ

In the N-Town plays, a suspicious Joseph returns home to find his wife, Mary, pregnant, and he knows full well that he cannot be the father of her child. When he asks her, "Whose childe is this?" (12.47), she answers with a long list of possible candidates: Joseph himself, the Holy Trinity, and the archangel Gabriel. Variations on this episode, which have been titled by modern editors "Joseph's Doubt," "Joseph's Jealously," or "Joseph's Troubles about Mary," expand on three lines from the Gospel of Matthew (1:18–20)—though in the Bible, Joseph never gives voice to his suspicions.[1,2] Early English drama throws off any such discretion and has Joseph speak "open words, contrary to scriptures," as the early modern reformer Christopher Goodman complained.[3] Indeed, N-Town's Joseph accuses Mary in no uncertain terms of sinning with "sum other man" (12.28) or "sum boy" (12.75). "Joseph's Doubt" draws on a long tradition within Christianity of doubts and accusations about the identity of Jesus's father. The N-Town manuscript in particular compiles these long-simmering insinuations into an extended running joke, accumulating more and more paternal candidates for the far-cically promiscuous virgin birth.

Joseph, God's Cuckold

According to the parsimonious principle of Ockham's razor, the simplest explanation is often the best. In the case of the virgin birth, that principle would seem to point directly to Joseph. When Mary is found to be pregnant, she and Joseph are betrothed and cohabitating: therefore, Joseph's paternity would seem to be the most obvious explanation. N-Town stages this knee-jerk first response: when the news of Mary's pregnancy begins to spread, the neighborhood immediately suspects Joseph.[4]

Apparently responding to the same suspicion, the Gospel of Matthew narrates the virgin birth as a sustained denial of Joseph's paternity. The argumentative thesis of verses 1:18 to 1:25 is that Joseph is most decidedly *not* Jesus's father.[5] The passage opens and shuts with clear-cut insistence on Joseph's noninvolvement: he had not consummated his marriage when Mary conceived; therefore, he could not be the father of her child. Later apocryphal emendations clarify that Joseph was not even present when Mary conceived but rather far, far away on a prolonged business trip.[6] The vehemence of this denial suggests the urgency of the suspicion to which it responds. Joseph poses a significant threat to the doctrine of the virgin birth. He provokes suspicion. Indeed, several early heretical sects (the Ebionites and, later, the School of Antioch, most importantly Nestorius and Diodorus of Tarsus) believed that Jesus was not the Son of God but rather the son of Joseph—biological rather than adoptive.[7]

And yet Joseph also keeps up appearances. As Thomas Aquinas himself pointed out, Joseph's legitimizing presence in the narrative of the virgin birth prevents every pregnant and unmarried Christian girl from claiming the Virgin as the exemplar and excuse for her dishonor.[8] In other words, Joseph offers Christianity some, if meager, protection from the virgin birth's enormous potential for scandal.

As Christianity flourished, so did Mary's purity. A standard of chastity acceptable in one century became insulting by the next. Following this pattern, the Gospel of Matthew's denial of Joseph's paternity, which had at first functioned as a defense of Mary's virginity, soon became cause for further denial. The problem: verse 1:25 of Matthew defends the virgin birth by specifying that Mary and Joseph did not consummate their marriage until *after* the birth of Jesus. This foundational claim defended but also limited the doctrine of Mary's virginity. Adding to the problem, all four Gospels refer repeatedly and casually to Jesus's siblings, the abundant fruit of the consummated marriage of Mary and Joseph.[9] Thus, Tertullian praises Mary for honoring Jesus with all of the "sacred titles": "mother and virgin and monogamous wife" (*matrem et virginem et univiram*).[10]

Quickly enough, however, Christianity's chaste ambitions outgrew these limitations. As early as the second century, the Church began to demand more and better virginity from and for the Virgin: *perpetua* (eternal) rather than limited until the birth of Jesus. The Parthenos was well on her way to becoming the *Aeiparthenos*, the Ever-Virgin. The second-century Gospel of James attempted to support this cause by adding an apocryphal backstory to the Nativity.[11] This Gospel introduces Joseph to Mary as an old widower with children from a previous marriage, indisposed toward consummating his second, very late-in-life marriage.[12] In fact, Joseph flat-out refuses to accept Mary's hand, protesting, "I have sons and am an old man; she is but a child. I do not want to become the laughingstock of Israel."[13] Only by threatening that the Lord might split open the earth and swallow him whole does the officiating priest change Joseph's mind. Thanks to these apocryphal emendations, Joseph went from being a disturbingly virile young man to being a reassuringly grouchy and elderly—and, by implication, impotent—widower.[14]

The pattern repeats. This fortification of Mary's virginity, like its predecessors, soon began to undermine itself. Although the apocryphal Gospel of James attempted to protect Mary's chastity by making Joseph old and impotent, Jerome found its best efforts deeply inadequate. Jerome saw that a doctrine as monumental as Mary's perpetual virginity could not be founded on the shifting sands of apocrypha; this fortress had to be deeply rooted in the self-evident truth of the canonical Gospels. The naked text, however, posed the very problem that the apocrypha had sought to correct in the first place. Therefore, Jerome came up with an ingenious interpretive solution: he retranslated (or rather, as he would have it, corrected the previous mistranslation of) the truth. Jerome argued that the Greek word for *until* in verse 1:25 of Matthew (Joseph "knew [Mary] not *until* she brought forth her first-born son") did not necessarily mean that "after the time indicated something had changed"—and that the word *brothers* (as in Jesus's brothers) did not necessarily mean biological siblings.[15] Thus, Jesus's brothers became his cousins and Mary's limited virginity became potentially limitless.

Problem almost solved. Jerome was also troubled by the apocryphal Gospels' depiction of Joseph as a once-fertile patriarch rendered celibate by physical decrepitude. He wanted much better security for Mary's virginity than Joseph's impotence. Old age, while taking away the means, does nothing about the will. Jerome understood that bridling Joseph's sexuality by rendering him decrepit and impotent has the unintended effect of magnifying the underlying insinuation of that bridling's necessity. Therefore, he internalized Joseph's chastity. Rejecting the legend of Joseph's first marriage, Jerome insisted that Joseph, like Mary, obeyed a pristine vow of lifelong virginity. He argued that "holy men" do not "fornicate"; therefore, a man as holy as Joseph must never have fornicated—an aggressive choice of words, considering that Joseph stood accused only of lawful marital intercourse.[16] Jerome concluded that Joseph must have kept his virginity perfectly intact, just like Mary: self-motivated and self-policing. He rewrote the marriage of Mary and Joseph as an ever-unconsummated *syneisaktism*, a spiritual or white marriage, between two like-minded virgins.[17]

Jerome would be pleased with the version of Saint Joseph venerated in contemporary Catholicism, as well as Christianity more broadly. Today, Joseph tends to be represented as a young, fair, blandly handsome man, situated in the center of the frame and set off by a golden halo. He cuddles with the baby Jesus, chaste lilies in hand; when Jesus grows older, father and son bond over carpentry. Modern iconography depicts the Holy Family as a nuclear family: Joseph takes care of Mary and Jesus, who revere his paternal authority. As the patriarch of the Holy Family, Joseph is respectable and respected. In 1870, Pope Pius IX officially declared Joseph the patron saint of the Universal Church—the father figure of Catholicism itself; in 1955, Pope Pius XII promulgated the feast of Joseph the (Anti-Communist) Worker—the Holy Family's (and Catholicism's) breadwinner.[18] Joseph no longer disturbs but rather upholds the chaste decorum of the Holy Family. It is all so very solemn and polite.

This triumph of decorum was not easily achieved. It took centuries to accomplish, largely because of the problem posed by the raucous late medieval period. During the late Middle Ages, Jerome's corrections circulated in tandem with the very problems that they sought to resolve. Both versions of Joseph got around: the apocryphal Gospels' old grouch and Jerome's chaste saint. Artists representing sacred scenes like the visit of the magi or the flight into Egypt could pick and choose from this composite tradition which qualities their Joseph would express. Early English biblical drama, for example, mixes and matches, representing Joseph as a wizened old man (following the apocryphal Gospels) *and* as a virgin (following Jerome).

In fact, contrary to Jerome's wishes, most late medieval artists, across many media, chose to make their Josephs elderly. Altarpieces, triptychs, alabasters, tapestries, stained-glass windows, misericords, and murals represent Joseph as a decrepit, and often fat, old man. Instead of a halo, he wears a *pileum cornutum*, a hat that marks him as Jewish.[19] Instead of the classical drapery appropriate to sainthood, he wears rags that mark him as Mary's social inferior—her servant, even.[20] His decrepitude provides comic relief in the midst of sacred scenes. Located in the margins of the frame, Joseph dozes off during the Nativity, huffs and puffs on the flight into Egypt, and eats his porridge sullenly in the corner—his back turned to Mary and Jesus, excluded (and apparently miffed) by their sacred embrace.[21] Despite Jerome's best efforts, the late medieval version of Joseph was no saint, at least not in the modern sense of the term.[22] He was, instead, a kind of sacred fool—emphasis on *fool*.[23]

What was it about old Joseph that struck medieval artists as being so funny? Joseph's role in the divine comedy of the virgin birth is inherently amusing—even (if not especially) in the context of the canonical Gospels themselves. The jokes write themselves. Joseph discovers that his bride is pregnant, and knows that he is not the father; he tries to extricate himself from this knot yet cannot escape—because God has made him his cuckold. This is the plot of a farce—specifically, Plautus's *Amphitryon*, a Roman comedy of mistaken identities (well known in the Middle Ages and adapted by Vitalis of Blois, Eustache Deschamps, and John Gower) in which Jupiter cuckolds Amphitruo and impregnates his wife, Alcumena, with the demigod Hercules.[24] The apocryphal Gospel of James only made this farce more farcical still by casting Joseph in the stock role of the *senex amans*, the grumpy old man, the butt of ancient comedy (as in Menander's *Dyskolos*, meaning "grouch" or "misanthrope") and ancient comedy's direct descendent, the medieval fabliaux.[25] Topsy-turvy fabliaux sexually humiliate grouchy old men—cuckolds, misers, misanthropes, and even clerks and philosophers—

with *contrapasso* comeuppances.[26] In perhaps the most paradigmatic example of this tendency, the fabliau heroine Phyllis rides old Aristotle like a beast of burden, asserting her dominance over his age and wisdom in a processional triumph.[27] The combination of Jerome's Joseph (the celibate cleric of the Holy Family) and the apocryphal tradition's Joseph (an impotent old grouch) sets up an irresistible comic premise. Joseph's impotence and authority pit him against Mary in a fabliau battle of the sexes, which—statistically speaking—the old cuckold tends to lose.[28]

Medieval representations of the infant Christ often show him clutching or playing with a goldfinch; this iconography foretells the Crucifixion, when—according to legend—a goldfinch stained its face with blood when it perched on the crown of thorns.[29] Yet sometimes a different bird accompanies the baby Jesus: a cuckoo.[30] The English word *cuckold* descends from the Old French *cucu*, or cuckoo, referring to an ancient (and not inaccurate) observation that cuckoos parasitically lay their eggs in other birds' nests, thereby outsourcing the burden of child-rearing.[31] By holding a cuckoo, the infant Christ flaunts his sacred illegitimacy. God laid his egg in Joseph's nest—a paradoxically humiliating honor. Keep an eye out and you will see just how often carved, painted, and woven medieval representations of Joseph can be found standing directly in front of a horned bull or a big-eared donkey; this is the medieval artist giving Joseph the horned hand, putting fingers up behind his head—marking him as God's cuckold.[32]

Adding insult to injury, medieval artists also encumber Joseph with ironic fertility symbols. The bundle he carries over his shoulder, the purse he wears around his waist, and the carpentry tools he holds in his hands (drills, saws, and so on) look suspiciously phallic or testicular.[33] Joseph is often shown using these oversize tools to comically underwhelming effect. For example, the fifteenth-century Mérode Altarpiece shows old Joseph drilling holes into a plank of wood as, in the very next room (or panel), the Holy Ghost (with the help of the attractive archangel Gabriel) is impregnating his beautiful young wife.[34] The unflattering contrast between Joseph's drilling of the plank and the Holy Ghost's impregnation of Mary insinuates Joseph's impotence. Furthermore, Joseph is shown in the process of making mousetraps, yet another joke at his expense.[35] According to Augustine, *muscipula diaboli, crux domini* (the Cross of the Lord was the devil's mousetrap); in other words, Jesus gained the advantage of surprise over the devil by disguising himself as a mortal man, as the natural-born son of Joseph—a nebbish whom Satan would never suspect of fathering the incarnated God.[36] Busy building this mousetrap at the very moment of the Annunciation, Joseph fulfills his role as God's fool. He is the front, the disguise, the beard—not the lover, not the father, not the man.

These farcical aspects of the virgin birth have inspired laughter for millennia, from the polemic of the second-century Greek philosopher Celsus to Monty Python's *Life of Brian*. When upright pillars of the Christian establishment (in the particular cases of Celsus and Monty Python, respectively, Origen and Arthur Mervyn Stockwood, the bishop of Southwark) have condemned this laughter, they have insisted that only Christianity's enemies could ever joke at the expense of the Virgin Mary's chastity.[37] Yet, more unmistakably than any other era, the late Middle Ages give the lie to that assumption. Middle English biblical drama makes use of every available comic trick to render Joseph as funny as possible—even when those jokes challenge the apologist mission of defending Mary's reputation from all and any threats. Rather than attempting to contain the virgin birth's scandalous potential, early English drama turns that potential into uproarious laughter.

N-Town's Miracle of the Blooming Rod

Perhaps the clearest example of N-Town's preference for laughter over decorum is the miracle of the blooming rod in the pageant of "The Marriage of Mary and Joseph," an episode ultimately derived from the apocryphal Gospel of James.[38] The miracle comes at the conclusion of a fertility contest held by the house of David in order to select Mary's bridegroom from among the princes of Israel—including impotent old Joseph. N-Town does not waste this choice opportunity to emphasize Joseph's decrepitude. When Joseph enters, he declares, "For febylnesse of age, my jorney I may not spede" (10.157). This is an understatement: dialogue soon reveals that Joseph not only "may not speed" but actually lies completely flat on the boards of the stage (10.159–60). He complains,

> Age and febylnesse doth me enbrase
> That I may nother well goo ne stond. (10.161–62)

Joseph makes similar complaints in the other English cycles: York's Joseph, for example, protests that he cannot step over two straws (13.13).[39] Having firmly established Joseph's ineligibility, N-Town forces him into the comic situation of the fertility contest. The angel of the Lord has commanded that all the eligible bachelors of the house of David compete for Mary's hand in marriage by bringing a "whyte yard" (10.128) or *virga* (which can mean "branch," "graft," "staff," or "male genitalia") to the Temple to see whose yard "doth blome and bere" (10.131).[40] The phallic symbolism at play here is not subtle. While the other heirs of King David hurry across the *platea* with their impressive yards firmly in hand, Joseph lies limp as a worm.

Joseph protests that he cannot sexually reproduce. "Abyl to be maryed," he says, "that is not I" (10.178). In other words, he can neither increase nor multiply. Joseph elaborates on the reason: he is "old and also colde" (10.189)— and therefore, according to Galenic medical theory, physically incapable of generating the heat necessary to turn blood into semen. As Peter Brown inimitably explains this theory, "To make love was to bring one's blood to the boil, as the spirit swept through veins, turning blood into the foam of semen."[41] According to N-Town, Joseph's body is simply too cold to enable this alchemical transformation. As the extremely influential late thirteenth- or early fourteenth-century medical tract *De Secretis Mulierum* has it, cold testicles can only generate semen "as thin as water" and "not fit for generation," thus causing infertility.[42] Joseph, in other words, argues that his physical incapacity ought to excuse him from the contest. Little does he know, however, that this incapacity is exactly what God is looking for—because, apparently, in the words of F. M. Salter, "in the Middle Ages God himself had a sense of humor."[43]

When Joseph's turn comes to offer his yard at the altar, he whines and stalls. "I am so agyd and so olde," he complains, "that both myn leggys gyn to folde" (10.226–27). Embarrassingly, he even loses (or worse, pretends to lose) his symbolic phallus: "I kannot my rodde fynde!" (10.235). The text describes Joseph's paltry offering as "a ded stok" (10.262), a stock polemical phrase for idols. N-Town's use of the phrase suggests that Joseph's sexuality is as useless as a false god, while Mary's sexuality, by contrast, is generative and efficacious.[44] N-Town represents Mary as the young, beautiful, blossoming flower of Christianity and Joseph as the superseded Old Testament— *old* taken to its comic extremity. Geriatric Joseph serves as a farcical analogue to the Christian iconographic representation of Judaism as Blind Synagoga, her eyes veiled and standard broken. Medieval depictions of Blind Synagoga sometimes replace the female allegorical figure with Moses or a generic old man, types that are visually and typologically comparable to Joseph: horned and ancient with a broken rod.[45]

This comic buildup climaxes in a startling inversion. Despite his hyperbolic decrepitude, Joseph (literally) rises to the challenge and wins the fertility contest. As he holds his rod up at the altar, it blossoms with white "flourys fre" (10.262), signifying that the Holy Ghost sits on his branch and thereby marks him as Mary's bridegroom (10.197).[46] At first glance, this inversion might seem rather straightforward: Joseph wins the contest because God needs an impotent and unthreatening stooge rather than a virile rival. Yet if we extrapolate tenor from vehicle, the metaphorical miracle mimes Joseph's phallus serving as a vessel for God's seed to enter Mary's body. Although Joseph could barely stand up before approaching the altar, once he reaches it and begins to pray, he stops complaining. At the end of his prayer, we learn that he has—miraculously—managed to hold his rod aloft throughout his speech: when the rod blossoms, he exclaims,

> I may not lyfte myn handys heye.
> Lo, lo, lo! What se ye now? (10.255–56)

In other words, Joseph holds his rod erect until it bursts into seminal white blossoms, at which point he drops his arms. This mime imitates the progress of intercourse from erection to ejaculation. God empowers and Joseph performs. Only afterward does Joseph revert to type, complaining about his aches and pains.

This miracle anticipates and reduplicates the virgin birth. God generates blossoms from Joseph's impotence and fruit from Mary's virginity. In one sense, then, the miracle of the blooming rod serves to explicate the impossible fertility of the marriage of Mary and Joseph: God supplies what Mary and Joseph lack, and their lack functions as proof of his supply. And yet the miracle also has the effect of interjecting Joseph into the process of Jesus's conception. In this sense, the incapacity of Joseph's impotence functions as the scope for God's potency to assert itself; God fulfills Joseph's impotence. Surprisingly (at least for us), God chooses to accomplish this fulfillment by puppeteering (rather than replacing or circumnavigating) Joseph's phallic symbol—by using Joseph's rod as a kind of syringe in a process of divine in vitro fertilization. This interjection of Joseph's genitals into a mime of Jesus's conception—even if symbolic and puppeteered—contradicts our modern understanding of Mary's inviolateness. Yet Joseph's assisted potency seems to be one of many ways that N-Town (and its apocryphal sources and late medieval analogues) imagines the virgin birth. Indeed, N-Town phrases this scene as yet another cuckold joke at Joseph's expense, an extension of the idea that God used Joseph as his tool.

Entering the Gate and Beating the Bush

As Jerome knew all too well, the apocryphal invention of Joseph's impotence created a loophole in the defense of Mary's virginity. Neutering Joseph amplifies the implication of the operation's necessity while at the same time proving utterly inadequate as a solution to the causal problem—and comically so. As the fabliaux teach us, impotence is not equivalent or even comparable to chastity. The old cuckolds of fabliaux are, in fact, notoriously lecherous.

Let me paint you a picture. William Dunbar's late fifteenth- or early sixteenth-century Middle Scots poem *The Tretis of the Twa Maritt Wemen and the Wedo* (N-Town's contemporary, if not its neighbor) explains in vivid detail how old cuckolds kiss, grip, clap, and shove the bodies of their poor wives—all to no avail, either orgasmic or reproductive.[47] The cuckold's "hard hurcheone skyn" (hard hedgehog skin) scratches his wife's cheeks and lips (107)—and yet, as one bride remarks, "soft and soupill as the silk is his sary lume" (his sorry tool is as soft and supple as a silkworm) (96). The fabliau genre runs on the perversely fertile lechery generated by impotent cuckolds. In fact, the impotent cuckold represents the very quintessence of lust—not despite but precisely because of his impotence. According to the fabliau template, these sexual misers stifle the community's reproductive economy by hoarding the most attractive and fertile maidens on the market. Utterly unproductive and unwelcome, their lechery is inexcusable, unjustifiable: it is the very worst, most excessive kind of lust.

By casting Joseph in the fabliau role of the old cuckold, biblical drama necessarily implies his lechery. This transference often becomes explicit. In the Chester cycle, Joseph complains,

> These XXX[tie] winters, though I would,
> I might not playe noe playe. (6.135–36)[48]

In other words, thirty years of impotence have deprived Joseph of the means but not the motivation. He *would* play the game if only he *could*. Here, Joseph expresses a stock cuckold sentiment: as Dunbar tells us, parodying Matthew 5:28, old cuckolds "may weill to the syn assent" (may well consent to the sin), but "sakles" (sinless) are their deeds (97). In other words, their sinlessness is hardly saintly. If we follow this thought through, we arrive at an inevitable question. Assuming (with the apocryphal Gospels) that impotence is a necessary defensive measure that functions to prevent Joseph from impregnating Mary, then what prevents him from subjecting her to his "sakles deidis" (sinless deeds) and his "sary lume" (sorry tool), impotence notwithstanding? In its fabliau vein, Middle English biblical drama answers that, frankly, nothing prevents Joseph's impotent advances. Contrary to our expectations, these texts seem to find Joseph's advances rather harmless—and even amusing.

Perhaps the clearest instance of biblical drama's tolerance of the possibility of Joseph and Mary's active although inefficacious sex life occurs in N-Town's play of "Joseph's Doubt." This pageant begins with Joseph banging on a locked door, shouting at Mary,

> How, dame, how! Undo youre dore, undo!
> Are ye at hom? Why speke ye notht? (12.1–2)

A servant answers, "Who is ther? Why cry ye so?" (12.3). Joseph retorts, even angrier,

> Undo youre dore, I sey yow to!
> For to com in is all my thought. (12.5–6)

Here we have a familiar farcical episode: the emasculated husband banging on his own door, trying to access house and housewife.[49] Perhaps the most famous iteration of this kind of lockout comes from Plautus's *Amphitryon*, in which Jupiter impersonates the absent husband in order to sleep with his wife; misunderstandings ensue when that husband returns home after seeming to have just left.[50] In "Joseph's Doubt," the Plautine gag of the locked door implies that although Mary has shut Joseph out (rejected and replaced him), he makes a concerted—though impotent—effort to get inside. Joseph wants in. As he says, "To com in is all my thought."

N-Town's depiction of Mary's body as a locked door intertwines biology and theology. *De Secretis Mulierum* explains that the vulva (which, as Danielle Jacquart and Claude Alexandre Thomasset note, "designated a rather vague semantic field") "is named from the word *valva*, folding door, because it is the door of the womb."[51] In the Old Testament, Ezekiel describes a gate that "shall be shut, [and] shall not be opened, and man shall not pass through it: because the Lord the God of Israel is entered in through it, and it shall be shut for the prince" (44:2). Ambrose glossed these lines as a reference to the Virgin: "Mary," he writes, "is the door which was closed and not to be opened."[52] In an earlier play, N-Town explicitly brings up this association, parading Ezekiel out in a pageant of Old Testament prophets to foretell the coming

> of a gate that sperd was trewly
> And no man but a prince myght therin go. (7.47–48)

God has passed through Mary's locked gate (her virginity) without unlocking it. God entered. Joseph, as it seems (and as we might expect), cannot.

Yet Joseph keeps on knocking. Even more surprisingly, he gets in. After charging the locked door with so much weighty typological meaning, N-Town has Mary open up and welcome Joseph home. When Mary makes her entrance onstage, she immediately says,

> It is my spowse that spekyth us to!
> Ondo the dore—his wyl were wrought!
> Wellcome hom, myn husbond dere! (12.7–9)

And in through the symbol of her impenetrable virginity he goes. Not only does Joseph's reentrance resonate with the conventions of medieval fabliaux and Roman farce, it also makes sound theological sense.[53] Mary is paradoxically virgin and wife, inaccessible and accessible. Although medieval imagery frequently depicts Mary as an enclosed space (a locked gate, or *hortus conclusus*), we must not repress the other half of her paradox. She is also wide open.

In medieval iconography, the Virgin sits with widespread knees and stands with outstretched arms in open arches and the open air.[54] The eleventh-century antiphon *Alma Redemptoris Mater* (familiar to readers of the *Prioress's Tale*) describes Mary as a permeable passageway to Heaven: *pervia caeli porta*.[55] As a traversable portal, she symbolizes Ecclesia, the welcoming Church whose door never closes.[56] N-Town interlaces this positive theological openness with the fabliau suggestion that Mary, after having taken a lover during her husband's absence, resumes her sexually active marriage upon his return. When N-Town's Ezekiel describes Mary as "a gate that sperd was trewly," he uses a verb with a double meaning: *sperd* means both "bolted shut" and "speared through."[57] Mary, miraculously, is both.

Why should Joseph not enter the locked gate? After all, he is Mary's lawful husband. She happens to have two spouses, one on earth and one in heaven. God, in a certain sense, seems open to sharing. After all, he set Mary up with Joseph in the first place. Joseph, however, grumbles. N-Town's God may find Joseph completely unthreatening, but the feeling, unsurprisingly, is not mutual. In "Joseph's Doubt," Joseph complains to the audience,

> Here may all men this proverbe trow:
> "That many a man doth bete the bow;
> Another man hath the brydde." (12.81–3)

He frames the proverb with a piece of advice. All men should trust in that maxim's truth, he says, because of what they see "here," in this play. If we follow Joseph's advice and apply the proverb to the pageant, it implies that Joseph beat the bush—in other words, Joseph did all the work—but his rival got the reward, the bird.

We could take this to mean that Joseph wooed Mary to no avail. But Joseph could also mean that he "bete the bow" by actively engaging in the toil of matrimony: working to provide food and shelter and laboring to pay the marriage debt. This reading would imply that Joseph had been attempting to impregnate Mary—to beget his own egg rather than selflessly devoting all his energy to caring for God's alien cuckoo. Here is Jerome's worst nightmare realized. Yet in N-Town, neither God nor Mary seems to mind Joseph's encroachment. In N-Town, the Mother of Mercy has more than enough love to go around. Mary's virginity tends to function here more like a transcendent power than a fragile membrane. Joseph's rod blooming, gate banging, and bush beating pose no threat to her perfection because her perfection is miraculously invulnerable. N-Town celebrates Mary's paradoxical incorruptibility by linking Jesus with one father after another after another. Since Mary's virginity cannot diminish, the more the merrier.

The Holy Ghost, God's Intermediary

In N-Town's play of "Joseph's Doubt," Mary tries to explain to Joseph that he himself, "the Fadyr of Hevyn," "swete Jhesus," and "the Holy Gost" are all the fathers of her unborn child.[58] Joseph rejects this explanation. Incredulous, he says,

> Goddys childe—thu lyist, in fay!
> God dede nevyr jape so with may! (12.43–44)

In other words, Joseph protests that God has never "japed" in this way with a maiden—*japed* meaning "to trick," "to joke," and "to have sexual intercourse with."[59] Joseph is, of course, in error: God may never have japed this way with a maiden before, but he has now. Mary is (as the archangel Gabriel hails her) God's one and only human "pleynge fere" (*fere* meaning "fellow," "companion," or "spouse")—God's playmate, in effect (11.315). Yet Joseph's initial take on the virgin birth has been understood as erroneous in another sense entirely—as a crude misreading of Mary's words, "as though she were saying that the Christian God had adopted the habits of Jove."[60] According to this take on the text, Joseph errs by insinuating that God sexually reproduced with Mary as Jupiter did with Leda, Danaë, Io, or any of his other victims.

Here we arrive at a much-disputed question: If not by means of sexual reproduction, then how did God cause the effect of the virgin birth? The Gospels remain discreetly vague on this sensitive subject. The Gospel of Luke tells us that the Holy Spirit will ἐπελεύσεται (*superveniet*, "come upon") and ἐπισκιάσει (*obumbrabit*, "overshadow") Mary (1:35), and the Gospel of Matthew states that "what is begotten [γεννηθεν, *natum*] in her is of the Holy Spirit" (1:20).[61] These verses have been understood to mean that the power of God caused Mary's pregnancy—not so intimately as to be improper, and not so abstractly as to be unexceptional.[62] After all, God abstractly intervened in other unvirgin births. He made Sarah pregnant when she was ninety years old (Genesis 17:15–17) and caused the barren Elizabeth to conceive (Luke 1:7–13).[63] While the Gospel of Matthew works to deny Joseph's paternity while still maintaining his legitimacy as Mary's husband, the Gospel of Luke has a different fine line to walk—between denying God's participation in sexual intercourse and insisting on his paternity. The Holy Ghost functions as the solution to this problem. Exegetical consensus on the Gospel of Luke maintains that a formless spirit representing the power of God, and not Jehovah the entity, impregnated Mary. Not a man with a white beard but rather the abstract, formless, and sexless Holy Ghost.

Yet the strategy of insisting on the presence of the amorphous Holy Spirit and the absence of the humanoid Jehovah at the scene of the Annunciation has never fully succeeded in preventing the inevitable comparison between the virgin birth and the rapes of Jupiter. Jupiter came to his victims wearing many clever disguises. He approached Leda as a swan and Danaë as a shower of gold—shapes that resemble the Holy Ghost. The New Testament itself gave form to this formless spirit, embodying the Holy Ghost in the form of a dove (Luke 3:22), an avian motif perpetuated in Christian iconography from the catacombs of late antiquity to the cathedrals of the Middle Ages.[64] Medieval representations of the Annunciation regularly depict the Holy Ghost as a dove perching on Mary's windowsill or as a golden ray of light beaming through her window—images not so far removed from an eagle or shower of gold.

The resemblance between the Annunciation and the rapes of Jupiter puts Christianity, a religion that prides itself on its exceptional chastity, in a difficult position.[65] The extant record of this difficulty reaches back as far as the second century, when Celsus allegedly accused the Christian evangelists of having recycled Greek myths (the rapes of Danaë, Melanippe, Auge, and Antiope) in fabricating the story of Jesus's conception.[66] In his response, Origen unsurprisingly dismisses the accusation as vulgar and ridiculous.[67] But he also takes up a less predictable strategy. In order to make the larger point that Christian scripture is no more incredible than pagan mythology, Origen stresses the similarities between the legendary births of Jesus and Plato.[68] He points out that while the Gospel of Matthew tells us that God sent a message to Joseph in his sleep not to consummate his marriage to the Virgin Mary until after the birth of Jesus, Greek legend tells us that Apollo sent a vision to Ariston in his sleep not to touch the virgin Perictione until after the birth of Plato.[69] Engaging in the same defensive strategy, Justin Martyr emphasizes that the myths of Zeus fathering Dionysus on Semele and Hercules on Alcumena strikingly resemble the story of God fathering Jesus on Mary.[70] And indeed they do—with the difference that Christianity has insisted with peculiar vehemence on the incomparable purity of its heroine.[71]

And yet, as the Middle Ages progressed, this vehement insistence did *not* have the effect of suppressing the many and various sexual implications of the mysterious virgin birth. Quite the contrary. Mary's ever-increasing purification excused and, in that sense, nurtured her scandalousness. In the fourth century, Ambrose identified Mary as the beloved in the Song of Songs, her womb like a mound of wheat surrounded by lilies (7:2).[72] In the twelfth century, Bernard of Clairvaux embroidered on this typological theme, ecstasiating about the special love between Mary, the virgin bride, and Christ, her bridegroom—a sweet wound of love that pierced and permeated her body and soul.[73] In his commentary on the Song of Songs, Bernard elaborates on Mary and Jesus's physical intimacy: "Happy indeed were the kisses [Jesus] pressed on her lips when she was nursing and as a mother delighted in the child in her virgin's lap. But surely will we not deem much happier those kisses which in blessed greeting she receives today from the mouth of him who sits on the right hand of the Father, when she ascends to the throne of glory, singing a nuptial hymn and saying, 'Let him kiss me with the kisses of his mouth'?"[74] Inspired by Bernard's effusions, the high Middle Ages reimagined the Annunciation as a "celestial wedding," as the twelfth-century English Cistercian Aelred of Rievaulx put it: "The bridegroom is God, the bride the virgin, and the bridegroom an angel!"[75] Or rather, as the twelfth-century Benedictine Godfrey of Admont clarifies, all three of the persons of the Trinity serve Mary as her lovers.[76] At the zenith of Mariology in the late Middle Ages, iconography represents the Incarnation as an incestuous and interspecies orgy of God the Father; Jesus, the handsome young man; the Spirit dove; and Mary, their beautiful bride, daughter, mother, and sister.[77]

N-Town engages in this devotional practice most spectacularly. In N-Town's pageant of Mary's Assumption, the Trinity, a chorus of martyrs, and orders of angels sing catches from the Song of Songs, identifying Mary as God's "bride of Lebanon."[78] The martyrs sing,

> Que est ista que assendit de deserto,
> Deliciis affluens, innixa super dilectum suum?
> Who is this who comes up from the wilderness,
> Flowing with delights, leaning on her beloved? (41.343–44)

A three-personed figure, Dominus, answers by singing to Mary,

> Veni tu electa mea et ponam in te thronum meum
> Quia concupivit rex speciem tuam.
> Come, my chosen one, and I will set you upon my throne
> Because the king has desired your beauty. (41.318–19)[79]

After summoning Mary's soul into his lap, Dominus hails her as "my dowe, my nehebor, and my swete frende" (41.510), crowning her as his queen and consort (4.526). As Gail Gibson writes, "Christ calls Mary to him in a liturgy of holy espousal and coronation that is the final and ecstatic triumph of her creating womb."[80] Mary's reproductive system is adoringly described by the Trinity as its "tabernacle of joye, vessel of lyf," and "hefnely temple" (41.511). This encomium neatly fits Leo Steinberg's definition of "genital theology," the late medieval veneration of Jesus's genitals (and, by extension, Mary's) as the symbolic nucleus of the mystery of the Incarnation, the redemption of the flesh.[81] Thanks to Mary's paradoxically fertile virginity, the late medieval cult of the Madonna ultimately did not need to not choose between the pleasures of carnality and chastity, comedy and piety. The Virgin Mother could accommodate both simultaneously.

The Science of the Virgin Birth

In N-Town's dramatization of the Annunciation, the Holy Spirit gives Gabriel two "tokyn[s]" to bestow on Mary as proof of the truth of his words (11.208). The first token, taken from the Gospel of Luke, is the pregnancy of Mary's barren and elderly cousin Elizabeth (11.208–10). The second token, *not* taken from the Bible, is orgasmic pleasure.[82] The Holy Ghost explains,

> Her body shal be so fulfylt with blys
> That she shal sone thynke this sownde credible. (11.211–12)

The Holy Ghost's phrasing stresses the carnality of Mary's experience: she will feel "blys" in "her body."[83] N-Town represents the moment of Mary's conception with an elaborate special effect: God the Father projects three rays of light into Jesus, who reflects and beams these rays into the Holy Ghost, who reflects and beams them into Mary's bosom.[84] Mary can only describe the feeling of being penetrated by these myriad celestial rays with the inexpressibility topos,

> I cannot telle what joy, what blysse
> Now I fele in my body! (11.305–6)

Here, Mary echoes back the emphatically carnal terms used by the Holy Ghost: she says that she feels "blysse . . . in [her] body." This explosion of bliss marks the moment of Jesus's conception and corresponds to an ancient and medieval medical theory that fertilization could not occur without mutual orgasm.

Medieval Scholastic theologians scrutinized the biological process of the virgin birth in explicitly gynecological and embryological terms. Scholastics investigated many such matters: how many angels could dance on the head of a pin, whether Christ would have decomposed if he had not been resurrected, and how Mary's reproductive system processed the conception of Jesus.[85] Most concluded that Mary had reproduced nonsexually by means of spontaneous generation. Yet others (including Rupert of Deutz, Amadeus of Lausanne, Hugh of Saint Victor, and Hildegard of Bingen) came to the very different conclusion that we have seen expressed in N-Town: that Mary and the Holy Ghost reproduced sexually—and yet sinlessly—by means of mutual orgasm.[86]

The medieval investigation of the virgin birth drew on the opposing theories of two ancient medical authorities: Aristotle and Hippocrates. Aristotle argued that male semen gives shape, motion, and life to raw female matter. In effect, Aristotle maintained that females do not actively contribute to reproduction.[87] By contrast, Hippocrates insisted that only the orgasmic mixture of male *and* female semen has the power to produce life.[88] Galen compromised between these two positions, claiming that female seed exists and contributes to reproduction but is too cold, scanty, and wet to "impress an artistic form" all on its own.[89] Yet ultimately Galen, like Hippocrates, believed that conception could not occur without the orgasmic emission of female as well as male seed. Like Hippocrates, Galen saw conception as a collaborative process.[90] By the late Middle Ages, "cautious Galenism" had become the consensus among natural philosophers.[91] Yet when attempting to explain the virgin birth in scientific terms, Aquinas (ever the Aristotelian) rejected this Galenic consensus and reverted to the reassuringly passive model put forward by Aristotle, which had long since been Christianity's preferred template for the virgin birth.

Origen was perhaps the first to explain the virgin birth in terms of Aristotelian science by drawing a comparison between Mary and the vulture, which was believed to reproduce without any copulation but rather thanks to the inseminating breath of the east wind.[92] Various comparisons between Mary and other such creatures followed—for example, the oyster, which was believed to conceive the pearl by opening its shell to the light of sun, moon, and stars.[93] In his *Life of Our Lady*, John Lydgate catalogs examples ("moo than two or three") of virgin births that occur in nature: trees that produce birds instead of fruit; soil that gives birth to snakes; ashes that re-create the phoenix.[94] According to the Aristotelian explanation of Christ's conception, the Holy Ghost played the role of the male seed ("the active principle in generation," *principium activum in generatione*) by catalyzing the separation of pure blood from Mary's menstrual matter like curds from whey and then impressing Jesus's embryonic form onto that purified blood.[95] In other words, Mary remained chastely impassive and insensible throughout the biological process of conception—as inert as the clay that God used to make Adam.[96] She did *not*, Aquinas emphasizes, ejaculate. "A certain concupiscence," Aquinas reminds us, accompanies the emission of female semen, and in "that virginal conception" of Jesus "there could be no concupiscence."[97] Instead, he maintains, "the blessed Virgin did not actively do anything in the conceiving."[98]

As Aquinas's anxious protestations indicate, the Hippocratic and Galenic models were not without their influence on the medieval understanding of the science of the virgin birth. N-Town is not alone in its representation of Mary's orgasm at the moment of conception. Nicholas Love's *Mirror of the Blessed Life of Jesus Christ* agrees that Mary's sensory explosion marked the exact moment of Jesus's conception: "Our Lady was fulfilled and enflamed with the Holy Ghost and in the love of God more burning than she was before, and feeling that she had conceived, kneeled down and thanked God."[99] Or, as the twelfth-century Cistercian Amadeus of Lausanne described it, the Virgin's "womb trembled and swelled at the touch of the Holy Ghost, and her spirit rejoiced, and her womb flowered" at the "divine infusion."[100] This same idea was also expressed by the twelfth-century theologian Hugh of Saint Victor, who argued for the validity of the Galenic model in all cases of reproduction, even in the exceptional case of the virgin birth. Hugh of Saint Victor maintained that love and only love, consummated mutually and joyfully, could persuade Nature to create new life.[101] To his mind, then, Mary's ardent desire had to have actively contributed to the virgin birth. Thanks to and because of her love, "in her flesh the virtue of the Holy Spirit worked marvelous things."[102] Without Mary's emissions of love and joy, Jesus could not have been conceived; Mary's ejaculate "glue[d]" the human to the divine.[103]

Hugh of Saint Victor clarifies that Mary's sacred pleasure had nothing to do with the lust of the flesh for the simple reason that she conceived not through love of man but rather through love of the Holy Spirit.[104] The phrasing of this distinction seems to suggest an underlying assumption that because Mary partnered with the Holy Ghost instead of with a mortal man, the otherwise unchanged process of copulation became its opposite: the transmission of original sin by means of sin turned into the communication of redemption by redeemed means.[105] A similar distinction is also made by Hildegard of Bingen, who interrupts her mystical panegyric to the orgasmic explosion of the virgin birth with disclaimers to the effect that Mary never felt any "human pleasure" during the process of conception.[106] Exactly what Hildegard means by this merits closer inspection.

Aristotle claimed that the heat of male seed (caused by the exhalation of warm, airy spirit, or *pneuma*) purified female menstrual matter into the concocted, refined blood necessary for forming a fetus.[107] From a medieval Christian perspective, however, this claim makes little sense, because sexual reproduction is seen as being necessarily corrupting, not purifying. Thus, in her theory of reproduction, Hildegard rewrites the Aristotelian moment of conception—the curdling of the menstrual blood—as the moment of original sin's transmission. She imagines, then, that in the exceptional case of the virgin birth, the heat of the Holy Spirit (much hotter than the heat of mortal *pneuma*) must have superpurified Mary's blood in Christian as well as Aristotelian terms, cleansing it of the foam (*spuma*) of lust.[108] The "unquenchable fire" of the Holy Ghost inflamed Mary's body (Hildegard uses the verb *incendo*), evaporating the frothy scum of sin that bubbled to the surface.[109]

This model of purification by divine fire echoes Hippocrates's description of an orgasm. Hippocrates understood the heat of *pneuma* as the prime mover of pleasure: he compares the orgasmic spike in sensation "at the moment the seed falls into the uterus" to the leap of flames when wine is poured onto a fire.[110] The purification of Mary's blood need not necessarily have produced an anesthetic effect, numbing her to all sensation. Instead, Hildegard's erotic lyricism suggests that evaporating sin from lust concocts intense and blameless pleasure of the highest grade—pleasure that only Mary, full of grace, has ever had the opportunity to relish.

According to this logic, Mary felt ardent desires, but not lustful desires; she experienced orgasmic bliss, but not concupiscent orgasmic bliss. These distinctions seem more than metaphysical: Mary's pleasures not only change their names (from sins to virtues) but also outdo themselves. One delightful distinction between Mary's exceptional sensations (which we might call supernatural or divine) and those sensations normally (which we might call natural or worldly) seems to be that the sensations feel even better when Mary experiences them; they improve in degree without changing in kind (though changing in category). In Mary's body, sinful lust becomes divine love without changing as a sensation except to upgrade. This pattern follows through in the N-Town plays, which seem much more interested in differentiating between the bliss Mary felt and the bliss felt by other, normal women in terms of quality and quantity rather than kind: she felt more and better bodily pleasure than anyone before or since.[111] Chaucer's Wife of Bath laments, "Allas, allas! That evere love was synne!"[112] For the Madonna of these branches of late medieval Mariology, it never was—her sexual adventures only ever rebounded to the amplification of her paradoxical purity. God's mediation through the Holy Ghost, like his manipulation of Joseph as his tool, may function in one sense to purify the virgin birth of the taint of sexuality, while in another only magnifying its promiscuous pleasures.

Gabriel, God's Wingman

After revealing that Joseph and the Trinity are the fathers of her child, N-Town's Mary still has one final paternal candidate left to name: Gabriel the archangel. When Joseph hears that an angel visited his wife during his absence, he draws his own conclusions. York's Joseph puts it most succinctly: "The aungell," he says, "has made hir with childe" (13.135). In the Towneley Annunciation, this thought staggers Joseph: he asks, incredulous, "Shuld an angell this dede haue wroght?" (10.293).[113] According to ancient Judeo-Christian legend, quite possibly. Genesis tells of angels who defied God by impregnating the daughters of men with mighty sons.[114] Midrashic legends warned maidens not to trust celestial messengers promising divine offspring. After all, the fallen angel used this very trick against Eve by introducing himself to her as God's messenger and then impregnating her with Cain, the spawn of Satan.[115] No wonder, then, that in the apocryphal Gospel of

James, Joseph suspects both angels and demons of having impregnated Mary. He fears to accuse her in case "the child in her is angelic" and therefore far beyond his jurisdiction.[116]

In the Gospel of Luke, neither God nor the Holy Spirit manifests any visible appearance to Mary; it is Gabriel alone who stands and speaks with her during the conception of Jesus. He is the only suspect perceptibly present at the scene of the crime. And what a sight he makes. The Gospel of Luke mentions that when Gabriel first spoke to Mary, she was troubled (*turbata*, "troubled, disturbed, disordered, agitated, excited") (1:29).[117] And yet, according to the second-century apocryphal Gospel of James, Mary received her daily sustenance from the hand of an angel.[118] Why, then, would the familiar sight of an angel upset her so? According to ancient and medieval exegetes, although angels attended Mary every day, Gabriel must have been the first to appear to her disguised as a man.[119] N-Town's Mary explains as much to the audience:

> Aungelys dayly to me doth aper,
> But not in the lyknes of man, that is my fer. (11.232–33)

And not in the likeness of just any man: the apocryphal Gospel of Pseudo-Matthew specifies that Gabriel appeared to Mary as "a young man of indescribable beauty."[120]

Medieval artists elaborated on this detail with enormous enthusiasm. Artists made the archangel ridiculously attractive, expending on him all their very best hairstyles and outfits. Chaucer captures Gabriel's signature look (as seen in the Mérode Altarpiece and so many late medieval images of the Annunciation) with his descriptions of the pretty boys Jankyn, with his "crispe heer, shynynge as gold so fyn," and Absolon, with his golden curls "strouted [stretched out] as a fanne large and brode" and parted in the middle.[121] In N-Town, Joseph grumbles jealously about Gabriel's "clene and gay" finery (12.76): the rich embroidery of gold on red edged in pearl, the ruby- and sapphire-encrusted diadem, the peacock feathers.[122] As the only visible and humanoid agent of God's envoy to the Virgin, Gabriel functions as an attractive showpiece—the Incarnation's representative male object of desire onto which the medieval erotic gaze transfixed its ardent attention.

In his commentary on the Annunciation, Ambrose elaborates that Mary's first sight of Gabriel's attractive disguise prompted a virgin blush: "It is the habit of virgins to tremble, and to be even afraid at the presence of man, and to be shy when he addresses her."[123] It all begins to sound so romantic, especially considering the setting. Medieval artists liked to locate the Annunciation in the intimate space of Mary's bedroom, the *thalamus virginis*, or bridal chamber of the Virgin.[124] Augustine drew a comparison between this larger architectural space and the smaller physical chamber of Mary's womb; riffing on this association, N-Town's Gabriel hails Mary as "Goddys chawmere and his bowre!" (11.316).[125] The Trinity consummate their marriage to Mary in this inner chamber of her body, where fetal Jesus will then live—like a monk in a cell—for nine months.[126] Amplifying this theme, late medieval artists filled Mary's bridal chamber with vaginal symbols: a ball of wax (representing Mary's Aristotelian matter), a volumetric flask (representing the "bridal union" of alchemical reaction), a uterus-shaped curtain sack, and a white pussycat.[127] God and Mary favor Gabriel with intimate access to this symbolic space. The archangel penetrates her virgin bower.

Twelfth-century theologians described the Annunciation as a courtly romance, according to the rules of which (as prescribed by Andreas Capellanus) every lover needs an intermediary—a Galehaut or Pandarus.[128] Aelred of Rievaulx identified Gabriel as God's angelic go-between and bridesman, his *paranymphus angelus*.[129] Yet as the legend of Tristan and Isolde attests, the courtly necessity of employing an intermediary puts the lover at great risk. When King Mark sent Tristan to woo Isolde on his behalf, Tristan wooed for himself. Small wonder, as the genre of courtly love tends to favor adultery over marriage. We all know how the story of the king, queen, and handsome knight tends to end. In N-Town, Gabriel pledges his service to Mary as a knight would to his lady. Mary instigates this pledge: she requests that Gabriel visit her regularly in her chambers (11.325–27), as "youre presence is my comfortacyon" (11.238). Gabriel vows to serve her, since she is

> the gentyllest of blood and hyest of kynrede
> That reynyth in erth in ony degree. (11.330–31)

This emphasis on her noble rank positions their relationship in a courtly milieu, setting up the generic expectation of an elegant affair. Chaucer's savvy Nicholas exploits the romantic appeal of Gabriel's courtly tête-à-tête with the Virgin, serenading Alisoun with *Angelus ad virginem*, playing Gabriel to her

Mary.[130] As Chaucer says of "hende [courteous] Nicholas," "Of deerne love he koude and of solas."[131]

And yet, departing from the generic conventions of courtly romance, the relationship between Mary and Gabriel is no secret, least of all to God. Unlike the average courtly king, God explicitly and intentionally orchestrates his queen's courtly liaison with his underling. God employs Gabriel in the collaborative effort of the virgin birth as the representative of his "hey inbassett" (high embassy) (11.213), an "ambassadour" or "procuratour" being "one who acts or speaks for another."[132] And while medieval interpretive consensus carefully separated Gabriel's diplomatic function from the Holy Ghost's role as the agent of conception, alternative readings confused these categories, making Gabriel yet another active participant in the group effort of Mary's impregnation.

The Gospel of John refers to Jesus as "the Word made flesh" (1:14). From this, exegetes concluded that the Word must have impregnated Mary. According to the theory of the *conceptio per aurem*, God's words (*Ave Maria, gratia plena*) acted as the seminal principle that sparked conception in Mary's eardrum, an unusual reproductive method also witnessed (according to the bestiaries) in the weasel.[133] The question then becomes whether it was the content of God's message that catalyzed conception or the potent medium of Gabriel's voice.[134] Medieval images of the Annunciation illuminate this confusion. While some show a speech scroll descending from the mouth of God the Father, others (like the fourteenth-century Annunciation by Simone Martini and Lippo Memmi) extend a scroll directly from Gabriel's mouth into the waiting ear of the Virgin.[135] As a thirteenth-century English lyric addressed to Mary puts it,

> Through thine ear thou were with child,
> Gabriel, he said it thee.[136]

Thus, in N-Town's pageant of the Annunciation, Mary thanks Gabriel for the deliverance of Jesus's orgasmic conception: "Aungel Gabryel, I thank *yow* for thys" (11.307).[137]

The theory of the *conceptio per aurem* reiterates our central theme: intermediation. In one sense, God's use of intermediaries in the collaborative effort of the virgin birth serves to fortify the purity of Jesus's conception. In this sense, these intermediaries insert a respectable distance between God and Mary—like chaperones at a dance. Yet in order for impregnation to oc-cur, as it must, these chaperones must facilitate, rather than prevent, the union of their charges. Each additional mediator—the Holy Ghost, Gabriel, and Joseph—actually augments the promiscuity of the virgin birth. The logic of generosity and excess, rather than of fragility or defensiveness, or-chestrates this mediation. In this sense, the superabundance of grace gush-ing from the very source and epicenter of redemption (the instant of the Incarnation's accomplishment) demands to be shared, freely and promiscu-ously. Overflowing with grace, Mary spreads it around.

"Sum Man in Aungellis Liknesse"

God wears many masks in the divine comedy of Mary's impregnation: he employs Joseph as his beard, Gabriel as his emissary, and the Holy Ghost as his agent—or some combination of these functions thereof. All this to ac-complish the ultimate impersonation: disguising Jesus in Mary's flesh. Me-dieval theologians explained these many machinations as necessary means to deceive the Deceiver.[138] In late antiquity, the plot was even thicker: con-spiratorial exegetes influenced by Gnosticism speculated that Gabriel could actually have been Jesus in disguise, and Mary the archangel Michael.[139] In the game of cosmic espionage, appearances deceive.

These hermeneutics of suspicion seem to have gotten to the Joseph of the apocryphal Gospel of Pseudo-Matthew. When Mary's handmaidens protest the innocence of their mistress, Joseph accuses them of attempting to deceive him (the verb used in Latin is *seduco*).[140] The handmaidens insist that only an angel could have impregnated Mary because no man ever touched her. Joseph answers, "Why are you misleading me, making me believe you, that an angel of God has made her pregnant? It could be that someone disguised himself as an angel and seduced her."[141] In other words, Joseph suspects that this "archangel Gabriel" was merely a disguise worn by some cad with bad intentions. With this remark, the Gospel of Pseudo-Matthew inspired a tra-dition of interpreting the mystery of the Incarnation in terms of the battle of the sexes. Joseph's suspicions about this so-called angel suggest a comic read-ing of the Annunciation as an elaborate ruse. According to theologians, the chicanery of the Incarnation duped Satan. Medieval fabliau retellings of the story, on the other hand, redirected the punch line, always at Joseph but sometimes also at Mary herself.[142]

Joseph's comment from the Gospel of Pseudo-Matthew, for example, targets Mary as the butt of the joke. By excusing his wife and blaming her handmaidens, Joseph implies that Mary was the victim of a long con. The York cycle dramatizes this particular interpretation of events. After interrogating Mary's handmaidens, Joseph claims to have figured out their ploy: "Thanne se I wele youre menynge is," he says, "som man in aungellis liknesse" beguiled Mary "with somkyn gawde [trick]" (13.134–37). Wise to the game (as he thinks), Joseph silences the handmaidens' protestations:

> We, why gab ye me swa
> And feynes swilk fantassy? (13.141–42)

You've been caught; why keep up the lie? York's Joseph seems to conclude that Mary's handmaidens are trying to shirk responsibility for their failure as chaperones: under their watch, "som man" deflowered the Virgin. Joseph interprets their account of the Annunciation as a crafty attempt to excuse their failure (and their mistress's shame) with outrageous lies.[143] He holds them responsible for the entire fiasco. Poor Mary may have been "beguiled," he says, but her handmaidens are crafty liars.

York's Joseph, then, not only accuses Mary's handmaidens of lying but also insinuates a deeper conspiracy. Since he charges the handmaidens with knowing full well that this "Gabriel" was no angel, he must assume that they had to have known as much all along. Therefore, Joseph suggests that a sexual predator masquerading as an angel must have corrupted Mary's chaperones in order to gain access to their innocent mistress. Such situations are not uncommon in fabliaux and courtly literature. Illicit romance depends on the corruptibility of handmaidens, a notoriously crooked type. In *The Romance of the Rose*, the suitor need only bribe La Vieille with compliments and promises in order to persuade her to leave the back door to the garden unlocked for his easy access to her unsuspecting charge.[144]

Biblical drama is not alone in its comic elaboration of Joseph's apocryphal suspicion that some man pretending to be an angel made a fool of Mary. Boccaccio unspools an entire fabliau from the notion.[145] The second tale of the fourth day in the *Decameron* recounts the story of an unscrupulous

Franciscan friar who exploits the Annunciation's utility as a blueprint for the seduction of virtuous Christian ladies.[146] This friar targets an especially credulous Venetian *madonna*, who considers herself (like the capital-*M* Madonna) paradisiacal in her exceptionalism.[147] The handsome archangel Gabriel holds a special fascination for this *madonna*: she "loved him and never let the opportunity go by to light a four-penny candle for him whenever she saw his image in a painting."[148] Parodying the Gospel of Luke, the friar presents himself as Gabriel's go-between—the messenger of God's messenger, the emissary's emissary—and makes an indecent proposal on behalf of the archangel. In a clever manipulation of the ambiguities of the virgin birth, the friar explains that if the lady sleeps with him, his body will serve as the vessel through which Gabriel communicates his intentions, just as Gabriel explained to Mary that he would function as the vessel through which God communicated *his* intentions. The *madonna* consents to this proposition on the condition that Gabriel abandon her rival, the Virgin Mary. Jealously, she complains that she has heard that Gabriel adores the Virgin, a rumor confirmed by the fact that "wherever she saw him, he was always on his knees in front of her."[149]

Boccaccio positions his *madonna* as the friar's gull, thereby implicating *the* Madonna as the dupe of a celestial sexual heist, in line with Joseph's worst suspicions. Much of the black humor of Boccaccio's fabliau derives from his reading of the Annunciation as a predatory fantasy. By contrast, the N-Town plays reverse the joke to score yet another point for Mary at Joseph's expense. In N-Town, Joseph chastises Mary's maid Sephor for putting "an aungel in so gret blame" (12.73) and accuses her of lying. He says,

> It was sum boy began this game
> That clothyd was clene and gay,
> And ye geve hym now an aungel name! (12.75–77)[150]

Unlike York's Joseph, N-Town's Joseph does not suspect that "Gabriel" came disguised as an angel, only that he was "clothed clean and gay." He was, in other words, as well dressed *as* an angel. Not supernatural—just stylish. Neither does N-Town's Joseph presume Mary's innocence. Rather, this version of Joseph seems to suspect the old trick of the spontaneous excuse, a mainstay of the fabliaux.[151] Fabliaux delight in the ingenious lie crafted in the very moment of discovery. The goal of the game is to invent an excuse that both assuages and humiliates the cuckold in equal measure. Almost an entire day of the *Decameron* is devoted to this art form. One especially masterful liar fornicates with her lover right in front of her husband and then manages to persuade the cuckold not to believe his own eyes.[152]

N-Town's Joseph suspects Mary and Sephor of practicing this feminine craft. He deduces that Sephor must have colluded with her mistress in order to arrange an assignation with some fancy-pants boy—and now, when the women are caught red-handed (with a visibly pregnant "virgin"), he assumes that Sephor is trying to dupe him with an insultingly ludicrous excuse. This suspicion places Mary among the ranks of fabliau and courtly heroines who, with the invaluable help of their trusty attendants, excel at outfoxing the tyrannical supervision of their husbands, brothers, and fathers. The Wife of Bath offers a tip to wise wives: handmaidens make the best witnesses. When a husband accuses his wife of infidelity, the Wife counsels, she should stick to her story,

> and take witnesse of hir owene mayde
> Of hir assent.[153]

The Romance of the Rose represents this craft as an oral tradition passed down from attendant to mistress, generation to generation. La Vieille teaches her charge how to drug a man with opiates, get him in through the window, and hide him under the roof or in a chest.[154] She knows all the best spots for secret assignations: cellars, woods, tents and hangings, wardrobes and attics, pantries and stables.[155] By accusing Sephor and Mary of being partners in crime, Joseph phrases Sephor as Mary's procuress, the fabliau correspondent to Gabriel, God's pander.

Chapter 2

Testing the Chastity of the Divine Adulteress

The catalog of Jesus's fathers listed in N-Town's pageant of "Joseph's Doubt" ends with a suspect nominated not by Mary but rather by her husband. After listening to Mary's many excuses, Joseph comes up with his own explanation: "sum boy" must have done the deed (12.75).[1] The allegorical gossips Raise-Slander and Back-Biter agree: "sum fresch yonge galaunt" must have impregnated the Virgin (14.87). Of all the rumors that have haunted the legend of the virgin birth, this one is by far the worst. It claims that Jesus was not the Son of God, an archangel, or his adoptive father—and that Mary was not impregnated by a deity, an archangel, or her betrothed husband. Instead, humiliatingly, it makes Jesus the son and Mary the victim of some nameless nobody who abandoned them to their shame. This rumor, in other words, demotes Jesus all the way from divinity to bastard, and Mary from virgin to adulteress. Historically, Christianity has not brooked this slander with equanimity; two millennia of precedent have established that outrage and even violence can follow fast upon its insinuation.

And yet if we follow the rumor of Jesus's illegitimacy back to its original source in the New Testament, we hear no furious denial—only a profoundly ambiguous silence. The Gospels of Matthew and Luke circumnavigate the possibility that Mary committed adultery, leaving the possibility unspoken.[2] The Gospel of Matthew will not even say *why* Joseph contemplated abandoning his bride upon discovering her pregnancy.[3] This circumlocution could be interpreted as high-minded refusal to dignify that basest calumny with a response. And yet by refusing to deny that Mary committed adultery, the Gospels effectively leave that possibility wide open.[4] Matthew's and Luke's only explicit denials stipulate that neither Joseph nor God the Father impregnated Mary by means of sexual intercourse; they do not completely foreclose the possibility of adultery. If we proceed backward from the doctrine of the virgin birth, then the solution to this riddle must be that the Holy Ghost (and neither Joseph nor God the Father) impregnated Mary by means of a miracle (rather than sexual intercourse).[5] But if we do not proceed from this foregone conclusion, then what the New Testament scholar Raymond E. Brown has called "a very unpleasant alternative" arises.[6] What if Mary sexually reproduced not with Joseph or with God the Father but rather with some anonymous third party—"sum boy," as N-Town puts it?

In the late twentieth century, New Testament scholars began to reconsider this ancient question from a feminist perspective.[7] Most famously, Jane Schaberg made a provocative and persuasive case for interpreting Mary as a survivor of rape by a Roman soldier.[8] According to Schaberg's reading, the Gospels represent the Virgin as yet another victim of circumstance condemned by society and yet exalted by God, the last link in the typological chain connecting Tamar, Rahab, Ruth, and Bathsheba, the foremothers listed in Matthew's genealogy of Jesus.[9] Furthermore, Schaberg interprets Mary's rape as the first iteration of the New Testament's many inversions of Roman violence, a pattern culminating with Jesus's Crucifixion, which, like his conception, turns guilt into innocence and shame into glory.[10]

This positive take on Jesus's illegitimacy, as Schaberg admits, remains elusive: a subtext hidden in silence.[11] Less difficult to discern are the insults that the Gospels report were shouted at Jesus by anonymous voices in the crowd. In John 8:41, someone cries out, "*We* were not born of fornication," implying the currency of a rumor that Jesus could not say the same for himself.[12] In Mark 6:3, hecklers call Christ "the son of Mary," departing from the Judaic convention of identifying sons by their fathers, and thereby insinuating that Jesus did not know his real father's name.[13] In these insults, we hear the unspoken alternative implied by Matthew and Luke given voice. A very specific voice: that of an enemy. When said out loud, the possibility of Mary's adultery sounds polemical.

And, indeed, these insults recur, much more elaborately and unmistakably, in polemical records external to the New Testament. Perhaps as early as the end of the first century, certain rabbinic texts refer to Jesus as "the son of Pantera" (or "Pandera") rather than the son of Joseph.[14] The medieval *Toledot Yeshu*, or *History of Jesus*, a controversial Hebraic parody of the New Testament, fleshes out the backstory behind this epithet.[15] The *Toledot Yeshu* claims that "a certain disreputable man" named Joseph Pandera of the house of Judah tricked Mary into granting him access to her private chamber by pretending to be Joseph, her betrothed husband. Once inside, he raped her. According to the *Toledot Yeshu*, this rape conceived Jesus, "an illegitimate child and the son of a *niddah*," an unclean woman.[16]

In the Gospels, Jesus refuses to respond to the insults of his detractors, just as he refuses to reply to the accusations of Herod and Pilate. But as early as the second century, Christianity stopped turning the other cheek to this particular slap and started fighting back. Ambiguous silence gave way to extensive and richly detailed denials. New evangelists (posing as old evangelists) felt the need to supplement the Gospels with additional, apocryphal proof of Mary's purity.[17] This additional proof necessitated the incorporation of additional doubts, because proof requires doubt's catalyst. According to the logic of the apocryphal Infancy Gospels, God only supplies evidence of Mary's virginity on demand. Therefore, the defenders of Mary's chastity had to take it on themselves to collect and construct, conserve and curate, and expand and disseminate a vast archive of accusations against the Virgin—some collected from the mouths of disbelievers and others invented in the fecund imaginations of the faithful.

The Trials of the Virgin from the Apocryphal Gospels to N-Town

First, the apocryphal Proto-Gospel of James (and, in turn, its Latin adaptation, the Gospel of Pseudo-Matthew) added a public trial to the story of the

Nativity, subjecting the pregnant Virgin to both an interrogation and an ordeal.[18] Trials of chastity tend to demand the impossible.[19] The vestal virgin Tuccia, according to legend, had to prove her virginity by carrying water in a porous sieve from the Tiber to the Temple of Vesta without spilling a drop.[20] Between 1166 and 1215 in England, wives tested by fire had to hold a red-hot iron without wounding their flesh, while those tested by water had to sink rather than float when submerged.[21] And, in the apocryphal Infancy Gospels, the people of Nazareth demand that Mary survive the ingestion of poison in order to prove herself innocent of the charge of adultery. Such tests frame innocence as a suspension of the laws of nature. According to the rules of this game, survival demands nothing less than a miracle.

As luck would have it, the Virgin is the mother of miracles. In the Protoevangelium Jacobi, Mary swallows the poison and survives, fully exonerated.[22] But her trials and tribulations have only just begun. Immediately after narrating the blessed event of the virgin birth, the apocryphal Proto-Gospel of James summons an expert witness to conduct an invasive, postpartum medical examination of Mary's genitals.[23] "Brace yourself," Salome the Doubting Midwife says to Mary, "for there is no small controversy concerning you."[24] Yet again, Mary passes the test, allaying all suspicions. Or at least for the time being.

All this evidence—legal, medical, and miraculous—could not satiate Christianity's hunger for proof of Mary's virginity. Late antiquity and the Middle Ages continued to supplement the supplemental apocrypha of James and Pseudo-Matthew with even more attacks, tests, and trials.[25] In the long-accumulated legendary life of the Virgin narrated by late medieval stained glass windows, wall paintings, altarpiece carvings, manuscript illuminations, hagiography, homiletics, and the living Bibles of civic drama, Mary submits to the insults, questions, and demands of one skeptic after another: her husband, her neighbors, her relatives, her bishop, her midwives, and even passing strangers.[26] In the legend of the Purification of the Virgin dramatized by the Chester cycle, the very first man that Mary meets after her ceremonial forty days of recovery from childbirth questions the doctrine of the virgin birth and demands yet another performance (or rather, technically, two back-to-back performances) of miraculous proof before he will recant—a demand that God accommodates yet again (and then again).[27] But it is never enough.

Although the trials of the Virgin abate while Jesus takes center stage during his ministry, Crucifixion, and Resurrection, old doubts resurface after his Ascension.[28] And with a vengeance. After such a long wait between proofs (decades in diegetic time and hours in performance), skepticism degrades into sheer aggression. In N-Town's pageant of the Assumption of the Virgin, Mary's detractors can barely articulate their allegations through their rage. Cursing and sputtering, they broadly accuse "Mary, that fise" (meaning fart), of spreading "myschefe," "stench," and "steyn" (41.83).[29] They plot violent attacks against her "bychyd body," which they long to torture, burn, and scatter to the winds (41.396).[30] Essentially, these detractors seek to test the inviolability of the Virgin in the most rudimentary way possible: by means of violation.

As Mary's funerary bier is carried through the streets by the apostles, these skeptics launch an assault against her coffin, "intending," as *The Golden Legend* tells the tale, "to overturn it and throw the corpse to the ground"—in essence, to humiliate her, to bring her down, both literally and symbolically.[31] But God will not allow it. The instant that their hands touch the bier, an "invisible sword of fire" cuts them off at the shoulders, leaving their severed limbs "hanging in the air beside the bed."[32] At long last, the sweet relief of proof. Glutted on this spectacular evidence, all the onlookers convert, finally fully convinced of Mary's virginity. Or rather, almost everyone, and only for a moment. Still unsatisfied, N-Town feels the need to top this gory showstopper by staging an even bloodier climax: the onstage vivisection of one final holdout, an especially recalcitrant skeptic (one "Princeps 3") who out-and-out refuses to repent.[33] Devils tear his body apart, set him on fire, and toss what is left into a boiling hellmouth, staging his dismemberment as proof of Mary's integrity.[34]

It does not end there. Even after God translates Mary's body and soul into paradise and crowns her as the Queen of Heaven, she must continue to prove her chastity to disbelievers back on earth. According to the apocryphal account of the Assumption of the Virgin, Doubting Thomas, true to his name, "refused to believe" that Mary had ascended into the clouds.[35] In order to put his mind at ease, Mary must descend from her heavenly throne and drop "the girdle that had encircled her body" into his waiting hands. This "intact" circle of fabric serves as evidence that the Virgin's hymen evaded the wormy penetrations of the grave.[36] With this final test, the trials of the Virgin end—until, of course, the narrative, iconographic, liturgical, or theatrical cycle begins again.

Perhaps unsurprisingly, the apocryphal Gospels at the root of these traditions express themselves rather defensively, in the rhetorical mode of apology.[37] After all, they have so much for which to apologize. These texts disparage the canonical Gospels by implying their insufficiency and forging their authority, flaunt the slander and abuse of the Mother of God, and demand an unending supply of miraculous proofs, taking nothing on faith alone. Jesus sharply rebuked the faithless Pharisees who tempted him to perform a miracle: "A wicked and adulterous generation seeketh after a sign," he said, "and a sign shall not be given it" (Matthew 16:4).[38] And yet the apocryphal Gospels boldly presume to coerce signs from God by effectively holding his beloved bride and mother hostage. When Mary Magdalene reached out to touch the body of the resurrected Christ, he chastised her: "Do not touch me" (John 20:17). And yet the apocryphal Gospels dare to grab the Mother of God by her genitals, grasping for carnal proof of her virginity. The Gospels of Matthew and Luke shrouded the miracle of the virgin birth in discreet ambiguity—in the words of Ignatius of Antioch, deep inside the profound "silence of God."[39] Yet the apocryphal Gospels rudely violate this silence, trading in mystery and dignity for embarrassingly rudimentary spectacles of hard evidence.

The apocryphal Gospels have a ready excuse for these suspect narrative choices. They frame each and every trial of the Virgin as an unavoidable and proportionate response to the malicious provocations of detractors. And they tend to identify these detractors as Jews.[40] The Proto-Gospel of James blames the first trial of the Virgin on "Annas the scribe," who sets the entire judicial process in motion by informing against Mary and Joseph to the Temple.[41] The subsequent ordeal is then pinned on the Law of Moses, which, as the Infancy Gospels stress, decrees that women suspected of adultery must face either trial by poison or death by stoning. The Gospel of Pseudo-Matthew goes on to describe Mary's Jewish midwives as stern and even sadistic enforcers of Jehovah's Curse of Eve, infuriated by Mary's disobedient lack of suffering.[42] Continuing this pattern, the apocryphal legend of the funeral of the Virgin identifies the assailant who attacks Mary's coffin as "a certain Hebrew named Jephonias" and the surrounding crowd of bystanders as "all the people of the Jews."[43] Not us but rather them. As these narratives have it, Jewish instigators and bystanders both produced and consumed the trials of the Virgin, while Christians—utterly passive and guiltless—merely reported the facts for posterity.

Making use of a strikingly similar excuse, the fathers of the Church who interrogated Mary's virginity for an audience of Christian readers tended to claim to speak to outsiders in Mary's defense: Justin Martyr blamed Trypho; Origen, Celsus; and Jerome, Helvidius—Jews, heathens, and heretics who, rather conveniently, could not speak for themselves.[44] In order to defend the Virgin, Origen felt that he needed to paraphrase and sometimes quote verbatim, at great length and in full detail, the horrible slanders written by his enemy, whom he identified as the second-century Greek philosopher Celsus.[45] No other record of Celsus's remarks survives. Effectively, Origen rescued Celsus's anti-Christian polemic from oblivion, not only preserving but also promulgating its slanders—just as the apocryphal Gospels elaborated and disseminated insults and accusations against Mary found nowhere else, integrating them inextricably into Christianity's mythology of the Virgin.

As part of his defense of Mary's chastity, Origen repeats what Celsus allegedly imagined a hypothetical Jewish interrogator might have said to Jesus had they had the opportunity to confer. This imaginary Jew accuses Jesus of having "fabricated the story of [his] birth from a virgin to quiet rumors about the true and unsavory circumstances of [his] origins," the awful truth being that "a Roman soldier named Panthera" impregnated, abandoned, and disgraced Mary.[46] In other words, a notorious bastard fathered an illegitimate faith. Having set Celsus's argument up for demolition, Origen proceeds to tear it down. And yet unlike the apocryphal Gospels, which respond to slanders against the Virgin with denials, Origen pursues a more complicated and paradoxical defensive strategy, as is his wont.[47] He celebrates rather than refutes the accusations that his opponent finds so damning.

For example, the apocryphal Gospels vehemently insist that the Virgin Mary derived from noble stock and lived like royalty.[48] Scholars have taken this insistence as evidence of the existence of a contrary polemical tradition external to Christianity.[49] And indeed, Celsus seems to prove this point. According to Origen, Celsus called Mary a "poor country woman who earned her living by spinning."[50] The apocryphal Gospels respond to this allegation by taking the opposite position: Mary was not poor but rather rich; not a peasant but rather a princess. By contrast, Origen takes the insult as a compliment. And why not? We need not seek out polemic external to Christianity in order to find the source of the tradition of Jesus's humble origins. The New Testament itself tells that story: "And she brought forth her firstborn son, and wrapped him up in swaddling clothes, and laid him in a manger; because there was no room for them in the inn" (Luke 2:7). Origen stands his ground in the face of Celsus's scorn, proudly celebrating Jesus for having risen from poverty and obscurity to "shake the world."[51]

In fact, Origen catalogs all Celsus's many aspersions against Jesus and Mary—including even the report of Jesus's illegitimacy—and concludes that "all of these things" in a "fundamental" sense actually harmonize with Christ's mysterious divinity.[52] In 1 Corinthians 1:23, Paul preaches Christ crucified, scandalous to the Jews and foolish to the Gentiles. Origen takes up this contrarian strategy, building his celebratory theology on the foundation of his enemies' laughter. At least for a moment, Origen seems to embrace the origin myth of scandalous adultery as an appropriate—and even ideal—exposition for the life of Jesus Christ.

This moment of possibility does not last long. After seeming to suggest that Jesus's illegitimacy only magnified his glory, Origen backtracks to clarify his position on Mary's virginity. Reversing his own logic, he argues that God the Father would never have subjected his Son to "a birth more shameful than any."[53] Upending his thesis, Origen insists that Jesus could not have been virtuous had his mother been impure. "The offspring" of an adulteress, he argues, would necessarily have been "some stupid man who would harm men by teaching licentiousness, unrighteousness, and other evils, and not a teacher of self-control, righteousness, and other virtues."[54] Rather than inverting Celsus's values by championing humility over glory and mercy over justice, Origen accepts the validity of Celsus's accusation. In this one instance, he denies the accusation's facticity without dismantling its logic. Apparently, Origen could stand for Jesus to bear any humiliation (including poverty, torture, and execution) except illegitimacy. That worst scandal he simply could not stomach—or at least not for long. As in the Gospels, the possibility of a redemptive reading of Jesus's illegitimacy remains elusive and insubstantial, unlike its overt manifestation as polemic.

Over time, polemic came to define the Virgin Mary. By the Middle Ages, the narratives of the life of the Virgin and the Miracles of Our Lady had become bloody battlegrounds.[55] Medieval Mariology produced an enormous catalog of hideous transgressions allegedly committed against the Virgin by heathens, heretics, Jews, and Muslims.[56] In such narratives, the enemies of Christianity desecrate the host, torture saints, poison wells, cannibalize infants, and insult the Virgin. In 850, Saint Eulogius of Córdoba claimed that the Qur'an described Muhammad's rape of Mary, a lie that energized an uprising against the caliphate.[57] In 1240, King Louis the IX of France put the Talmud on trial.[58] When its alleged slanders against the Virgin were read aloud in court—that Miriam had been a lowly hairdresser, an adulteress, and a *sotah* (outcast)—the audience exploded with rage, and the Talmud was sentenced to the bonfire.[59] In fifteenth- and early sixteenth-century England, the Inquisition accused heretics of remarkably similar crimes. It was reported that one Lollard had used her last words to proclaim that Mary had conceived Jesus in sin, and that this heretic had thereby infected another heretic, who subsequently took to promulgating Jesus's illegitimacy in the streets.[60] The "govundy syght" (gunky, infected sight) of heretics, John Lydgate complained, "ne may not systeyne / For to beholde, the clennesse" of the Virgin.[61] Instead, he implies, Christianity's blind enemies beheld the filth of whoredom.

The study of the allegation of Mary's adultery has tended to restrict itself to this polemical nether sphere of lies and nightmares.[62] When limited to this context, aspersions against the purity of the Virgin become nothing more than trumped-up falsehoods motivated by hatred, projected onto imaginary others, and punished on the innocent bodies of scapegoats. Strangely enough, this interpretive method overlaps, to a certain extent, with the apologetic strategy employed by the apocryphal evangelists and the patristic fathers in their defenses of Mary's virginity. Both methods depend on the assumption that Christianity's interactions with outsiders inspired and sustained the rumor of Jesus's illegitimacy—as if Christianity could have no reason to put Mary on trial for adultery other than to shame its enemies or frame its victims.

And yet contradictions of the doctrine of the Madonna's virginity do not restrict themselves to purely polemical contexts. Rather, once embedded within hagiography, iconography, and liturgy, the accusation of Mary's adultery took on an uncanny life of its own. Case in point: Late medieval sacred drama—and N-Town in particular—compiles, extends, and embellishes insults against the Virgin accumulated for more than a millennium, translating and updating these slurs into the choicest terms of the local vernacular. Vulgarized, poeticized, and played for laughs, these slanders seem to function as crowd pleasers and even as a kind of devotional practice. Upon closer examination, it begins to look as if these insults celebrate and venerate the adulterous Virgin denied but also preserved and promulgated by centuries of apologists. Perhaps this scandalous version of the Virgin survived and thrived not only because she made such an effective polemical tool, whether defensive or offensive, but also because sinners loved the way she made them feel: amused, aroused, understood, and forgiven.

In N-Town's Nativity pageant, Mary laughs as she gives birth to Jesus. Rather than bringing forth her child in sorrow, she flaunts her triumph over the Curse of Eve. Startled by this merry miracle, Joseph demands an explanation: "Why do ye lawghe, wyff?" (15.182). As the stage directions specify, Mary replies, smiling (*Hic Maria subridendo, dicat*),

> The chylde that is born wyl preve his modyr fre,
> A very clene mayde, and therfore I smyle. (15.180–81)

Over the course of the N-Town manuscript, this prophecy comes true, but not how we might expect. Yes, God proves his mother's virginity—but never once and for all, only time and again. The cyclical pattern of the liturgical and civic calendar can only have amplified this sense of repetition, as reenactments of Mary's series of trials looped through the years, decades, and centuries. And yet N-Town's Mary does not seem to mind this unending cycle of interrogations, inquisitions, examinations, and ordeals—all this ranting and raving, poking and prodding, badgering and fisting. Rather, she seems to tolerate the farce of her persecution with equanimity, if not also (as her laughter would seem to suggest) amusement and even enjoyment.

In this spirit of good-humored tolerance, N-Town tends to reward rather than punish Mary's detractors.[63] In the entire compilation, only three perpetrators are ever punished for their crimes against the Virgin. After the trial by water, God tortures (and then heals) Raise-Slander; after the midwives' examination, God withers (and then restores) Salome's offending hand; after the assault against Mary's corpse, devils drag Princeps 3, Mary's unrepentant attacker, to hell.[64] But no one else is punished: not the bishop who accused Mary of fornication; the summoner or the three lawyers who called her whore; Back-Biter, who slandered her name; Zelomy, the first midwife, who subjected her to a postpartum gynecological examination; Simeon, who twice denied the virgin birth; or Princeps 1 or 2, who both assaulted her coffin.

Nor, for that matter, Joseph. And yet Joseph abuses Mary repeatedly. First, he publicly accuses her of deceptive, adulterous, and even murderous inclinations.[65] Second, he charges her with adultery and threatens to have her stoned to death.[66] Third, in a sudden rage, he revokes his vow to protect and provide for the mother of another man's child.[67] An unexceptional woman, in these situations, might find herself abandoned, ruined, and destroyed. But for the grace of God, Joseph could have done some serious damage. Yet he goes entirely unpunished, and is even rewarded, for his offenses. God dignifies each of Joseph's outbursts with a generous response, patiently providing three miraculous demonstrations of Mary's virginity. Following suit, Mary responds to her husband's threats and insults with thanks, hugs, and kisses.[68] It is as if she finds his abuse endearing.[69]

Perhaps this is because she cannot be abused. The Virgin, like her virginity, is invulnerable. Frustratingly for the green-eyed monster of jealousy, the purity of unexceptional women remains "an essence that's not seen" (as Iago put it to Othello) unless made manifest by the red evidence of the hymen's destruction.[70] Transferring the logic of blood on the sheets, ancient and medieval exemplars of virginity put their faith in the proof of gore. Lucretia and her many imitators verified their innocence by opening their veins; blood-spurting decapitations ratified the purity of the virgin martyrs.[71] These evidentiary methods give and yet they take away, leaving witnesses bereft of the very jewel whose value has just been so incontrovertibly proved.[72] Thus the unnatural delight of Mary and her perpetual virginity, which even the most violent investigative penetrations could not damage. After each assault, Mary is always like a virgin yet again, as if touched for the very first time, despite so much manhandling. Her magical invulnerability turns the trial by ordeal into a harmless game, violence into play, tragedy into comedy.

Inquisition and Ordeal in N-Town's "Trial of Mary and Joseph"

N-Town sets its pageant of "The Trial of Mary and Joseph" here and now rather than long ago and far away: in fifteenth-century East Anglia rather than first-century Nazareth.[73] Relatively little effort is made to distance the trial from its audience or to shift blame onto an externalized other.[74] On the contrary, the pageant forces its spectators to actively participate in Mary's persecution. The dramatic action begins with an injunction spoken directly to the audience by a summoner:

> Avoyd, serys, and lete my lorde the buschop come
> And syt in the courte, the lawes for to doo! (14.1–2)

We know this type well from the genre of estates satire: a summoner is an un-christian Christian, a caricature of the institutional failures of contemporary canon law.[75] This familiar figure refers to the arena that he enters as "this place" (namely, the makeshift *platea* shared by actors and audience) and summons the spectators to an ecclesiastical court presided over by a bishop (Episcopus Abizachar) and his legal minions (a team of canon lawyers, or *legis doctores*), thereby blurring the distinction not only between the past and the present but also between this theatrical performance and the civic rituals of daily life.[76] "I warne yow here all abowte," he says, "that I somown yow all the rowte!" (14.5–6).

The summoner then produces a book of records and prepares to call out the names of those accused by their neighbors.[77] For a moment, the summoner seems poised to hail members of the audience by name.[78] But instead, he identifies them by type—a more flexible approach. He summons the local butcher and miller ("Bertylmew the bochere" and "Miles the myllere"), as well as the local liar and cheat ("Luce Lyere" and "Geffrey Gyle"). Gossip is the thematic focus of his roll call of sins. As Richard Moll has pointed out, the names that he reads off his list suggest the clanging of pots and pans ("Tyndere" and "Pottere"), the chattering of idle tongues ("Cakelere" and "Mylkdoke"), and the cruelty of gossip ("Smalfeyth" and "Lytyl Trust").[79] (A "milk-duck," by the way, is a time waster and, in this context, a gossip.)[80] When the spectators answer his summons and approach the scaffold, they identify themselves as telltales, blabbermouths, and scandalmongers. As such, they become defendants, informants, and witnesses, tightly entangled in the net of the ecclesiastical judicial system and the reenactment of the Virgin's persecution.

In the apocryphal Gospel of James, "the sons of Israel" discover Mary's pregnancy and assume the worst.[81] But in N-Town, it is the audience who commits this crime. At the scaffold, N-Town's spectators encounter their own sins made manifest in the stock allegorical figures of Raise-Slander and Back-Biter, "kyd and knowyn in many a place" (14.63).[82] After establishing a bond with the audience, these Vices begin to spread vicious rumors about the Virgin Mary. When Back-Biter asks for the newest gossip, Raise-Slander tells him to prepare to "lawgh ryght wel" (14.69)—words also peculiarly applicable to spectators gathered to enjoy a farce. "Mayd Mary," he says, swore to keep her virginity intact, and yet "her wombe doth swelle" (14.80).

As Raise-Slander reminds us, N-Town's Mary and Joseph made mutual vows of abstinence at the public ceremony of their *syneisaktism*, or white marriage.[83] In late medieval culture, breaking such an oath constituted a mortal sin and, perhaps worse, a scandal. Records demonstrate that white marriages incited such aggressive skepticism and scrutiny from servants, neighbors, and summoners that couples tended to hide their virtuous continence like a dirty secret.[84] When the secret of Margery Kempe's marital abstinence got out, it brought down an onslaught of surveillance, ostracism, and humiliation.[85] Here, N-Town's audience puts Mary in a similar position. Simply by passively listening to Raise-Slander and Back-Biter, the spectators actively accuse the Virgin of breaking her oath of virginity. According to late medieval English canon law, gossip becomes defamation when it is spoken publicly, in the hearing of "good and serious persons," and defamation necessitates a trial.[86]

In the second-century Gospel of James's account of the trial of the Virgin, Mary reacts to her neighbors' and relatives' accusations with bitter tears.[87] But when the Gospel of Pseudo-Matthew retold the story several centuries later, her tears had already dried, and she spoke to her detractors with "firm conviction."[88] By the time of N-Town, at the height of her power, Mary welcomes her trial with open arms, greeting her enemies as friends. When summoned to court in N-Town's "Trial of Mary and Joseph," she calmly pronounces, "Almyghty God shal be oure frende / Whan the trewthe is tryed owth!" (14.180–81), thereby describing the trial as a beneficent revelation of divine truth rather than a terrifying ordeal. Later, during her interrogation by the bishop and canon lawyers, she goes even further and represents the trial as a blessed purgation:

> I hope thurowe Goddys sonde
> Here to be purgyd before youre syght,
> From all synne clene. (14.291–93)

Her phrasing implies that the imputation of adultery has sullied her virginity, just as slander mars a spotless reputation or sin dirties the soul. We might expect N-Town to maintain that Mary's transcendent purity remains completely untouched by slander. As V. A. Kolve expresses this reading, "But Mary knows she is pure, and so do we."[89] Yet here in the text, Mary herself suggests that she needs to purify her honor, which has been tainted and besmirched.[90]

In fact, she aggressively insists on it. Mary interrupts her interrogators to demand the bottle of poison. "Here shal I drynke beforn youre face," she says, "I pray yow, lett me nought" (14.295). At first, her persecutors resist, shocked by her audacity. One berates Mary for being blasphemously presumptuous:

> Se, this bolde bysmare wolde presume
> Ageyn God to preve his myght! (14.298–99)

Another accuses her of irreverence: "With Goddys hygh myght loke thu not jape" (14.314). But Mary is fearless; she *will* jape with the high might of God. The late medieval Church forbade the ecclesiastical courts from tempting divine intervention with trials by fire or water. "Secret and unknown crimes," the Vatican had decreed, "should be left to God, who alone knows the hearts of men."[91] Yet N-Town's Mary does not heed this injunction. She demands purgation by ordeal. She prays to God, "Send me this day thin holy consolacyon / That all this fayr peple"—the audience, in other words—"my clennes may se!" (14.337). Whereas natural virginity cannot withstand touching or testing, Mary's supernatural virginity seems to benefit from both—just as the phoenix, her emblem, thrives on fire.[92] Proof improves, rather than endangers, her chastity.

The Virgin then proceeds to her trial by ordeal, a ritual that ultimately derives from the book of Numbers.[93] There, Jehovah tells Moses what to do should "the spirit of jealousy stir up the husband against his wife" (Numbers 5:14). First, a priest must brew a concoction of "most bitter waters, whereon he hath heaped curses with execration" (Numbers 5:18). Should an innocent drink those bitter waters, God promises, "she shall not be hurt, and shall bear children" (Numbers 5:28). But in a guilty body, the concoction works differently. "The malediction shall go through her, and her belly swelling, her thigh shall rot: and the woman shall be a curse, and an example to all the people" (Numbers 5:27). "This," Jehovah concludes, "is the law of jealousy" (Numbers 5:29).

The apocryphal Gospels, apparently fearful of arousing God's wrath (though not enough to forgo the test entirely), carefully dilute these bitter waters. The Gospel of James gives Mary the re-named "Lord's water of refutation" rather than the "bitter" and "cursed" waters of jealousy.[94] No mention is made of any heaping of maledictions or rotting of thighs. The Proto-Gospel merely stipulates that this sacred water has the power to "reveal sin." The text does not say how, but it is vaguely implied that this revelation might manifest itself in the form of bodily injury or even death. (Mary only proves her innocence by "coming back whole"—in short, by surviving and remaining intact—thereby suggesting that death or disfigurement would have demonstrated her guilt.) Even more circumspect than its progenitor, the Gospel of Pseudo-Matthew dilutes "the Lord's water of refutation" even more, turning it into the bland "water of drinking."[95] This innocuous beverage, the text reassures its readers, can only cause "a certain sign" to appear on a liar's face. Mary, in other words, is never in any real danger.

By contrast, N-Town seems to think nothing of endangering the Virgin. Consistently, N-Town treats Mary like any other suspected adulteress—assuming the worst, calling her a whore, and menacing her with violence. When the summoner arraigns Mary and Joseph, he pauses to threaten Mary with yet another ancient penalty for adultery: mutilation of the face. "And ye were myn," he promises her,

> I wolde ech day beschrewe youre nose
> And ye dede brynge me such a pak. (14.192–93)

Shreuen, meaning "to curse," is often used in prohibitive threats.[96] The summoner's words recall one of the many punishments prescribed for the harlot Israel in Ezekiel: "And I will set my jealousy against thee, which they shall execute upon thee with fury: they shall cut off thy nose" (23:25). Nor was this punitive practice absent from late medieval life. The historian Valentin Groebner has compiled an extensive catalog of instances of husbands cutting off their wives' noses to punish them for suspected acts of adultery.[97]

Persisting in this uncompromising vein, N-Town represents the "potacyon" that Mary must drink as "Goddys vengeauns" in liquid form, thereby restoring (and even raising) the high stakes set by the book of Numbers (14.234). The bishop characterizes this potion of vengeance as both an indicator and a toxin. As an indicator, the potion exposes sin: "Pleyn in his face shal shewe it owth" (14.241). And, as we soon learn, sin looks like agony. When Mary drinks her "large draught," she circles the altar seven times with perfect composure, completely unaffected (14.330). Whether we are meant to conclude that the poison targets only sinful atoms, or that the panacea of virginity defends the immune system from toxins, or that God has miraculously arrested the venom's chemical progress in Mary's body—or even that Mary possesses incredible powers of stoical endurance—when Raise-Slander takes the same test, his skull burns with invisible fire:

> Out, out! Alas, what heylith my sculle?
> A! Myn heed with fyre me thynkyht is brent! (14.364–65)

Thrillingly, Raise-Slander's body fully registers the consequences of the violence that the court so impotently (and, apparently, therefore disappointingly) inflicted on the invulnerable Virgin.[98]

N-Town neither pulls its punches nor minces its words. Instead, the text comes at Mary with every dirty joke that it can dredge up from the lowest registers of obscenity. Raise-Slander and Back-Biter fantasize about the intimate details of Mary's alleged adultery in graphic detail. They go on at some length imagining "sum fresch yonge galaunt" shooting his bolt into her ticklish tail.[99] Raise-Slander paints a picture for the audience:

> Such a yonge damesel of bewté bryght
> And of schap so comely also
> Of hir tayle ofte tyme be light
> And rygh tekyl undyr thee, too! (14.94–97)

After establishing this vivid image, Raise-Slander opens up the fantasy by switching to direct address in the second person (14.97). He says that the Virgin Mary's "light" (easy or lascivious) tail would be right "ticklish" (responsive or exciting) under *you*. His phrasing invites spectators and readers to imagine Mary's tail tickling them—or rather *us*. We might expect the text to turn here—to silence, chastise, and punish. Yet it continues to draw out the titillating slander. Back-Biter responds in kind:

> Be my trewth, al may wel be,
> For fresch and fayr she is to syght,
> And such a mursel—as semyth me—
> Wolde cause a yonge man to have delyght! (14.90–94)

Back-Biter's response (like Raise-Slander's initiating call) translates the standard epithets of Mariology (fresh, bright, fair, and so on) into a lower register (shapely, ticklish, and light), arousing a mouth-watering hunger for a "morsel" (from *mordeo*, meaning "to bite") of the Virgin's delectable flesh.

This sexual harassment of the Madonna might at first seem straightforwardly disparaging. And yet N-Town's insults resonate with positive theological significance. Arousing an audience's desire to devour the Virgin serves a higher calling. Theologically, Mary's flesh is Jesus's flesh and Jesus's flesh is the Eucharistic wafer, which Christians eat. Augustine urged sinners to worship the earthly flesh of Mary through carnal consumption, because Christ "received his flesh from the flesh of Mary" and "gave us that same flesh to eat for our salvation."[100] Or, as Richard of Saint-Laurent puts it in his thirteenth-century *De laudibus sanctae Mariae* (which was attributed by the Church to the higher authority of Albertus Magnus until the twentieth century), "In the sacrament of her Son we also eat and drink her flesh and blood."[101] N-Town insistently reminds us of this equation, describing Mary as "food" (15.145) and as "whyte . . . lave," or bread (10.275). Drooling for a bite, Back-Biter promulgates a sacred craving.[102] Whereas natural virginity diminishes when consumed, Mary's miraculous purity rewards gluttonous enjoyment. As Shakespeare said of another exceptional queen, she makes hungry where most she satisfies.[103]

The Devotional Practice of Ritual Humiliation

Unlike its sources and analogues, N-Town neglects to apologize very convincingly for the events that transpire in "The Trial of Mary and Joseph." In Lydgate's *Life of Our Lady*, a neighbor and contemporary of the N-Town plays, the "dismayed" onlookers of Mary's trial fall to the ground and literally beat themselves up about their misdeeds: "They bonche ther brestez with fistez wondir sore."[104] By contrast, N-Town's bishop falls to his knees (not the ground) and prays for grace with more equanimity of temper. He says, "All cursyd langage and schame onsownd, / Good Mary, forgeve us here in this place" (14.372–73), pointedly using the metatheatrical term *place* to draw a protective circle of exemption around both actors and audience.

In every version of the story, from the Proto-Gospel of James to Lydgate's *Life of Our Lady*, the Mother of Mercy forgives her detractors. In N-Town, however, she also rewards them with thanks and blessings. When N-Town's bishop commends Mary for her "good hert and gret pacyens" (14.379), Mary returns his thanks: "I thank yow hertyly of youre benevolens" (14.382). Continuing to demonstrate her extraordinary good humor, Mary goes on to formally bless the actors and spectators by generously offering to intercede with God on their behalf. She prays,

> He mote yow spede that ye not mys
> In hevyn of hym to have a sight. (14.392–93)

Mary's trial always ends happily.[105] The Gospel of Pseudo-Matthew concludes with a parade: "And all the crowd, along with the priests and all the virgins, led her home with exaltation and joy, crying out and saying to her, 'May the name of the Lord be blessed, for he has revealed your holiness to the people of Israel.'"[106] Lydgate's *Life of Our Lady* celebrates the festive "noyse" that made the heavens ring after Mary's victory:

> And euery wightys tunge
> For Ioye and myrthe, gan hym gloryfie
> And all the day, thus in meloydye,
> Thay led further, tyl it drewe to eve.[107]

Turning these descriptions into dramatic action, N-Town's pageant of "The Trial of Mary and Joseph" concludes with the stage direction "Explicit cum gaudio" (It ends with joy). As if carried away by the feeling, the scribe has decorated these words with a frame of happy squiggly embellishments, a rare flourish in an otherwise rather plain manuscript.[108]

N-Town presents its obscene and violent harassment of the Virgin as a festival endorsed by Mary herself, who rewards the audience for their accusations, insults, and threats with thanks, blessings, and festivities. In the context of medieval devotional practices, this is not so very strange. The historian Patrick Geary has demonstrated that in the thirteenth century, Christians (both clerical and lay) regularly engaged in what he calls "ritual humiliation": the abuse of relics and icons for the purpose of "forc[ing] them to carry out their duties."[109] In 1250, the archbishop of Rouen reported that whenever crops failed, villagers would excoriate, topple, and whip their local statue of the Madonna.[110] Although the pope forbade such customs in 1274, his prohibition did not end the practice all at once. Instances of ritual humiliation are documented as late as the early sixteenth century, as when locals (led by their vicar) in Pamiers threw the Black Madonna of Foix to the ground because of bad weather.[111] In fact, Helen Parish has collected extensive evidence of the pervasive influence of ritual humiliation on late medieval English sermons, art, hagiography, and theater.[112]

Especially theater. Early English playscripts call for actors to stab Eucharist wafers, torture the body of Jesus, and humiliate the Virgin Mary, abuses that incur miraculous special effects and moral edification—instruction and delight rather than wrath or punishment.[113] In the late medieval Cornish *Beunans Meriasek* (The Life of Saint Meriasek), a desperate supplicant kidnaps the image of the baby Jesus from a statue of the Madonna and Child and holds it ransom, thereby motivating the Virgin in heaven to answer the kidnapper's prayers.[114] An evil tyrant, King Massen, has imprisoned the woman's son and plots to have him hanged, drawn, and quartered. When the woman's prayers to Mary fail, she decides to take more drastic measures: "Mary, these many times have I prayed to you for my son, but where is the gift of your consolation? Can it be that you are unmoved by my tears? If there is such a thing as mercy, why, Mary, won't you hear me this night? Mary, I am left with no choice since to pray is useless. My son is in chains, Mary, listen and believe. In place of my precious child, your little one shall go home with me today."[115] This bold strategy works. In response, Mary immediately explodes the doors of the tyrant's prison and zaps the fetters from its prisoner's legs. The Virgin says to the son, "Tell [your mother] that although I may have seemed slow in giving heed to her prayers, it was never my wish to forget her."[116] Far from being insulted, Mary seems apologetic and even impressed.

The practice of ritual humiliation blurs the line between devotion and desecration. Many late medieval English records describe scenes of violence in churches and shrines while ascribing no motive to the crimes, leaving historians somewhat baffled. In Byfield, Northamptonshire, in 1416, a parish clerk decapitated a statue of Mary and then set the severed head on fire; in Exeter in 1421, someone (the perpetrator was never caught) shredded an image of Mary in a Franciscan friars' close.[117] Both cases have been studied as potential examples of Lollard iconoclasm, and yet historians acknowledge that there is no undeniable evidence of heretical motives in the records of either incident.[118] Many impulses could have motivated these crimes. On the one hand, yes, they resemble the iconoclastic attacks against images perpetrated by Lollards.[119] Then again, they also recall devotional (if heterodox) acts of ritual humiliation. Yet again, they could also be classified under the broad rubric of mischief and merriment.[120] (Some incidents more clearly than others: in 1441, one Hugh Knight, husbandman, used candle smoke to paint a bushy black beard on a statue of the Madonna and then said loudly, "Mable, ware thy berde"—Mable, wear your beard.)[121] Early English drama's trials of the Virgin combine all these many impulses—comical, mischievous, iconoclastic, and devotional. Yet most fundamentally of all, they seem to express a form of desire so intense that it crushes its beloved—or rather, that might crush another object of devotion, but not this one. Mary remains perpetually unharmed and unoffended.

The practice of ritual humiliation helps to explain the behavior reported of spectators at performances of theatrical trials of the Virgin. Although medieval audience response is so often invoked in early English drama studies, we have very little evidence of how spectators actually behaved.[122] One rare record, an early fifteenth-century note from the *A/Y Memorandum Book*, records a complaint from the goldsmiths and masons of York about their assigned pageant, the apocryphal funeral of the Virgin—and specifically about its violent assault against Mary's corpse.[123] First, the goldsmiths and masons grumble about the indignities of performing legends "not contained in the sacred scripture." The Lollard movement had revitalized Jerome's ancient dismissal of the Infancy Gospels as apocrypha, inspiring a resurgence of protestations against the most flagrant "superstitions" narrated in the life of the Virgin—like the "miracles of mydwyves" at "the lulling of oure Ladye" and other such old wives' tales.[124] For their part, the goldsmiths and masons allege that the performance of this particular apocryphal scene caused "more noise and laughter than devotion," resulting in disruptive "quarrels, disagreements, and fights . . . among the people."[125]

This precious description of late medieval English audience response offers no further explanation, leaving many questions unanswered.[126] What made the spectators laugh? The absurdity of apocryphal error (the reading pushed by the motivated authors of the record), the clownish antics of the actors, or something else entirely? And why, for that matter, did they brawl? Are we really meant to understand, as the goldsmiths and masons would have us believe, that debates about scriptural canonicity erupted into violence, or that the performance of apocrypha inherently and necessarily encourages bad behavior? Whatever the cause, this record indicates an audience response so engaged and enthusiastic as to constitute a disturbance of the peace—rather like the contemporary phenomenon of football hooliganism. And while the goldsmiths and masons strictly differentiate between the people's "noise and laughter" on the one hand and "devotion" on the other, we might well ask how the people in question would have described their noisy response. Would they agree that their laughter precluded their devotion? Probably not. The Wife of Bath, who behaves so badly at "pleyes of myracles" (and everywhere else too), reminds us of the merciful capaciousness of medieval devotion: "God clepeth folk to hym in sondry wyse."[127] In any case, this report suggests that theatrical trials of the Virgin were received (by and large, though not by all) in a carnivalesque spirit of play and misrule. Perhaps for that reason, when the city of Chester repackaged its biblical pageantry after the Reformation, the new banns attempted to excuse the trials of the Virgin as jokes, harmless and entertaining. Although, the banns admit, the scriptures "waarant not of the Mydwyfes reporte," the people of Chester should not make earnest of game. "Take it in sporte," the banns advise.[128] In other words, let's have fun with this old game, like we used to.

Carnal Knowledge in N-Town's "Nativity"

In N-Town's pageant of the Nativity of Christ, two midwives probe the vaginal orifice of the Virgin Mary in search of proof of her postpartum virginity.[129] N-Town takes this remarkable theatrical tradition, rooted in the apocryphal Infancy Gospels, to its furthest documented extremity. Other dramatic representations of this trial show much more restraint. The Chester cycle, for example, reduces the number of gynecological exams from two to one and then stops that one before it can even begin. Just as the first and only doubting midwife reaches out to touch Mary's body, her hands wither. The stage directions read, "Then Salome shall attempt to touch Mary in her private parts [*in sexu secreto*], and at once her hands shall dry up."[130] Clarifying the point, Salome tells the audience,

> My hands be dryed up in this place,
> that feeling none haue I! (6.555–6)

In other words, no contact was made. Even more discreetly, Continental Nativity pageants often redirected the midwife's touch to the baby Jesus or hid the entire procedure from the audience by means of a screen.[131] But not

N-Town. N-Town goes so far that scholars tend to describe it almost as an impossibility—as a transgression of human reason, the utterance of the unmentionable, and a performance of the unperformable.[132] And yet there it is, in black and white.

N-Town wants the audience, like the midwives, to experience palpable, transparent, and reproducible evidence of Mary's virginity—as Elina Gertsman puts it, "to experience the tangibility of salvation, to touch the imaged Word."[133] In this spirit, Joseph invites the first midwife, named Zelomy, to approach and see the miracle for herself: "I pray yow," he says, "com to us more nere" (15.199). But seeing is not enough for Zelomy, who answers,

> With honde lete me now towch and fele
> Yf ye have nede of medycyn. (15.218–19)

Her phrasing here sounds like a request, but really it constitutes a demand. She does not ask whether she may but rather announces that she is about to "towch and fele." Although Zelomy uses a diplomatic conditional ("if"), she unavoidably implies that she doubts the doctrine of Mary's perpetual virginity, positing touching and feeling as the foundational requirements on which her conditional possibilities depend. *If* the test establishes that Mary has need, *then* Zelomy offers to help:

> I shal yow comforte and helpe ryght wele
> As other women, yf ye have pyn. (15.220–21)

This offer of assistance, as Jerome argued, is insulting. Jerome condemned "the nonsense of the Apocrypha" for claiming that Joseph and Mary let midwives anywhere near the scene of the Nativity. "There were no women attendants present," he insisted, because Mary—unlike all other women—did not require any assistance.[134]

However, unlike Jerome, N-Town's Mary does not take offense at Zelomy's lack of faith. Rather, she encourages Zelomy to put her to the test, saying, "Tast with youre hand yourself alon" (15.225). The multivalent verb *tast* suggests both tasting and testing, and it has strong sexual connotations.[135] In John Gower's *Confessio Amantis*, for example, Amans confesses that he has "tasted / In many a place" and yet never cared for any of his conquests.[136] Here, Mary's use of the word emphasizes the eroticism of the midwife's proposition. Zelomy wants to taste Mary's virginity by handling the most intimate part of her body. Taking Mary up on her invitation, Zelomy touches: "Hic palpat Zelomye Beatam Mariam Virginem." Upon contact, Zelomy's arm does not wither. She goes entirely unpunished. In fact, Mary rewards Zelomy for her doubts by inviting her to "fele and se" the miracle of the virgin birth with her own hands (15.228). When she tastes Mary's body, Zelomy experiences the very first—and by far the most intimate— communion in Christian history.

The pageant's spectators are not so fortunate. They can only access Zelomy's privileged experience of tasting and touching by listening and watching.[137] For Salome, the second midwife and avatar for the audience's frustration, that is not enough. Unsatisfied by Zelomy's verbal testimony, Salome boldly demands a hands-on experience of her own:

> I shal nevyr trowe it, but I it preve
> With hand towchynge, but I assay.
> In my conscience it may nevyr cleve
> That sche hath chylde and is a may. (15.246–49)

Salome speaks in emphatically erotic terms. As Helen Cushman has pointed out, N-Town repeatedly makes use of the sexual sense of the verb *assay* (to have intercourse with) in conjunction with its rhyming partner *may* (meaning "maiden") in reference to Mary's virginity.[138] Joseph, for one, has repeatedly protested that he never assayed this maid.[139] But now, finally, the maid will be assayed. Furthermore, English translations of the Bible, from the Wycliffite to the King James, used the verb *cleave* to Anglicize Genesis's definition of the covenant of marriage: "Wherefore a man shall leave father and mother, and shall cleave to his wife: and they shall be two in one flesh" (2:24). In Hebrew (as in Latin and English), this verb recurs in the Old Testament as a description of Israel's marital bond with Jehovah.[140] An autoantonym, *cleave* can mean "to cling together" or "to split apart," "to marry" or "to divorce."[141] With her use of this word, Salome suggests that only carnal consummation with the New Law can break the ancient covenant between her heart and the Old Law. In order to cleave from Jehovah, she must cleave to Mary, becoming two in one flesh.

Even though Salome phrases her demands so much more aggressively, even rudely, than did her predecessor, Mary acquiesces yet again:

> Yow for to putt clene out of dowth,
> Towch with youre hand and wele asay:
> Wysely ransake and trye the trewthe owth
> Whethyr I be fowlyd or a clene may. (15.250–53)

In Middle English, the word *ransack* means, as it does for us, "to plunder," but it can also suggest investigation, scrutiny, or (as seems most relevant here) the medical examination of a wound.[142] In medieval romance, festering lacerations are healed when ransacked by pure hands—as when Lancelot heals Sir Urry in Thomas Malory's *Le Morte d'Arthur*.[143] The double meanings of words like *cut*, *slit*, and *gash* demonstrate the long-standing sematic association between wounds and female genitalia—in Latin, *vulva* and *vulnus*.[144] Here, Mary's repetition of the word *clean* associates the purity of her virginity with the purity of the kind of certainty that only hands-on experimentation can afford.[145] In this exceptional case, penetrative assaying will cleanse rather than pollute both Mary's honor and Salome's doubts. Thus, Mary asks Salome to be thorough, to take her time—to "wysely ransake" and "wele assay." Throughout both the trial by ordeal and the midwives' examinations, Mary encourages and celebrates testing—because even the most aggressively penetrative probes defend rather than endanger her unnatural virginity.

To Zelomy, Mary said, "Tast with youre hand" (15.225); to Salome, she says, "Towch with youre hand" (15.251)—just as Jesus will say, many pageants later, to Doubting Thomas,

> Put thin hool hand into my ryght syde,
> And in myn hert blood, thin hand that thu wynde. (38.339–40)[146]

N-Town repeatedly emphasizes, and iconography confirms, that this is to be done with their whole hands.[147] The *Holkham Bible Picture Book* depicts Mary's attendant with what looks like a prop hand dangling off her wrist, suggesting the logistics of a special effect—as if the performer playing her part popped off a spring-wound dummy appendage at the climactic moment.[148] In murals and manuscript illuminations, Salome displays a stump severed at the wrist or even farther up the arm.[149] These details imply that artists imagined Salome thrusting her arm into Mary all the way from the tips of her fingers to her wrist or even up to her elbow—just as N-Town's

Doubting Thomas puts his arm so deep into Jesus's side wound that he reaches his heart's blood. In many ways, these two holes are one and the same: late medieval exegesis and iconography often represented Christ's side wound as the cosmic vagina that gave birth to salvation, the mirror image of Mary's vulva.[150] As Karma Lochrie writes, devotional texts instructed sinners to "touch, kiss, suck, and enter the wound of Christ," just as Mary invites her midwives to taste, assay, and ransack her vaginal opening.[151] This intercourse does not deflower or ruin; instead, it purifies and heals.

God punishes Salome for her transgression, withering her flesh: "Myne hand," she exclaims, "is ded and drye as claye!" (15.256). The Chester pageant of the Nativity lets us know exactly why: "Unbeleeffe," its Expositor proclaims, "is a fowle sinne" (6.721). In the Chester Nativity, the first midwife takes the truth of Mary's virginity on faith alone, while the second insists on a gynecological examination; in response, God rewards one and punishes the other.[152] But in N-Town, as in Pseudo-Matthew, both midwives conduct examinations of Mary's body, but only one is punished. Why? Scholars have tended to argue that the first midwife, unlike the second, tests Mary politely, "in a spirit of reverence."[153] But the difference may have more to do with luck. Zelomy gets there first and delivers the good news of her findings to Salome. Salome then finds herself in the position of every other Christian given written or oral secondhand reports of spectacular firsthand experiences. In this sense, God's punishment of Salome teaches self-restraint. As Augustine argued, Christianity may depend on the proof of miracles, but not every Christian can demand miraculous proof.[154]

Yet this limitation hardly limits. N-Town's Nativity pageant caves to Salome's demand for a second trial. Salome receives the proof that she demands, despite God's slap on the wrist. Even God's chastisement of Salome functions as yet another token of proof, a provision that implies an underlying assumption that readers and spectators—still unsatisfied even after so many trials of the Virgin—always hunger for more. Though N-Town may (briefly) penalize Salome, it never punishes the audience for their implicit demands; rather, it depends on the infinitude of their craving, as well as the inexhaustibility of the Virgin's (and, for that matter, theater's) capacity to both whet and satiate that hunger.

The Privities of the Virgin in Chaucer's "Miller's Prologue"

Chaucer's Miller prefaces his tale with some advice:

> An housbonde shal nat been inquisityf
> Of Goddes pryvetee, nor of his wyf.[155]

Pryvetee can mean "private affairs," "sacred mysteries," or "genital organs," and here it multitasks as the possessive complement of both God (God's privity) and the wife of the inquisitive husband (his wife's privity).[156] In effect, the Miller preaches the virtue of Christian humility. Just as pastors taught their flocks not to question the impenetrable mysteries of doctrine, the Miller advises husbands not to pry into their wives' private affairs.

And yet the secrets of wives are no secret. The Miller has already told us what an inquisitive husband would find, were he to seek: "Who hath no wyf, he is no cokewold."[157] In other words, all husbands are cuckolds, and every daughter of Eve an adulteress. Knowing this awful truth, the Miller seeks refuge in denial. Although he has a wife and knows what that means, he likes to think that he has not been made a fool: "I wol bileve wel that I am noon."[158] He turns a blind eye to the truth and pretends to believe in lies—a trick that he claims to have learned from Christianity and, specifically, from the Virgin Mary.[159] The sacred mysteries of which the Miller speaks remind him of a wife, her genitals, and her secrets—details that suggest the enigmatic miracle of the virgin birth.[160] In his satire of Our Lady of Walsingham, Erasmus puns on the same ambiguity: pilgrims, Erasmus winks, approach the shrine panting with desire to see "the virgins secrets."[161] When the Miller advises men not to be "inquisityf / Of Goddes pryvetee," he postpones the punch line: "nor of his wyf."[162] Dangling at the end of the sentence, this phrase's referent becomes ambiguous: it could refer to the "pryvetee" of "his wyf," as in the husband's wife, or God's wife—the Virgin Mary.[163] The Miller has Mary on his mind. These comments preface "a legende and a lyf / Bothe of a carpenter and of his wyf," a sly reference to Joseph the carpenter, God's cuckold, and to Mary, the divine adulteress.[164]

Echoing the Miller's words, late medieval English homilists instructed their listeners not "to be to inquisitiff how that itt may be that the virginitie and the moderhede be both in Oure Lady."[165] This tradition of representing the virgin birth as a black box extends far back in the Christian tradition, all the way to the silence of the Gospels of Matthew and Luke. Celebrating the evangelists' reticence, Ignatius of Antioch described the virgin birth as a secret concealed by God in unfathomable mystery.[166] The patristic fathers urged Christians not to give in to the suspicions provoked by scripture's ambiguity but rather to let their faith in Mary's purity transform confusion and shock into awe and reverence. "Do not discuss the Virgin's conception," Peter Chrysologus wrote, "but believe it."[167] Others reiterated this injunction. "Believe! Believe strongly! Do not question," the Syriac theologian Jacob Bar-Salibi advised; "Neither Gabriel nor Matthew was able to say *how* [the virgin birth] happened."[168] These many warnings provoke a question: Why not? What might an inquisitive Christian discover?

Is it not obvious? We all know where babies come from. Boethius taught the logic of cause and effect with this commonsense example: "From an antecedent an argument is taken. If she has borne a child, she has lain with a man. I take the antecedent: but she has borne a child; I take the consequent: therefore she has lain with a man. From consequences in this way, I take the consequent: but she has not lain with a man; I conclude the antecedent: therefore, she has not borne a child."[169] Mary's persecutors in N-Town often make this very point. One of her interrogators asks,

> How shulde thi wombe thus be arayd—
> So grettly swollyn as that it is—
> But if sum man thee had ovyrlayd? (14.214–16)

How indeed?

The Miller's sly joke suggests that medieval Christians suspected Mary of adultery to the same extent that husbands suspected their wives: constantly. And yet, as his tone implies, their suspicion articulated itself not as anger or despair but rather in a comical spirit of playfulness—a kind of playfulness that deeply informed their understanding of Christianity. The thought that Mary might have committed adultery seems to have tickled the medieval sense of humor and even strengthened, if not constituted, their faith.

Chapter 3

The Second Eve

In the book of Genesis, the subtle serpent tempts Eve to eat the fruit of the tree of knowledge, or, as N-Town calls it, the tree of cunning (2.38).[1] N-Town represents the serpent as "a werm with an aungelys face" (2.220).[2] In medieval iconography, this hybrid creature wraps its serpentine body around the trunk of the tree and leans down through its branches to bring its beautiful face closer to Eve's.[3] Whispering in her ear, the serpent tells Eve that God lied.[4] Eating the forbidden fruit will not bring death, as God claimed, but rather knowledge that will make Eve and Adam "be as gods"—*eritis sicut dii*, in the words of the Vulgate (3:5).[5] N-Town lovingly expands on the serpent's temptation of Eve, tripling its length:

> Of this appyl—yf ye wyl byte—
> Evyn as God is, so shal ye be!
> Wys of connyng—as I yow plyte—
> Lyke onto God in al degré!
> Sunne and mone and sterrys bryth,

> Fysch and foule, bothe sond and se,
> At your byddyng bothe day and nyth:
> Allthynge shal be in yowre powsté. (2.100–107)

Eve cannot resist this proposition. "So wys as God is," she says, "and felaw in kunnyng fayn wold I be" (2.113–14)—she yearns to be God's fellow in cunning, and his "pere of myth" or equal in power (2.121). Motivated by this ambition, Eve disobeys God's injunction and takes a bite of the delectable fruit of knowledge, described by Genesis as "fair to the eyes" and "delightful to behold" (3:6).[6] In retaliation for this crime, God curses Eve and all the race of women to bear children with "gret gronynge, / in daungere and in deth dredynge" (2.256–57), and to serve man as his "undyrlyng" (2.253–54).

As we know, the fathers of the Church tended to interpret the third book of Genesis as a parable about the evils of womankind.[7] According to this reading, God made woman lesser, and Satan exploited that weakness. As Tertullian put it, "Woman! You are the devil's gateway" (Tu es diaboli ianua).[8] The serpent waited to find Eve alone, knowing that Adam would never fall for such tricks—unless, of course, Eve herself became the agent of Adam's temptation. Unfortunately for Adam, God made woman corruptible, as well as irresistibly attractive. So many passages from patristic exegesis argue that Eve's beauty and lustfulness (categories often collapsed by misogynist discourse) caused the Fall of Mankind. According to this reading, Eve's hunger for the knowledge and power of God and for the enticing forbidden fruit caused not only all mankind's misery—shame, death, and toil—but also the suffering of Jesus on the Cross. As the Wife of Bath reads from her husband's "Book of Wicked Wives," "Womman was the los of al mankynde."[9]

Typology demands balance. In Simone de Beauvoir's words, Mary must serve as the "inverse figure of the sinner Eve"—"the mediator of salvation, as Eve was of damnation."[10] Or, as the prophet Micah has it in N-Town, Eve is the "modyr of wo," and Mary the "modyr of blyss" (7.53–56). Exegetes began to construct this typological opposition as early as the second century.[11] Justin Martyr argued that Mary was a second Eve just as Jesus was a second Adam: while the first Eve "conceived the word of the serpent, and brought forth disobedience and death," the new Eve conceived the word of God and brought forth salvation.[12] Mary reverses Eve, an inversion most succinctly expressed by the scriptural anagram of Ave and Eva. In the Vulgate, Gabriel's first word to Mary is "Ave," which, reversed, spells "Eva."[13] As Gabriel says to Mary in N-Town's Annunciation, "Here, this name *Eva* is turnyd *Ave*" (11.219)—Eve becomes Mary, or rather, Mary undoes Eve.

The typology of Eva and Ave gives new meaning to God's curse of the serpent in Genesis 3:15: "It will crush your head," God promises, "and you will snap at its heel."[14] At first, patristic exegetes interpreted these words as a messianic prophecy about the "seed of the woman," Jesus Christ, who would crush Satan under his foot.[15] But with the rise of Mariology, this prophecy also became a reference to Mary, the heroine who would defeat Satan once and for all—thereby undoing what Eve, her foremother, had done. As Irenaeus had it, the knot of Eve's disobedience was dissolved by Mary's obedience: "For what the virgin Eve had tied up by unbelief, this the virgin Mary loosened by faith."[16]

Yet Eve is not only Mary's opposite but also her mirror image—reversed and yet identical.[17] In an elaborate illumination from the fifteenth-century Salzburg Missal, Mary and Eve pluck different fruit from the same tree.[18] Mary, the Mother of the Church, plucks a Eucharist wafer from the foot of the Cross (the planks of which, according to exegetes, came from the tree of knowledge), while Eve plucks the apple of Death from the serpent's mouth, much to the delight of the grinning skeleton standing over her shoulder.[19] Adam, meanwhile, lies prone at their feet, looking rather dazed and helpless.

Despite their many differences, these mirror images of Mary and Eve reflect each other in every gesture and feature. After all, typology, double-edged, cuts both ways. Opposition is always also comparison.[20] The exegetical imagination delights in matching every detail of Genesis to the Gospels, constructing an overwhelming impression of providential confluence. As Justin Martyr wrote, God likes for typology to repeat itself always in "the same manner in which it had originated."[21] In the streamlined iconography of the mass-produced *Biblia Pauperum* (fifteenth-century block-book picture bibles), the image of the Fall of Eve mirrors the Annunciation: Eve becomes Mary, the serpent becomes Gabriel, the apple becomes the Word, and God's curse becomes his blessing.[22] Medieval Christianity's typological twinning of Eva and Ave compared and even collapsed what it simultaneously contrasted. Hence the difficulty of telling Eve and Mary apart. In one fifteenth-century stained-glass window from Norfolk, we see a beautiful woman in blue spinning flax in a green garden.[23] Is it Eve fulfilling the terms of God's curse, laboring in the sweat of her brow, or Mary allegorically unraveling that curse by spinning the body of Jesus, clothing him in her flesh and blood?[24] Who can tell?

Both Eve and Mary were propositioned, even seduced (as certain Rabbinic and Christian texts claimed)—Eve by the serpent and Mary by Gabriel.[25] "Eve," Tertullian wrote, "believed the serpent; Mary believed Gabriel."[26] Both suitors claimed to be angelic messengers—and neither lied, though one of those two angels had fallen from God's grace. Both Eve and Mary, according to the tradition represented in the Salzburg Missal, were impregnated by their supernatural encounters: Eve by Death and Mary by Life.[27] And both Eve and Mary were promised deification. The serpent promised Eve that she would become like a god, while Gabriel promised Mary that she would become the Theotokos, the God-Bearer. According to even the most Christocentric late medieval theologians, the Incarnation purified Mary's body of original sin and metamorphosed her matter into an embryonic, incarnated deity. Her body became Jesus. In this sense, then, Mary fulfilled the serpent's prophecy. The second Eve became as God.

Much to the horror of early modern reformers, the Virgin's medieval devotees all but explicitly made this claim. Medieval theologians flirted with the concept of a "Quaternity" (rather than a Trinity), wavering back and forth between the orthodox position that the Virgin occupied a "fourth hierarchy" (*quarta Hierarchia*) below the Trinity but above the orders of angels and the heterodox belief that she enjoyed "an equal participation of the regal glory."[28] In a prayer directed at the heavens, the twelfth-century theologian Peter of Celle asked Mary, "O Virgin of Virgins, where are you?" Sitting beside the Trinity as an equal, he wondered, or kneeling before them as a supplicant? Peter answered his own question with a careful hypothetical: "*If* the Trinity admitted in any way an external Quaternity, you alone would complete the Quaternity."[29] Others believed unwaveringly. Eadmer of Canterbury saw Mary sitting on a cosmic throne, "by motherly right presiding with her Son over heaven and earth" as "the mother and mistress of all things" (*mater et domina rerum*).[30] Eagerly taking part in this tradition, the N-Town plays venerate the Virgin as the "Qwen of Hefne, Lady of Erth, and Empres of Helle" (11.335).

Some late medieval theologians even went so far as to hail the Virgin as the Creator of the Universe—or rather, even better, its Recreatrix, "the Mother of re-created things" (*mater rerum recreatarum*).[31] Anselm of Canterbury argued that the Incarnation of Jesus in Mary's body re-created both the Creator and his entire Creation, restoring or renewing (Anselm uses the verb *renovo*) the fallen universe with its full Edenic potential, lost since Eve's transgression.[32] Anselm and Eadmer thanked Mary for the Re-creation, attributing its cause to her overflowing merit rather than exclusively and directly to the power of God.[33] God, they argued, made the universe out of nothing by means of force (*potentia*) but refused to remake it that way—choosing instead to become the son of his most beloved creature, through whom the universe was finally redeemed.[34] In other words, God acknowledged that his first attempt at creation had failed. As Peregrinus put it, Eve had turned God's Edenic green world into a barren wasteland "withered in sin" and blighted by divine punishments (the Curse of Adam and Eve, Noah's Flood, the razing of Sodom and Gomorrah, the Plagues of Egypt).[35] Learning from experience, God decided not to repeat his mistake. Instead of attempting to refashion the universe alone, he elected another, better creator—because, in the words of Bernardino of Siena, "it was quite impossible for God to do such a thing by himself."[36]

As Hildegard of Bingen describes it, God

> gazed on his fairest daughter
> as an eagle sets its eye upon the sun.[37]

In the bestiary tradition, when the sharp-eyed eagle grows old and blind, he must fly toward the sun until its rays burn away the mist from his eyes and restore his power.[38] In Hildegard's image, God is the old and blind eagle, and Mary the rejuvenating sun. Old and weak, God looked to Mary for salvation. God, Hildegard argues, first created life from primordial matter, building Adam out of clay. But Mary's merits endowed her clayey flesh with a new luminosity, a light capable of breathing virtue into the material universe.[39] Adam was made of earth, but Jesus was made of Mary. As Jesus is to Adam, Hildegard concludes, so is Mary's luminous Re-creation compared to God's drossy rough draft.[40]

In light of the theory of the Re-creation, the transgression of Eve begins to sound less like a tragic disaster and more like a lucky break—or, as Saint Ambrose had it, a *felix culpa*.[41] After all, had Eve not fallen, Mary would never have had the opportunity to rise. As an anonymous late medieval lyric has it, had Eve not taken the apple ("Ne hadde the appil take ben"), Our Lady would never have been the Queen of Heaven ("Ne hadde never our lady / A ben hevene qwen"). Therefore, the lyric concludes,

> Blyssed be the tyme
> That appil take was![42]

Thank God for that apple. Theologians following this logical thread tend not only to argue that Eve's fall fortunately and fruitfully set the stage for Mary's triumph but also to suggest a more intentional and even premeditated alliance between the first and second Eve. Irenaeus calls Mary Eve's "advocate," suggesting that Mary negotiated with God on Eve's behalf—a special interest in her broader advocacy for all mankind.[43] Late medieval art and literature take that notion a step further—especially the N-Town plays, which represent Mary as the triumphant fulfillment of the charming promises made to Eve in the Garden of Eden by the cunning serpent. Mary not only imitates but also avenges her foremother.

The Miracle of the Cherry Tree

N-Town's pageant of the Nativity of Christ begins with yet another complaint from the long-suffering husband of the Virgin. Joseph complains to the audience that "oure emperour," Caesar Augustus, has demanded tribute. Born of the blood of David, Joseph says, "The emperorys comawndement I must holde with" (15.8). Joseph lives in fear of his two masters: the law of Moses and the law of Caesar. Crippled by the heavy Curse of Adam, he must bend his body in servile labor. Mary, by contrast, takes a very different tone. Like Pollyanna, she sees the brighter side of things. "It wolde be grett joye onto me," she says, to see the sights of the city of Bethlehem and to catch up with old friends (15.15–18). What aggravates Joseph can only delight Mary. His prison is her unfallen earthly paradise.

At first, Joseph refuses to allow Mary to accompany him to Bethlehem. He protests that pregnant women should not go gallivanting all over the countryside. "For mesemyth," he says, "it were werkys wylde" (15.19). That adjective, *wild*, is of great importance in N-Town's Marian pageants. We expect to hear Mary described as "mild," not "wild." Yet repeatedly, N-Town has skeptics express their suspicions about the Virgin by means of this rather unexpected adjective.[44] Even Mary's own mother warns her to be "sad and sobyr and nothyng wylde," as if in response to some clear and present danger (10.394). In Middle English, *wild* has a wide range of meanings, from "bestial" to "rebellious."[45] Here, Joseph seems to use *wild* in its sense of "rash" or "reckless," perhaps even "mad" or "insane," yet he uses it as part of a stock phrase ("werkys wylde") in which it usually tends to mean "lascivious" or "wanton."[46] Pregnant women worry Joseph, what with their intense cravings and violent mood swings. With these concerns in mind, Joseph suddenly changes his tune, saying,

> But yow to plese ryght fayn wold I.
> Yitt women ben ethe to greve whan thei be with childe. (15.20–21)

In other words, he finds himself stuck in a trap: because Mary is "wild," he dare not risk denying any request that she might make, no matter how "wild."

Why not? Beyond Joseph's fear that Mary will beat him ("clowte [his] cote"—tan his hide) if he dares chide or cross her (10.282), medieval medical theory promulgated many dire warnings against the terrible dangers of denying a pregnant woman her desires. *De Secretis Mulierum* cautions the reader that irresistible cravings so overpower pregnant women that the smallest dissatisfaction—the failure to fulfill one request for a fresh apple, for example—can cause immediate disaster.[47] The *Trotula* warns that "care ought to be taken that nothing is named in front of her which she is not able to have, because if she sets her mind on it and it is not given to her, this can occasion miscarriage."[48] Natural philosophers referred to this medical condition as *pica*, a term derived from the Greek word for *jay* or *magpie*, a noisy bird that will eat absolutely anything.[49] The pregnant woman suffering from *pica* craves all manner of strange things, from charcoal to unripe apricots. Aristotle warned that women, unlike all other animals save the mare, even crave coition during pregnancy—so ravenous are their appetites.[50] Hunger for one thing suggests hunger for another. Or, as Chaucer's Wife of Bath puts it, "A likerous mouth mosten han a likerous tayl"—a likerous (lecherous) mouth denotes a likerous tail.[51] N-Town's Joseph seems to have taken all this advice very seriously and fearfully, though with every request Mary makes, his acquiescence becomes more and more grudging and exasperated. He simply cannot keep up with Mary's wild desires.

As they go along, Mary (who, naturally, is hungry) spies a cherry tree on a hill. In a detail found in N-Town's telling of this legend, the tree, as Joseph remarks, is out of season—its unripe fruit cannot "fede" Mary's "fylle" (15.27).[52] Like the fruit of the tree of knowledge, these cherries are off limits. The seasonal rules of Nature forbid their consumption, as the commandments of God forbade the apple to Eve. Or perhaps not necessarily the *apple* as such. Medieval iconography did not fixedly identify the fruit of knowledge as any one fruit in particular; it was sometimes represented as a pear, a grape, a date, or even a cherry.[53]

In the wider context of late medieval English literature, cherries symbolized worldly brevity and sweetness. "This life, I see," as one anonymous fifteenth-century lyric puts it,

> is but a chery fayre.
> All things passene.[54]

In lyrical blazons, the mouth of the beloved is invariably a ripe, red cherry.[55] In Hieronymus Bosch's *Garden of Earthly Delights* (a near contemporary of the N-Town plays), frolicking bathers wear humongous cherries atop their heads like crowns and wild dancers brandish cherries in their hands like maracas. Late medieval artists attempting to capture the love shared by the Madonna and Child often put cherries in their intertwined fingers—seven for the Sorrows of the Virgin, five for Jesus's wounds on the Cross, three for the Trinity, and two for Christian chastity's paradoxical fertility. In this spirit, in the Towneley *Second Shepherds' Play*, Coll gives the baby Jesus "a bob of cherys" (13.1036).[56] The Flemish artist Quentin Massys paints Mary and the infant Christ kissing as Mary holds two ripe, red cherries between her thumb and forefinger—making an unflattering contrast to the two rotten pears (representing his defunct testicles) offered up by Saint Joseph in the *Holy Family* attributed to the workshop of Gerard David.[57]

And then the miracle happens. Mary calls out to Joseph, who apparently has his back both to his wife and to the cherry tree,

> Turne ageyn, husbond, and beholde yon tre,
> How that it blomyght now so swetly! (15.28–29)

As usual, Joseph, focused intently on his cursed responsibilities to the letter of the law, misses the pageant's lovely special-effects miracle. Even after

Mary calls to him, he refuses to turn around. "Cum on, Mary," he says (15.30), urging her forward to Bethlehem and the commandment of Caesar. Joseph, playing the thankless role of the anti-Judaic stereotype, stubbornly refuses to hear the good news. The miracle that he misses recalls several episodes from the Gospels involving fig trees, perhaps most strikingly the miracle of the fig tree.[58] Hungry on the road to Jerusalem, Jesus spots a barren fig tree. Angered by its unaccommodating fruitlessness, he curses the tree, which withers and dies. The fathers of the Church understood this barren fig tree as a sign of the Jewish people, who refused to bloom for the Messiah, thereby incurring his wrath. Here, in N-Town, Mary does Jesus one better. The barren tree, which would not bloom for Christ, blooms for the Recreatrix. Her sacred pregnancy inspires the landscape, which imitates her virginal fertility by blossoming out of season.

Famished, Mary insists that Joseph stop. She makes her desires clear: "to have therof ryght fayn I wold" (15.34), she says—she really wants those cherries. Politely yet firmly, she says that she hopes that it will please Joseph "to labore so mech" for her as to climb the tree and harvest the miraculous crop (15.35). Joseph finally gives in, halting their urgent progress to Bethlehem and promising to do his best to fulfill Mary's desires: "Youre desyre to fulfylle I shal assay, sekyrly" (15.36). Unsurprisingly, however, Joseph fails most humiliatingly in this attempt. He cannot—and has never been able to—fulfill Mary's desires. In yet another mime of impotence, Joseph cannot get up the tree. It is too high and too hard, he protests (15.38). Alas, even the tree is more potent than poor old Joseph. Repeating his earlier phrase, he calls the task that Mary has set before him "a werk wylde" (15.37)—a crazy, perverse, and lascivious request.

In anger, Joseph then speaks some rather "unkynde wurdys" to his spouse (15.45). "Lete hym pluk yow cheryes," he says, "begatt yow with childe" (15.39)—let the man who impregnated you pluck you your cherries. Joseph's phrasing here suggests a pun at Mary's expense: let the man who plucked your cherry pluck your cherry.[59] Lo and behold, another miracle. God, the father of Mary's child and the plucker of her cherry, satisfies her craving: he blooms the tree and then bends the branches so she can gather the crop and "etyn [her] fylle" (15.43). "Ow!" says Joseph—oops! "I know weyl," he says, that "I have offendyd my God in Trinyté" (15.44). And indeed he has. Apparently, God wants all Mary's desires fulfilled—no matter how wild.

This is the miracle of the cherry tree, a narrative derived from the apocryphal Gospel of Pseudo-Matthew's account of the flight into Egypt.[60] In the apocryphal Gospel, Mary craves ripe dates out of reach in the branches of a palm tree. The baby Jesus asks the palm tree to bend down and refresh his mother, and it bows its top to Mary's feet. Although this story was often retold in late medieval English literature, only N-Town and one other text (the "Cherry Tree Carol," still sung at Christmas) turn it into a kind of farce about the December–May marriage of Mary and Joseph.[61] In N-Town and the "Cherry Tree Carol," the tone becomes comical, the dates become cherries, the occasion shifts from the flight into Egypt to the Nativity, and Joseph turns from passive bystander to motivating antagonist.[62] His skepticism and grouchiness provoke the miracle: by criticizing and begrudging Mary's desires every step of the way, Joseph prompts the deus ex machina. And most importantly, N-Town's adaptation of the apocryphal miracle of the palm tree effectively flips the script of Genesis. When Eve craved the forbidden fruit, God punished her—yet he satisfies Mary's wild and carnal desire for out-of-season cherries. In N-Town's Nativity, God seems to reward Mary for reenacting the scene of Eve's transgression.

One might well protest that the differences between Eve and the apple on the one hand and Mary and the cherry on the other are too manifold and obvious for this comparison to work.[63] Most importantly, sin motivated Eve's desires, while virtue motivated Mary's. Yet the optical illusion of typology, as ever, can shift from contrast to comparison with the blink of an eye. The Nativity pageant consistently phrases Mary as a lawbreaker, like Eve before her: against Joseph's better judgment, Mary sets off, nine months pregnant, across the desert; dawdles along the way in defiance of Caesar's urgent deadline; and demands that her ancient husband scale a tall tree to fetch her unripe, inedible cherries. She is, as Joseph repeatedly gripes, "wild": rebellious, untamed, crazy, perverse, and wanton. Joseph, the obedient subject of the laws of Caesar and Moses, cannot govern her. In the Old Testament, God stood behind the Law and punished Eve for her transgression. But in the New Testament (at least according to a certain kind of late medieval Mariology), God takes a very different approach: mercy rather than punishment, indulgence rather than judgment. In N-Town's Nativity pageant, old Joseph effectively functions as a parody of God's first round against Woman, as well as of his failed strategy of strictness, grouchiness, and chastisement. Having punished the first Eve with less than successful results, God indulges the second. He condemned Eve, but he bends to Mary's will—bowing the branches of the tree to kiss her feet.

Why? What changed God's mind? Beyond reductive binaries (Eve bad, Mary good; Eve proud and concupiscent, Mary humble and chaste), another and more intriguing pattern emerges. First and foremost, N-Town blurs the distinction between Eve's concupiscence and Mary's chastity by phrasing Mary's craving for the cherries as an emphatically carnal urge. When Joseph first notices that Mary is pregnant, he exclaims, "Thi wombe to hyghe doth stonde!" (12.26), and then repeats a variation on this exclamation several lines later: "Thy wombe is gret; it gynnyth to ryse!" (12.30). This image of Mary's womb visibly rising and engorging recurs yet again in the manuscript. In "The Trial of Mary and Joseph," Raise-Slander reiterates this description, remarking to Back-Biter that Mary's "wombe doth swelle / And is as gret as thinne or myne!" (14.80–81), interpreting her swollen belly as a symptom of gluttony. These descriptions by Joseph and Raise-Slander characterize Mary's risen womb as a kind of female erection, the telltale sign of her "fals delyght" (14.301).[64]

Neither is the distinction between Mary's humility and Eve's pride as sharp as it may at first appear. In medieval Mariological discourse, the Virgin's humility and obedience go hand in hand with her cosmic power and supreme might. For the literal-minded architects of the Protestant Reformation, this paradox made little sense: Luther insisted that the humble Virgin earn her reputation for humility by giving up her crown and throne and taking up a broomstick and apron.[65] By contrast, the medieval Virgin, unfettered by literalism, radiated both power and humility—the honor of being the humblest and also the most exalted.[66] We should not bring a limited understanding of Mary's chastity or humility to the medieval typology of Eva and Ave. Medieval Mariology assumes the irrefutability of Mary's goodness. Therefore, Eve's reach beyond her grasp can register as lustful pride while Mary's desire for forbidden fruit counts in her favor as chaste humility.

The point, then, is not so much that Mary did no wrong but rather that Mary could do no wrong—that Mary possessed a special talent for getting off scot-free. Contemplating the parallelism of the typology of Mary and Eve, some medieval exegetes arrived at an idea that sounds extraordinary to modern ears, if not downright shocking.[67] Bernardino of Siena argued that God failed to punish Mary because she seduced him with her sexual charisma and bewitched his better judgment: "O incogitabilis virtus Virginis matris! . . . Una mulier Hebraea fecit invasionem in domo Regis aeterni; una puella, nescio quibus blanditiis, nescio quibus cautelis, nescio quibus violentiis, seduxit, decepit et, ut ita dicam, vulneravit et rapuit divinum cor, et divinam sapientiam circumvenit."[68] (O unthinkable power of the Virgin Mother! . . . One Hebrew woman invaded the house of the eternal King; one girl, I know not by what caresses, I know not by what promises, I know not by what violations, she seduced, deceived, and, if I may say so, wounded and ravished the divine heart, and overcame God's wisdom.)[69] Bernardino explains the Incarnation of Jesus and Redemption of Mankind as the indulgences of a besotted lover. According to this interpretation of Christian mythology, Mary used her feminine wiles to trick God into granting mankind undeserved forgiveness. Or, as Chaucer's Prioress puts it, Mary "ravysedest" the Holy Ghost "doun fro the deitee" and into her body, thereby redeeming humanity.[70] In other words, Christendom owes its salvation not only to Jesus's bloody sacrifice but also to Mary's ravishing powers of attraction.

The "Mystic Hunt of the Unicorn"

The allegory of the "Mystic Hunt of the Unicorn" features some of the late medieval period's most explicitly sexual imagery of the Incarnation and derives from ancient Mediterranean animal lore.[71] The *Physiologus* tells us that hunters cannot approach the mighty *monoceras*—literally, "the one-horn," translatable as "unicorn" or "rhinoceros."[72] The distinctive horn of this "ryght cruell beast," John of Trevisa explains, extends four feet in length, "so sharpe and so stronge" that it can kill an elephant.[73] "With this mighty and potent horn," an early thirteenth-century French translation of the *Physiologus* adds, the unicorn "tears and shreds through anything in its path."[74] Therefore, hunters pursuing this beast must abandon force and resort to duplicity.

The *Physiologus* teaches that only a beautiful (and, ideally, naked) virgin can capture a unicorn.[75] Unicorns, apparently, cannot resist this bait. "As soon as the unicorn sees her," Richard de Fournival explains in his thirteenth-century *Bestiaire d'amour*, "it comes to her."[76] Why? As Hildegard of Bingen tells us, it is because "he perceives that [maidens] are enticing and delightful."[77] Once the unicorn approaches, Richard de Fournival suggestively continues, "the maiden opens her lap to it. And the beast bends its legs in front of the maiden and puts it head in her lap."[78] Other versions of the story add that the unicorn will then "suck the breasts of the maiden and conduct himself familiarly with her."[79] Afterward, the unicorn falls fast asleep in the maiden's embrace. It is at this point that the crafty maiden must grab the unicorn by the horn, rendering him utterly helpless. Only then can the monster finally be captured and caged—or (as Hildegard of Bingen advises in her *Physica*) disemboweled and harvested for the precious medicinal properties of his skin, hooves, and horn.[80]

The sexual valence of this narrative is hard to miss. The unicorn functions as a symbol of masculine fecundity: his whiteness and wildness signify his purity (purity primarily in the sense of untapped potency ripe for fertilization), and his four-foot-long horn makes for a rather obvious phallic symbol. The unicorn's horn, as the art historian Christian Heck discreetly puts it, "evokes another kind of appendage."[81] This phallic fertility monster can only be subdued by coitus, represented by the encircling and suckling of the animal in the embrace of a naked virgin. Depictions of the encounter between the maiden and the unicorn are often adorned with marginal symbols of fecundity: cherries, bunnies, oranges, fountains, nightingales, and all manner of medieval aphrodisiacs.[82] Indeed, images of the "Hunt of the Unicorn" (like, for example, the Unicorn Tapestries held at the Cloisters) actually functioned as literal accessories to the sacrament of marriage.[83] When the maiden encircles the captured unicorn's neck with a golden collar, she allegorizes the plighting of troth, exchanging of rings, and carnal consummation.

Contrary, perhaps, to modern expectations, medieval exegetes saw this explicit fertility ritual of the maiden and the unicorn as an apt allegory of the Incarnation.[84] "Our Lord Jesus Christ," as the bestiaries have it, "is the spiritual unicorn."[85] Just as the unicorn put his horn into the grip of the maiden, the Savior (as the *Physiologus* explains) put his "horn of salvation" into the womb of the Virgin Mary.[86] In the sixth century, Gregory the Great elaborated on this comparison, adding that the mighty *monoceras* "lost all his swelling pride" when the Virgin opened her bosom and enveloped the Wisdom of God in her flesh.[87] In other words, the allegory of the "Mystic Hunt of the Unicorn" represents the wrathful God of the Old Testament as a wild and dangerous beast, and the Virgin Mary as the irresistible bait that lured him into the double-hinged trap of the Incarnation and Crucifixion.

This erotic allegory of the Incarnation flourished in medieval literature, homiletics, and iconography. A fourteenth-century Middle English lyric (perhaps William of Shoreham's translation of a poem by Robert Grosseteste) thanks the Virgin for having "aleyd," "ytamed," and "istyld" (allayed, tamed, and stilled) the "unicorn that was so wyld" with the "melke of thy breste." In other words, the poet thanks Mary for having subdued the jealous and avenging Jehovah and for having transformed him into the sweet and harmless infant Christ mewling and suckling at her breast. The Virgin pacified God's anger:

> Ine thee hys God bycome a chyld,
> Ine thee hys wreche bycome myld.[88]

Inside her body, Mary transformed God's vengeance into mercy, and his terrifying might into adorable infancy. Perhaps the Franciscan Bernardine of Busti put it best: "As a rhinoceros, on seeing a holy virgin, puts away his fury and meekly lies in the lap of the virgin, so God, seeing this most holy virgin, touched by love of her, laid aside all indignation and wrath and descended into her womb, laying down the rod of his anger [*virgam furoris*]."[89] To repeat: God put his angry rod into the womb of the Virgin. Bernardine reads Jehovah's Old Testament wrath against mankind (the Curse of Adam, Noah's Flood, the Plagues of Egypt) as a kind of misdirected libidinal urge. All God's anger dissipates once he succumbs to his overpowering desire to be and be inside his most beautiful creature.

In his *Life of Our Lady*, an important analogue of the N-Town plays, the English poet John Lydgate thickens the plot by adding Adam to the allegorical scene of the "Mystic Hunt."[90] Adam, Lydgate writes, escapes the forest "free from every trappe" while Christ the Unicorn sleeps in the lap of Virgin Mary.[91] Mary's lap, it would seem, entraps Jesus, allowing Adam to escape. This triangulation of Jesus, Mary, and Adam casts Adam in the role of the hunter with whom the Virgin colludes. The Virgin's lap, Lydgate continues, "wraps" the unicorn's horn, exactly where that horn "was wont to slee by violence."[92] The extraordinarily multivalent verb *wrappen* can signify embracing, entrapping, lulling, healing, and disguising—ambiguities that express so many of the complexities of the Incarnation.[93] In other words, the unicorn lays down his horn in the same place where he used to wield it as a weapon of death.

In a literal sense, Lydgate refers to a detail found in the bestiaries: the notion that the unicorn could bring down an elephant by stabbing it in the womb with its horn.[94] Thus, the unicorn demonstrates his change of heart by surrendering to, rather than stabbing, his old foe. In an allegorical sense, however, Lydgate refers to the Curse of Eve. With that curse, Jehovah turned the female reproductive system into a factory of death, the anatomical means by which original sin increased and multiplied. Then what better place to undo the Curse of Eve? Typology likes to come full circle. "By Christ's birth," Proclus writes, "the door of sin was made the gate of salvation."[95] In the moment of the Incarnation, God returns to his primal scene. The unicorn sheaths his horn in the vaginal scabbard. Or rather, to look at it another way, the female reproductive system finally gets its revenge. Lydgate's rhyme scheme suggests this *contrapasso* reading: the lap wraps and traps. It grabs back.[96]

In a late fifteenth-century Swiss tapestry of the "Mystic Hunt," Mary sits in a *hortus conclusus*, holding the unicorn's horn with a firm grip and pointing it directly at her womb.[97] The unicorn leaps with joy (rearing on its hind legs) toward the Virgin's lap. Clarifying that the capture of the unicorn signifies the moment of the Incarnation, a homunculus-Christ armed with a cross and an avian Holy Ghost can be seen diving down from a cloud toward the Virgin's body. Adam and Eve (both labeled with name scrolls) play the role of the hunters pursuing the unicorn through the forest. As the Virgin pulls the unicorn by the horn, Adam stabs the distracted animal in the breast. A ribbon of text unspools from Adam's mouth: "He is wounded because of our sins" (Ipse autem vulneratus est propter iniquitates nostras) (Isaiah 53:5). Eve, smiling serenely at the bottom of the frame, collects the unicorn's spurting blood in a golden chalice. Her speech scroll reads, "And by his blood we are saved" (Et livore eius sanati sumus) (Isaiah 53:5). This visual narrative provides us with the bait's motivation. Apparently, the maiden entraps the unicorn in order to feed his precious blood to her favorites, Adam and Eve. In other words, Mary seduced, ravished, and sacrificed Jesus in order to save her true love, mankind.

The allegory of the "Mystic Hunt" assumes an underlying and ambient antagonism between the human and the divine, cast in the roles of predator and prey. In the allegory, Mary and mankind (the hunters) join forces to hoodwink God the Father and Son (the hunted). Were we to transpose this allegory of the Incarnation into the plot of a medieval farce, God the Father would play the role of the old cuckold facing off against his young wife and her coconspirators: her lover and her lady-in-waiting. Indeed, in some representations of the "Mystic Hunt," Eve implicitly plays the stock fabliau role of the crafty handmaiden. In a fragment of the tapestry series of the Hunt of the Unicorn held at the Cloisters, Mary embraces the unicorn around its neck while Eve (standing beneath an apple tree enriched with silver-gilt threads) signals for Adam the Hunter to enter the *hortus conclusus* and capture his prey.[98] Her eyes looking sidelong and the corner of her mouth upturned in a half smile, the crafty Eve beckons the hunter into the garden with a gesture that also registers as a reach for one of the apples above her head.[99] Perhaps this confluence between the standard love triangle of the fabliaux or courtly romance on the one hand and the allegory of the "Mystic Hunt" on the other explains why certain medieval artifacts (such as ivory jewel boxes, enameled silver cups, and adjoining misericords) reflect the image of Tristan, Isolde, and King Mark with a parallel image of Love the Hunter, the Virgin Mary, and the unicorn as Christ.[100]

This playfulness did not survive the Reformation.[101] Barbara Newman writes, "A beleaguered Church could no longer sustain the freewheeling play of imagery that had been such a characteristic feature of late medieval religious culture."[102] In 1563, the Council of Trent abolished the production and exhibition of images that, as their decretum put it, "support false doctrine and give occasion of dangerous error to the uneducated."[103] The council particularly sought to eliminate all iconography that smacked of "lasciviousness." The sacred would no longer, the council warned, "be painted or adorned with a beauty exciting to lust." The council wanted the profane, the indecorous, and even the unusual banished from the house of God. So much for the imagery of the "Mystic Hunt," which vanished by the end of the sixteenth century.[104]

The "Parliament of Heaven"

To the left of the maiden and the unicorn in the Swiss tapestry of the "Mystic Hunt," just outside the walls of the *hortus conclusus*, the archangel Gabriel appears as a hunter, blowing a ribbon of text from his horn that reads, "Ave Maria."[105] Gabriel also appears in the fourth tapestry of the Hunt of the Unicorn series held at the Cloisters as a hunter blowing his horn, identified as a type of the archangel by the scabbard that hangs between his legs, on which is written the inscription, "Ave Regina C[aelorum]"

(Hail, Queen of the Heavens).[106] In the Swiss tapestry, "Gabriel the Heavenly Hunter" (as the minnesinger Konrad von Würzburg calls him), his head encircled by a garland of roses, reins in four eager hunting dogs, each biting down on an identifying scroll.[107] The hounds are labeled as follows: Veritas (Truth), Misericordia (Mercy), Justitia (Justice), and Pax (Peace).[108] They represent, in other words, the Four Daughters of God and refer to another, interlocking medieval allegory of the Incarnation: the "Parliament of Heaven," a scene lavishly staged in N-Town's dramatization of the Incarnation.

In N-Town's pageant of the "Parliament of Heaven," Pater, Filius, and Spiritus Sanctus debate the fate of mankind with the four allegorical Daughters of God: Truth, Mercy, Justice, and Peace.[109] Having received countless petitions from sinners, saints, prophets, and angels to forgive Adam and Eve, God the Father decides that—4,604 years after the Expulsion from the Garden—the time for "reconsyliacyon" between heaven and earth has come (11.52).[110] In the parliamentary debate that follows, Truth and Justice argue against mankind's salvation, maintaining that the progeny of Adam and Eve deserve their "endles punchement" (11.93). Taking the opposite position, Mercy begs God the Father to pardon "thi love, man"—mankind, God's beloved (11.88). Peace agrees with Mercy, admitting that although Truth and Justice "sey grett resoun," Mercy "seyth best to my pleson" (11.116–17). In other words, although Peace acknowledges the rationality and legality of the argument made by Truth and Justice, she finds Mercy's argument more pleasing and therefore most persuasive. "The pes of God," Peace concludes, "overcomyth all wytt" (11.115).[111] Her words come true. God forgives mankind, motivated not by truth or justice but rather by love and mercy. At the end of the parliament, the Four Daughters of God and the three members of the Trinity all kiss and make up (*et hic osculabunt pariter omnes*) and begin the reproductive process of the Incarnation.[112]

The "Parliament of Heaven" (or *Procès du paradis*) ultimately derives from the Psalms, which describe a reconciliation between God and Israel: "Misericordia et veritas obviaverunt sibi, iustitia et pax osculatae sunt" (Mercy and Truth are met together; Justice and Peace have kissed) (84:11). Midrashim expanded these verses into an allegorical debate held in heaven, a tradition imported into Christianity in the twelfth century by Hugh of Saint Victor and Bernard of Clairvaux.[113] In Bernard's "Parliament of Heaven," Jesus (whom Bernard calls *regem Salomenem*, King Solomon) must resolve two irreconcilable ultimatums.[114] Truth and Justice insist that they will cease to exist if the Trinity forgives mankind; Mercy and Peace insist that *they* will cease to exist if the Trinity does *not* forgive mankind. As Bernard puts it, "The one side says, 'I perish if Adam does not die,' and the other, 'I perish if he does not receive mercy.'"[115] The new Solomon writes his judgment in the sand, thereby typologically layering the judgment of Solomon (1 Kings 3:16–28) on top of Christ's exoneration of the adulteress (John 7:53–8:11).[116] The judge decrees the Incarnation, Crucifixion, and Harrowing of Hell: "If one, himself guiltless, should die out of love for man, Death could not hold him, for Love, being stronger than Death, would enter Death's home and bind him, and so free the dead."[117] Love, in other words, will triumph.

Late medieval English literary adaptations of the "Parliament of Heaven" tend to depart from Bernard's representation of the judge's dilemma. Whereas Bernard describes the scales as perfectly balanced (with the death of two Daughters of God poised in equal weight on either side), late medieval literary adaptations tend to tip that balance in Mercy's favor. N-Town, for example, diminishes the case put forth by Truth and Justice by pointedly phrasing their problem in the past tense. As N-Town has it, Truth and Justice *would have perished* had God not cursed Adam with mortality after the Fall (11.139–40). With this shift in tense, N-Town hints that Truth and Justice have already been compensated—and for 4,604 years, no less. And yet, as Jesus adds, "yiff another deth come not" (that is, if no more men perish), then Truth and Justice would "chastyse foly" (11.141). To paraphrase, Jesus implies that if he forgave Adam (as he would like to do), Truth and Justice would chastise his folly: they would criticize his decision and accuse him of being foolish. They would make fun of him for doting on mankind and for sparing the rod. In Bernard's version of the allegory, the very existence of two out of the four Daughters of God hangs in the balance of Jesus's decision. In N-Town, by contrast, Jesus faces the much less awe-inspiring risk of incurring some scornful teasing. N-Town stacks the rhetorical deck against Truth and Justice, representing their ultimatum as excessive and unreasonable—even as mean-spirited.

And not just mean—late medieval English literary adaptations of the "Parliament of Heaven" turn Truth and Justice into shrewish caricatures.[118] N-Town's Justice cannot control her temper, devolving at one point into simply yelling, "Nay, nay, nay!" (11.96). *The Castle of Perseverance*'s Justice expresses her anger in an even lower register. She promises,

For though [Man] lie in hell and stinke,
It schal me nevere overthinke.
As he hath browyn [brewed], lete him drinke![119]

In his *Life of Our Lady*, Lydgate portrays Truth as a victim of imbalanced humors,

almost in a rage
of cruell Ire, and of malencholye.[120]

In *Piers Plowman*, Truth and Justice simply abuse their sisters Mercy and Peace, answering measured arguments with childish insults. "That thow tellest," Truth says, "is but a tale of waltrot!"[121] Justice comes on even stronger: "What, ravestow?" she asks Peace, "or thow art righty dronke?"[122] Late medieval English literature, in short, represents Truth and especially Justice as harridans so exasperating that they provoke even Peace and Mercy. In *The Castle of Perseverance*, Peace is moved to shushing her sister: "I preye you, Ritwisnes, be stille!" (3204). In N-Town's "Parliament of Heaven," Mercy goes a step further and chastises Justice outright: "Systyr Ryghtwysnes! Ye are to vengeabyl!" (11.105). Truth and Justice quickly reveal their true faces: they are Wrath and Vengeance, thinly disguised.

Late medieval English literature, in other words, takes Mercy's part, describing the parliament of heaven as a done deal from the outset. N-Town's pageant, for example, clarifies that God the Father assembles the heavenly parliament for the express purpose of reconciling God and Man (11.52). The decision has already been made. The only remaining question is how to satisfy Truth and Justice, not whether to forgive mankind. The Trinity needs complete consensus, not an answer to an open question. And although Jesus must intercede when Mercy fails to persuade her sisters, in a sense, Mercy has actually already won, because she has already persuaded the judge. In Lydgate's version of the parliament, God insists that he cannot forgive mankind "by favour" without the consent of Truth and Justice.[123] But *with* their consent, he can. Thanks to the nature of allegory, the consent of Truth and Justice has the power to render a verdict true and just—even a verdict explicitly motivated by favoritism. In *The Castle of Perseverance*, the Father enthroned in Judgment admits that his verdict—made, as he puts it, in "bliss" and not "aftyr deservinge" (3565)—mingles all Peace, some Truth, some Justice, "and most of my Mercy" (3572).

These literary adaptations of the "Parliament of Heaven" understand Mercy as the very heart of Christianity. As N-Town's Mercy puts it, "Above all hese werkys, God is mercyabyl!" (11.107).[124] Lydgate's Mercy asserts that she is "chefe" in God's favor.[125] In *The Castle of Perseverance*, she says, "I, Mercy, pase al thing" (3453). In the fifteenth-century allegory of *The Court of Sapience*, Mercy describes herself as "the pure avaunt" (the pure pride) of the godhead, the "tresour" of God's deity, and the "gemme celestyal" in his heavenly crown.[126] The Trinity does not disagree: Mercy holds a special place in God's favor. In turn, she spreads that favor around—promiscuously and indiscriminately. There seems to be no limit to her leniency. Not only does Mercy argue that God should forgive mankind for the transgression in Eden, she also argues for the policy of forgiveness much more broadly. In *The Castle of Perseverance*, Mercy takes the position that God should indulge mankind's every desire: "To no man" she argues, "schuld be say nay" (3139). Justice, outraged, protests that such a policy would encourage sin:

> Thanne every man wold be bolde
> To trespas, in trost of forgevenesse. (3277–78)

Yet Mercy remains firm in her softness, reminding her sister that God himself put mankind in Mercy's power, "beside al His Ryth" (3462)—beyond Truth and Justice.

In the allegory of the "Parliament of Heaven," Mercy effectively plays the role of the Virgin Mary. Mercy advocates for the election of the Virgin as the mother of the Incarnation: thus, Mercy passes the torch, as it were, to Mary. But more broadly, Mercy represents the Virgin's primary function in the bureaucracy of heaven. According to late medieval theology, Mary—"the Mother of Mercy"—intercedes between God and man, tirelessly advocating for leniency and forgiveness.[127] Eadmer of Canterbury argued that salvation comes more quickly when sinners invoke the name of the Virgin rather than the name of God.[128] The sinner who prays to "the Lord and Judge," Eadmer argues, subjects himself to a thorough process of "just judgment"—while the prayers of the sinner who invokes the name of the Virgin get fast-tracked.[129] So effective is Mary's advocacy, Eadmer claims, that she can save even the undeserving.[130] Eadmer explains how this loophole works: when a sinner invokes the name of the Virgin, her exceptional merits spring up in the mind's eye of the judge, motivating him to answer that sinner's prayers immediately—truth and justice notwithstanding. In effect, Eadmer advises sinners to exploit God's besotted adoration of the Virgin for their own ends. Drop her name and watch God's frown turn into a smile. According to this understanding of intercession, Mary's seduction of God not only saved Adam and redeemed mankind—her gift also keeps on giving. As Richard of Saint Laurent put it, "Mary has so softened the Lord, and still continues to do so by her merits and prayers, that he now patiently tolerates even great sins, whereas before he mercilessly avenged even quite small ones."[131]

In at least one version of the allegory of the "Parliament of Heaven," Mary replaces the figure of Mercy entirely. The late medieval Dutch "Play of Masscheroen," a play within the play *Mariken van Nieumeghen* (entitled *Mary of Nemmegen* in its Middle English translation), stages a legal drama in a heavenly court, pitting Lucifer's lawyer, Masscheroen, against the Virgin, mankind's defense attorney.[132] Arguing before the highest judge, Masscheroen makes a strong case for Lucifer's right to punish humanity for its sins, while the Virgin, unsurprisingly, demands mercy. Masscheroen tempts God to return to his vengeful old ways: "It was only in the time of Abraham, Moses, and David," he taunts, "that You could be called truly righteous!"[133] Since the Incarnation, Masscheroen says, God has gone soft, even though the humiliation of the Crucifixion ought to have made him "more strict and angry than before."[134] At first, God seems to find Masscheroen's arguments persuasive and begins to consider smiting mankind with his "powerful sword of justice." Only thanks to the intervention of the Virgin does he back down and cool off. "Remember the breasts at which You nursed!" Mary says to her Son, "Remember the womb which carried You!"[135] These anatomical reminders from God's "dear mother" work quickly and completely. After hearing the Virgin's plea and, as ordered, contemplating her breasts and womb, God enthusiastically recommits to the Christian strategy of mercy, reconfirming the promise made in the New Testament to forgive any sinner who sincerely repents—much to Masscheroen's disappointment.

In the "Play of Masscheroen," as in N-Town's "Parliament of Heaven," the forces of mercy triumph over truth and justice. Favoritism, motivated by love and not by law or reason, wins the day and saves mankind. Across the spectrum of so many allegories and typologies that seek to explain Christianity's supersession of Judaism (the anagram of Eva and Ave, the "Mystic Hunt of the Unicorn," and the "Parliament of Heaven"), Mary and Mercy find themselves opposed by a wide variety of antagonists ranging along a

sliding scale from God the Father to the devil himself. While some medieval images of the Virgin crush the satanic serpent beneath their feet, others
trample on the face of an old and bearded sage who looks suspiciously like
Jehovah.[136] Mary triumphs not only over evil but also over Judaism, Justice,
Truth, and the God of the Old Testament. According to these understandings
of the supersession, Mary functions as Christianity's purest extremist, its
bleeding edge. Jesus is the new Solomon who compromises between old and
new, between Justice and Mercy—while Mary is the antinomian force pulling the Trinity from its established position toward universal salvation.

The struggle between Mercy and Justice is cosmic as well as personal,
anagogical as well as tropological. In a tropological sense, the "Parliament
of Heaven" is the small psychomachia that plays out every time reason succumbs to sin. As Thomas Aquinas explains in the *Summa*, the temptation
of the flesh cannot lead to the commitment of a mortal sin without the consent of reason.[137] Following Augustine, Aquinas compares sin's seduction of
reason to Eve's temptation of Adam in the Garden of Eden. When a sinner
beholds an object of desire and appreciates the sensations of its powers of
carnal attraction, Augustine argues, "I deem this to be like as though the
woman alone had partaken of the forbidden fruit."[138] Or, as the Parson puts
it in Chaucer's *Canterbury Tales*, Eve represents "the delit of the flessh"—
what Aquinas calls "the lower reason."[139] Only when the higher reason, the
judge that sits in the supreme court of each soul, consents to temptation has
Adam fallen or does sin become deadly. Thus, each mortal sin represents the
triumph of temptation over wisdom.

Building on this premise, God the Father in N-Town's "Parliament of
Heaven" argues that only the power of wisdom can resolve the discord between Mercy, Peace, Truth, and Justice. After all, God points out, "in wysdam
was [Adam's] temptacyon" (11.174).[140] Wisdom defeated Adam fourfold: the
cunning serpent ingeniously tempted Eve with promises of godlike knowledge, thereby leveraging her sexual magnetism against Adam's capacity for
higher reasoning. Therefore, according to the circular paradigm of typology, wisdom must solve the problem that wisdom caused. The clever compromise offered by Jesus (who is called "Wisdom" for the duration of this
pageant) represents that solution. Adam, embodying mankind's power of
reason, consented to sin in the Garden of Eden; therefore, Jesus, exemplify-
ing an even higher form of wisdom, must consent to the Incarnation and
Crucifixion in the parliament of heaven. Jesus must not depart from but

rather fulfill Adam's pattern. The first Adam fell from grace, so the second Adam must fall to earth. Adam fell for love of the first Eve, and so must Jesus fall for love of the second Eve, his bride and mother. Adam's wisdom turned to folly, and Wisdom must become Love, the blindly doting bridegroom of mankind.[141] Like a lovesick knight, as the *Ancrene Wisse* has it, Christ must come to earth "to pruvien his luve" (to prove his love) with chivalrous deeds and joust at the tournament of the Crucifixion.[142] Or, to use the metaphor of the "Mystic Hunt," the unicorn must rest his horn in the lap of a virgin. Effectively, the parallelism of Eve's temptation of Adam and Mary's seduction of God metamorphoses sin into grace. In a sense, then, Eve failed because she seduced only Adam. Mary succeeded because she overthrew the wisdom of God himself.

In his *Troilus and Criseyde*, Chaucer offers up a prayer to the goddess Venus, celebrating her dominion over the universe. Love's influence, Chaucer writes, moves heaven, earth, and hell, as well as every living thing therein, from the fish in the sea to God in heaven. Pointedly using the word *God* rather than *Jove*, Chaucer concludes, "God loveth, and to love wol nought werne"—God loves and can deny love (or rather Love, as in the goddess Venus) nothing (3.12). Without pausing to acknowledge his conflation of Christian and pagan mythology, Chaucer then goes on to describe the rapes of Jupiter. Venus, he writes, made Jove desire mortal things (3.18) and metamorphosed him into "a thousand formes" (3.20)—swan, bull, eagle, shower of gold. She brought Jove down from heaven to earth, mad for love. Boccaccio, Chaucer's source, adds that Venus made Jove "gentle towards the harmful works of us mortals, turning the weeping we merit into glad and delightful rejoicings."[143] Between them, Chaucer and Boccaccio conflate Venus and the Virgin, creating one overarching fertility goddess to reign over Jove, Jehovah, and Jesus.[144] And why not? In both cosmologies, pagan as well as Christian, Love made God amorous and vulnerable and brought him down from heaven to earth in the shape of a mortal creature. Since that metamorphosis, Love reigns, replacing deserved punishments with unmerited blessings.

Chaucer's "Merchant's Tale"

The plot of the "Parliament of Heaven" (and all its manifold typological reflections and refractions) can so easily be translated into a dirty joke, which is exactly what Chaucer does with it in his "Merchant's Tale."[145] In this fabliau, the pagan deities Pluto and Proserpina take over the role played by the Trinity in the "Parliament of Heaven" by adjudicating an infraction committed by a man and wife in an Edenic garden. Like the first Eve, the heroine of Chaucer's fabliau (named May—Mary minus only one letter) suffers from a "greet appetite" for forbidden fruit.[146] And like the second Eve, May finds herself matched against her similitude with an impotent old cuckold, whom Chaucer names January—thereby creating a happy confluence of initials: Mary and Joseph, May and January (or, for that matter, Jehovah).[147]

In a clever attempt to escape her blind old husband's jealous supervision, May pretends to suffer a potentially lethal craving for "smale peres grene" high up in a tree so that she may climb beyond his reach to an assignation with her young lover up in its branches.[148] The pears encapsulate several symbolic meanings simultaneously: they represent the forbidden fruit of the tree of knowledge of good and evil; concupiscence (Augustine's reading of that fruit's significance); and the object of May's concupiscent lust, her lover Damian (and specifically his testicles).[149] Drawing on the template of the cherry tree miracle, May convinces impotent old January that pregnancy motivates her craving.[150] Just as Mary had to have those cherries, May suggests, she has to have those pears. "Help," May pleads, pointedly, "for love of hir that is of hevene queene!"[151] An unconvincing excuse, especially considering January's impotence: May's pregnancy seems as improbable as the Virgin's. Yet blind January blindly believes—"for," as Chaucer has it, "love is blynd alday, and may nat see."[152] In his dotage, January has faith that his barren rod, like that of Saint Joseph, will miraculously bear fruit.[153] Bursting with pride, he happily stoops over to serve as the footstool by which his wife climbs into the tree and her lover's embrace.

Witnessing this reprisal of the Fall of Man (a pattern "perennial in human experience," as D. W. Robertson puts it), Pluto reacts very much in the style of Jehovah—wrathfully and vengefully.[154] "Th'experience," he concludes,

> so preveth every day
> The tresons whiche that wommen doon to man.[155]

In addition to experiential evidence of woman's perfidy, Pluto also calls on the authority of the wise King Solomon to support his argument. Quoting from the book of Ecclesiastes, Pluto reminds his wife that Solomon found one good man in a thousand, but not one good woman.[156] Doubling down on God's Curse of Eve, Pluto threatens to punish woman for her treachery with even more pain and suffering, perhaps in the form of a nasty new venereal plague: "a wylde fyr and corrupt pestilence."[157] At the very least, he vows to remove the scales from the eyes of old January, whom love has made so blind, foolish, and helpless.[158]

Proserpina—who plays Mercy to Pluto's Justice, Mary to his Jehovah—intervenes. She asks, "What rekketh me of youre acutoritees?" She dismisses Solomon outright as a "Jew" and "ydolastre."[159] Pluto's argument, she implies, is unchristian: it is pagan (idolatrous) and Jewish (in the polemical, anti-Judaic sense of strict and cruel). Having undermined the ethos of her opponent's authority, she then doubles back in order to reinterpret Pluto's passage from Ecclesiastes exegetically rather than literally, finding its spiritual fulfillment in the New Testament—specifically in Mark 10:18. There, Jesus asked, "Why callest thou me good? None is good but one, that is God." Thus, Proserpina argues, when Solomon said that all women were evil, what he *really meant*, in the truest and most Christian sense of his "sentence," was that no one, "neither he nor she," is good save God alone.[160] Finally, Proserpina rhetorically moves to occupy the grounds of experience, reminding her husband that she is a woman and will not brook misogyny "for no curteisye."[161] Confronted by Proserpina's multipronged defense, Pluto surrenders with comical alacrity. "Dame," he pleads,

> be no lenger wrooth;
> I yeve it up![162]

Yet, he insists, he cannot break his word, and so must stand by his promise to restore January's sight. May, it seems, will be caught in flagrante delicto.

Like the new Solomon in the "Parliament of Heaven," Proserpina comes up with a solution that cleverly circumvents truth and justice without technically breaking the law. She blesses May, "and all wommen after," with "suffisant answere"—with the grace to brave out any and every accusation with ingenious and shameless lies.[163] Proserpina's gift extends even to those caught in the act. She vows that

> though they be in any gilt ytake,
> With face boold they shulle hemself excuse,
> And bere hem doun that wolden hem accuse.[164]

Here, Chaucer invents an origin myth for that staple of the fabliaux, the adulteress's cunning and spontaneous excuse. "For lak of answere," Proserpina promises, "noon of hem shal dyen."[165] Her merciful gift of mendacity will save lives. The threat of death to which Proserpina refers resonates on several levels: in one sense, God punished Eve with mortality; in another, Leviticus prescribes death by stoning as the lawful punishment for adultery.[166] In another still, Proserpina might refer to the ambient threat that haunts the fabliau genre: the often unspoken but never forgotten expectation that the old cuckold is quite likely to kill his young wife in a jealous rage.[167] Proserpina saves May, and womankind, from all three threats—the threats posed by her husband, the law, and God himself.

Proserpina's salvation of May embodies Christianity: Christian mercy motivates her decision, and Christian craftiness enables and constitutes her gift. When Pluto restores January's sight, the old cuckold gapes up and sees with his own eyes his squire swiving his wife.[168] Making good use of Proserpina's blessing, May coolly explains to her husband,

> Ful many a man weneth to sen a thyng,
> And it is al another than it semeth.[169]

This excuse—that things are not always what they seem—works just as well for the virgin birth, implying a confluence between the excuse made by the Virgin (the Annunciation and Incarnation) and the excuses made by every other daughter of Eve when caught red-handed. N-Town makes this association explicit by comparing Mary's explanation for her pregnancy to a familiar fabliau, "The Snow Drop," or "De l'enfant qui fu remis au soleil," in which an adulteress tries to convince her husband that she conceived her bastard child by accidentally swallowing a snowflake.[170] Appropriately, Chaucer concludes the "Merchant's Tale" with a prayer to the Virgin:

> Thus endeth heere my tale of Januarie
> God blesse us, and his mooder Seinte Marie![171]

May and Proserpina's sophistry—like Mary's redemption of mankind—outmaneuvers truth and justice. Love conquers all. For sinners in the fallen world, what glad tidings.

Chapter 4

IMITATIONS OF THE VIRGIN

According to the apocryphal traditions that N-Town inherits, Mary's purity depends on the exclusion of many threats.[1] In the Proto-Gospel of James, Saint Anne turns the infant Virgin's bedroom into a high-security sanctuary. Anne protects Mary from contact with all and any contaminants, including the presence of men, the touch of unclean women, and the ingestion of impure food. When Mary takes her first steps at six months, Anne lifts her up and says, "You will not walk at all on this ground until I have taken you to the Temple of the Lord"—as if the earth itself threatened to sully her daughter's purity.[2] When Mary turns three, she is finally permitted to walk, but only on cloistered and consecrated ground.[3] Between the ages of three and fourteen, Mary lives within the Temple's walls, supervised by five virgins, seven priests, and innumerable hosts of angels.[4] "Ye shal nevyr, Lady," N-Town's guardian angel assures her, "be lefte here alone" (9.275). Angels feed Mary manna from heaven (represented, as N-Town's stage directions specify, by *confeccyons*, or prop Eucharistic wafers), forbidding worldly stuff to pass through her lips.[5] Since manna was believed to produce no waste, this exclusive diet of "aungelys mete" ensures that Mary never digests, never burps or farts, and never defecates.[6] The Virgin's body remains untouched by unclean hands, food, soil, and air.

In one sense, these ascetic practices—dietary restrictions, constant surveillance, and strict enclosure—prepare Mary to become the *inventrix virginitatis* (inventor of virginity), Christianity's first nun.[7] Before leaving Mary at the Temple, N-Town's Anne asks her daughter, "Wole ye be pure maydyn and also Goddys wyff?" (9.33). Here, Anne echoes the ceremonial vows sworn by novices—then and now—in the *consecratio virginum*.[8] The three-year-old child enthusiastically agrees to remain "Goddys chast servaunt" forever, unstained and unspotted (9.36). While her peers preserve their virginity for the harvest of marriage, Mary vows to keep her chastity for God.

According to the apocryphal legends of the life of the Virgin, Mary might have remained cloistered within the Temple forever were it not for Jewish law, which expelled her from God's sanctuary before the onset of puberty and the defilement of menstruation.[9] In N-Town's pageant of "The Marriage of Mary and Joseph," the high priest Ysakar orders Mary to leave the Temple and obey the Mosaic law of universal procreation.[10] (This is not an actual Judaic law but rather a polemical Christian misrepresentation.)[11] But Mary refuses to break her vow of virginity and chastises Ysakar for crossing her. "Such clene lyff," she tells him,

> shuld ye nouht,
> In no maner wyse, reprove. (10.72–73)

Thrown by Mary's "grett wytt," Ysakar acknowledges that a certain line from the Psalms does seem to suggest that God permits his creatures to make and keep vows, not coincidentally citing the very passage—Psalm 75:12 (in the Vulgate)—used by Augustine to justify clerical celibacy.[12]

Thus far, the legend of the Virgin's childhood seems set on representing Judaism's insistence on procreation as wrongheaded and mean-spirited, and Mary's commitment to celibacy as pioneering and righteous. And yet, as we know, God will not invite Mary to keep her vow of celibacy forever cloistered in his Temple, liberated from the troubles and responsibilities of domesticity and motherhood. Christianity's supersession of Judaism demands much more complex negotiations. Indeed, N-Town's high priests face a seemingly unsolvable dilemma: Psalm 75:12 demands that Mary keep her vow of celibacy, and yet Genesis 1:28 demands that she marry and reproduce. Flummoxed by this apparent inconsistency in the word of God, the priests of the Temple appeal directly to the heavens and ask for a sign.[13] Annunciating angels and spectacular miracles manifest on the page and stage to explain God's multipronged solution: the *syneisaktism* or white marriage of Mary and Joseph, the miracle of the Incarnation, and the redemption of mankind.[14] In short, God solves Mary's problem with paradoxes (a sexless marriage, a virgin mother, a human God) that make the impossible possible. Rather than choosing between the mutually exclusive categories of fertility and virginity, God breaks the rules of precedence and nature in order to choose both.[15]

In this sense, the paradox of Mary's virginal and yet fertile body brokers a dynamic and tenuous compromise between Jewish and Christian sexual values. As a mother, Mary obeys the oldest law, God's first commandment: in the Vulgate, *crescite et multiplicamini* (Genesis 1:28).[16] Second Temple Judaism understood this commandment to mean that God blessed and even demanded lawful sexual reproduction.[17] By giving birth to a son of the house of David, Mary fulfills her responsibility to perpetuate the chosen seed. Yet, as a perpetual virgin, Mary also follows the chaste example set by Jesus, who—in apparent defiance of the Old Law—never married or procreated.[18] Rather than reproducing carnally, Jesus increased his flock spiritually by means of the sexless process of conversion. He called his disciples away from their families and made them "eunuchs for the kingdom of heaven" (Matthew 19:12). Imitating Christ and his apostles, the elite forces of Christianity (saints, hermits, monks, and nuns) made oaths of celibacy, keeping themselves clean for the eagerly anticipated apocalypse.[19]

Whereas Judaism interpreted marriage as a reflection of God's sacred covenant with Israel, early and medieval Christianity saw it as a necessary evil. "It is better," Saint Paul wrote, "to marry than to burn" (1 Corinthians 7:9).[20] However, despite Christianity's perennial commitment to celibacy, very few Christian sects have ever abandoned marriage and reproduction completely.[21] No exception to this rule, the medieval Church hedged its bets, delegating the lower, carnal task of fertility to the laity and the loftier, spiritual work of chastity to the clergy. Jerome explained this compromise as a happy collaboration: "Marriage replenishes the earth, and virginity replenishes paradise."[22] And yet the disparagement of marriage inherent in this compromise left the laity in a double bind. By obeying Jehovah, they disappointed Jesus.

The miracle of the virgin birth seeks to reconcile these irreconcilable differences, accommodating both the Old Law and the New Law, both Jewish family values and the Christian preference for celibacy. Perhaps for this reason, the distinction between Judaism and Christianity sometimes fleetingly disappears in N-Town's pageants about the childhood and adolescence of the Virgin. Although the text describes Ysakar as a Jewish priest of the Temple and firm pillar of the law of Moses, it also explicitly identifies him as a "Crysten" bishop who worships the Trinity, administers the sacraments, and quotes the New Testament chapter and verse.[23] In a fifteenth-century altarpiece dedicated to Mary's mother, Ysakar stands in the doorway of a Gothic cathedral wearing the robes and miter of a medieval bishop; above his head, a figure of Moses smiles down on him, revealing to him the tablets of the Ten Commandments.[24] Momentarily, Ysakar becomes a Jewish Catholic, a Catholic Jew. Mary's paradox makes this impossibility possible. Her miraculous double identity (virgin and mother) innovates and yet also conserves, enabling the inauguration of the celibate priesthood without forsaking the institution of reproductive marriage.[25]

And yet this solution has its limits. The prevailing orthodox interpretation of the Virgin maintains that no one else, either before or since, has ever been or will ever be able to obey both the Old Law and New Law so harmoniously. The virgin mother is inimitable: alone among mortals and, even more importantly, "alone of all her sex" (*sola sine exemplo femina*).[26] According to overwhelming consensus, Mary's miraculous exceptionalism opened the doorway to redemption, but not too wide. As a nonpareil, Mary serves to inspire hope, but also humility—and shame.[27] Early Christian and medieval sermons and conduct manuals exhorted sinners, and especially girls and women, to emulate the Virgin but never to expect to compare to her incomparability.[28] The fathers of the Church recognized the apparent contradiction inherent in their advice. "Someone will say," Saint Ambrose acknowledges, "Why have you brought forward the example of Mary, as if anyone could imitate the Lord's mother?"[29] Misogynists offered a simple solution to this riddle: Mary was the only good woman, the exception that proves the rule of female depravity.[30]

But this is not the only way to interpret the Virgin Mother. Mary's paradoxical sexuality has the potential to redistribute perfection rather than restrict it to one unique exception. When the angel of the Lord announces the conception of the Virgin in N-Town, he reveals that "God is avengere of synne and not nature doth lothe" (8.178). In other words, God hates sin, not nature. This distinction invites an interpretation of Mary's paradox as a double endorsement and not as a divisive contradiction. If N-Town understands Mary's virginity as proof of God's approval of virginity and her fertility as proof of God's approval of fertility, then her paradox extends rather than limits sanctity's borders.[31] And indeed, N-Town often seems to represent Mary as a sign that God loves both virgins and wives, not one at the other's expense. Dissatisfied by Judaism's universal imperative to marry and reproduce, N-Town's Virgin institutes new Christian practices (lifelong virginity, the celibate priesthood, the second order of nuns, and spiritual marriage) in addition to, rather than in place of, the old. And it hardly stops there. In the High and late medieval period, a certain strain of devotion, art, and literature extended Mary's sanctifying influence much further.

Disturbed by these attempts, Bernard of Clairvaux tried to point out the problem, as he saw it, with opening up Mary's singularity. Bernard asked a rhetorical question, intended to sound ridiculous: "What if someone, following this line of reasoning," he wrote, should extend the honor due only to Mary to "each of her parents, then her grand-parents, and then their parents, and so on ad infinitum?"[32] What then? "Such joy," Bernard answers, "would be more fitting for heaven than for earth, for citizens rather than exiles." Sharing Mary's grace, in other words, would make this fallen world far too delightful. Unsurprisingly, not everyone found this possibility distasteful. Bernard's reductio ad absurdum rather precisely maps the narrative trails blazed by medieval legends, revelations, images, and pageants that extended Mary's perfection back to her father and mother, Saint Anne, and then back to *Saint Anne's* mother and father, Saint Fanuel, and then back to *Saint Fanuel's* mother, the daughter of Abraham, and so on and so forth, all the way back to Eve and the Garden of Eden.[33]

According to this particular branch of Mariological mythology, a seed from Eden's tree of life (guarded, according to Genesis, by fiery cherubim and forbidden to the exiled children of Adam and Eve) took root in Abraham's garden.[34] The aroma of that flower then impregnated Abraham's virginal daughter. In an explosion of birdsong and flowers, she gave birth to Saint Fanuel, who impregnated his thigh (like Zeus with Dionysus) when he wiped it with a knife wet from cutting apples. From the smell of this flower and the juice of this fruit derived Saint Anne, who gave birth to the Virgin Mary, *flos florum*, flower of flowers.[35] This genealogy makes Mary the child of Adam, Eve, and the tree of life, which is also the Arbor Annae (the tree of Anne), Jesus's matrilineal bloodline (as opposed to Jesus's patrilineal family tree, the Stem of Jesse, which charts his adoptive rather than biological heritage). Thanks to the tree of Anne, mankind never fell—not completely. One strain of flesh, the future flesh of the Virgin, remained sinless and yet earthbound for generations on generations, reproducing sinlessly in defiance of God's curse—and then finally, by means of the Incarnation, disseminating itself throughout mankind.

The Immaculate Conception

Inter faeces et urinam nascimur—we are born between urine and feces, shit and piss.[36] This truth poses a messy problem for Christianity, whose God, unlike his rivals (Jehovah and Allah), chose to be incarnated. In late antiquity, the Christian claim that God had descended into the body of human woman horrified outsiders. Porphyry, for example, gagged at the thought of a celestial deity gestating inside a womb, "made filthy by the blood of the choron and bile and even worse things."[37] In a similar vein, the *Book of Nestor the Priest* taunts Christians with graphic images of the fetal Jesus listening to Mary's "flatuses when she moved her bowels" and pushing his mouth and nose against her urethra as he emerged into the corrupt world through her bloody birth canal.[38] As Alexandra Cuffel has shown, the concept of the Incarnation provoked an onslaught of nasty polemic, to which, by and large, orthodox Christianity responded with capitulation.[39] Rather than maintaining that Mary drenched the infant Christ with her bodily filth in the manger at Bethlehem, the apocryphal Gospels clarified that Jesus emerged from Mary's body in a blinding flash of light, without pain, pollution, or loss of virginity.[40]

By the twelfth century, the virgin birth had been purified of invisible as well as visible contaminants.[41] Anselm of Canterbury claimed that while the Virgin was born with the stain of original sin, God washed that spot away at the moment of the Annunciation, thereby exempting his mother from the Curse of Eve.[42] Anselm argued that Mary had to have been cleansed of all impurities—even and especially the original—in order to become worthy of bearing the Christ Child. It would not have been seemly, he reasoned, for God to take up residence in a cursed and filthy edifice; thus, it must be assumed that the Trinity would have had the place thoroughly scrubbed and scoured in preparation for Jesus's arrival. (As Boccaccio puts it in his *Corbaccio*, God prepared a hostelry "worthy of abode for such and so great a King, in order not to come and inhabit the pigsty of modern womanhood.")[43] While formulating these ideas, Anselm was very careful to forestall any implication of Mary's divinity. "Christ's mother's purity," he writes, "by which he was pure, was only from him, whereas he was pure through and from himself."[44] Mary's sinlessness, in other words, came from God, for God— not from herself or for herself.

But these restrictions on Mary's powers and privileges could not hold for long. Within one generation, Anselm's student Eadmer of Canterbury was already pushing back against his teacher's limits and threatening to turn Mary's purification into deification.[45] Eadmer argued that God would not have waited to purify his mother until the moment of the Annunciation but rather would have eagerly bestowed this special favor much earlier—in fact, as early as possible: in Mary's mother's womb at the moment of Mary's conception. This claim raised the same question that Mary asks the archangel Gabriel in the Gospel of Luke: How might this be? Circumnavigating specifics, Eadmer compared the embryonic Virgin inside her mother's body to the white fruit of a chestnut inside its dark and spiky husk. If God lets the milky chestnut grow inside but unharmed by thorns, he asked, then why would he not let his own mother grow "among the thorns of sin" and yet "immune from their pricks"?[46] God could do it, Eadmer argued, and, therefore, "if he willed it, he did it" (*potuit, voluit, ergo fecit*).

Eadmer's theory of the Immaculate (literally, spotless or unstained) Conception of the Virgin shocked and appalled many of the most celebrated theologians of the period, including Bernard of Clairvaux, Peter Lombard, Alexander of Hales, Albertus Magnus, Bonaventure, and Thomas Aquinas.[47] It was not Eadmer's argument that Mary had been cleansed and purified before the Annunciation that provoked offense. On the contrary, that aspect of his theory met with almost universal approval. Most everyone agreed that God would have exempted the Virgin from the Curse of Eve as early as possible, long before Mary's pregnancy. The question was *when* that moment of possibility began. While Eadmer nominated the moment of Mary's conception inside her mother's womb, his opponents insisted instead on the instant of her animation (roughly eighty to ninety days after conception in the case of a female fetus, according to the rules of

Aristotelian science).[48] Why the delay? Because the maculists (those who opposed the theory of the Immaculate Conception) stood by a maxim that they attributed to Augustine: "Omnem quae de concubitu nascitur, carnem esse peccati" (All flesh born of intercourse is of sin).[49]

"How can there not be sin," Bernard of Clairvaux asked, "when there is carnal lust?"[50] Aquinas agreed: Mary had to have contracted original sin because "she was conceived in sexual desire and the joining of husband and wife."[51] From the perspective of Bernard and Aquinas (and the maculists more broadly), it was one thing to claim that God had purified the embryonic Virgin in her mother's womb but quite another to propose that God had sanctified Mary's parents' carnal emissions in the very moment of their fertilizing orgasmic climax. The latter implies that, at least once, God consecrated sexual intercourse, liberating coitus from the bonds of sin and elevating it to the status of the sacred.[52] Reason, Bernard concluded, forbids it—"Nec hoc quidem admittit ratio."[53]

Maculists and immaculists continued to debate the issue of Mary's conception for centuries.[54] The pope did not make a definite decision on the matter until 1854, when the Immaculate Conception (carefully defined and declawed) finally became dogmatic.[55] Before then, however, the Vatican avoided taking sides. The controversy burned especially hot during the fifteenth century, inspiring petitions, polemics, excommunications, and accusations of heresy.[56] In this fog of war, confusion abounded. Maculists complained about the strange errors circulating among the rude and vulgar people: chief among them, the idea that Anne had, like her daughter, conceived without sexual intercourse by means of the Holy Ghost—specifically while sharing an innocent "Kiss of Cleanness" with her husband at the Golden Gate of Jerusalem.[57] And, even worse, that Saint Anne's father, King Fanuel, had *also* conceived without sexual intercourse. And, worse still, that *his* mother had as well. Virgin births, the maculists complained, were breeding in Mary's family tree like rabbits.[58]

This fecund multiplicity, the maculists protested, detracted from the chaste and singular honor of the Virgin, rendering her unique perfection unexceptional and therefore less valuable.[59] And yet despite their contempt for these "fables," maculists actually agreed with the assumption underlying the very "superstition" that they excoriated: the assumption that only a virgin birth, enabled by the Holy Ghost and unsullied by sexual intercourse, could possibly be considered immaculate.[60] But not everyone made this assumption. Saints and mystics like Bridget of Sweden and Margery Kempe, wives and mothers themselves, tended to interpret the mechanism of the Immaculate Conception not as miraculous but rather as natural.[61] According to their interpretation of the Immaculate Conception, Mary's parents managed a feat more surprising and unprecedented, within the logic of Augustinian Christianity, than the virgin birth itself. After the Fall of Man, they reproduced without a spot of sin.[62] No miracle, just self-control. And while the Church neglected to discipline those who perpetuated the legends of the virgin births of Mary's mother, grandfather, and great-grandmother, claims of immaculate procreation were taken more seriously—that is, when they were acknowledged at all. The Inquisition condemned heretics like John of Brunn and Bloemardine of Brussels for their alleged promulgation of sanctified sexuality and regularly interrogated suspects about their views on sin and reproduction.[63]

Despite the risk, mystics, saints, and artists persisted in their belief that Anne and Joachim had conceived the Virgin Mary sexually and yet sinlessly. In the *Liber Celestis*, Saint Bridget explains her theory of the Immaculate Conception in great detail, an explanation that she claimed to have received in a revelation from the Virgin Mary.[64] In Bridget's vision, Mary begins with a puzzle. Let us say that a hungry servant vowed to mortify his flesh by fasting but then received a command from his sovereign to eat. What should he do? Keep his vow or obey his king? He should obey and eat, Mary answers, because fasting, in this case, would constitute disobedience. Likewise, she argues, God prefers the obedience of the reproductive to the abstinence of the celibate. Anne and Joachim, Mary explains, were more than capable of fasting (that is, preserving their virginity), but they virtuously chose the more difficult path: they reproduced, as God commanded in Genesis. And, like true athletes of God, they managed to do so sinlessly, in a spirit of purely pious obedience (unlike the celibate clergy, Bridget pointedly implies, who boast of their chastity and yet flee from the challenge of coitus like cowards). A sixteenth-century French theatrical cycle from Valenciennes dramatizes a similar take on the Immaculate Conception, staging the intimate scene as a psychomachia fought between chaste angels and lusty devils over the marital bed.[65] Anne and Joachim's good angels trounce the demons of lust and heroically expel them from the stage. Then the couple proceeds to have perfectly natural—and perfectly immaculate—sexual intercourse.

Seeking enlightenment through meditation, the pregnant fifteenth-century English mystic Margery Kempe asked God to direct her thoughts. "Jhesu," she asked, "what schal I thynke?" Jesus answered, "Dowtyr, thynke on my modyr."[66] Contemplating the Virgin, Margery beheld a vision of Mary inside the womb of Saint Anne.[67] In the sight of this image of sacred fertility, Margery dared to ask Jesus a burning question. Why, she asked, would God deign to speak to an unworthy wife and mother? Saying exactly what Margery most wanted to hear, Jesus said, "I lofe wyfes also"—"as wel as any mayden in the world."[68] Not only virgin martyrs and desert hermits but also wives and mothers. In this vision, Jesus promises Margery that bringing forth fruit within the bond of marriage is "no synne" but rather "mede and meryte."[69] Saint Anne delivered the same good news to Bridget: "I ame Anne, ladi of weddid folk," she said (Ego sum Anna, domina omnium coniugatorum)—patron saint of all those who "bring furth froite to the wirshipe of Gode."[70] To a lay audience of spouses and parents, the Immaculate Conception and the interconnected cult of Saint Anne represented the theological viability of distinguishing between reproduction and sin—and even of sanctifying the pleasures of sexuality beyond its reproductive office.[71]

The Legendary Life of Saint Anne

Wives and mothers are few and far between in the litany of the saints. According to several statistical studies, you could count them on the fingers of one hand.[72] When dealing with these rare few, hagiographers tend to exercise extreme caution. The late medieval hagiographers of the saintly mothers Elizabeth of Hungary and Bridget of Sweden insist that filial obedience, rather than love or desire, forced their heroines to enter into the state of matrimony.[73] These chaste wives, it is strongly emphasized, never paid more than the bare minimum installments on their sexual debts. Elizabeth was "bound to the law of the conjugal bed," her hagiographer writes, but not "bound to enjoyment."[74] In order "to quell all carnal desire," we are told, she often rose from her husband's side at night to pray on her knees, sleep on the floor, nurse dying lepers, and mortify her flesh with floggings.[75] So too did Bridget prefer to "wake the most part of the night" prostrated in prayer or scourged by cruel discipline.[76] As these hagiographers have it, such practices did not hinder but rather helped conception. God rewarded Elizabeth with three children and Bridget eight (including another saint, Karin of Sweden). The message seems clear: God condones lawful reproduction but not carnal delights.

The legend of Saint Anne—especially as N-Town dramatizes it—departs from this paradigm. Although Anne's late medieval hagiographers may preach ascetic values, their running commentary in praise of renunciation frames an ill-fitting sequence of events. As Virginia Nixon has shown, Anne's vitae often begin with the familiar claim that she married only in order to obey her father and the Father, thereby fulfilling her duty to perpetuate the chosen seed.[77] And yet in Saint Anne's case, hagiographers cannot support that claim with the usual reproductive evidence, because Anne produced no heirs. According to a tradition derived from the apocryphal Gospels, God kept Anne's womb closed for many, many years, like those of Sarah, Rebecca, Rachel, and Hannah before her.[78]

As the story of the apocryphal Infancy Gospels goes, and as Anne's hagiographers must repeat, Anne and Joachim lived for decades on decades as the only infertile couple in Israel.[79] In his *Life of Saint Anne*, the fifteenth-century East Anglian friar Osbern Bokenham (N-Town's contemporary and neighbor) describes Anne and Joachim as the perfect match: alike in status, temperament, and age—as "lyche to lychee" as two billing swans.[80] Bokenham's phrasing, harking back to Chaucer's maxim that "man sholde wedde his simylitude," implies Anne and Joachim's sexual harmony.[81] Yet this harmony jars against God's commandment. Their love neither increases nor multiplies but rather stagnates. Rabbinic law advises that a husband should divorce his wife if their marriage has not produced children after ten years.[82] Legends of the life of Saint Anne exaggerate that advice, turning it into a universal imperative.[83] In N-Town's pageant of "Joachim and Anne," the high priest of the Temple proclaims that "amonge all this pepyl, barreyn be no mo" (8.106)—among Jews, infertility is not allowed. And yet despite this enormous pressure to reproduce, Joachim fails to divorce his barren wife, even after twenty years of infertility, double that ten-year limit.

This discrepancy between law and practice puts Anne's hagiographers in an awkward position. When Bokenham relates that Anne and Joachim lived together for so long "wythout issw," he anxiously adds, "in chast maryage and not vycyous."[84] But what does the phrase "chaste marriage" mean in this context? Bokenham certainly does not mean that Anne and Joachim practiced celibacy. Several leaves later, Bokenham's Joachim complains to God that he has sown his seed "wyth gret dilygence" in a barren field, watering his crop "eche day" and yet never harvesting a crop. Here, Joachim implies that he "labouryde in vayne" to impregnate his wife on a daily basis for twenty years.[85] We might ask why he continued to plough for so long and with such zeal if he knew the ground was barren. He does not say. He only says that he drank from the sea to quench his thirst.[86] Drinking only ever made him thirstier.

As far as their neighbors can tell, Anne and Joachim are shameful sexual deviants. This is unsurprising, really. Sexual deviancy and bad reputations run in the Holy Family, from the four depraved foremothers listed in the Gospel of Matthew's genealogy of Jesus (Tamar, Rahab, Ruth, and Bathsheba) to the Virgin Mary herself.[87] Dramatizing the events narrated in the apocryphal Gospels, N-Town's pageant of "Joachim and Anne" revolves around Judaism's persecution of Mary's parents for their flagrantly illicit marriage.[88] First, the high priest publicly humiliates Joachim and exiles him from the Temple. Ysakar tells Joachim that infertility is a "tokyn" of being "cursyd" by God (8.104). Until an angel intervenes, Anne and Joachim are racked with shame.[89] The "grett slawndyr" (8.62) and "fowle fame" (8.127) of their infertility make Anne weep and quake with dread.[90] Joachim's despondency drives him from his wife and into his pastures, where stares "al hevely" at his sheep, which are "lusty and fayr and grettly multyply" (8.136–37)—the task at which he has so miserably failed.[91]

When the adolescent Virgin Mary looks back on her infancy and narrates the history of her birth, she says that her parents were cruelly "revylyd" and called "wykkyd and wylde."[92] Yet Mary does not deny the charge that they broke the law for the sake of love. There is no need to protest. Despite the rules, God is always on Mary's side. Exegetes compared the Virgin to the Old Testament's Queen Esther.[93] King Ahasuerus forbade, on pain of death, that any supplicant ever enter his presence uninvited. Yet when his beloved wife broke that rule to save her people, he made an exception. "This law was not made for you," Ahasuerus told Esther, "but for all others" (Esther 15:13). This moment prefigured the exceptionalism of the Virgin, the only uncursed daughter of Eve. Legends of Saint Anne extend this exceptional privilege. Anne and Joachim broke the law, scandalizing their neighbors and incurring the wrath and judgment of the high priests. And yet God rewards them for their disobedience, sending them "both seed and flowre" of the "Savyour unto al mankende."[94] If God's election of Mary suggests his approval of both virginity and maternity, then his election of Anne would seem to demonstrate his tolerance of—and even admiration for—infertile pleasures.

Appropriately, then, N-Town's pageant of "Joachim and Anne" emphasizes and celebrates carnal joys. When the angel announces the coming of Mary, he tells Joachim that his "blyssd wyf" shall bear a child "which shal be blyssyd in her body" (8.191). Joachim echoes back the phrase "blessed body," praying, "A, Anne, blyssyd be that body of thee shal be bore!" (8.204). After hearing this good news, Anne and Joachim joyfully reunite at the Golden Gate of Jerusalem. Weeping with joy, Joachim says to his wife, "Have this kusse of clennesse, and with yow it kepe" (8.241). Completing his rhyme (and echoing his "joy"), Anne exclaims, "Ther was nevyr joy sank in me so depe!" (8.243). Anne's choice of verb, *sank*, can mean "to become submerged," "to penetrate," and "to make an impression on the mind, feeling, or senses."[95] In other words, Joachim's kiss deeply penetrates Anne's body, taking root there. This Kiss of Cleanness—so often depicted in late medieval murals, altarpieces, stained-glass windows, and the Hours of the Virgin—symbolically represents the Immaculate Conception, Anne and Joachim's sexual congress unsullied by sin.[96] And while Anne's late medieval hagiographers insist that she felt no lust in this blessed moment, they do not tend to stipulate that she felt no pleasure.[97] Instead, the cult of Saint Anne magnified her joys. Like Chaucer's Wife of Bath, Anne ecstatically heeds God's call to use her sexual instrument "in the actes and fruyt of marriage."[98] Not for nothing was she venerated as the patron saint of good fortune.[99] N-Town's Anne asks the audience, "Ho myth have joys more?" (8.234).[100] Her labors of love, practiced and perfected in childless peace over decades of infertility, helped to save mankind.

Anne loved marriage so much that she married three husbands. In this, as in other things, she is an outlier. As a rule, the saintly wives venerated in the later Middle Ages tended to end their days as celibate widows. After the death of her husband in the Crusades, Elizabeth of Hungary left her children behind and fully committed herself to brutal asceticism; after her husband fell ill and died, Bridget of Sweden distributed all her goods and became the celibate bride of Christ.[101] Even wives aiming merely to be good, rather than blessed or saintly, were discouraged from remarriage; Jesus, Saint Paul, and the Church fathers united their voices in praise of celibate widows, whose reward in heaven would multiply sixtyfold (less than the hundredfold merited by virginity but double the thirtyfold awarded to wives).[102] The Wife of Bath proves hard of hearing when it comes to this counsel. She prefers to heed "that gentil text," Genesis 1:28: "God bad us for to wexe and multi-plye."[103] Saint Anne, apparently, agreed. Like the Wife of Bath, Anne returned to the marriage market after the death of her husband—and not once but twice, her *trinubium* (or triple marriage) only two husbands shy of the Wife of Bath's quintuple.

When Jerome retranslated (or rather corrected, as he would have it) the Gospels' references to Jesus's siblings, he successfully augmented the purity of the Virgin.[104] But he also expanded the Holy Family—provoking the question, who were these cousins of Christ? It was quickly decided that they had to be the sons of Mary's sisters. The Gospel of John refers to a sister of the Virgin Mary: Mary Cleophas, who witnessed the Crucifixion (John 19:25). And when describing the same moment, the Gospel of Mark refers to the presence of another woman, named Salome (Mark 15:40). From these small seeds, medieval exegetes constructed an elaborate family tree of which Anne formed the trunk. In the ninth century, the Benedictine Haimo of Auxerre charted his theory of the *trinubium*, the three blessed marriages of Saint Anne: first, Anne married Joachim and gave birth to the Virgin Mary, the mother of Jesus Christ; then, after the death of Joachim, Anne married Joachim's brother, Cleophas, her second husband, and gave birth to Mary Cleophas, the mother of James the Lesser, Jude, Simon, and Joseph the Just; finally, after the death of Cleophas, Anne married Salome, her third husband, and gave birth to Mary Salome, mother of James the Greater and John the Evangelist.[105] All told, that is three holy marriages, three sainted children, and seven sainted grandchildren.

Marginalia in the N-Town manuscript lovingly delineates this matrilineal system with a genealogical chart connecting Jesus, the fruit, back to Mary, the flower, and Anne, the stem.[106] Images of this Holy Kinship proliferated in the late Middle Ages: illuminations, altarpieces, woodcuts, and stained-glass windows represent Anne surrounded by her many children and grandchildren, sisters and cousins.[107] Fertility fills and overflows these crowded family portraits: babies cuddle and wriggle in the laps of their mothers and crawl around the edges of the frame, peering out from under their grandmother's skirts; children run around playing with toys, fruit, and puppies. Irrepressibly, the fertility that Jerome diverted from the Virgin

Mary jetted up not so very far away, in the adjacent and interconnected cult of her mother.

And for a time, at least, the doctrine of Anne's triple marriage flew—despite the outraged protestations of those (including Fulbert of Chartres, Jean de Fribourg, and Aquinas) who found it atrociously indecorous and even whorish.[108] Anne sometimes saw to these complaints personally. Saint Colette of Corbie, disgusted by the apparent inchastity of the *trinumbium* (which, as Colette herself admitted, reminded her of her own mother's irritating remarriage), refused to pray to Anne, until the saint appeared before her surrounded by her glorious progeny.[109] Dazzled, Colette fell into line. Not all skeptics fared so well: according to one legend, an English bishop fell off his horse and broke his neck after casting aspersions about Anne's excessive enthusiasm for the joys and fruits of marriage.[110]

But times changed, and quickly.[111] Caught in a terrifying thunderstorm in 1505, Martin Luther made Saint Anne a promise: "Help, dear Saint Anne—I'll become a monk!"[112] Twenty years later, he had changed his tune. By the 1530s, Luther had come to see Anne as an upstart idol.[113] He was not alone. After the Council of Trent, Pope Pius V suppressed the feast of Saint Anne and removed the Office of Joachim from the breviary; the iconography of the Kiss of Cleanness, the Triple Marriage, and the Holy Kinship diminished, if not vanished, soon thereafter.[114] Mary's exceptionalism became singular rather than plural, hers alone rather than hers and her mother's, and her father's, and his mother's, and Eve's, and everyone's.

Bad Wives: Eve, Norea, Gill, and Mary

Mary bears the fruit not only of a matrilineal bloodline but also an exegetical genealogy. Medieval exegetes represent Noah's wife as the centerpiece of a typological triptych, connected backward to Eve and forward to Mary. Eve and Noah's wife, the mothers of mankind, populate the earth before and after the Flood, and then Mary repeats their pattern with a difference by giving birth to salvation. As the *Bible moralisée* has it, "Noe significat Christum, uxor eius beatam Mariam" (Noah signifies Christ, and his wife the blessed Mary).[115] Considering this framework, we might expect early English biblical drama to represent Noah's wife as an exemplary prototype of the Virgin. And, indeed, the N-Town pageant of Noah's Flood (following the pattern of Continental drama) takes this approach, praising Noah's wife as a paragon of virtue, her husband's pride and joy.[116] But N-Town's English peers—the plays of York, Chester, and Towneley—take a different approach. These texts pillory Noah's wife, characterizing her as a caterwauling shrew, enemy to man and God.[117] She curses, kicks, and bites. She refuses to heed her husband's warnings or obey his commands. Instead, she sabotages God's plans and, in a fragment from Newcastle, even goes so far as to join forces with Satan. Thanks to these plays, Noah's wife became a byword for shrewishness in late medieval English culture. "Hastow nat herd," Chaucer's Nicholas asks,

> the sorwe of Noe with his felaweshipe,
> Er that he myghte gete his wyf to shipe?[118]

The question is rhetorical; everyone (even and especially simple John the Carpenter) knew the story of Noah's wife, the paradigmatic scold.[119]

What does this shrew have to do with the Blessed Virgin?[120] In a nutshell, both are types of Eve.[121] Gnostic heretics associated the wife of Noah with their heroine Norea, the daughter of Eve and manifestation of Sophia, Wisdom's divine emanation.[122] We first hear of Norea in the fourth-century heresiography of Epiphanius of Salamis, who dismissed the Gnostic "nonsense" that Noah's wife, named Noria, set fire to the ark three times.[123] This Gnostic reinterpretation of Noah's Flood (later fleshed out by the discovery of the Nag Hammadi library in 1945) characteristically inverts Judeo-Christian values, casting Jehovah as the villain, Noah as his wicked accomplice, and Norea as humanity's last hope of achieving true enlightenment.[124] When God and Noah plot to drown Norea by refusing her passage onto the ark, she repeatedly sabotages the ship until Noah throws up his hands and lets her come aboard. Thus, Norea thwarts Jehovah's evil plan and lives on to fight for truth and wisdom another day. Somehow, by unknown twists and turns, this Gnostic myth made its way to late medieval England, where it resurfaced, recognizable though changed, in two fourteenth-century illuminated manuscripts (Queen Mary's Psalter and the Ramsey Abbey Psalter) and in the Newcastle play of Noah's Flood.[125] These three adaptations fitted their source's most basic plot points into the template of the Temptation in the Garden, reimagining Norea as a satanic temptress rather than an en-lightened savior—in other words, as a second Eve.

Imitating the exposition of the Fall of Man, these adaptations of Noah's Flood begin with a prohibition: the angel of the Lord instructs Noah not to tell anyone about the ark (just as God commanded Adam not to eat the fruit of the tree of knowledge). Desperate to uncover God's secret, Satan seeks out Noah's wife (just as the serpent sought out Eve), because, as he says in the Newcastle fragment, "she is both whunt and slee"—both wise and sly, the devil's natural ally.[126] Satan then recruits Noah's wife (as he did Adam's) with truthful lies. Exploiting God's insistence on secrecy, Satan casts Noah's mysterious absences in a sinister light. In Queen Mary's Psalter, he tells Noah's wife, "He is gone to betray thee and all the world," a falsehood not so very far from the truth.[127] In the next scene, Noah's wife cozies up to her husband and slips him a truth serum.[128] Queen Mary's Psalter depicts her as a seductress who presses her lips to Noah's, one arm snaked around his neck and the other holding the forbidden fruit (in this case, the drugged chalice).[129] As in so many late medieval images of the Flood, the psalter repre-sents Noah as old and bearded (like Joseph) and Noah's wife as young and beautiful (like Mary).[130] All three of these narratives (the psalters and the fragment) end with Noah inviting his corrupted wife—now the devil's "own dear Dame"—onto the ark.[131] In the Newcastle play, Satan stands by her side; in the Ramsey Abbey Psalter, he clings to her back.[132] According to Gnostic myth, Eve and Norea outwitted the tyrant Jehovah, liberating the fruit of knowledge from his clutches and escaping his Flood. But from the Christian perspective articulated in Queen Mary's Psalter, the Ramsey Abbey Psalter, and the Newcastle fragment, their trickery serves Satan. Thanks to Noah's wife, the serpent wins again. Twice, God gave mankind a perfect world; twice, woman took it away.

Not much distance separates the satanic seductress of Newcastle from the slapstick shrew of York, Chester, and Towneley.[133] Although the shrew does not take orders directly from Satan, she continues to thwart God's plan. Al-though her ultimatum changes (from demanding to refusing passage), she continues to sabotage Noah's progress. And most importantly, she continues to reiterate the pattern of Eve, that "begynnar of blunder" (Towneley 3.587). The comedy of Noah's wife that we see in York, Chester, and Towneley re-frames a cosmic struggle between good and evil as a domestic battle of the sexes. In York, Chester, and Towneley, Noah (like Adam before him) tries his best to serve his righteous God, while his contrarian wife (like Eve before her) undermines him at every turn. Such, we are to understand, is the curse of marriage, purgatory on earth.[134] Trapped in this cage match, Noah and his wife toil away in misery, struggling to survive, always at odds.[135] Their division divides the audience: Noah's wife appeals directly to the "wifys that ar here," and Noah to their husbands (Towneley 3.568). She riles up her base ("We all wish our husbands were dead, am I right?"), and he his ("Take my advice and tame your wife while she's young").[136] Their conflict quickly turns violent, and they beat each other black and blue in an elaborate knockabout routine for the entertainment of the crowd, thereby embodying the acrobatic images of domestic violence that decorated so many medieval margins and misericords.[137]

In this darkly comic tradition, as V. A. Kolve aptly writes, "husbands and wives brawl simply because they are married to each other."[138] Marriage equals violence, and fisticuffs euphemistically represent the reciprocation of the cursed conjugal debt. Noah and his wife exchange blows, back and forth, using language reminiscent of the Wife of Bath's nostalgia for Jankyn's abuse. He broke my ribs, she remembers, and I punched him in the face; "I loved hym."[139] Campaigning in the same war, Noah pounds his wife and gets pounded in return. Noah's wife promises, "I shall not in thi det / Flyt of this flett"—I will not flee this battlefield in your debt (Towneley 3.322–23). True to her word, she gives him a kick in the pants, which he returns, which she repays with a "three for two" deal, which he "quits" evenly.[140] "Ar strokys good? say me!" Noah screams: Do you like that? (Towneley 3.553). Their double meanings and obscene acrobatics climax when Noah's wife finally pins him underneath her, and he gives up, his back broken. "Se how she can grone," Noah complains, "and I lig under"—see how she can groan, and I lie under (Towneley 3.592–93). Here, Noah scoffs at his wife's sounds of pain, pointing out to the audience that, despite her ruse of weakness, she has him tightly locked in a submission hold. And, continuing the routine's extended double entendre, Noah suggests his wife's preference for being on top.

All this obscenity, violence, and bad behavior, it has been argued, should disqualify this particular version of Noah's wife from her traditional position as a type of the Virgin. There is no resemblance between them, it has been said.[141] And yet Mary's own husband cannot tell them apart. When first introduced to Mary, Joseph does not recognize her singularity. On the contrary, he sees yet another daughter of Eve. He sees Noah's wife. Joseph fully expects Mary to repeat the sins of her foremothers: to "clowte [his] cote" (clout his coat) and "blere [his] ey" (blear his eye)—in short, to abuse and deceive him (N-Town 10.282–83). Neither does Mary reverse those expectations. Rather, she confirms her husband's worst fears. She saddles him with a child he did not father and subjects him to the scorn of his neighbors. All men, he says, call me "olde cokwold" (N-Town 12.55), a valid complaint that might have been realized in real time by jeers from the crowd.

Utterly defeated by his wife's tactics, Joseph relinquishes his sovereignty, vowing to serve Mary as an abject underling.[142] Performing this promise, Joseph stoops to kiss his wife's "swete fete" (N-Town 12.185). Later centuries coined a descriptive term for this pattern of behavior: *henpecked*, a word that often comes up in scholarly commentary on these pageants.[143] When Noah's wife boasts of her talent for subverting her husband's authority with "gam and gyle" (game and guile), she anticipates the complete triumph of the Virgin, who dominates not only helpless old Joseph but also God himself (Towneley 3.310). Mary may not wrestle her husband into submission, but, then again, she has no need for fisticuffs. When Joseph turns against Mary, swift angels descend from the clouds to intervene on her behalf. When he picks a fight, miracles quickly bring him to his knees. In Mary, shrewishness has its fulfillment. She perfects its potential, bending the entire universe to her will.

In the pageant of the flight into Egypt, Joseph, like Noah, attempts to obey God's command—not to build an ark, in this case, but rather to flee Judea. And like Noah's wife, Mary gets in the way and stalls his progress. We must flee, Joseph tells her, *now*. In response, Mary dissolves into tears and lamentations. "We, leve Marie, do way," Joseph says, "late be, I pray thee, leve of thy dyne" (York 18.147–48). Here, Joseph echoes Noah, who likewise silenced his wife: "Late be thy dyne" (York 9.271). We have to go, Joseph repeats; help me pack our things. Mary refuses. "I may not bere," she says (York 18.162). I cannot bear it, but also, I do not schlep. Joseph grumbles ("God it wote I muste care for all") but obeys (York 18.164). Such is his lot. Mary, still weeping and wailing, asks (again) where they are going. I just told you, Joseph says, to Egypt. Mary, continuously hyperventilating, pesters her husband with questions: why, when, and where. "Leve, Marie, leve thy grete," Joseph snaps—stop howling (York 18.192). The Towneley Joseph sums it up roundly: "This helpys noght"—you are not helping (15.91). Husbandry,

Joseph concludes, repeating the sentiments of his forefather Noah, is a bad bargain.[144] Even, it seems, when you're married to the unparalleled Virgin Mary—or rather especially then.

The late medieval iconography of the flight into Egypt lends support to Joseph's complaints. In altarpieces, illuminations, and transept bosses, Mary glides through the landscape on her otherwise unencumbered donkey, kissing and caressing the radiant infant Christ, while Joseph trudges ahead or behind on foot like a beast of burden, hefting provisions and equipment.[145] Here, devotion resembles parody. In his early sixteenth-century woodcut of the flight into Egypt, Albrecht Dürer depicts Mary sitting astride her donkey, cradling the baby Jesus in her arms, and looking ahead toward Egypt and salvation.[146] When he parodied this image, the satirist Cornelis Anthonisz made only the thriftiest of alterations.[147] He flipped Dürer's donkey around (to face the sinister left rather than the righteous right); swapped out the infant Christ for a squealing pig, meowing cat, and squawking parrot; and labeled his broadsheet "Saint Aelwaer," meaning Saint Shrew—the name of a popular "mock saint" (like Saint Lazy, Saint Spendthrift, or Saint Foutin, "the Little Fucker"), patroness of scolds, prostitutes, Beguines, and minstrels, players, and playwrights.[148] In Hieronymus Bosch's *Temptation of Saint Anthony*, the image of the flight into Egypt devolves even further, metamorphosing the Virgin into a monstrous, withered tree trunk with a thick, reptilian tail.[149]

In one sense, these parodies contrast saints with sinners and paragons with monsters. But in another, they condense every variable into one punch line: women are all the same, including the Virgin Mother of God. While on the surface it might seem as if this joke could only be made at Mary's expense, the infinitude of her late medieval account—in both the theological terms of her treasury of merit and the sociological terms of her cultural capital—rendered loss impossible. On the contrary, she turned detraction into devotion and misogyny into a strange kind of tolerance, if not celebration and even veneration. Mary's perfection served not only to shame all lesser mortals but also to elevate by association. Her grace spilled over, anointing all her many "deformed adumbrations," from Eve to Saint Aelwaer.[150]

Sacred drama literalized this transformation by turning sinners from cities and villages across Europe into the immaculate Virgin. Locals like "Rychard Byrscrow" from Coventry, "Robert Gallyn" from Kent, and "Gleyns daughter" and "Elyn Tuck" from London played the role of Our Lady for the entertainment and edification of their friends and neighbors.[151] Records indicate that both boys and girls played Mary in England at least until she reached her fourteenth year (her age at the Nativity, according to the *Golden Legend*), if not also beyond.[152] And yet, by and large, scholarly consensus has long maintained that male performers dominated medieval English theater, including the playing of the Virgin, presumably because of "the low reputation of female 'tombesteres' and other professional entertainers, of whom we know very little, but whose name seems to have been synonymous with 'harlot.'"[153] Supporting that notion, the fifteenth-century English-Latin glossary *Catholicon Anglicum* defines "an Harlott" as (among many other things) a kind of professional comedienne.[154] And yet the solution of all-male casting only amplifies the scandal inherent in theatrical performance.[155] Deuteronomy 22:5 prohibited cross-dressing, yet another rule broken by Mary when she disguised the Second Person of the Trinity in the costume of her flesh, encouraging medieval performers to follow suit.[156]

What did officials in charge of casting look for in a Madonna? One fourteenth-century record from Beverley's Guild of Saint Mary advises appointing "a certain member of the Guild," "the most suitable for this role who may be found," to play Mary at the ceremony of the Purification.[157] The record does not go on to specify the qualities that would make a certain member of the guild suitable for this role. But an account of a performance of a civic passion play in Grenoble in 1535 praises the actress who played the Virgin, one Françoise Buatier, for enchanting *tous les spectateurs* with *les gestes, la voix, la prononciation, le débit* (her gestures, voice, pronunciation, and flow).[158] Another account of a performance of the Presentation from Avignon in 1372 celebrates the actor playing Ecclesia for the beauty of his beardless face and the elegance of his wig (made from "the most beautiful hair of a woman").[159]

So, grace and beauty seem to have been in order. Yet that record from Beverley almost seems to suggest that the role plays itself. The "certain guildsman" cast to play Mary, the record emphasizes, must be "most nobly and appropriately robed and arrayed in the likeness of the glorious Virgin Mary." This phrasing implies that Mary's glory amounts to a particular costume of robes, ornaments, and tresses—a costume that need only be put on in order to work its magic. The community made that costume by collecting from its members the most well-crafted fabrics, sumptuous jewels, and loveliest hair (in the case of Lucerne, by sending out periodic inquiries into the countryside).[160] Gilded diadems were bequeathed to moving images of the Virgin made of flesh, as well as to statues made of wood. For example, in 1499, one William Brokshawe of East Retforth bequeathed a "serkelett" of gilt and stones to the image of the Blessed Virgin in the procession of the feast of Corpus Christi, on the feast of All Saints, in the play called Mankind (*in ludo de Mankynd*), and other plays (*et aliis ludis*).[161] (Except, of course, during times of plague, when all this intimate sharing threatened to spread disease from the bodies of actors to the families of the "knights and gentlemen" who furnished the gems and silks of their costumes.)[162] The community (whether in Avignon, Beverley, Lucerne, or East Retford), in short, made its local imitations of the inimitable Virgin Mary out of itself.

Before the Reformation, it was not so unusual to invite comparison between the Queen of Heaven and mere mortals. In the thirteenth century, Queen Blanche of Castile commissioned a portrait of herself as the Virgin, veiled in blue, pleading for mercy before her enthroned son, Louis IX of France.[163] In the fifteenth century, the Duke of Orleans did not think it inappropriate when courtly poets called his newborn daughter Marie "immaculate."[164] Anne Boleyn, like Margaret of Anjou before her and Elizabeth I after, played the role of the Virgin in her royal pageantry.[165] Anne imitated Mary not only during public rituals but also during private flirtations. When Henry VIII inscribed a missive in Anne's Book of Hours under the image of the Man of Sorrows, complaining of his lovesickness, Anne wrote back under the Annunciation (featuring a dark-haired Virgin who resembled Anne more than a little),

> By daily proof you shall me find
> To be to you both loving and kind.[166]

In other words, Anne promised to requite her king's love as obediently as Mary did the King of Heaven's, as well as to bear him a son and heir. Making an even naughtier allusion to the Virgin, the French painter Jean Fouquet used the king's mistress, the beautiful Agnès Sorel, as his model for a bare-breasted portrait of the Madonna Lactans.[167] Indeed, from the perspective of early modern reformers, Catholic images of the Virgin Mother, Mary Magdalene, and Mary of Egypt looked like nothing so much as "notorious harlots." Puritans complained that papist painters collected all the "daintiest Wenches" from their communities and compiled the Madonna from their choicest parts ("from one he borrowed her high forehead, from another her sparkling eyes, from a third her pretty long nose, from a fourth her smiling mouth, from others a dimpled chin, and other parts of the body"), immortalizing "such creatures" into "the beautiful object of Our Lady."[168] Not so far from the truth. Chaste and unchaste, rich and poor, male and female—it seems that almost any sinner could serve as a type of the Virgin. Not so exceptional or inimitable after all.

The Towneley Second Shepherds' Play

The diptych-like structure of Towneley's *Second Shepherds' Play* requires that two of its actors play double roles.[169] Mak the sheep thief and his shrewish wife, Gill, disappear just before the appearance of Joseph and the Virgin Mary.[170] This dual casting embodies the typological comparison that the text implies: Gill is another Mary, the last—and the least.[171] Her husband swears to it: there is, he says, no worse wife than Gill (13.358–9). She is, in his words, "a fowll dowse" (literally, a foul sweet, translated by David Bevington as "foul slut") who eats, drinks, and breeds him out of house and home (13.356).[172] She is a parasite, he complains, who only "lakys, / And clowse hir toose"— nags, and scratch her toes (13.597–98). "We must drynk as we brew," Mak sighs (13.723). The curse of marriage repays Mak's conjugal deposits with unwanted children, too many to feed. If only, he wishes, the devil would knock out their brains.[173] Adam made the bed, and Mak lies in it, forever bound to the no-good race of Eve. Mak offers up a prayer:

> Yll spede othere good
> That she will do! (13.345–46)

In short, Mak asks God to sabotage the saboteur. Stop her, he prays, before she ruins anything else.

And yet, in a Mariological turn, it turns out that Gill is Mak's only hope of salvation. Mak, after all, is no saint himself. After the Fall, God sentenced mankind to hard labor. But Mak refuses to toil. Instead, he steals from his neighbors, thereby "earning" (as he has it) more in a day "than thay that swynke and swette" (13.450). I am, he boasts, full of "sich grace" (13.453). When Mak returns home with a stolen sheep, Gill (busy spinning, like Eve and Noah's wife before her) points out that he failed to think things through.

"By the naked nek," she says, "art thou lyke for to hyng" (13.445–46). When this reality sinks in, Mak panics and begs his wife for help. He puts his fate in a woman's hands—like a hunter in pursuit of a unicorn, or any sinner desperate for the Virgin's intercession. The pageant of the *Second Shepherds' Play* is crammed full of proverbs about the irrevocability of error. We must drink as we brew, spend as we earn, and reap as we sow.[174] "Ill-spon weft, iwys, / Ay commys foull owte"—an ill-spun weft, to be sure, always comes out badly (13.848–9).[175] In short, good cannot come from evil. And yet, thanks to a *felix culpa*, these saws prove untrue—luckily for Mak, as for mankind. From Eve's fall came Mary's rise. Gill, like the second Eve, turns bad into good.

"Bot I play a fals cast," Gill promises, "trust me no more"—in other words, unless I play with false dice, never trust me (13.645–46). Making good on that promise, Gill comes up with an ingenious lie designed to save Mak's skin. "A good bowrde have I spied," Gill says, "syn thou can none" (13.478–79). This is the first of many compliments that the text bestows on Gill's "good bowrde" (meaning "game," "jest," or "trick"). It is also called "a good gyse," meaning "device" or "disguise" (13.491); "a far-cast," meaning "a long throw," as of a dart—a nice shot, in other words (13.492); and "a qwantt gawde" (13.855). That last phrase puns on the double meaning of *queinte*, which connotes both "quaint" ("a clever or curious device or ornament; a trick") and "cunt," in the sense of female genitalia. This is a pun beloved by Chaucer and Shakespeare (and Middle and early modern English poetry more broadly) for its tight encapsulation of the notion that trickery inheres in womankind as universally and inextricably as their reproductive organs.[176]

What is this amazing trick? Gill stages a Nativity scene. She wraps the stolen sheep in swaddling clothes, costuming herself as Mary and Mak as Joseph, ready to lullaby on cue. With this pageantry, Gill demonstrates the easiness of imitating the supposedly inimitable Virgin Mother—especially for a duplicitous and sluttish shrew. Like Mary, Gill gives birth to a sacrificial lamb, conceived without intercourse and delivered without pain or pollution. When Mak announces the good news of this birth to the shepherds, they come bearing gifts for the child. Triumphant, Gill crows, "Yit a woman avyse / Helpys at the last"—so, a woman's advice helps after all! (13.493–94).[177] Alas, Gill claims this glory for womankind a little too quickly. The shepherds soon see through her stratagem to the horned changeling behind the little daystar and the "fals skawde" behind the saintly mother (13.861). Yet they are not unimpressed. "It was a hee frawde," Gyb admits (13.857). Not quite good enough. Although the shepherds take mercy on Mak, tossing him in a blanket rather than hanging him from the gallows, Gill's trick fails in the end. Her theatrical illusion cracks. Nevertheless, when she vaunts, "If it were a gretter slyght / Yit couthe I help tyll," her words ring true (13.625–26). Her boast anticipates the coming of an even better trick.

In their second visitation of the evening, the shepherds bear witness to that highest and most immaculate deception: the adulterous and yet virginal birth of Christ, scandalous and sacred.[178] In the presence of God disguised as an infant, Coll makes a speech in praise of craftiness. He thanks Jesus for beguiling the beguiler and deceiving the deceiver. Satan, Coll knows, will never see Christ coming.[179] In response to this encomium to trickery, the baby Jesus laughs and makes merry. Apparently, Christ appreciates a good joke. "Lo, he merys," Coll says, "Lo, he laghys, my swetyng!" (13.1032–33). Coll then bestows his humble gift: "a bob of cherys" (13.1036)—the miraculous fruit that ripened for the Virgin in midwinter. With Jesus on her knee, Mary promises to intercede for the shepherds with God in Heaven. "He kepe you fro wo! / I shall pray hym so," she says (13.1072–73). Yet another quaint gaud. Thanks to the Mother of Mercy, God rewards sin with salvation.

Chapter 5

Promiscuous Mercy

The Gospel of Matthew tells us that when Joseph first discovered Mary's pregnancy, "being a just man, and not willing publicly to expose her," he decided to "put her away privately" (1:19).[1] Or, as John Lydgate puts it in his *Life of Our Lady*, Joseph, being "rightfull," did not "be traye" Mary with word or action.[2] In other words, he did not visibly react. If he had, he would have exposed Mary to accusations of adultery, because the literal level of the virgin birth so precisely resembles that crime. Under the Old Law, the punishment for adultery is death: "They shall cast her out of the doors of her father's house, and the men of the city shall stone her to death, and she shall die" (Deuteronomy 22:21).[3] In N-Town, Joseph tells the audience that he is bound by the letter of the law to inform against Mary to the local authorities and have her "quelled" (killed) "with stonys" (12.97). Yet the Gospel of Matthew implies that by hiding Mary from the law's eye, Joseph proved himself "just"—in Greek, δίκαιος, meaning "one obedient to the commands of God, an upright man, a man of character."[4]

Patristic commentary on Matthew 1:19 offers various explanations for this apparent contradiction.[5] Jerome, for one, argued that Joseph demonstrated his righteousness by humbly "concealing in silence that mystery which he did not know about."[6] Joseph, Jerome maintained, remained fully confident in Mary's purity yet was "perplexed" by the specifics. Thus, wisely, he did nothing, said nothing, and thought nothing. Others, like Chrysostom, interpreted Joseph's failure to react as a silent protest against the cruelty of the law of Moses.[7] Joseph's kindness, Chrysostom argued, superseded truth and justice, heralding the coming of Christ's mercy like the light that brightens the world before the sunrise. In other words, Chrysostom understood Matthew 1:19 to mean that Joseph assumed Mary's guilt and yet protected her anyway, in spiritually righteous though technically criminal defiance of the law. This way of reading the text baffled Jerome, who asked, "If this is so, why is Joseph recorded to be just, when he is concealing the crime of his wife?"[8] After all, Jehovah inscribed his prohibition against the crime of adultery with his own finger on the stone tablets of the law, a condemnation confirmed by Christ.[9] Then why would the Gospel of Matthew praise Joseph for breaking the rule that prescribes adultery's punishment? For Jerome, the answer to that question was clear. "This is a testimony to Mary," he concluded, that Joseph remained perfectly confident in her innocence despite all the apparent evidence of her guilt.[10]

But what if Mary *had* been guilty of adultery? Would it still have been "just" to evade the law then? Jesus offers an ambiguous answer to that question in the Gospel of John. In an episode called Christ and the adulteress (or the Pericope Adulterae), scribes and Pharisees bring Jesus an unquestionably guilty adulteress—"taken even now in" the very act—and ask for his verdict, hoping to catch him in a trap.[11] Augustine explains Christ's dilemma: if Jesus lets the adulteress go unpunished, he breaks the law of Moses; if he condemns her to death, he contradicts his own message of mercy.[12] Ingeniously, the new Solomon finds a loophole in the law, as he is wont to do. Jesus redirects: "He that is without sin among you, let him first cast a stone at her" (John 8:7). No one can lift a finger against the prisoner, despite her guilt. Technically, Jesus could, as he is without sin. But he does not. Instead, he tells her, "Neither will I condemn thee. Go, and now sin no more" (8:11). The adulteress departs unpunished, and Jesus avoids answering the Pharisees' underlying question. What punishment does adultery deserve under the New Law?

At least on the surface, Jesus's actions would seem to suggest that adultery deserves no punishment whatsoever—good news to some, but not all. The upright Ambrose admitted, "There is an uneasiness . . . when we see Christ send the adulteress away without condemnation."[13] This uneasiness was exacerbated by the fact that verses 7:53 through 8:11 are missing from the earliest surviving witnesses to the Gospel of John, an absence noticed as early as the fourth century.[14] This lacuna casts doubt on the authority and legitimacy of an already suspicious passage, making it all too easy to dismiss the story of the adulteress as an adulteration of the word of God—as a forgery. Augustine countered these suspicions with suspicions of his own. He suggested that "some men of slight faith, or, rather, hostile to the true faith, fearing, as I believe, that liberty to sin with impunity is granted their wives, remove from their Scriptural texts the account of our Lord's pardon of the adulteress."[15] With this comment, Augustine repurposed the difficulty of the text as a test separating the faithful from the faithless. Heathens, he argues, may shrink away in disgust, but the righteous dare to embrace Christ's radically—and even scandalously—promiscuous message of mercy.

Within limits. In his commentary on the Gospel of John, Augustine faces the burning question that the Pericope Adulterae provokes. "What does it mean, O Lord? Do you, therefore, countenance sins?"[16] For a moment, the possibility of a "yes" hovers in the air. But not for long. "Certainly not," Augustine reassures himself. If God favored sin, he reasons, then Jesus would have said, "Go, live as you will." But instead, Jesus commanded that the adulteress "sin no more." In this command, Augustine hears the inexorable approach of Doomsday, when the guilty adulteress will finally pay for her crime. Therefore, he concludes, Christ did not grant wives the liberty to sin with impunity, despite appearances to the contrary.

And yet Christ's apparent tolerance—or even penchant—for guilty adulteresses comes up more than once in the New Testament. Jesus fraternized with so many women of ill repute: the Samaritan woman with five husbands (John 4:4–42), the outcast with her alabaster box of ointments (Luke 7:37–38), and Mary Magdalene with her seven devils (Luke 8:2)—women interpreted by patristic commentary and medieval exegesis as adulteresses and prostitutes.[17] These two identities (adulteress and prostitute), according to certain ancient and medieval habits of thought, differ in degree but not in kind. Canonists defined both adultery and prostitution more in terms of promiscuity, notoriety, and deception than remuneration.[18] In a sense, then, the interrelated crimes of adultery and prostitution simply take the wicked inclinations of Eve to their logical extremity. "Woman," as the eloquent twelfth-century misogynist Marbod of Rennes wrote in *De meretrice*, "subverts the world; woman, the sweet evil, compound of honeycomb and poison."[19] And yet, to the shock of his allies and enemies alike, Jesus allowed these sinful daughters of Eve to hear his words, anoint his skin, kiss his feet, cover his expenses, and travel by his side.[20]

In fact, Mary Magdalene (or rather the composite Magdalene pieced together by exegetes, hagiographers, and homilists) seems to have been Christ's very favorite disciple—the only witness (in the canonical Gospels) of his life, death, and resurrection.[21] This preference once led Martin Luther to quip over dinner that Jesus clearly had a weakness for bad girls.[22] Elaborating on the thought, Luther amused himself by spinning a story about Jesus's string of affairs, first with the Samaritan woman at the well, and then Mary Magdalene, and finally the adulteress "whom he let off so easily." Luther's little joke (painful to its editors, who insist that the recorder of the comment must have misheard or misunderstood) takes part in an ancient, if now somewhat obscure, comical tradition internal to Christianity: laughing at the indignity of Christian mercy.

Christianity, as Dante knew, is a comedy—a divine joke. When he labeled Virgil's *Aeneid* as a tragedy and his own *Inferno* as a *commedia*, Dante implied a cosmic scheme of generic classification.[23] Christianity, unlike paganism, has a happy ending.[24] From an eschatological perspective, all Christian stories will turn out for the best, and so all Christian stories are comedies. (And all other stories are tragedies; Christianity, in other words, gets the last laugh.) Mary's apparent dishonor, Jesus's execution, and the humiliations of the Roman arena may seem tragic, but Christian hermeneutics seek and find the spiritual punch line behind the literal catastrophe.

Comedy suits Christianity in form as well as content. Comedy, as Aristotle and Horace taught, is low and ugly, and tragedy noble and sublime.[25] Christianity upended this hierarchy, choosing the despised style of comedy to express its sublime mystery.[26] This is Incarnational logic at work: tragedy becomes comedy, God becomes man, death becomes life, and shame becomes honor. When excusing the earthy obscenity of his pilgrims, Chaucer reminds us that

> Crist spak himself ful brode in hooly writ,
> And wel ye woot no vileynye is it.[27]

Jesus communicated his good news in the flesh and the vernacular, telling folksy parables about seeds, sheep, and taxes to children, lepers, and prostitutes. Outsiders found both Jesus and his followers scandalous and laughable (Acts 2:13).[28] Luckily for Christianity, humility thrives on mockery. In the words of Bernard of Clairvaux, "It is humility alone that exalts."[29] Small wonder, then, that the Pericope Adulterae courts scandal and laughter. Preaching decorously and solemnly would defeat the purpose.

In this humble and comical spirit, the New Testament associates Christ with prostitutes and adulteresses from the very beginning, even before his birth. The Gospel of Matthew's genealogy of Jesus includes four scandalous foremothers: Tamar, Rahab, Ruth, and Bathsheba—"sinful women" as Jerome calls them, "whom Scripture reprehends."[30] In the book of Genesis, the outcast Tamar (in the words of Melissa Jackson, a "trickster matriarch") plays the part of a prostitute in order to seduce Judah and earn a place in his tribe.[31] In the book of Joshua, Rahab, a Canaanite harlot with a heart of gold, betrays king and country to protect Joshua, her Israelite customer.[32] In the book of Ruth, the Moabite Ruth conceives Obed, the grandfather of David, by seducing Boaz on the threshing floor.[33] And in the books of Samuel, the enchanting Bathsheba catches David's eye, a look that leads to the birth of Solomon and heralds the birth of the new Solomon, adultery's fulfillment.[34] These foremothers contributed to the sacred Stem of Jesse by means of enchantment, trickery, and seduction. We could interpret their depravity as a foil setting off the jewel of Mary's perfect chastity.[35] Or we could focus on the unbroken pattern that connects these types together.[36] Mary's ways, like those of Christ's foremothers, seemed scandalous until exempted and exalted by God's grace. The Virgin realizes the promise of these progenitors not only by departing from precedent but also by repeating history.

N-Town's "Woman Taken in Adultery"

Uniquely in the tradition of early English drama, N-Town devotes an entire pageant to the episode of Christ and the adulteress, expanding eleven lines from the Gospel of John to almost three hundred.[37] Also uniquely, N-Town frames this pageant as a continuation of its meditation on the Virgin Mary. As David Bevington writes, "The adulterous woman recalls Eve as a fallen woman, and yet by her dignity in the face of oppression she also reminds us of the Virgin Mary bravely facing her detractors."[38] In both "Woman Taken in Adultery" and "Trial of Mary and Joseph," a sympathetic heroine suffers the cruel insults of a brutal and invasive ecclesiastical court. In both pageants, this heroine stands accused of adultery. Verbal echoes bind these accusations. Both Mary and the adulteress are insulted with the same slurs: "scowte," a variation on *scold*; "bysmare," meaning "a person worthy of scorn"; and "quene," an autoantonym that signifies both "queen," as in empress, and "quean," as in whore.[39]

"Com forth, thu scowte," the adulteress's persecutors shout (24.145), echoing Mary's detractors, who respond to the Virgin's protestations of innocence with scorn: "Ya, on this wyse excusyth here every scowte" (14.182). The canon lawyers who interrogate Mary call her "bolde bysmare" (14.298), the same phrase thrown at the adulteress: "Com forth, thu bysmare and brothel bolde!" (24.146). The enemies of the adulteress and the Virgin alike speak of "that quene"—unwittingly hailing the Queen of Heaven with an appropriate devotional epithet.[40] (Interestingly, this use of the word *quene* in "The Woman Taken in Adultery" has been taken as evidence that the adulteress in question is a prostitute. However, according to that logic, so is the Virgin Mary.[41]) Both sets of detractors harass their victims with a common store of nasty names, dirty jokes, and violent threats. In short, N-Town seems to compare the Virgin Mary and the woman taken in adultery by subjecting them to the same humiliating ordeal.

Jesus opens N-Town's pageant of "The Woman Taken in Adultery" with a sermon preached directly to the audience or reader:

> Man, I cam down all for thi love!
> Love me ageyn—I aske no more.
> Thow thu myshappe and synne ful sore,
> Yit turne agen and mercy crave.
> It is thi fawte and thu be lore:
> Haske thu mercy and thu shalt have. (24.19–24)

Invoking the tradition of the Christ Knight, N-Town depicts Jesus as a lover begging mankind to requite his love.[42] In exchange, he offers mercy and, ultimately, the bliss of paradise. He adds only one stipulation to this extremely generous proposal, warning that he will deny mercy to mankind if and only if mankind denies mercy to his neighbors. As Jesus puts it,

> What man of mercy is not tretable
> Whan he askyth mercy, he shal not spede. (24.35–36)

With this caveat, Jesus outlines an opposition between Christian mercy on the one hand and the unforgivable sins of "cruel jugement" (24.8), vengeance (24.25), and "wrath" (24.31) on the other.

Jesus identifies these sins as being broadly unchristian, and specifically Jewish. The vices of judgment, vengeance, and wrath quickly materialize in the forms of the anti-Judaic stereotypes Scriba and Phariseus. (The York manuscript simply labels these characters as "III Judeus" and "IV Judeus"— Jew Number Three and Jew Number Four.) Scriba and Phariseus overhear Jesus's message of mercy and dismiss it as "his dalyauns" (24.101), meaning "amorous talk," "flirting, coquetry," or even "sexual union."[43]

> On hym beleve many a score:
> In his prechynge he is so gay,
> Ech man hym folwygh ever more and more!
> Agens that he seyth, no man seyth nay. (24.53–56)

Scriba and Phariseus satirize Jesus's message with winking accusations of sexual deviancy: the word *gay* can mean "joyous" and "merry," but also "wanton," "lewd," and "lascivious."[44] They accuse Jesus's "gay" evangelism of seducing "many a score" of converts with its suspiciously irresistible charms and irresponsibly permissive promises of mercy. Christianity, they insinuate, wins its converts promiscuously: too many too quickly and too easily. Indeed, Scriba and Phariseus seem to interpret Christianity as a kind of wildly proliferating orgy. In response to this burgeoning threat, they come up with their plot to entrap Jesus. Their stratagem pairs Christ's mercy with the adulteress's guilt; they hope to use one kind of harlotry to expose another.

This accusation extends back to Christianity's earliest days.[45] In a letter to the emperor Trajan, Pliny the Younger darkly referred to "the vices with which the name Christian is associated."[46] According to Origen, "malicious rumors" of cannibalism and "unrestrained sexual intercourse" tainted the first century of Christian evangelism. "Even now," he writes, "it still deceives some who by such stories are repelled from approaching Christians even if only for a simple conversation."[47] Polemicists circulated lurid reports of ritual murder, incest, and orgies. "In the shameless dark," it was said, "with unspeakable lust they copulate in random unions."[48] Soon enough, orthodox Christians turned this polemic against the heretics in their midst, whom they suspected of the same crimes of which they themselves had been accused, and worse.[49] Epiphanius of Salamis claimed that the heretical sect of the Phibionites reenacted the Last Supper as an orgy culminating in a feast of semen and menstrual blood ingested in place of the body and blood of the incarnated Christ.[50] These slanders make sense: of course polemicists, from both within and without, tarred Christianity with that particular brush. Accusations of cannibalism and orgiastic promiscuity—two variations on the theme of communion—hit close to home. Christianity advertised its promiscuous mercy, its open incorporation of Jew and Gentile, slave and master, and man and woman into the ecstatic communion of Christ's body (Galatians 3:28).

Not only does N-Town's pageant of "Woman Taken in Adultery" repeat these ancient slanders, it also proves them right—or at least to a certain extent. Remember that in his commentary on the Gospel of John, Augustine insisted that, despite appearances, the story of Christ and the adulteress did not condone adultery or encourage sin. If Jesus did favor sin, Augustine argued, he would have said, "Be without anxiety as regards my liberation. However much you sin, I shall free you from all the punishment of Gehenna and the tortures of Hell."[51] But this is not what Jesus said in the Gospel of John, as Augustine emphasizes. However, it is exactly what Jesus says in the opening speech of N-Town's "Woman Taken in Adultery." N-Town's Jesus explicitly promises, "Iff thu aske mercy, I sey nevyr nay" (24.16). N-Town preaches this message of mercy so enthusiastically that at least one edition of the play feels the need to protest that the text "does not condone sexual promiscuity."[52] A necessary disclaimer, considering the content of the pageant. N-Town removes the safeguards so carefully constructed by centuries of patristic commentary, restoring the story of Christ and the adulteress to its full potential for scandalousness.

N-Town's "Trial of Mary and Joseph" and "Woman Taken in Adultery" mount a sustained satirical assault against the sin of "cruel jugement" (24.8) as represented by a wide array of villains: anti-Judaic stereotypes (Scriba and Phariseus), allegorical gossips (Raise-Slander and Back-Biter), and officers of the late medieval ecclesiastical court system (the bishop, canon lawyers, and summoner). N-Town, in other words, figures its anti-Judaism both literally and figuratively: in the form of Jewish characters (like the Pharisees) as well as allegorical abstractions (like Raise-Slander) and contemporary Christians (like the canon lawyers) characterized as being Jewish in spirit.[53] Their crime is their obedience to the letter of the law, against which the accused adulteress's fornication and Jesus's mercy stand firmly united in their deviancy.[54] Exploiting this sympathy between adultery and Christianity, N-Town's Jesus uses the adulteress's transgression as an opportunity for conversion, substituting his "dalyauns" for her lusty lover's. At the beginning of the pageant of "The Woman Taken in Adultery," Jesus asks the audience to return his love. By the end, the adulteress fulfills his request by turning her affections from Juvenis to Jesus, from one lover to another—just as Mary Magdalene, in the Digby play, looking for a new "valentine," finds Christ, the ultimate paramour.[55]

This switch between Jesus and Juvenis works so well because the variables are interchangeable. N-Town repeatedly identifies Jesus as a "harlot." In "The Trial before Herod," the tyrant refers to Jesus as an "onhangyed harlot" (30.221); in "The Procession to Calvary," "Judeus 2" calls him "harlot" yet again (32.33).[56] We could translate this insult as "scoundrel," thereby purging the term of its sexual valence. Yet the *Middle English Dictionary* demonstrates that by the early fifteenth century, *harlot* could also mean either "a female prostitute" or "a man of licentious habits," as when Chaucer's Parson tut-tuts at "thilke harlotes that haunten bordels of thise fool wommen."[57] In his study of several hundred defamation cases from late medieval England, the historian L. R. Poos confirms that although *harlot* had once been a gender-neutral and nonsexual term, it had accrued strong sexual connotations by the late fifteenth century.[58] This valence would explain why N-Town uses the term to describe the adulteress's lover as he exits the stage with his shorts in his hands (*et braccas in manu tenens*, as the stage directions specify). His accusers cry, "Stow that harlot!" (24.125). N-Town pointedly and consistently transforms slurs like "harlot," "warlock," and "heretic" into badges of honor worn in solidarity by Jesus, Mary, the apostles—and the adulteress.[59]

In an infamously ambiguous passage from his thirteenth-century Arthurian romance *Tristan*, Gottfried von Strassburg attempts to explain Jesus's tolerance for adultery with the image of a windblown sleeve.[60] This description immediately follows the ordeal of the red-hot iron, in which Isolde cheats on a test of chastity. First, she arranges for her lover Tristan to disguise himself as an ancient pilgrim. Then, as she approaches the site of her public trial, she purposefully trips and falls into Tristan's arms. Finally, she swears to God that she has never lain in the arms of any man save her husband—and, of course, the poor pilgrim into whose arms she just fell. God, apparently pleased with Isolde, allows her to hold the red-hot iron without burning her flesh, thereby proving her innocence—despite her guilt. "Thus," Gottfried explains (perhaps sarcastically, perhaps not), "it was made manifest and confirmed to all the world that Christ in His great virtue is pliant as a windblown sleeve. He falls into place and clings, whichever way you try Him, closely and smoothly, as He is bound to do. He is at the beck of every heart for honest deeds or fraud. Be it deadly earnest or a game, He is just as you would have him" (15737–748).[61]

This is the promiscuously merciful Christ celebrated in N-Town, courtly romance, and the cult of the Virgin—as easily moved as silk in the wind. Gottfried's image recalls the tokens bestowed on knights by ladies, like the sleeve that Chaucer's Criseyde faithlessly gives to Diomedes, much to Troilus's woe.[62] The love of Christ is like a woman's favor: changeable. To faithful and old-fashioned lovers hung up on eternal covenants (like Troilus or Jehovah), this promiscuity might seem terribly tragic.[63] But to the newfangled and promiscuous (like Criseyde or the Gospel of John's adulteress), these are tidings of great joy.

The Harlot Israel

Israel, Jehovah says, is an unclean vessel (Hosea 8:8), a wanton heifer (Hosea 4:16), and a brazen harlot (Jeremiah 3:3). The Old Testament often uses graphically sexual imagery to describe the covenant between God and Israel, comparing monotheism to marriage and idolatry to adultery—a parallelism evident in image (the commandment against idolatry reflecting that against adultery across the first and second tablets of the law) and in language.[64] When Israel betrays her promise to worship the God of Judaism alone, backsliding into promiscuous paganism with graven images, Jehovah falls into a jealous rage. He imagines Israel, mad with lust, drenched in the fornications of "beautiful young men" (Egyptian princes, Assyrian captains, Chaldean horsemen, the sons of Babylon), glutting herself on their flesh ("like the flesh of asses") and semen ("like the issue of horses") (Ezekiel 23:20–3). Sometimes, despite all these many sins, Jehovah asks Israel to come home: "Thou hast prostituted thyself to many lovers: nevertheless, return to me, saith the Lord, and I will receive thee" (Jeremiah 3:1). At other times, he threatens annihilation: "They shall cut off thy nose and thy ears: and what remains shall fall by the sword: they shall take thy sons, and thy daughters, and thy residue shall be devoured by fire" (Ezekiel 23:25). Like an old cuckold in a fabliau, God wavers back and forth between desperation and fury, violence and abjection.

To a certain extent, Jesus follows in his father's footsteps, using erotic language to hail Ecclesia, the new Israel, as the bride of Christ. Yet while Jehovah spoke to Israel as a jealous husband, Christ must speak to the object of his affections as a supplicant. Until Doomsday, Jesus cannot command; he must entreat. Unlike Jehovah, Christ never sealed a blood covenant with his beloved. He has no chosen seed, no tribe. Instead, Jesus must win the love of all mankind, one soul at a time—Jew and Gentile, slave and master, man and woman (Galatians 3:28). The Old Testament's prohibitions against meddling with strangers no longer apply (1 Kings 11:2): Saint Paul urges Christians to evangelize by means of seduction, marrying heathens into the fold (1 Corinthians 7:14). Christianity depends on mankind's promiscuity. If she were not open to change, she could not be seduced and converted. In order to tempt mankind away from her husband and lovers (Jehovah, idols), Jesus must play the harlot, not the husband.

Paul argues that this particular kind of spiritual adultery supersedes the law. Jews who convert to Christianity, Paul writes, "become dead to the law by the body of Christ," like a widow liberated from marriage by the death of her husband (Romans 7:4). In other words, the convert's true love for the body of Christ, consummated in carnal communion, effectively kills her spiritual bond to Judaism, her wedded husband—who is very much alive, though dead to his wife. As long as you follow your heart, Paul promises, cheating does not really count as cheating. In spirit if not in fact, the beloved of Christ is not the wife of a jealous husband, bound by the law, but rather a merry widow, free to choose.

This is also the logic of courtly love—that "parody, or imitation, or rivalry—I know not what to call it—of the Christian religion," as C. S. Lewis described it.[65] When Thomas Malory decries the factually accurate accusations of adultery leveled at Lancelot and Guinevere as false slanders, he means "false" in a spiritual rather than a literal sense. It may look like adultery, but to call it adultery reveals an embarrassingly literalist and ignoble frame of mind. As Andreas Capellanus argues, courtly love refines the mind, revealing in adulterous passion "the virtue of chastity," or rather, precisely as he puts it, "quasi chastity."[66] When ninety-six out of one hundred ladies (including Queen Isolde) fail a test of chastity at King Mark's court in Malory's *Book of Tristam*, Mark wrathfully sends all ninety-six to burn at the stake. How uncourteous and unchristian, his barons and the narrator protest. Such tests, they agree, are "false," "enemy to all trew lovers."[67] *True* meaning "false," and *false* meaning "true." From the refined perspective of a courtly lover, the spiritual truth supersedes the base facts. What could be more Christian? "For the letter killeth, but the spirit quickeneth" (2 Corinthians 3:6).

The New Testament figures mankind's betrayal of Jehovah for Jesus as the inevitable culmination of so many prophecies, so many signs: Eve's transgression, Israel's harlotry, Bathsheba's adultery. In fury, Jehovah commanded the prophet Hosea to "find a wife of whoredom and have children of whoredom," a prophecy fulfilled in Mary and Christ, who revealed themselves in the likeness of an adulteress and her bastard (Hosea 1:2). When Paul delivers God's new message, he revises those very lines from Hosea: "I will call that which was not my people, my people; and her that was not beloved, beloved" (Romans 9:25). In other words, the God of the New Testament vows not only to forgive the harlot Israel for her crimes, as was promised in the Old, but also to change his ways. "The Virgin," Bernardino of Siena wrote, transformed the Lord into "the form of a servant."[68] Transformed from a jealous husband into a servile lover, God imitates Israel's promiscuity, opening his arms to Jews and Gentiles, Samaritan adulteresses and Ethiopian eunuchs.[69] "God, the figurative husband of Israel," as Catherine E. Winiarski argues, crosses over "to the opposite side of the analogy, entering into the human world as a divine adulterer, breaking, in paradigmatic fashion, the human laws of marital monogamy to establish a new covenant."[70] Mary, the second Israel, turns adultery into chastity and sin into salvation, a paradox encapsulated in her impossible virginity.

In the book of Jeremiah, God says to Israel, "If a man put away his wife, and she go from him, and marry another man, shall he return to her anymore? Shall not that woman be polluted, and defiled?" (3:1). The question is rhetorical. A human husband, we are to understand, would never return to an adulterated, polluted, and defiled wife. But God is different. Magnanimously, God promises to rise above the petty jealousy of a mortal man and to take Israel back, despite all her crimes—if she repents. In order to return, God emphasizes, Israel must reform: "Know that I am the Lord, / that thou mayest remember, and be confounded, and mayest no more open thy mouth because of thy confusion" (Ezekiel 16:62–3).

For a certain kind of medieval Christian, the terms of this covenant demanded revision. When the thirteenth-century *Ancrene Wisse* translated God's promise to Israel from the book of Jeremiah into Middle English, it added a new bonus. In this revision, God vows to not only forgive Israel but also restore her virginity. In fact, the *Ancrene Wisse* extends this offer to all women. The text promises, "Ne beo neaver his leof forhoret mid se monie deadliche sunnen, sone se / ha kimeth to him ayein he maketh hire neowe meiden" (As soon as Christ's beloved returns to him, even though she prostituted herself with so many deadly sins, he makes her a new virgin) (7.130–31). Christ, the text rejoices, is nothing like a husband. "Monnes / neoleachunge maketh of meiden wif, ant Godd maketh of wif meiden" (Husbands turn virgins into wives, but Christ turns wives into virgins) (7.132–33).

Here, the *Ancrene Wisse* applies Christian hermeneutics to the hymen, arguing that the spiritual truth supersedes the literal facts. The question underlying this claim had long been disputed in Christian circles. Can God restore virginity to a woman who has lost it? The *Ancrene Wisse* may say yes, but Jerome thought not. In a letter to Saint Julia Eustochium, a Roman virgin of tender years, Jerome warned, "Although God can do all things, He cannot raise up a virgin after she has fallen. He is able to free one who has been corrupted from the penalty of her sin, but he refuses her the crown."[71] In other words, she may repent, and God may forgive her, but he cannot restore what has been lost, nor refund the hundredfold reward that her hymen would have reaped in paradise.[72] Jerome argues that at least in this regard, the covenant established between Jehovah and Israel in the Old Testament transfers, largely unchanged, to the New. A reformed and penitent harlot can be forgiven, but not exalted. She can regain a place in the fold, but not the place she once had. Augustine agreed: once lost, virginity remains forever "lost beyond any hope of recovery."[73]

Medieval Scholastics, on the other hand, tended to disagree, although to different extents.[74] Some (such as Thomas Aquinas and Peter Abelard) maintained that God could forgive sins and restore hymens but could not change the past.[75] Others (such as Peter Damian and William of Auxerre) argued that God could restore virginity not only *juxta carnem* (according to the flesh) and *juxta meritum* (according to merit) but also perfectly and utterly, as if nothing had ever been lost. In fact, Peter Damian accused his opponents of insulting the purity of the Virgin Mary by disputing the question. He wrote, "The God-Man has been able to come forth from the womb of a virgin, while leaving intact her virginity, so will He not be able to repair the loss of virginity which has been violated?"[76] In other words, if God could make Mary a virgin, then he can make anyone a virgin.

Taking this logic to its extreme, medieval hagiographers restored virginity to reformed prostitutes left and right—to Mary of Egypt, Thais the Courtesan, Pelagia the Harlot, and Mary Magdalene.[77] In these legends of "holy harlots," as Ruth Mazo Karras calls them, Christ not only restores what was lost but rewards beyond measure, as if he preferred penance to innocence and reformed harlots to unspotted virgins. Indeed, Jesus says as much in the Gospel of Luke. In his parable of the two debtors, Jesus explains why he loves the sinner at his feet (interpreted by glossators as an adulteress or prostitute) more than the respectable Pharisee scandalized by her presence. Just as a debtor released from a great sum returns more gratitude than one released from a small sum, Jesus argues, the fallen woman has more love to give than the clean-living Pharisee (Luke 7:47). In other words, sins—and preferably the titillating sins of a harlot—better prepare the soul for the pleasures of Christianity than righteousness or innocence.[78]

At first glance, the cult of the Virgin would seem to depart from this paradigm by celebrating untouched and unspotted purity above all else.[79] And yet, in a sense, the Virgin Mother represents an even more indulgent understanding of Christian mercy than Mary Magdalene, Thais the Courtesan, or Pelagia the Harlot.[80] These reformed prostitutes wept for their sins. The Virgin Mary, by contrast, plucked sin up by its root and remade the law in her image. They fell and then rose, while the Virgin altered the laws of God's universe, turning falling into rising. The Madonna perfects the type of the penitent harlot, exceeding all expectations. The God of the Old Testament promised to forgive Israel but not to restore her crown. The Virgin Mary, the new Israel, explodes this prophecy. According to the logic of late medieval Mariology, the Virgin's sexual charisma overcame God's wisdom and toppled his strength.[81] The harlot took the throne and crowned herself with new names: Virgin Mother, God-Maker, Recreatrix, Queen of Heaven, Immaculate. God cannot forgive this new Israel, because, under the terms of her reign, there are no sins to forgive, only virtues to praise.

The Mother of Mercy

Exegetes heard in Ezekiel 44 a reference to the Virgin:

> And the Lord said to me: This gate shall be shut, it shall not be
> opened, and no man shall pass through it: because the Lord
>   the God of Israel hath entered in by it, and it shall be shut
> For the prince. (Ezekiel 44:2–3)

As Ambrose glossed these lines, "The gate is Mary, through whom Christ entered this world when he was brought forth in a virgin birth without loosening the closed genitals of virginity."[82] In Ambrose's formulation, then, Mary's reproductive organs function as a synecdoche for Mary herself, and this synecdoche serves as the tenor of an exegetical metaphor: Mary is her womb, and her womb is Ezekiel's gate. And although ancient and medieval anatomical terms can cover wide territories of meaning (*womb*, for example, can refer to the abdomen, heart, or uterus), the image of the gate implies an entranceway rather than an enclosure.[83] While other emblems of the Virgin (such as the tabernacle, fountain, or *hortus conclusus*) evoke the shape of the uterus (seen by natural philosophers as a hollow receptacle), the image of the gate suggests the cervix, the vaginal canal, or the vulva—understood by etymologists as the gate or *valva* of the womb.[84] Associated metaphors compare Mary to an aqueduct carrying the water of life (that is, Jesus) from heaven to earth, and to a neck (in Latin, *cervix*) connecting the head of Christ to the body of the Church.[85] These images emphasize Mary's role as the *mediatrix*, or intermediary, between God and man, this world and the next.

In an anagogical or eschatological sense, Mary's cervix or vulva is the *porta caeli*, or "gate of salvation."[86] An anonymous fourteenth-century Middle English translation of the ancient Marian hymn "Quem terra, pontus, aethera" puns especially cleverly on this multivalence.[87] The lyric directly addresses the Virgin: "Thow art in hevene an hole imad / Thorw which the senful thorwgeth glad" (You are in heaven a hole that has been made / through which the sinful go gladly). This pun works acoustically: the phrase "hole imad" registers in our ears as "holy maid" and "hole y-made." Mary, in other words, is the holy maid through whose hole (in a double sense, anatomical and allegorical) sinners will someday gain entrance to paradise.[88] As Proclus of Constantinople explains, the gate of Eve marks the entrance into the fallen world, and the gate of the Virgin the entrance to bliss. As he puts it (and as the hymn "Alma Redemptoris Mater" repeats), "The door of sin becomes the gate of salvation," and the path taken by Jesus *in* becomes the path taken by sinners *out*.[89] Thus, Mary's hole mediates all Christian intercourse between the realms of the human and the divine—whether of deities, souls, or prayers.

According to the Mariology that developed over the course of late antiquity and the Middle Ages, sinners' daily prayers ascended upward, passing first through Mary, then through Jesus, and ultimately to God the Father.[90] This intercessional system based itself on the premise that no sinner, "not one," merits salvation (Mark 10:18). Hence the necessity of corruption. It was believed that God the Father would bend the rules only for the sake of his son, and Jesus only for the sake of his mother, but that the promiscuous Virgin, thankfully for Christendom, would take pity on just about anyone who asked for her help. And so, sinners directed their prayers to the Virgin, the only opening in an otherwise impenetrable criminal justice system.

"Look after us, Mary," Eadmer prayed, "lest we perish."[91] Late medieval images of the double intercession of Christ and the Virgin represent dense crowds of sinners cowering before Mary, who is kneeling, with lactating breasts exposed, before Jesus, who is praying, with wounds bleeding, before God.[92] Thanks to Mary, her devotees believed, this system could not fail, and not only because Mary triangulated the nepotism on which everything depended. As Anselm wrote in a prayer to the Virgin, "It is not possible that whatever turns to you and you regard with favor, should perish."[93] Here, Anselm suggests that Jesus could not resist his mother's petitions—it was simply "not possible." Bolder voices—such as that of the twelfth-century Benedictine Guibert of Nogent—elaborated on Anselm's implication, claiming that Mary would "preside over heaven, command on earth, and afflict hell," "not by asking but by demanding."[94] Guibert describes the Trinity as a kind of puppet government and Mary as the power behind the throne, an idea that circulated in England as early as the ninth century.[95] Those who believed in the supremacy of the Queen of Heaven, *omnium potentissima* (the most powerful of all), celebrated this happy corruption in heavenly politics and trusted that any prayer directed to Mary would evade justice.[96]

Or any soul, for that matter. On Doomsday, it was believed, Mary's favorites would finally escape justice forever. While eschatologists debated the role that Mary would play during the sorting of the souls, her most committed enthusiasts maintained that the Queen of Heaven would extend her daily function as Intercessor by claiming final jurisdiction over mercy, leaving the administration of justice to Jesus. As explained in a sermon traditionally attributed to the authority of Bonaventure (but later disavowed for its heterodoxy), "The blessed Virgin chose the best part, because she was made Queen of Mercy, while her Son remained King of Justice."[97] And just as Mary surpasses Jesus, the sermon reasons, so too "mercy is better than justice."[98] In effect, this sermon suggests that on Doomsday Mary would orchestrate mercy and salvation, delegating the lower work of justice and condemnation to her son. Late medieval altarpieces depicting this theoretical division split the frame, separating Jesus the Judge from Mary the Mother of Mercy, kneeling before the saved and the gate to paradise.[99] Thus, the sermon concludes, "no one enters heaven except through her."[100]

According to this way of thinking, the Virgin Salvatrix gave birth to the Christian hope of salvation not only by delivering Jesus but also by poking a hole in the fabric of heaven—a vaginal or bureaucratic loophole through which sinners could escape God's prison and enter his heavenly kingdom.[101] The proponents of this theory believed that the irresistible influence wielded by this holy maiden (and specifically by her holy hole) over the besotted Trinity would reach its fulfillment at the *discretio spirituum*, when Christ would ultimately find himself incapable of crossing his bride and mother. (Our vernacular offers us a ready—if, unfortunately, pejorative—descriptive term for the Trinity in this situation: *pussy-whipped*.) As yet another treatise traditionally attributed to Bonaventure (but later disavowed) prophesies, on that day Mary will "prevent her son from striking" and fearlessly "hold back the Lord," reversing his guilty verdicts as she sees fit.[102] Late medieval artists represented the Madonna della Misericordia, or "Modyr of Mercy," protecting throngs of sinners under her magical mantle (symbolizing her redeemed flesh) from volleys of deathly arrows fired by Christ and armies of angels.[103] In a late fourteenth-century Genovese altarpiece attributed to Barnaba da

Modena, the darts snap in half upon contact with the circumference of Mary's robe, their power—like God's—utterly castrated.[104]

In a heartfelt prayer to the Virgin, Eadmer begs Mary to save his soul on the Day of Judgment even if Christ should condemn him to hell—because he, like so many others, believed that she could.[105] Catholics still joke about this let-out clause today. In one such joke, Jesus asks Saint Peter, "How did all these sinners get into heaven?" And Saint Peter answers, "Your mother keeps letting them in through the back door."[106] This polite little joke, tame enough for Sunday school, does not exploit the obscene anatomical reference at its disposal—Mary's back door. But late medieval Mariology so often made its obscene anatomical reference explicit and even paramount—though it had a different orifice in mind: that all-important synecdoche of the Virgin, the vaginal hole represented by the images of the neck, aqueduct, and gate. So irresistible to the Trinity, and so indulgent to mankind.

The Patroness of Sinners

The legend of Theophilus—perhaps the most important Miracle of the Virgin in the medieval tradition—tells the Faustian tale of Mary's salvation of a sinner who seemed lost past all hope of recovery.[107] As the story goes, Theophilus contracted his soul to Satan and renounced Christ and Mary. Yet despite this exchange, Mary not only saved Theophilus's soul but also descended into hell and stole back his covenant with Satan. Allegorically, this narrative tells the story of Mary's salvation of mankind. In his Epistle to the Romans, Paul promised, "But now we are loosed from the law of death, wherein we were detained; so that we should serve in newness of spirit, and not in the oldness of the letter" (7:6). In the Theophilus legend, Mary fulfills this promise, breaking mankind's contract with Satan. As one medieval English prayer to the Virgin put it, Mary "destroyed the old signed document of diabolical surrender and came to the assistance of the entire world."[108]

In her capacity as mankind's advocate and Satan's adversary, Mary cheats, fixing the scales of justice, hiding fugitives, and tampering with evidence. In a fifteenth-century wall painting from the Church of Saint James in South Leigh, Oxfordshire, a soul sits in the balance of the scales of justice, Mary to the right of Saint Michael and a host of devils to his sinister left.[109] The devils conspire to tip the scales in their favor, making the soul's sins outweigh its good deeds. One demon pushes down with both hands on the scale of sin while another pulls it with a rope toward the toothy, gaping mouth of hell. Yet their fiendish efforts are in vain, because Mary has tricks of her own. She subtly lets her rosary rest on the right arm of the balance beam, which tips the scales in favor of her client's good deeds.[110] Such is the power of even one bead of her prayers. Satan may be tricky, but—thankfully for mankind—Mary, his nemesis and counterpart, is far trickier. The Trinity may plan to punish the guilty and reward the innocent on Doomsday with fair and empirical tools like weights and scales, but neither Satan nor Mary is bound by the rules of truth or justice. Rather, they are willing and able to use any means necessary to achieve their ends. The devil wants to drag every soul to hell, by hook or by crook— and Mary wants to save her clients: every soul who ever asked for her help.

She does it all for love. Late medieval Miracles of the Virgin advertise Mary's smitten devotion to mankind. Unlike the lady fair of courtly romance, the tender-hearted Queen of Heaven never hesitates to say yes.[111] Her suitors need not perform chivalrous deeds, carry out impossible tasks, or suffer abject humiliation in order to win her favor. All they have to do is ask. In the prologue to the *Cantigas de Santa Maria*, King Alfonso X sings, "No one ever failed to receive [her blessing] who humbly begged for it, for such a prayer She always heard."[112] In some Miracles of the Virgin, simply calling Mary's name—even after death—makes all the difference between damnation and redemption, no matter how unlikely or unworthy the supplicant.[113] Medieval Miracles of the Virgin trumpet Mary's weakness for the worst of the worst: thieves, murderers, incestuous infanticides, incontinent monks, and pregnant nuns. As R. W. Southern put it, "Like the rain, the protective power of the Virgin falls on the just and the unjust alike—provided only that they have entered the circle of her allegiance."[114] And entering that promiscuous circle could not be easier. It seems that Mary can refuse mankind no better than Jesus can refuse her. Thus goes the cosmic love triangle: God loves Mary best, but Mary loves mankind more.

Perhaps the miracle of Beatrice helps to explain why. As told in the Middle English mid-fifteenth-century *Alphabet of Tales*, this narrative begins with a beautiful nun named Beatrice, who struggles to keep her vows of celibacy.[115] When Beatrice's willpower finally cracks, she stops on her way out the door of the nunnery to explain to a statue of the Madonna that she "may no langer susteyn the temptacion of [her] flesh."[116] Once deflowered and abandoned by her faithless lover, Beatrice falls into destitute prostitution. Yet when she walks by the nunnery fifteen years later, she discovers that the nuns believe that she has been there all along, keeping "clene & in gude name." The statue of Mary, it turns out, covered for her, disguising herself in Beatrice's "clothyng & in abbett" and "fulfill[ing] [her] offes." Mary and this fallen woman, in other words, are indistinguishable from one another. In Beatrice, it seems, Mary admires her own reflection.

This resemblance between "the patroness of sinners" and the sinners she patronizes is made even clearer in "The Miracle of the Pregnant Abbess."[117] In this Miracle of Our Lady, a pregnant abbess begins to show, and her nuns tattle and summon the bishop. But before he arrives, the Virgin steps in, delivering the child, whisking him away to a hermitage, and scouring the birthing bed of all evidence of the Curse of Eve. In one version of the story, Mary even spares the abbess from the pains of childbirth.[118] When the bishop storms in, the abbess and her bedchamber appear as immaculate as Mary and the stable in Nazareth after the birth of Jesus. The abbess, like Mary in the apocryphal Infancy Gospels, finds herself subjected to a postpartum gynecological exam orchestrated by stubborn skeptics. Her body, again like Mary's, triumphantly bears "no sygne that sho sulde be with childe."[119] The Virgin arranges a perfect crime—her own. At first blush, it might seem as though Miracles of the Virgin contrast Mary's perfection with human frailty. And yet these particular Miracles of the Virgin—the legends of Beatrice and the pregnant abbess—suggest that her understanding derives from experience rather than innocence. Beyond these two examples, medieval Miracles of the Virgin celebrate Mary's sacred criminality, cheering her on as she dupes the devil, circumnavigates Jesus in Judgment, and destroys all evidence of her clients' misdeeds. Mary pays it forward, extending her exceptional grace to protect other criminals from judgment, beginning with Adam and Eve and continuing through to their latest descendants.

N-Town's "Judgment Day"

Despite N-Town's extraordinary devotion to the Virgin, she fails to appear in its final and arguably most important pageant. N-Town's "Judgment Day" departs from the message of mercy preached so consistently throughout the rest of the manuscript, leaving no place for the Mater Misericordiae. As the banns promise, there is "no grace" to be found on Doomsday (0.515). The resurrected lament, "It is to late to aske mercye!" (42.39). Earlier on, in "Christ and the Woman Taken in Adultery," Jesus wrote the crimes of the adulteress's persecutors in the sand, horrifying them with the sight of their own misdeeds.[120] The audience, however, could not read the words; the truth remained a secret. But now, on Doomsday, as the archangel Gabriel says,

> All your dedys here shal be sene
> Opynly in syght. (42.21–22)

Black letters materialize on the skin of the condemned, revealing hitherto private sins "opynly" for all to see (42.78). The damned become open books, and devils amuse themselves (and the spectators) by reading the dark words branded on their foreheads.

In total, N-Town's devils read aloud from the bodies of seven condemned sinners, each of whom represents one of the Seven Deadly Sins. The first six follow a tight rhetorical pattern: the devils identify the body of an actor as an allegory of a particular vice (pride, covetousness, wrath, and so on) and then proceed to read a four- or five-line satirical stanza about that vice from their branded foreheads. But the pattern breaks with the seventh sin, lust. Rather than hailing this last actor with an abstract noun (Lechery), the devils call her by name: "Sybile Sclutte," "salte sewe"—Sybil Slut, lecherous pig (42.118). The devils then arraign this personification of lust for nine lines (double the length of the previous six stanzas):

> All youre lyff was leccherous lay;
> To all youre neyborys, ye wore a shrewe;
> All youre pleasauns was leccherous play. (42.119–21)

These are the very crimes that Christ refrained from inscribing in the sand in the Pericope Adulterae: the crimes of an adulteress. Now, those long-held-back accusations pour forth. Finally, N-Town seems ready to realize Augustine's reading of Christ's exoneration of the woman taken in adultery: Jesus let her go, but not forever. Now, on Doomsday, her time has come.

And yet that is not exactly how things turn out in the end. The damned beg for mercy one last time, exclaiming, "We aske thi mercy and not thi ryght" (42.128). At any other point in the manuscript, this plea might persuade the God of N-Town. Mercy over justice is, after all, the text's favorite sermon. And yet now it finally seems "to late to aske mercye" (42.39). Or is it? In Miracles of the Virgin, it is never too late for the Mother of Mercy to save a soul. But, then, Mary is missing from N-Town's Doomsday. What chance do the guilty stand in her absence? None, it seems. Immediately after the final plea of the damned, at the very bottom of the page, a speech marker reads "Deus." God is about to speak, and to pronounce his final judgment.

Yet if you turn over the leaf to read God's words, you will find that nothing follows. The N-Town manuscript abruptly ends. Presumably, the final leaves or quire became detached from the rest of the compilation at some point between the fifteenth and the nineteenth centuries.[121] One editor has written, "Little of the plot is lost: only the condemnation of the bad souls and their capture by the demons is missing."[122] But what a difference that little loss makes. As Paul promised in Colossians 2:14, and as devotees of the Virgin repeated, "the handwriting of the decree that was against us" has been blotted out. In the N-Town manuscript, thanks to a happy accident, judgment never comes, and Sibyl the Slut goes entirely unpunished. To me, that sounds suspiciously like a Miracle of the Virgin.

Chapter 6

THE WHORE OF BABYLON

The Virgin Mary never set foot on the floorboards of Shakespeare's Globe or, for that matter, those of any other commercial theater in early modern London.[1] The Protestant Reformation, slowly but surely, brought an end to the sacred drama of the Middle Ages.[2] In some cases, as in Wakefield in 1576, ordinances specifically and explicitly criminalized the playing of God, banning the theatrical representation (or "counterfeiting") of "the majesty of God the father, God the son, or God the holy ghost . . . or anything played which tend to the maintenance of superstition and idolatry."[3] Protestant reformers had little patience for those who prayed to their local statue of the Madonna instead of God in heaven, or who imagined Jesus as their neighbor in a mask ("some base fellowe [playing] Christe," in the words of the antitheatricalist Stephen Gosson) rather than the Word revealed in the naked text of the canonical Gospels.[4] In 1644, a Puritan named John Shaw claimed to have come across an old man—the lingering vestige of another time—who, thanks to his medieval miseducation, barely recognized the name of Jesus Christ. "I think I heard of that man you speake of," the old man said, "once in a play at Kendall, called Corpus-Christi play, where there was a man on a tree, & blood ran downe."[5] As reformers saw it, Catholicism had replaced the heavenly Creator with his earthly creations, and scripture with idolatry. The walking, talking icons of sacred drama—papism's most animated idols, more dexterous even than the mechanized Marionettes (literally, "little Marys") that enlivened Nativity tableaus—must have rankled especially painfully.[6] These breathing images dared not only to impersonate God but also to abuse his dignity and mangle his inerrant word. They had to go.

Over the course of the sixteenth century, Protestant reformers and their Catholic opponents paid particular attention to the pageantry of the Virgin Mary. For this reason, her plays changed with the wind. After the coronation of Edward VI, the city of York subtracted three especially objectionable pageants of Our Lady ("that is to say, the deying of Our Lady, assumpcion of our Lady, and Coronacion of our Lady") from its roster.[7] When the Catholic Queen Mary ascended to the throne, these plays were reinstated, only to be censored yet again—and this time permanently—during the reign of Elizabeth I.[8] Probably not coincidentally, the leaves containing these same three pageants—"The Death of the Virgin," "The Appearance of Our Lady to Thomas," and "The Assumption and Coronation of the Virgin"—appear to have been cut out of the Towneley manuscript. These plays are lost to history.[9] When Chester pruned its roster of pageants during the 1540s and 1550s, the Assumption of the Virgin was removed and her Purification chopped.[10] Ultimately, these piecemeal attempts at compromise failed. In 1572, Edmund Grindal, the puritanical archbishop of York (having put a stop to the York mysteries several years earlier), commissioned the reformer Christopher Goodman to compile a comprehensive list of the "errors" and "absurdities" of the recalcitrant Chester plays, some twelve of which directly involved the pageantry of the Virgin.[11] Three years later, in 1575, Chester played its mysteries for the last time.[12]

By the dawn of the seventeenth century, only a handful of towns and cities (including Kendal and Preston) continued to perform the mysteries at all, and those last few soon died away too.[13] Recusants and antiquarians managed to rescue only a handful of playscripts from oblivion, secreting them in private libraries, far from the public eye.[14] Everything else was stripped for parts. Actors, playwrights, and impresarios decontextualized and reappropriated the theatrical traditions of the Middle Ages for London's commercial playhouses.[15] Many of the old tricks and types—such as the three-tiered cosmic stage, blood-filled pigs' bladders, the cat-tearing tyrant, and the antic devil—played on largely unchanged.[16] But not the Virgin. She appeared to vanish.

And not only from the stage. The late medieval Catholic cult of the Virgin—or, rather, the idolatry of the Virgin, as polemicists put it— threatened the Protestant doctrine of Christ alone, *solus Christus*. Reformers accused Catholics of having "eclips[ed] the glory of God's mercy and the worthiness of Christ's satisfaction" by making Mary their supreme "Goddess."[17] This crime demanded proportionate punishment. Over the course of the sixteenth century, innumerable images of the Virgin were destroyed across England: "that ladye in that place and that ladye in that," as John Bale put it.[18] Iconoclasts attacked these images with chisels and axes, chopping off noses, breasts, arms, and heads.[19] John Foxe, for one, began his career as a reformer by personally breaking the "olde superstitious and idolatrous Lady of Ouldsworth, an Image, or Idoll Saint," destroying "her name, her place, [and] her power."[20] Records specify that the infant Christ was often found missing from Mary's wooden embrace—perhaps because the sight of Jesus nursing at her breast made reformers choke with rage.[21] "And yet must he now," William Crashaw asked, "after 1606 years *still* be an infant in his mother's arms?"[22] No longer. Iconoclasts pried their deity out of his arrested development, liberating him from the clutches of his mother.

Antipapist polemicists tended to interpret statues of the Virgin as idols and whores—in their mouths, synonymous terms, since the word *avowtery* meant both "fornication" (the misplacement of sexuality outside the lawful bonds of marriage) and "idolatry" (the misplacement of devotion beyond the monotheistic covenant between man and God).[23] During the sixteenth century, polemicists (both Lollards and reformers) habitually referred to icons of the Madonna as prostitutes, pilgrims as johns, and shrines as brothels. In 1511, one Elizabeth Sampson of London confessed that she had described Our Lady of Willesden as a "brent-ars Elfe" (a burnt-ass elf)—in other words, a pagan imp infected by a burning venereal disease.[24] Sampson saw the dark surface of England's black Madonnas (Our Lady of Willesden, Our Lady of Crome, Our Lady of Muswell) not as the color of the wood from which they were constructed or the paint with which they had been decorated but rather as soot accumulated from the candles of countless idolaters and, figuratively, as the rot of the pox.[25]

The 1528 polemical satire *Rede Me and Be Nott Wrothe* confirmed Sampson's diagnosis:

> As for whordom and letcherousnes,
> [Our Lady of Willesden] is the chefe lady mastres,
> Common paramoure of baudry.[26]

Yet whereas Sampson took the statue for a whore, *Rede Me and Be Nott Wrothe* calls Our Lady of Willesden a bawd, charging her with the crime of arranging for wives to breed bastards "under color of devotion." In 1563, Thomas Cromwell's propagandist William Grey added yet another offense to the list, accusing Our Lady of Walsingham of abandoning her pedestal to fornicate "very oft" by night with the Rood of Boxley, an infamously lifelike articulable image of Christ on the Cross.[27] In 1565, James Calfhill expanded that allegation to include all statues of Jesus and Mary, which, he wrote, "run in the night-time" from one chapel of the cathedral to another to meet for amorous trysts, like lecherous mice.[28] Bale and Foxe went even further, claiming that friars "fondled" and "milked" the breasts of images of the Virgin, with whom they fornicated "as familiarly" and "customarily" as husband and wife.[29]

Cromwell, the mastermind behind what the historian Helen Parish has called 1538's "long summer of iconoclasm," arranged for the righteous punishment of these whorish idols of the Madonna to resemble the humiliation of the harlot Israel in the book of Ezekiel:[30]

> Behold, I will gather together all thy lovers with whom thou hast taken pleasure, and all whom thou hast loved, with all whom thou hast hated: and I will gather them together against thee on every side, and will discover thy shame in their sight, and they shall see all thy nakedness. And I will judge thee as adulteresses, and they that shed blood are judged: and I will give thee blood in fury and jealousy. And I will deliver thee into their hands, and they shall destroy thy brothel house, and throw down thy stews: and they shall strip thee of thy garments, and shall take away the vessels of thy beauty: and leave thee naked, and full of disgrace. (Ezekiel 16:37–39)

Obeying these instructions, the reformer Hugh Latimer, the bishop of Worcester, had the Madonna of Worcester stripped of her vestments and ornaments and left standing naked and humiliated on her pedestal.[31] Records

suggest that Cromwell's agents invited the witnesses of this kind of iconoclastic spectacle to participate by stripping and smashing the idols with their
own hands, thereby playing the role of Israel's lovers-turned-punishers.[32]
This collective violence allegedly exposed the awful truth. According to
chronicles of the Reformation written by the victors, Our Lady of Worcester
was revealed, under her finery, to be neither Madonna nor mannequin but
rather the grotesque "similitude of a bishop, like a giant, almost 10 ft. long."[33]
In other words, a monster.

Although in this particular case, that monster turned out to be a strange
episcopal giant, as a rule, reformers tended find another beast entirely when
they unmasked idols of the Virgin: the Whore of Babylon foretold in the
book of Revelation, scripture's last type of the harlot Israel.[34] Revelation describes "that great harlot" as an allegory of a decadent and corrupt city
"which hath kingdom over the kings of the earth" (17:18). Ancient and medieval exegetes had interpreted this city as the fallen world or, more specifically, as the Babylonian or Roman (or any other relevant) Empire.[35] But to
reformers, the Whore of Babylon was none other than the pope and his
Church.[36] And, to their eyes, she bore a particular resemblance to Catholicism's best-beloved idol, the Queen of Heaven and Empress of Hell, who
glittered on many a pedestal, worshiped by kings and "clothed round about
with purple and scarlet, and gilt with gold, and precious stones and pearls"
(Revelation 17:4).[37]

Revelation prophesies that, at the end of days, the ten horns of the seven-
headed scarlet beast on which the Whore of Babylon rides shall turn against
their mistress and "shall make her desolate and naked, and shall eat her
flesh, and shall burn her with fire" (17:16)—thereby finally fulfilling the
terms of the punishment of the harlot Israel foretold in the Old Testament.
Following this typological script, iconoclasts ended their rituals of punishment by setting ablaze the idols that they had stripped and mutilated. In
1538, Latimer advised Cromwell that England's statues of the Virgin (Our
Lady of Worcester, "her old sister of Walsingham, her young sister of Ipswich,
with their other two sisters of Doncaster and Penrice"), having tempting so
many souls to hellfire, should burn, making "a jolly muster in Smithfield."[38]
In other words, Latimer suggested that they should suffer the spectacular
punishment reserved for traitors, heretics, witches, and the Whore of Babylon: death by fire.[39] Cromwell took this suggestion, and the Madonnas of
Walsingham, Worcester, Ipswich, Doncaster, and Penrhys (if not also Ber-

mondsey, Boxley, Islington, and many others—it is hard to tell how many) were publicly burned at the stake in London the following year.[40]

While iconoclasts incinerated these Romish harlots, reformers labored to rehabilitate the chaste, silent, and obedient mother of Jesus that they found in the canonical Gospels. Scripture, Martin Luther argued, represented Mary not as a mighty queen or goddess but rather as a humble handmaiden, "milking the cows, cooking the meals, washing pots and kettles, sweeping out the rooms."[41] (Although, it must be said, scripture does not actually describe Mary performing any of these tasks.) Reformers saw Mary as "a weak, stupid human being"—a mere "creature," "no better than other women."[42] Whereas Catholic theologians believed that God had chosen Mary to be his consort because of her exceptional merits, reformers followed the theory of human depravity, arguing that no mere mortal, not even the Virgin, could possibly deserve or earn God's favor.[43] While Catholics venerated Mary for having freely chosen to bear Christ and help save mankind, Luther maintained that God never needed her help and had not waited to ask for her consent.[44] Luther praised the Virgin not for her excellence but rather for her abjection—for reacting to the news of her impregnation without the smallest hint of resistance.[45] No one, Luther wrote, was ever more submissive.

Reformers claimed that this true and humble version of the Virgin was on their side, weeping in heaven at the sight of Catholicism's perversion of her image.[46] (Or, alternatively, chortling with glee as God "laid [the Holy Roman Empire's] tottering kingdom flat on the earth.")[47] And yet it often proved quite challenging to separate the modest virgin from the brazen whore.[48] When glossing Jesus's several rebukes of his mother in the Gospels ("Woman, what have I to do with thee?"), reformers tended to conclude that Mary "was pricked with vain-glory" and "no doubt had a smell of ambition" about her—sins that foreshadowed her future transgressions.[49] In other words, they admitted that even the supposedly benign Virgin of the Gospels often let slip the meretricious tendencies of Catholicism's Whore of Babylon. With this in mind, reformers took it upon themselves to follow Jesus's example and discipline even the best and truest versions of Mary with sharp rebukes, thereby keeping her wicked inclinations in check. They stripped not only her idols of their silks and gems but also her cult of its prayers, festivals, rituals, legends, and doctrines.[50] Only the pillars of Mariology that provided necessary structural support for the maintenance of Christology were allowed to remain standing.[51] Latimer, leading by example, vowed to "give as little to [Mary] as [he could] (doing her no wrong), rather than Christ her Son and Savior shall lack any parcel of his glory."[52] Or minus that parenthetical "doing her no wrong." God would understand, Crashaw prevaricated, if iconoclasts happened to "blemish" the Virgin in their righteous fury—"For what will not a Christian man's zeal cause him to do, when he seeth his God dishonored?"[53]

The Reformation's two-pronged strategy against the Virgin Mary—on the one hand, the punishment of her whorish pride and, on the other, the celebration of her chaste abjection—split her multivalence into a confusingly twinned binary opposition. The two halves of the divided Madonna—virgin and whore—looked disturbingly alike. The cunning whore, reformers warned, could flawlessly imitate her chaste sister, making them as difficult to tell apart as truth from error.[54] Which was which? Which Una and which Duessa?[55] In his *Holy Sonnets*, John Donne begs God to answer the question:

> Show me deare Christ, thy spouse, so bright and cleare.
> What, is it she, which on the other shore
> Goes richly painted? or which, rob'd and tore,
> Laments and mournes in Germany and here?[56]

Donne imagines these brides of Christ as difficult-to-distinguish but definitively separate figures (one painted in Catholic France or Italy and another naked in Protestant England or Germany), each claiming the same identity. But the schism in Christianity could also split perception more deeply, creating two in one. Depending on what one heard or read, the Protestant martyr Anne Askew was either a chaste and obedient wife or a coy and wanton shrew—and likewise for the Catholic martyr Margaret Clitherow.[57] England's Protestant and Catholic queens found themselves similarly doubled and yet also divided, their images fractured "in mirrours more then one."[58] "Bloody" Mary Tudor was both Deborah and Jezebel, Elizabeth I both Gloriana and Lucifera.[59] These divisive doublings drove men horn-mad.[60] In early modern literature, the smallest sign—a glance, gesture, or missing handkerchief—transforms idolatrous devotion into frenzied paranoia and violent punishment. Confounded by the indistinguishability of "the divine Desdemona" and "that cunning whore of Venice," Othello turns to murderous iconoclasm.[61]

In the English drama that preceded the Reformation, putting the Virgin to the test did little harm. Neither slanders, nor trials, nor assaults could diminish her power or purity. Unfazed and even amused by obscenity and violence, Mary always survived the attacks of her detractors with her indestructible virginity perfectly intact. Looking back, Donne remembered this impossible paradox with fondness: the Madonna who was neither virgin nor whore but both—"most trew" when "embrac'd and open to most men."[62] But by Donne's time the tide had turned. Although the old pattern of miraculous resilience continued to repeat itself in early modern performance (for example, in the resurrections of Shakespeare's slandered wives: Hero, Helena, Imogen, and Hermione), another, newer ending also became attached to the ancient ritual.[63] In this new grand finale, types of the Virgin did not get back up after being struck down. You can knock idols down thrice, iconoclasts taught, and "they cannot rise, not once, to save themselves."[64] Proving this point, painted images of women played by boys died in erotic climaxes of brutal iconoclasm on the London stage, stripped of all their whorish lies.[65] Exploiting the shock of this change from comic resilience to tragic fragility, Shakespeare's martyred Desdemona revives old expectations by briefly coming back to life, only to die again, and this time forever. For a moment, neither Othello nor the spectators can believe that she is really gone. "Methinks," Othello says,

> it should be now a huge eclipse
> Of sun and moon, and that th'affrighted globe
> Should yawn at alteration. (5.2.99–101)

But the world spins on.

For a while, at least, the loss of the medieval Madonna—human and divine, humble and imperious, promiscuous and chaste—seems to have been keenly felt.[66] When craftsmen with chisels and axes entered the rood loft of Saint Nicholas's priory in Exeter in 1536 to carry out the orders of the Crown, they were met by a gang of local women who protected the images of the saints so fiercely that one iconoclast felt the need to jump out of the window in order to escape their blows.[67] After Cromwell's agents stripped Our Lady of Worcester, a recusant named Thomas Emans entered the shrine and kissed the bare feet of the image.[68] In his confession, Emans later admitted to having said, "Lady, art thou stripped now? I have seen the day that as clean men hath been stripped at a pair of gallows as were they that stripped thee."[69] Emans then turned to the spectators that had gathered and tried to persuade them that the Madonna was "no worse to pray unto" naked than she had been clothed.[70] In his eyes, iconoclasts had merely restaged an old pageant of the Virgin. The violence and obscenity with which the image had been assaulted did her no dishonor, as he saw it, but only glorified her purity and rebounded against her persecutors. But Emans found himself out of step with the times. In Walsingham, villagers continued to attribute miracles to the missing statue of their Madonna for some time after she had been carted off to London and reduced to ashes. In a letter to Cromwell, Sir Roger Townshend complained, "I cannot perceive but the seyd Image is not yet out of sum of ther heddes."[71] But in her long absence, the memory of the promiscuous Virgin faded.

Shakespeare's Joan of Arc

Although the Virgin Mary does not seem to appear in the plays of Shakespeare, appearances can be deceiving. The Flower Portrait appears to be an authentic seventeenth-century painting of the features of Shakespeare derived from the Droeshout engraving in the frontispiece to the First Folio.[72] Yet x-ray analysis reveals a late medieval icon of the Madonna and Child hiding underneath what turned out to be a nineteenth-century forgery.[73] Mary lies just under the surface—often, in this instance as in others, literally. Recusants buried relics under floorboards, iconoclasts whitewashed frescoes, and the thrifty recycled antique canvases.[74] Excavation yields results.

In his plays, Shakespeare mentions the Virgin by name fewer than a dozen times—usually in offhand oaths ("By holy Mary") or place-names ("Saint Mary's chapel").[75] The majority of the remainder occur in the first part of his three-part history of King Henry VI.[76] There are more references to the Virgin in *1 Henry VI* than in any other play attributed to Shakespeare. Although she never makes an entrance or speaks a line, Mary makes her presence felt in this text. She speaks through her minion and mirror, Joan of Arc, who repeatedly declares herself to be a type of the Virgin. Joan is the clearest and closest analogue in the work of Shakespeare to the Madonna of earlier English drama—a resemblance that has gone largely unnoticed.[77] If you presume that medieval drama handled Mary with nothing

but the most pious and decorous respect, never calling her names or batter-
ing her with violence, then she and Shakespeare's Joan would appear to
have very little in common.[78]

Shakespeare's polemical portrait of Joan of Arc has tended to baffle contemporary readers and spectators, who find her "schizophrenic," "contradictory," and "disjunct."[79] For the first several acts of the play, Joan appears to
be a miraculous and saintly virgin sent from heaven. And yet over the course
of the performance, she degrades, finally revealing herself to be a promiscuous sorceress: "puzel" (whore) rather than *pucelle* (virgin).[80] The reversal, it
is often argued, comes in the fifth act when Joan consorts onstage with
demons, nursing them with her blood.[81] For modern readers primed to
idealize (if not idolize) both Joan and Shakespeare, this scene comes as a
shock. Some have even refused to accept its legitimacy, maintaining their
faith, despite the play's conclusion, in Joan's virtue and Shakespeare's gal-
lantry.[82] And yet in the end, Joan confesses her crimes and, humiliated and
reviled, heads off to burn at the stake—and, presumably, thereafter in hell.

Joan's disjunction should come as no surprise. The only canonized heretic
in Church history, she is nothing if not contradictory.[83] From the very beginning, Jeanne d'Arc struck some as saintly and others as satanic—some
as whorish and others as chaste.[84] The Hundred Years' War and Protestant
Reformation only exasperated this double effect. The city of Orléans remembered La Pucelle as a virgin martyr, annually commemorating her victory
over the English with pageantry and panegyrics.[85] English chroniclers, on
the other hand, vilified the "maide of God" as a whorish and murderous
monster, "an orgayne of the devill, sent from Sathan, to blind the people and
bryng them in unbelife."[86] This angry dispute constructed Joan's mythology,
which, at least until the early twentieth century, remained quite fraught.[87]
Especially during the first several centuries of Joan's reception history, neither panegyric nor polemical accounts of her life could manage to narrate
an account entirely pure of the opposition's influence. Even the virulently
anti-French and antipapist chronicle of Raphael Holinshed feels the need
to admit that Joan *seemed* virtuous "by hir holie words, hir fasting and prai-
ers," and, most crucially, "by hir virginitie," which was proved (as the text
acknowledges) by medical examination.[88] But, as Holinshed's account of history reminds its reader, seeming is suspect. "Satan," the text warns, "can change
himselfe into an angell of light, the déeplier to deceiue."[89] Who knows
what words Joan really whispered when she seemed to pray to God—or the

awful truth behind her seeming chastity.[90] Like an idol of the Virgin, English chroniclers insisted, Joan excelled at bewitching the untrained eye.

This is the polemical strategy that Shakespeare pursues in *1 Henry VI*, representing Joan's seeming virtues as hidden vices, at first thinly veiled and then at last fully exposed. When introduced by the Bastard of Orleans (Jean de Dunois), Joan is described as "a holy maid" (1.2.51)—a phrase designed to provoke suspicion in ears attuned to the teachings of antipapism. The reformed had been taught to distrust the apparent holiness of Catholic maidenhood. Luther roundly condemned the celibacy practiced by the Romish clergy and, leading by example, renounced his vows and married an escaped nun from the Cistercian cloister of Marienthron, the Throne of the Virgin.[91] While he acknowledged Paul's preference for the perfection of virginity over the compromised state of matrimony, Luther did not share the Catholic Church's belief in mankind's ability to live up to that ideal. "It is impossible," he argued, "that the gift of chastity is as common as the convent."[92] Far from it. Luther (participating in a long-standing and widespread polemical tradition) intimated that convents' thick walls hid appalling acts of sodomy, bestiality, and infanticide from the public eye.[93] William Tyndale, harping on the same string, accused the Vatican of harboring within its precincts "stews of twenty or thirty thousand whores" and "stews of young boys, against nature."[94] Likewise, Thomas Becon listed fornication, adultery, whoredom, incest, sodomy, bestiality, masturbation, and every attemptable "kynde of unclenness" as the direct results of Catholicism's misguided policy of "feigned chastity."[95]

Protestant polemicists railed against the hypocrisy of the clergy so successfully that they made celibacy code for lechery, purity for impurity. Reformers inverted the meaning of Catholic sexual values, first and foremost by compiling enormous catalogs of alleged virgins from Church history and then proving these saints to be, in the words of John Bale, "whoremongers, bawds, bribers, Idolaters, hypocrites, trayters and most filthy Gomoreanes"—either by pointing out (or inventing) narrative discrepancies in their vitae or simply by scoffing.[96] For example, in his *Discouerie of Witchcraft*, Reginald Scot interprets the old legend that one "Saint Christine" had selflessly offered to swap beds with a maiden troubled by an incubus to mean that Christine wanted that virile imp all to herself. These so-called saints, he concludes, are as "holy and chaste as horses and mares."[97] When Bale read Revelation's description of the golden cup of the Whore of Babylon, "full of the abomination and filthiness of her execrable whoredom," he saw her chalice brimming with the Catholic pretense of "perpetual virginity of life," which "seemeth gold" but hides "prodigious beastliness in lecherous living under colour of chastity."[98]

The Protestant doctrine of depravity made vows of celibacy sound inherently suspect. Only angels, Luther argued, could keep such vows—not men. "Purity," he wrote, "does not exist."[99] Mere mortals, he advised, should check themselves into the "hospital" of matrimony in order to treat the disease of lust through lawful purgation, a process as necessary for fallen sinners as "emptying the bowels and bladder."[100] Blocking the flow, he warned, would not purify but rather pollute and poison the body—especially the cold, watery, and sluggish female anatomy.[101] Singing the same tune, physicians instructed good Protestant girls to rid themselves of their hymens as quickly and respectably as possible in order to avoid the putrefaction of stifled humors and the displeasure of God Almighty. ("Virginity," as Shakespeare's straight-talking Parolles has it, "breeds mites, much like a cheese.")[102] Those who died intact, it was proverbially said, would "lead apes in hell"—in other words, suffer the condign punishment of rape by lecherous monkeys.[103]

In short, virginity became tainted by its associations with disease, pride, hypocrisy, and whoredom. So, when the Bastard calls Joan "a holy maid," his seeming praise begins the work of her condemnation. The insult behind his compliment becomes more explicit when the Bastard repeats himself later on in the play. Observing Joan and the Dauphin (surprised by a midnight attack) running together across the stage, he quips, "Tut, holy Joan was his defensive guard" (2.1.50). In this context, the adjective *holy* means not only sanctified but also full of holes.[104] The Bastard insinuates that Joan kept the Dauphin safe not only with her sword but also within the protection of her vaginal sheath.[105] His second use of the adjective *holy* to describe Joan follows inevitably from the first. According to this play's interconnected systems of iconoclasm and misogyny, Joan's vaginal hole makes holiness impossible. In *Othello*, Iago riffs on the same theme. When Roderigo protests that Desdemona's "most blessed condition" belies Iago's slanders, Iago rejoins, "Blessed fig's-end!" (2.1.249). In other words, Desdemona is no more blessed than the tip of a fig, a particularly obscene slur for the female genitals.[106] The fallen body, in short, is incapable of sanctity. To think otherwise is to fall into idolatry's snare.[107]

Shakespeare represents Joan as a seductress who tempts the French to join forces with Satan in exchange for power, glory, and sexual satisfaction.[108] To reformers and iconoclasts, no other agent of Satan seemed as bewitching or dangerous as the papist idol of the Madonna, Catholicism's most irresistible honey trap.[109] Therefore, upon making her first entrance, Joan extensively compares herself to Mary, boasting about her humble origins, exceptional merits, and divine election. She retells the story of the Annunciation and Nativity with herself playing the role of Mary and Mary playing the role of God, parodying the Catholic habit of generating apocrypha from scripture, and replacing *Dominus* with *Domina*.[110] "Our Lady," Joan claims, descended from Heaven "in complete glory" with tidings of great joy (1.2.83): La Pucelle's delivery of France from England (rather than Christ's of mankind from Satan). Whereas the historical Joan of Arc testified before the Inquisition that she had received her visions from Saint Margaret, Saint Catherine of Alexandria, and the archangel Michael, early modern English polemicists preferred to insist that Joan had named the Virgin Mary as her primary source of otherworldly inspiration.[111] Shakespeare follows suit, representing Joan as the second coming of the Madonna. "Christ's mother helps me," she says, "else I were too weak" (1.2.106).

Crucially, Joan claims that Mary "infused" her with "clear rays" of divine light and metamorphosed her from a "black and swart" peasant, her cheeks scorched by the "sun's parching heat," into a rare beauty, miraculously fair and royal (1.2.77, 84–85). These signs bode ill. First and foremost, Joan outs herself as an upstart. She brags that she has risen from a "contemptible estate" and "base vocation" to impersonate her betters with the aid of suspect supernatural powers, revealing that same vice that reformers identified in the Virgin Mary of both the Gospels and the Catholic Church: meretricious pride. This pride manifests itself in Joan's transformation from shepherdess to knight and black to white, recalling the biblical maxim that leopards cannot change their spots nor Ethiopians their skin (Jeremiah 13:23).[112] If black cannot become white, then Joan's apparent whiteness must read as hypocritical rather than miraculous—as the deceptive surface of a whitewashed sepulcher (Matthew 23:27). She is that "white devil" or "fair devil" so often decried in early modern invectives against hypocrisy, the serpent lurking underneath the flower.[113]

Specifically, when Joan professes to have undergone a miraculous process of purification and transformation, she echoes the late medieval Catholic doctrines of the Immaculate Conception and Assumption of the Virgin.[114] According to these doctrines, God spared Mary from the curses of Adam and Eve and raised her from Nazareth to rule the universe by his side in paradise—transforming her, in other words, from mortal to immortal, from nobody to queen. Medieval exegetes compared Mary to the beloved of the Song of Songs, who says, "Nigra sum sed formosa" (I am black but beautiful) (1:4), glossing her darkness as a sign of humanity, humility, earthiness, and sinfulness, often with a strong sexual valence.[115] Premodern climate theory understood blackness as an effect of exposure, a notion that associated whiteness with untouched purity and darkness with experience.[116] With these associations in mind, Abelard imagined that the skin of Solomon's black beloved would be sweeter and more delightful to touch than the skin of a white woman—because he believed that blackness could channel the pleasures of worldly love better than whiteness.[117] Thus the color scheme of the medieval English cult of the Madonna, who was black but beautiful, worldly but heavenly, and promiscuous but chaste.[118]

Early modern reformers saw things differently. In their eyes, an earthly body, blackened by sin, could not hope to achieve the beauty of immaculate purity. If humble and modest, a maiden should marry, reproduce, and know her limits. To imagine oneself exceptional and to make boasts of virgin sanctity despite the universal taint of original sin was to expose one's pride. Reformers identified that vainglorious impulse as the very root and essence of whoredom. Hence the offense caused by the doctrine of the Immaculate Conception.[119] On this subject, Crashaw writes, "Let [Catholics] . . . speak and write that [Mary] was conceived without sin original, and have a holy day for it, but they cannot prove it . . . though the whore of Babylon, affirm as much of herself, yet was she never so impudent, as to conclude it an article of the faith."[120] Crashaw identifies the self-proclamation of sinlessness as an essential characteristic of sexual promiscuity. Every whore, he assumes, is likely to try to pass off her blackness as whiteness in order to win more love and devotion from her victims. But the Virgin Mary, he argues, is by far the worst (the most "impudent" and therefore the most whorish), because she went so far as to make her lie an article of the faith.[121] Even the Whore of Babylon, as Crashaw has it, would never dare. But the Virgin has no shame. And neither has Joan, who vaunts (about herself, speaking in the third person),

> Joan of Arc hath been
> A Virgin from her tender infancy,
> Chaste and immaculate in very thought. (5.5.49–51)

When she seduces the Dauphin, Joan pointedly uses the language of Mari-ology. "Thou shalt find," she promises with a wink, "that I exceed my sex" (1.2.90)—not in virtue but in harlotry.

Captivated by Joan's enticements, the Dauphin sells his soul. "Whoe'er helps thee," he says, "'tis thou that must help me" (1.2.107), recklessly vow-ing to serve Joan as his sovereign goddess. This is the pyramid scheme of papism as reformers understood it: Satan controls Mary, who controls Joan, who controls the Dauphin—each idol lower than the last. Polemicists told horror stories about sinners turning from the Creator to some creature (like the human mother of God) and then "the very pictures of creatures."[122] The idolatrous cult of the Madonna, Crashaw reported, led the villagers of Sichem on the Continent to worship an image of Mary that stood in the hollow of an oak tree, and then (when the idol disappeared) the oak tree itself, and then (when the oak died), even tinier idols whittled from rotten branches and twigs.[123] Similarly, Joan's idolatry of Mary spawns the Dau-phin's idolatry of Joan. Sinking further and further into fleshliness, the Dauphin burns with the desire to worship Joan's bodily relics. He eagerly anticipates idolizing her corpse and entombing her ashes in an immense "pyramid," even "statelier" than that of Rhodopis, the legendary prostitute in whose honor and with whose riches (it was believed) the pyramid of Memphis had been built (1.7.21–22).[124] In *1 Henry VI*, Catholicism back-slides easily into ancient Egyptian paganism, represented as a cult of dead courtesans. Or worse. Joan names "Christ's mother" as the source of her power, but the Dauphin echoes back "who'er" (1.2.107). Blinded by lust, he does not care from whence Joan's powers derive—whether from Christ, his mother, or Satan himself. Moments later, the Dauphin hails Joan as "the Bright star of Venus, fallen down on the earth" (1.2.144)—in other words, light-bringing Lucifer, the black devil shining like a bright star.[125]

"Now Heaven Forfend! The Holy Maid with Child!"

Throughout *1 Henry VI*, Joan does her best to revive earlier English drama's lost pageantry of the Virgin. Up to a certain point, she succeeds—not only in her triumphs but also in her humiliations. Like Mary before her, Joan finds her claims of virginity met with scorn, laughter, and threats of violence from enemies and allies alike.[126] When finally captured by the English, Joan fiercely defends her virgin innocence, as would any saintly martyr taken by a tyrant. Richard, the Duke of York, dismisses her protestations with a bored, "Ay, ay," and then turns to the guards to order her immediate execution (5.5.54). Yet Joan's words move the Earl of Warwick, although not enough to save her life. Persuaded of her chastity but not her innocence, Warwick mercifully orders the guards to douse the stake with pitch in order to hasten her demise, "because she is a maid" (5.5.55).

It is at this point that Shakespeare introduces a slander invented by English chroniclers in the decades following Joan's death: the claim that she pled her belly at the foot of the gallows.[127] According to this version of history, the fear of death motivated Joan to lie by pretending pregnancy in order to gain the customary nine-month reprieve granted to expectant mothers awaiting execution.[128] By "seeking to eetch out life as long as she might . . . though the shift were shamefull," in the words of Holinshed's chronicle, Joan proved herself guilty.[129] Technically virginal, but whorish through and through.

Shakespeare hitches this plot point to earlier theatrical traditions. When Joan pleads her belly in *1 Henry VI*, she and her detractors rehearse the dialog of medieval drama's pageant of "Joseph's Trouble about Mary." Like Mary before her, Joan tries her best to spin the "infirmity" of pregnancy, Eve's curse, as an exceptional "privilege" that transcends the power of law (5.5.60–61). She claims that she, a virgin, has conceived and that salvation (her own, as well as that of France) is therefore at hand. This announcement provokes the same response with which the good news of the virgin birth is met by the people of Nazareth and Bethlehem in N-Town: laughter. York sneers at Joan, "Now heaven forfend! the holy maid with child!" (5.5.65). His joke cuts right to the point. Virgins, as we know, cannot bear children. It is impossible. Mary's detractors said the same to her. Salome protested, "It may nevyr be" (15.242), and the summoner scoffed, "Ya, on this wyse excusyth here every scowte" (14.182)—all whores tell the same preposterous lies. York and Warwick would appear to agree.

Incensed by Joan's scandalous confession, the English decide to expedite rather than delay her execution in order to rid the world of the bastard of Charles the Dauphin, whom they assume to be the father of her unborn child. Apparently hoping for better luck with a different name, Joan says,

> You are deceived, my child is none of his.
> It was Alençon that enjoy'd my love. (5.5.72–73)

When this strategy fails as well, Joan tries yet again:

> 'Twas neither Charles nor yet the duke I named,
> But Reignier, King of Naples, that prevail'd. (5.5.77–78)

By this point, the situation has become farcical. York and Warwick laugh that Joan seems to have had so many lovers that she cannot tell with which she conceived. And then the punch line: "And yet, forsooth," York adds, "she is a virgin pure" (5.5.83).

Just so with the Virgin Mary in early English drama—only her list was longer. When N-Town's Joseph dismissed Mary's first attempt at an explanation (his own name), he prompted the Virgin Mother and her handmaidens to name another father (God the Father), and then another (Jesus), and then another (the Holy Ghost), and then another (the archangel Gabriel) in an increasingly desperate attempt to prove her innocence. None of these excuses managed to assuage Joseph in the slightest. On the contrary, Joseph, York, and Warwick all respond by extending the lists with which they have been provided even further, adding more suspects of their own: some boy, some man, the entire French army. In neither N-Town nor *1 Henry VI* does anyone take the word of a pregnant virgin on faith alone.

Turning this scene from a comedy to a tragedy requires only the slightest of alterations. The Virgin's paradoxical multivalence had always inspired shock, anger, and laughter as well as adoration, and her cult encouraged ritual abuse. Very little separates medieval Catholic pageants devoted to the Virgin from early modern spectacles of iconoclasm. It is only in Joan's final moments that the crucial difference between the two finally becomes clear. Whereas medieval pageants of the Virgin conclude with last-minute divine interventions that spare Mary from certain ruin, in the end, Joan finds herself abandoned by all higher powers: Satan, God, and the playwright. The Catholic drama of the Middle Ages taught spectators to expect Mary to thrive when attacked and remain immaculate when defiled. And yet without the help of an angel descending from the heavens, a man playing God behind the curtain, or a prop cherry tree bending to the floorboards of the stage, Joan must face the fate that the medieval Virgin always managed to escape: the punishment for avowtery. The law finally catches up with its slipperiest antagonist. Like the black Madonnas of Willesden, Crome, and

Muswell, Joan burns. "Break thou," York says to her, "in pieces and consume to ashes" (5.5.92).

Until this sharp divergence, the devotional pageantry of the Virgin and the iconoclastic spectacles of the Reformation run tightly parallel. Like the tyrants in saint plays, iconoclasts hack at the breasts of virgin martyrs.[130] Like the desperate mother in the Cornish *Beunans Meriasek*, they kidnap the baby Jesus from his mother's arms.[131] And like Mary's detractors in biblical drama, they call the Virgin a whore and menace her with the punishments prescribed by God for the harlot Israel and the Whore of Babylon. But whereas these antics merely tickled the invulnerable Virgin of the Middle Ages, they destroyed her early modern descendants. In N-Town, Mary laughs to think that the miracle of the virgin birth "wyl preve [her] fre" (15.180)—"free," in this sense, meaning exempt from the laws of nature, man, and God.[132] Joan is also proved free, but in a very different way. Just before he sends Joan to the stake, Warwick concludes that she "hath been liberal and free" (5.5.82). In his mouth, "free" means whorish—and whorish means flammable.

The joke had always been on Mary, but not on her alone. The medieval comedy of the virgin birth made fun of Christianity itself, and especially its embarrassingly fleshly and farcical origins in Mary's suspect ways and private parts—"Goddes pryvetee," in Chaucer's words. Before the Reformation, the joke of the Virgin's promiscuity and Christianity's adulterousness pleased all kinds of sinners—theologians and artists, actors and audiences, husbands and wives. Its playfulness taught Christians a funny kind of humility and hope. But the joke did not amuse the puritanical sensibilities of early modern iconoclasts. The medieval Madonna made iconoclasts laugh, but in a different spirit and with a different punch line. When they performed the ritual of her humiliation, their violence broke the game.

NOTES

Abbreviations Used in the Notes

EEBO   Early English Books Online
EETS   Early English Text Society
MED   *Middle English Dictionary*
OED   *Oxford English Dictionary*
PL   *Patrologia Latina*
REED   Records of Early English Drama
TEAMS   Consortium for the Teaching of the Middle Ages

Introduction

1. Studies of the Madonna are many—too many to name here—but, among this multitude, I relied most extensively on the following: Hilda Graef, *Mary: A History of Doctrine and Devotion*. 1963, 1965. Rev. ed. with a new chapter covering Vatican II and beyond by Thomas A. Thompson (Notre Dame, IN: Ave Maria, 2009); Julia Kristeva, "Stabat Mater," trans. Arthur Goldhammer, *Poetics Today* 6, no. 1/2 (1985): 133–52; Marina Warner, *Alone of All Her Sex: The Myth and Cult of the Virgin Mary* (New York:

Knopf, 1976); Miri Rubin, *Mother of God: A History of the Virgin Mary* (New Haven, CT: Yale University Press, 2009); and Elina Gertsman, *Worlds Within: Opening the Medieval Shrine Madonna* (University Park: Pennsylvania State University Press, 2015).

2. For more on this painting, see Carol Becker, "Brooklyn Museum: Messing with the Sacred," in *Chris Ofili* (New York: Skira Rizzoli, 2009), 78–84; Alicia Ritson, "Between Heaven and Hell: *The Holy Virgin Mary* at the Brooklyn Museum," in *Chris Ofili: Night and Day*, ed. Massimiliano Gioni (New York: Skira Rizzoli, 2014), 164; and Jennifer Glancy, *Corporal Knowledge: Early Christian Bodies* (Oxford: Oxford University Press, 2010), 134–36.

3. Floyd Abrams, *Speaking Freely: Trials of the First Amendment* (New York: Penguin, 2006), 188–230.

4. Rudolph W. Giuliani, *Leadership* (New York: Hyperion, 2002), 225–26.

5. *OED*, s.v. "defile." This and all subsequent references to the OED refer to the online edition.

6. Quoted in Abrams, *Speaking Freely*, 195–7; Giuliani, *Leadership*, 226.

7. This book depends on the foundational work that established medieval and early modern virginity studies around the turn of the last century: Karen Winstead, *Virgin Martyrs: Legends of Sainthood in Late Medieval England* (Ithaca, NY: Cornell University Press, 1997); Kathleen Coyne Kelly and Marina Leslie, eds., *Menacing Virgins: Representing Virginity in the Middle Ages and Renaissance* (Newark: University of Delaware Press, 1999); Cindy L. Carlson and Angela Jane Weisl, eds., *Constructions of Widowhood and Virginity in the Middle Ages* (New York: St. Martin's, 1999); Kathleen Coyne Kelly, *Performing Virginity and Testing Chastity in the Middle Ages* (New York: Routledge, 2000); Sarah Salih, *Versions of Virginity in Late Medieval England* (Cambridge, UK: D. S. Brewer, 2001); Jocelyn Wogan-Browne, *Saints' Lives and Women's Literary Culture, 1150–1300: Virginity and Its Authorizations* (Oxford: Oxford University Press, 2001); Kathryn Schwarz, "The Wrong Question: Thinking through Virginity," *differences: A Journal of Feminist Cultural Studies* 13, no. 2 (2002): 1–34; Anke Bernau, Ruth Evans, and Sarah Salih, eds., *Medieval Virginities* (Toronto: University of Toronto Press, 2003); and Ruth Evans, "Virginities," in *The Cambridge Companion to Medieval Women's Writing*, ed. Carolyn Dinshaw and David Wallace (Cambridge: Cambridge University Press, 2003), 21–39.

8. Gregory D. Black, *The Catholic Crusade against the Movies, 1940–1975* (Cambridge: Cambridge University Press, 1997), 66–102; William Bruce Johnson, *Miracles and Sacrilege: Roberto Rossellini, the Church, and Film Censorship in Hollywood* (Toronto: University of Toronto Press, 2008), 259. See also Laura Wittern-Keller and Raymond J. Haberski, *The Miracle Case: Film Censorship and the Supreme Court* (Lawrence: University Press of Kansas, 2008).

9. William Johnson, *Miracles and Sacrilege*, 259, 271.

10. Wittern-Keller and Habersku, *Miracle Case*, 138.

11. Reid Mortensen, "Art, Expression, and the Offended Believer," in *Law and Religion*, ed. Rex J. Ahdar (Burlington, VT: Ashgate, 2000), 181–93; Bernadette Courtney, "An Artist Shrouded in Mystery," *Dominion*, April 4, 1998, available on ProQuest; "Campaigners Seek Legal Advice on Virgin Statue," *Dominion*, March 17, 1998, available on ProQuest.

12. Jeroen Temperman, "'Mother of God, Drive Putin Away': On Blasphemy and Activist Art in the Jurisprudence of the European Court of Human Rights," in *Blasphemy and Freedom of Expression: Comparative, Theoretical and Historical Reflections after the Charlie Hebdo Massacre*, ed. Jeroen Temperman and András Koltay (Cambridge: Cambridge University Press, 2017), 311. See also Nicholas Denysenko, "An Appeal to Mary: An Analysis of Pussy Riot's Punk Performance in Moscow," *Journal of the American Academy of Religion* 81, no. 4 (2013): 1061–92.

13. S. Brent Plate, introduction to *Religion, Art, and Visual Culture: A Cross-Cultural Reader*, ed. S. Brent Plate (New York: Palgrave, 2002), 2; Becker, "Brooklyn Museum," 84.

14. For more on the history and science of the hymen as a sign of virginity, see Giula Sissa, "Maidenhood without Maidenhead: The Female Body in Ancient Greece," in *Before Sexuality: The Construction of Erotic Experience in the Ancient Greek World*, ed. David M. Halperin, John J. Winkler, and Froma I. Zeitlin (Princeton, NJ: Princeton University Press, 1990), 339–64; and Bianca R. van Moorst et al., "Backgrounds of Women Applying for Hymen Reconstruction, the Effects of Counselling on Myths and Misunderstandings about Virginity, and the Results of Hymen Reconstruction," *European Journal of Contraception and Reproductive Health Care* 17, no. 2 (2012): 93–105, esp. 94.

15. For more on disenchantment, see Max Weber, *The Protestant Ethic and the Spirit of Capitalism*, trans. Talcott Parsons (New York: Routledge Classics, 2001); Marcel Gauchet, *The Disenchantment of the World: A Political History of Religion*, trans. Oscar Burge (Princeton, NJ: Princeton University Press, 1999); Charles Taylor, *A Secular Age* (Cambridge, MA: Harvard University Press, 2007), esp. 80–88, 553; and Janet R. Jakobsen and Ann Pellegrini, eds., *Secularisms* (Durham, NC: Duke University Press, 2008).

16. Ritson, "Between Heaven and Hell," 165.

17. Wittern-Keller and Habersku, *Miracle Case*, 71; William Johnson, *Miracles and Sacrilege*, 244–45, 249.

18. Rebecca Fortnum, *Contemporary British Women Artists: In Their Own Words* (New York: Palgrave Macmillan, 2007), 122–23; Jeremy Miller and Philip Hoare, *Tania Kovats* (Oxford: Ruskin School of Drawing and Fine Art, 2010), 9–10, 70–73.

19. Denysenko, "Appeal to Mary," 1069.

20. My thinking here owes a great debt to James Simpson's illuminating *Under the Hammer: Iconoclasm in the Anglo-American Tradition* (Oxford: Oxford University Press, 2010), esp. 39–48.

21. Cennino D'Andrea Cennini, *The Craftsman's Handbook "Il Libro dell' Arte,"* trans. Daniel V. Thompson Jr. (New Haven, CT: Yale University Press, 1933), 36–39; Michel Pastoureau, *Blue: The History of a Color* (Princeton, NJ: Princeton University Press, 2001), 50–55.

22. For more on the black Madonna, see Lucia Chiavola Birnbaum, *Black Madonnas: Feminism, Religion, and Politics in Italy* (Boston: Northeastern University Press, 1993); Monique Scheer, "From Majesty to Mystery: Change in the Meanings of Black Madonnas from the Sixteenth to Nineteenth Centuries," *American Historical Review* 107, no. 5 (2002): 1412–40; and Malgorzata Oleszkiewicz-Peralba, *The Black Madonna in Latin America and Europe: Tradition and Transformation* (Albuquerque: University of New Mexico Press, 2007).

23. Walter Besant, *Mediaeval London*, vol. 2, *Ecclesiastical* (London: Adam and Charles Black, 1906), 187–88; Ean Begg, *The Cult of the Black Virgin*, 2nd ed. (London: Arkana, 1996), 164–66. Not enough work has been done on medieval England's black Madonnas; see Mary Lee Nolan and Sidney Nolan, *Christian Pilgrimage in Modern Western Europe* (Chapel Hill: University of North Carolina Press, 1989), 204 (map 6-2); and Begg, *Cult of the Black Virgin*, 164–66. The most widely agreed-on example is Our Lady of Willesden, thanks to an early sixteenth-century Inquisitional record; see Shannon McSheffrey, *Gender and Heresy: Women and Men in Lollard Communities, 1420–1530* (Philadelphia: University of Pennsylvania Press, 1995), 146–47.

24. Harold Kane, ed., *The Prickynge of Love*, 2 vols. (Salzburg: Institut für Anglistik und Amerikanistik der Universität Salzburg, 1983); Walter Hilton, *The Goad of Love*, ed. Clare Kirchberger (London: Faber and Faber, 1952); Katie L. Walter, "The Child before the Mother: Mary and the Excremental in *The Prickynge of Love*," in *Words and Matter: The Virgin Mary in Late Medieval and Early Modern Parish Life*, ed. Jonas Carlquist and Virginia Langum (Stockholm: Sällskapet Runica et Mediævalia, 2015), 149–63.

25. Kane, *Prickynge of Love*, 1:191, lines 2–4.

26. Lisa Lampert, *Gender and Jewish Difference from Paul to Shakespeare* (Philadelphia: University of Pennsylvania Press, 2004), 52.

27. Roger Hutchinson, *The Works of Roger Hutchingson*, ed. John Bruce (Cambridge: Cambridge University Press, 1842), 148. For more on the ancient association between womb and sewer, see Glancy, *Corporal Knowledge*, 120–124.

28. Jerry Saltz, *Seeing Out Loud: The "Voice" Art Columns, Fall 1998–Winter 2003* (New York: The Figures, 2003), 326.

29. Guillaume de Lorris and Jean de Meun, *Le Roman de la Rose*, ed. André Lanly (Paris: Librarie Honoré Champion, 1975), 2.1.114; Guillaume de Lorris and Jean de Meun, *The Romance of the Rose*, trans. Frances Horgan (Oxford: Oxford World's Classics, 2008), 106–9.

30. Nicholas Love, *Love's Mirror of the Blessed Life of Jesus Christ: A Critical Edition Based on Cambridge University Library Additional MSS 6578 and 6686*, ed. Michael G. Sargent (New York: Garland, 1992), 34. See also Gertsman, *Worlds Within*, 94–100.

31. Alexandra Cuffel, *Gendering Disgust in Medieval Religious Polemic* (Notre Dame, IN: University of Notre Dame Press, 2007), 59–63; Tertullian, *Contre Marcion*, ed. René Braun, Sources Chrétiennes 399 (Paris: Éditions du Cerf, 1994), 3.11.6–9. See also Glancy, *Corporal Knowledge*, 94, 124, 127–28.

32. Rubin, *Mother of God*, 212.

33. Gary Waller, *The Virgin Mary in Late Medieval and Early Modern English Literature and Popular Culture* (Cambridge: Cambridge University Press, 2011), 34–37, 57, 78; Gertsman, *Worlds Within*, 70–77.

34. Leo Steinberg, *The Sexuality of Christ in Renaissance Art and in Modern Oblivion*, 2nd ed. (Chicago: University of Chicago Press, 1996), 3–5; Gail McMurray Gibson, "Scene and Obscene: Seeing and Performing Late Medieval Childbirth," *Journal of Medieval and Early Modern Studies* 29, no. 1 (1999): 7–24; Gary Waller, "The Virgin's 'Pryvytes': Walsingham and the Late Medieval Sexualization of the Virgin," in *Wals-*

ingham in Literature and Culture from the Middle Ages to Modernity, ed. Dominic Janes and Gary Waller (Farnham, UK: Ashgate, 2010), 113–30.

35. Donna Spivey Ellington, *From Sacred Body to Angelic Soul: Understanding Mary in Late Medieval and Early Modern Europe* (Washington, DC: Catholic University of America Press, 2001), 61–62.

36. Waller, *Virgin Mary*, 36; Gertsman, *Worlds Within*, 94.

37. Jos Koldeweij, "'Shameless and Naked Images': Obscene Badges as Parodies of Popular Devotion," in *Art and Architecture of Late Medieval Pilgrimage in Northern Europe and the British Isles*, ed. Sarah Blick and Rita Tekippe, 2 vols. (Leiden: Brill, 2004), 1:506; Albrecht Classen, introduction to *Sexuality in the Middle Ages and Early Modern Times: New Approaches to a Fundamental Cultural-Historical and Literary-Anthropological Theme*, ed. Albrecht Classen (Berlin: Walter de Gruyter, 2008), 19–21.

38. Ritson, "Between Heaven and Hell," 180.

39. Roberto Santiago, Mike Claffey, and Bill Hutchinson, "Virgin Mary Canvas Defaced in Brooklyn," *New York Daily News*, December 17, 1999.

40. Ibid.

41. My understanding of this shift depends on the work of Huston Diehl and Frances Dolan. See Huston Diehl, *Staging Reform, Reforming the Stage: Protestantism and Popular Theater in Early Modern England* (Ithaca, NY: Cornell University Press, 1997), 158–72; and Frances Dolan, *Whores of Babylon: Catholicism, Gender, and Seventeenth-Century Print Culture* (Ithaca, NY: Cornell University Press, 1999), 102–18. For more on the Reformation's broader effects on the Virgin, see Christine Peters, *Patterns of Piety: Women, Gender, and Religion in Late Medieval and Reformation England* (Cambridge: Cambridge University Press, 2003); Helen L. Parish, *Monks, Miracles and Magic: Reformation Representations of the Medieval Church* (London: Routledge, 2005); and Beth Kreitzer, *Reforming Mary: Changing Images of the Virgin Mary in Lutheran Sermons of the Sixteenth Century* (Oxford: Oxford University Press, 2004).

42. Waller, *Virgin Mary*, 12–17; Diehl, *Staging Reform*, 162–63.

43. Rubin, *Mother of God*, 400–412; Ellington, *From Sacred Body*, 142–43; Peters, *Patterns of Piety*, 217.

44. Johan Huizinga, *The Autumn of the Middle Ages*, trans. Rodney J. Payton and Ulrich Mammitzsch (Chicago: University of Chicago Press, 1996), ix–x.

45. Marina Warner, *Alone of All Her Sex*, 81–102, 315–31; Waller, *Virgin Mary*, 32; Sara Ritchey, *Holy Matter: Changing Perceptions of the Material World in Late Medieval Christianity* (Ithaca, NY: Cornell University Press, 2014), 13–15.

46. *OED*, s.v. "Mariolatry"; Dolan, *Whores of Babylon*, 103.

47. For a representative back-and-forth on this question, see Waller, *Virgin Mary*, 33–34, and Rachel Fulton Brown's response in the *Medieval Review* 12.02.29 (2012). Fulton Brown admits that "Waller is right," although she finds his reasoning (atheist instead of orthodox, psychoanalytic instead of theological) wrong.

48. Graef, *Mary*, 169–71; Eadmer, *Liber de excellentia Virginis Mariae*, in *PL*, ed. J.-P. Migne (Paris: Imprimerie Catholique, 1854), 159:570B.

49. For a polemical early modern take on this comparison, see William Crashaw, *The Iesuites Gospel* (London, 1610), 37–100, available on EEBO.

50. Mary Clayton, *The Cult of the Virgin Mary in Anglo-Saxon England* (Cambridge: Cambridge University Press, 1990), 114; Barbara Newman, *God and the Goddesses: Vision, Poetry, and Belief in the Middle Ages* (Philadelphia: University of Pennsylvania Press, 2003), 254–73.

51. Graef, *Mary*, 249; Rubin, *Mother of God*, 299; Ritchey, *Holy Matter*, 13–15; Bernardino of Siena, *De superadmirabili gratia et gloria Matris Dei*, in *S. Bernardino Senensis Opera Omnia* (Florence: Quaracchi, 1950–65), 2:376.

52. John Foxe, *The Second Volume of the Ecclesiastical History Containing the Acts and Monuments* (London: John Daye, 1570), 1774–77, available on EEBO.

53. For two examples of this language, one medieval and one modern, see Jean Gerson, "Sermo de nativitate Domini," in *Opera Omnia*, ed. L. Ellies du Pin (Antwerp: Sumptibus Societatis, 1706), 3:947; and Graef, *Mary*, xv.

54. Bernard of Clairvaux, "Epistola 174: Ad Canonicos Lugdunensis, de conceptione S. Mariae," in *PL*, ed. J.-P. Migne (Paris: Imprimerie Catholique, 1859), 182:332D–333A; Bernard of Clairvaux, *The Letters of Bernard of Clairvaux*, trans. Bruno Scott James (Kalamazoo, MI: Cistercian, 1998), 292.

55. James France, "The Heritage of Saint Bernard in Medieval Art," in *A Companion to Bernard of Clairvaux*, ed. Brian Patrick McGuire (Leiden: Brill, 2011), 329–35.

56. Sarah Jane Boss, *Empress and Handmaid: On Nature and Gender in the Cult of the Virgin Mary* (New York: Cassell, 2000), 123–55; Nancy Mayberry, "The Controversy over the Immaculate Conception in Medieval and Renaissance Art, Literature, and Society," *Journal of Medieval and Renaissance Studies* 21, no. 2 (1991): 208–9.

57. McSheffrey, *Gender and Heresy*, 146–7; Karma Lochrie, *Heterosyncracies: Female Sexuality When Normal Wasn't* (Minneapolis: University of Minnesota Press, 2005), 54–55; John F. Davis, "The Trials of Thomas Bylney and the English Reformation," *Historical Journal* 24, no. 4 (1981): 779, 781.

58. Of the many studies of the Virgin Mary in late medieval England, I owe the most to the groundbreaking work of Gail McMurray Gibson, from her dissertation, "The Images of Doubt and Belief: Visual Symbolism in the Middle English Plays of Joseph's Troubles about Mary" (PhD diss., University of Virginia, 1975), to her forthcoming *Medieval Drama in Afterlife*, and above all to *The Theater of Devotion: East Anglian Drama and Society in the Late Middle Ages* (Chicago: University of Chicago Press, 1989). The work of Theresa Coletti has also been invaluable, especially "A Feminist Approach to the Corpus Christi Cycles," in *Approaches to Teaching Medieval English Drama*, ed. Richard K. Emmerson (New York: Modern Language Association of America, 1990), 78–89, and "Purity and Danger: The Paradox of Mary's Body and En-gendering of the Infancy Narrative in the English Mystery Cycles," in *Feminist Approaches to the Body in Medieval Literature*, ed. Linda Lomperis and Sarah Stanbury (Philadelphia: University of Pennsylvania Press, 1993), 65–95. See also Waller, *Virgin Mary* and *Walsingham and the English Imagination* (Burlington, VT: Ashgate, 2011). For more on the phrase "dower of the Virgin," see Edmund Waterton, *Pietas Mariana Britannica: A History of English Devotion to the Most Blessed Virgin Marye Mother of God* (London: St. Joseph's Catholic Library, 1879), 11–17; and Dillian Gordon, "The Wilton Diptych: An Introduction," in *The Regal Image of Richard II and the Wilton Diptych*, ed. Dillian Gordon, Lisa Monnas, and Caroline Elam (Coventry, UK: Harvey Miller, 1997), 24–26.

59. Gail McMurray Gibson, *Theater of Devotion*, 138.

60. Mayberry, "Controversy," 208–9. For a more lurid account, see Henry Charles Lea, *A History of the Inquisition of the Middle Ages* (New York: Macmillan, 1906), 3:596–612.

61. Peter of Celle, *Epistola 171*, in *PL*, ed. J.-P. Migne (Paris: Imprimerie Catholique, 1855), 202:614A–B; Graef, *Mary*, 196–97.

62. Georgiana Donavin, *Scribit Mater: Mary and the Language Arts in the Literature of Medieval England* (Washington, DC: Catholic University of America Press, 2012), 3; Gertsman, *Worlds Within*, 44–46, 132–35. See also Henry Adams, "The Dynamo and the Virgin," in *The Education of Henry Adams* (New York: Modern Library, 1931), 384–85.

63. Ritchey, *Holy Matter*, 14–15, 89–90.

64. For more on gender, embodiment, and medieval Christianity, see Caroline Walker Bynum, *Jesus as Mother: Studies in the Spirituality of the High Middle Ages* (Berkeley: University of California Press, 1982), *Holy Feast and Holy Fast: The Religious Significance of Food to Medieval Women* (Berkeley: University of California Press, 1987), and *Fragmentation and Redemption: Essays on Gender and the Human Body in Medieval Religion* (New York: Zone, 1991); Barbara Newman, *Sister of Wisdom: St. Hildegard's Theology of the Feminine* (Berkeley: University of California Press, 1987), *From Virile Woman to WomanChrist: Studies in Medieval Religion and Literature* (Philadelphia: University of Pennsylvania Press, 1995), and *God and the Goddesses*; and Dyan Elliott, *Fallen Bodies: Pollution, Sexuality, and Demonology in the Middle Ages* (Philadelphia: University of Pennsylvania Press, 1999), *Proving Woman: Female Spirituality and Inquisitional Culture in Late Medieval Europe* (Princeton, NJ: Princeton University Press, 2004), and *The Bride of Christ Goes to Hell: Metaphor and Embodiment in the Lives of Pious Women, 200–1500* (Philadelphia: University of Pennsylvania Press, 2012).

65. For more on English Miracles of the Virgin, see Beverly Boyd, *The Middle English Miracles of the Virgin* (San Marino, CA: Huntington Library Press, 1964); R. M. Thomson and M. Winterbottom, eds., *William of Malmesbury: The Miracles of the Blessed Virgin Mary* (Rochester, NY: Boydell, 2015); and Adrienne Williams-Boyarin, ed., *Miracles of the Virgin in Middle English* (Peterborough, ON: Broadview, 2015) and *Miracles of the Virgin in Medieval England: Law and Jewishness in Marian Legends* (Cambridge, UK: D. S. Brewer, 2010). For more on Miracles of the Virgin beyond England, see Claire Waters, *Translating "Clergie": Status, Education, and Salvation in Thirteenth-Century Vernacular Texts* (Philadelphia: University of Pennsylvania Press, 2016), 164–207; Gautier de Coinci, *Les miracles de Nostre Dame*, ed. Frédéric Koenig, 4 vols. (Geneva: Droz, 1955–70); and Kathy M. Krause and Alison Stones, eds., *Gautier de Coinci: Miracles, Music, and Manuscripts* (Turnhout: Brepols, 2006).

66. M. R. James and E. W. Tristram, "The Wall Paintings in Eton College Chapel and in the Lady Chapel of Winchester Cathedral," *Volume of the Walpole Society* 17 (1928–29): 27. See also Michael Camille, *The Gothic Idol: Ideology and Image-Making in Medieval Art* (New York: Cambridge University Press, 1989), 220–41; and Gertsman, *Worlds Within*, 122, 133–35.

67. Alfonso X, *Songs of Holy Mary of Alfonso X, the Wise: A Translation of the Cantigas de Santa Maria*, trans. Kathleen Kulp-Hill (Tempe: Arizona Center for Medieval and Renaissance Studies, 2000), 2, 442.

68. Jan M. Ziolkowski, "Juggling the Middle Ages: The Reception of *Our Lady's Tumbler* and *Le Jongleur de Notre-Dame*," *Studies in Medievalism* 15 (2006): 158–59; Gautier de Coinci, *Of the Tumbler of Our Lady & Other Miracles*, trans. Alice Kemp-Welch (London: Chatto and Windus, 1908); Alfonso X, *Songs of Holy Mary*, 13–14.

69. Williams-Boyarin, *Miracles of the Virgin*, 10, 90–91, 103. For more on this kind of comic trickery in the Judeo-Christian tradition, see Melissa Jackson, *Comedy and Feminist Interpretation of the Hebrew Bible: A Subversive Collaboration* (Oxford: Oxford University Press, 2012).

70. Nicholas Constas, *Proclus of Constantinople and the Cult of the Virgin in Late Antiquity* (Leiden: Brill, 2003), 301–2; Gustaf Aulen, *Christus Victor: An Historical Study of the Three Main Types of the Idea of Atonement* (London: SPCK, 1953), 63–71; John Parker, *The Aesthetics of Antichrist* (Ithaca, NY: Cornell University Press, 2007), 169–77.

71. It has been widely acknowledged for quite some time that these texts represent the Virgin in a fabliau "frame," "context," or "paradigm." See, for example, Joseph L. Baird and Lorrayne Y. Baird, "Fabliau Form and the Hegge *Joseph's Return*," *Chaucer Review* 8, no. 2 (1973): 159–69; Gail McMurray Gibson, "Images of Doubt and Belief," 3, 131–32, 256; Coletti, "Purity and Danger," 65, 72; and Emma Lipton, *Affections of the Mind: The Politics of Sacramental Marriage in Late Medieval English Literature* (Notre Dame, IN: University of Notre Dame Press, 2007), 104, 119–22. It has often been argued that the text "inverts," "resolves," "rebukes," and "conquers" its fabliau predilections—a self-fulfilling interpretation, as the critic becomes the agent of that inversion and resolution. Departing from this paradigm, I have taken Coletti's advice to "give comedy its due"; "Purity and Danger," 65.

72. Carol Symes, *A Common Stage: Theater and Public Life in Medieval Arras* (Ithaca, NY: Cornell University Press, 2007), 80–92. See also *OED*, s.v. "jongleur," "juggler," and "jangler"; and *MED*, s.v. "janglere."

73. Symes, *Common Stage*, 90.

74. My understanding of Mary in early Christianity owes an enormous debt to the pioneering work of Jane Schaberg, especially *The Illegitimacy of Jesus: A Feminist Theological Interpretation of the Infancy Narratives*, 2nd ed. (Sheffield, UK: Sheffield Phoenix, 2006). For more on Mary as Theotokos, see Susan Wessel, *Cyril of Alexandria and the Nestorian Controversy: The Making of a Saint and of a Heretic* (Oxford: Oxford University Press, 2004), 76–81.

75. John 8:41; Mark 6:3; Schaberg, *Illegitimacy of Jesus*, 138–45. For an introduction to Mary in the New Testament, see Raymond E. Brown et al., eds., *Mary in the New Testament* (Philadelphia: Fortress, 1978), and Beverly Roberts Gaventa, *Mary: Glimpses of the Mother of Jesus* (Minneapolis: Fortress, 1999).

76. For the episode of the finding in the Temple, see Luke 2:41–52. This and all subsequent quotations from the Bible in English, unless otherwise noted, are taken from the Douay-Rheims, available on the Bible in English Database.

77. Mark 3:31–5; Raymond Brown et al., *Mary in the New Testament*, 167–70.

78. This translation is taken from the King James Bible, available on the Bible in English Database. See also Ernst Haenchen, *John 1: A Commentary on the Gospel of John, Chapters 1–6*, trans. Robert W. Funk, Hermeneia (Philadelphia: Fortress, 1984), 172–73.

79. See Terry Jones et al., *Monty Python's Life of Brian*, Criterion Collection 61 (New York: Janus Films, 1999). See also Max Ernst, "The Blessed Virgin Chastising the Child Jesus before Three Witnesses," in Anthony Julius, *Transgressions: The Offences of Art* (Chicago: University of Chicago Press, 2003), 159–60; and Leo Steinberg, "Max Ernst's Blasphemy," *New York Review of Books*, September 22, 2005.

80. Geoffrey Chaucer, *Troilus and Criseyde*, 3.12–21. This and all subsequent quotations from Chaucer are from Larry Benson, ed., *The Riverside Chaucer*, 3rd ed. (Boston: Houghton Mifflin Press, 1987). See also Giovanni Boccaccio, *Il Filostrato*, trans. Robert P. Roberts and Anna Bruni Seldis (New York: Garland, 1986), 172–73 (3.76); Camille, *Gothic Idol*, 220–41.

81. Graef, *Mary*, 249; Bernardino of Siena, *De superadmirabili gratia et gloria Matris Dei*, 2:376.

82. For an introduction to the study of early English drama, see Janette Dillon, *The Cambridge Introduction to Early English Theatre* (Cambridge: Cambridge University Press, 2006); and Richard Beadle and Alan J. Fletcher, eds., *The Cambridge Companion to Medieval English Theatre*, 2nd ed. (Cambridge: Cambridge University Press, 2008). For more on the association between theater and the Incarnation, see Sarah Beckwith, *Signifying God: Social Relation and Symbolic Act in the York Corpus Christi Plays* (Chicago: University of Chicago Press, 2001), esp. 59–60; and Gertsman, *Worlds Within*, 94–96.

83. For more on the festival of Corpus Christi, see Miri Rubin, *Corpus Christi: The Eucharist in Late Medieval Culture* (Cambridge: Cambridge University Press, 1991); Sarah Beckwith, *Christ's Body: Identity, Culture and Society in Late Medieval Writings* (London: Routledge, 1996); and Clifford Davidson, *Festivals and Plays in Late Medieval Britain* (Aldershot, UK: Ashgate, 2007), 49–79. For an important caveat, see Alexandra F. Johnston, "What If No Texts Survived? External Evidence for Early English Drama," in *Contexts for Early English Drama*, ed. Marianne G. Briscoe and John C. Coldewey (Bloomington: Indiana University Press, 1989), 11–12.

84. Frederick W. Fairholt, ed., *The Civic Garland: A Collection of Songs from London Pageants*, in *Early English Poetry, Ballads, and Popular Literature of the Middle Ages* (London: Percy Society, 1846), 19:xxxiii. For more on this sacrificial imagery, see Merrall Llewelyn Price, "Re-membering the Jews: Theatrical Violence in the N-Town Marian Plays," *Comparative Drama* 41, no. 4 (2007–8): 454; Gertsman, *Worlds Within*, 50–53, 70–71, 75–76; and Cleo McNelly Kearns, *The Virgin Mary, Monotheism and Sacrifice* (Cambridge: Cambridge University Press, 2008).

85. Gail McMurray Gibson, "Writing before the Eye: The N-Town 'Woman Taken in Adultery' and the Medieval Ministry Play," *Comparative Drama* 27, no. 4 (1993): 401; Gail McMurray Gibson, *Theater of Devotion*, 156–66; Gertsman, *Worlds Within*, 56.

86. Douglas Sugano, ed., *The N-Town Plays*, TEAMS Middle English Texts (Kalamazoo, MI: Medieval Institute Publications, 2007), 12.31. Unless otherwise noted, all subsequent references to the N-Town plays refer to Sugano's edition. Other scholarly editions include K. S. Block, ed., *Ludus Coventriæ: or, The plaie called Corpus Christi: Cotton ms. Vespasian D. VIII*, EETS (London: Oxford University Press, 1922); Peter Meredith and Stanley J. Kahrl, eds., *The N-Town Plays: A Facsimile of British Library MS Cotton Vespasian D VIII*, Leeds Texts and Monographs: Medieval Drama Facsimiles 4 (Leeds: University of Leeds, 1977); Stephen Spector, ed., *The N-Town Play: Cotton MS*

Vespasian D. 8, 2 vols., EETS (Oxford: Oxford University Press, 1991); and Peter Meredith, ed., *The Mary Play from the N. Town Manuscript* (London: Longman, 1987). In this book, I have not made use of Meredith's *Mary Play*; I agree with Gail McMurray Gibson's take on this edition; *Theater of Devotion*, 212.

87. N-Town 11.78, 11.201–2; *MED*, s.v. "wede" 2; *OED*, s.v. "weed" 2. See also Beckwith, *Christ's Body*, 61; Gertsman, *Worlds Within*, 94.

88. Julian of Norwich, *The Writings of Julian of Norwich*, ed. Nicholas Watson and Jacqueline Jenkins (Philadelphia: Pennsylvania State University Press, 2005), 2.2079.

89. Erich Auerbach, *Mimesis: The Representation of Reality in Western Literature*, trans. Willard R. Trask (Princeton, NJ: Princeton University Press, 2003), 151.

90. For representative carnivalesque readings of medieval drama, see Mikhail Bakhtin, *Rabelais and His World*, trans. Helene Iswolsky (Bloomington: Indiana University Press, 1984), 15; and Kristina Simeonova, "The Aesthetic Function of the Carnivalesque in Medieval Drama," in *Bakhtin, Carnival and Other Subjects*, ed. David Shepherd (Atlanta: Rodopi, 1993), 70–79.

91. Alexandra F. Johnston and Margaret Rogerson, eds., *York*, REED (Toronto: University of Toronto Press, 1979), 1:47–48, 2:732; Margaret Rogerson, "Audience Responses and the York Corpus Christi Play," in *Staging Scripture: Biblical Drama, 1350–1600*, ed. Peter Happé and Wim Hüsken (Leiden: Brill, 2016), 360–83.

92. Chaucer, "Wife of Bath's Prologue," *Canterbury Tales*, 551–59; Lynne Staley, ed., *The Book of Margery Kempe* (Kalamazoo, MI: Medieval Institute Publications, 1996), 1.1.1613–25, 1.2.3302–13. All subsequent quotations of Kempe derive from this edition. See also Jesse Njus, "Margery Kempe and the Spectatorship of Medieval Drama," *Fifteenth-Century Studies* 38 (2013): 135.

93. Liana De Girolami, ed., *Giorgio Vasari's Prefaces: Art and Theory* (New York: Peter Lang, 2012), 144, 159; Giorgio Vasari, *Le Vite de' più eccellenti pittori, scultori, e architettori da Cimabue insino a' tempi nostril* (Turin, Italy: Einaudi, 1986), 1:100; Edmund Burke, *A philosophical enquiry into the origin of our ideas of the sublime and beautiful*, 2nd ed. (London: R. and J. Dodsley, 1759), 2.4.109.

94. Margaret Kean, ed., *John Milton's "Paradise Lost": A Sourcebook* (London: Routledge, 2005), 28; M. de Voltaire, *An Essay upon the Civil Wars of France, Extracted from Curious Manuscripts* (London: Samuel Jallasson, 1727), 103; George Gordon Byron, *Cain, A Mystery* (London: H. Gray, 1822), v. See also James Wright, *Historia Histrionica* (London: G. Croom, 1699), 17–18; Thomas Warton, *The History of English Poetry, from the Close of the Eleventh to the Commencement of the Eighteenth Century*, 3 vols. (London, 1778), 2:373–74.

95. For more on this treatise, see Sharon Aronson-Lehavi, *Street Scenes: Late Medieval Acting and Performance* (New York: Palgrave Macmillan, 2011). "A tretise of miraclis pleyinge," in *Selections from Wycliffite Writings*, ed. Anne Hudson, Medieval Academy Reprints for Teaching 38 (Toronto: University of Toronto Press, 1997), 97–104.

96. Ibid., p. 97, line 28.

97. Ibid., p. 99, lines 92–93.

98. Ibid., p. 99, lines 73–74.

99. Ibid., p. 98, lines 44–45.

100. N-Town 12.315; *MED*, s.v. "fere."

101. N-Town 12.43–46; *MED*, s.v. "japen."

102. As Sarah Kay writes, Mary "specializes in lost lives and lost souls"; *Courtly Contradictions: The Emergence of the Literary Object in the Twelfth Century* (Stanford, CA: Stanford University Press, 2002), 184.

103. Margaret M. Raftery, ed., *Mary of Nemmegen* (Leiden: E. J. Brill, 1991); Therese Decker and Martin W. Walsh, eds., *Mariken van Nieumeghen: A Bilingual Edition* (Columbia, SC: Camden House, 1994).

104. Raftery, *Mary of Nemmegen*, 34.

105. Waller, *Virgin Mary*, 55, 67–68.

106. For more on the *Miracles de Nostre Dame par personnages*, see Gaston Bruno Paulin Paris, Ulysse Robert, and François Bonnardot, eds., *Miracles de Nostre Dame par personnages* (Paris: Firmin Didot et Cie, 1876), and Donald Maddox and Sara Sturm-Maddox, eds., *Parisian Confraternity Drama of the Fourteenth Century: The Miracles de Nostre Dame par personnages* (Turnhout: Brepols, 2008). For more on Lincoln, see Alan H. Nelson, *The Medieval English Stage: Corpus Christi Pageants and Plays* (Chicago: University of Chicago Press, 1974), 100–118; and James Stokes, ed., *Lincolnshire*, 2 vols., REED (Toronto: University of Toronto Press, 2009), 2:409, 2:413–16.

107. Stokes, *Lincolnshire*, 1:143, 2:417; Kenneth M. Cameron and Stanley J. Kahrl, "Staging the N-Town Cycle," *Theatre Notebook* 21 (1967): 130; Nelson, *Medieval English Stage*, 105, 110–11.

108. For representative critiques along these lines, see Graef, *Mary*, 250; Huizinga, *Autumn of the Middle Ages*, 182; and R. W. Southern, *The Making of the Middle Ages* (New Haven, CT: Yale University Press, 1953), 248.

109. For more on this sense of shock, see Evans, "Virginities," 21–22.

110. For a comparison of English and Continental theatrical representations of the Virgin during this period, see Elizabeth A. Witt, *Contrary Marys in Medieval English and French Drama* (New York: Peter Lang, 1995), esp. 4, 97, 131; and Lynette Muir, *The Biblical Drama of Medieval Europe* (Cambridge: Cambridge University Press, 1995), esp. 89–91, 93–95, 98–101.

111. See, for example, V. A. Kolve, *The Play Called Corpus Christi* (Stanford, CA: Stanford University Press, 1966), 139; Eleanor Prosser, *Drama and Religion in the English Mystery Plays: A Re-evaluation* (Stanford, CA: Stanford University Press, 1961), 96; and Rosemary Woolf, *The English Mystery Plays* (Berkeley: University of California Press, 1972), 79.

112. See, for instance, William Hone, *Ancient Mysteries Described: English Miracle Plays Founded on Apocryphal New Testament Story* (London: printed for William Hone, 1823), 204–5. For more on antipapism's influence on academic medievalism during this period, see Eamon Duffy, "A. G. Dickens and the Late Medieval Church," *Historical Research* 77 (2004): 98–110.

113. For more on obscenity in late medieval literature and culture, see Nicola McDonald, ed., *Medieval Obscenities* (Rochester, NY: Boydell for York Medieval Press, 2006); Nicole Nolan Sidhu, *Indecent Exposure: Gender, Politics, and Obscene Comedy in Middle English Literature* (Philadelphia: University of Pennsylvania Press, 2016); Carissa Harris, *Obscene Pedagogies: Transgressive Talk and Sexual Education in Late Medieval Britain* (Ithaca, NY: Cornell University Press, 2018).

114. Hence the association between the Virgin/Maid Marian and Robin Hood. See Anthony James Pollard, *Imagining Robin Hood: The Late-Medieval Stories in Historical Context* (London: Routledge, 2004), 14–15.

115. For more on these rituals of humiliation, Patrick Geary, *Furta Sacra: Thefts of Relics in the Central Middle Ages* (Princeton, NJ: Princeton University Press, 1978), 134–35. See also Patrick Geary, "Humiliation of Saints," in *Saints and Their Cults: Studies in Religious Sociology, Folklore, and History*, ed. Stephen Wilson (Cambridge: Cambridge University Press, 1983), 123–40; and Lester Little, *Benedictine Maledictions: Liturgical Cursing in Romanesque France* (Ithaca, NY: Cornell University Press, 1996), 26–30, 83–85, 133.

116. For an introduction to the N-Town plays, see Theresa Coletti, "N-Town Plays," in *Dictionary of Literary Biography: Old and Middle English Literature*, ed. Jeffrey Helterman and Jerome Mitchell (Detroit: Gale Research, 1994), 146: 405–14. For an exhaustive study of N-Town in its geographic and historical context, see Penny Granger, *The N-Town Play: Drama and Liturgy in Medieval East Anglia* (Cambridge, UK: D. S. Brewer, 2009).

117. Lawrence Clopper, *Drama, Play, and Game: English Festive Culture in the Medieval and Early Modern Period* (Chicago: University of Chicago Press, 2001), 186–87; Gail McMurray Gibson, "Manuscript as Sacred Object: Robert Hegge's N-Town Plays," *Journal of Medieval and Early Modern Studies* 44, no. 3 (2014): 503–29.

118. For more on the function of banns, see Matthew Sergi, "Beyond Theatrical Marketing: Play Banns in the Records of Kent, Sussex, and Lincolnshire," *Medieval English Theatre* 36 (2014), 3–23. For more on N-Town's title, see Walter Wilson Greg, *Bibliographical and Textual Problems of the English Miracle Cycles* (London: Alexander Moring, 1914), 365.

119. For more on civic records and the York cycle, see Nicole R. Rice and Margaret Aziza Pappano, *The Civic Cycles: Artisan Drama and Identity in Premodern England*, ReFormations: Medieval and Early Modern (Notre Dame, IN: University of Notre Dame Press, 2015). For evidence of the performance of the N-Town plays, see Spector, *N-Town Play*, 1:xxiii–xxiv, 2:544–47.

120. Gail McMurray Gibson, "Bury St. Edmunds, Lydgate, and the N-Town Cycle," *Speculum* 56, no. 1 (1981): 56–90; Douglas Sugano, "'This Game Wel Pleyd in Good A-ray': The N-Town Playbooks and East Anglian Games," *Comparative Drama* 28, no. 2 (1994): 230–31. See also Ken Farnhill, *Guilds and the Parish Community in Late Medieval East Anglia, c. 1470–1550* (Rochester, NY: Boydell, 2001).

121. Gail McMurray Gibson, "Manuscript as Sacred Object," 504. For more on East Anglia, see Gail McMurray Gibson, *Theater of Devotion*, esp. 19–46; Richard Beadle, "Prolegomena to a Literary Geography of Later Medieval Norfolk," in *Regionalism in Late Medieval Manuscripts and Texts*, ed. Felicity Riddy (Woodbridge, UK: Brewer, 1991), 89–102; Victor Scherb, *Staging Faith: East Anglian Drama in the Later Middle Ages* (Madison, NJ: Fairleigh Dickinson University Press, 2001); Theresa Coletti, *Mary Magdalene and the Drama of Saints: Theater, Gender, and Religion in Late Medieval England* (Philadelphia: University of Pennsylvania Press, 2004), esp. 36–49; and Granger, *N-Town Play*, esp. 40–50.

122. This is often said. See, for example, Theresa Coletti, "Devotional Iconography in the N-Town Marian Plays," *Comparative Drama* 11, no. 1 (1977): 22; Gail McMurray

Gibson, *Theater of Devotion*, 1–2; Waller, *Virgin Mary*, 55, 62–79; and Sidhu, *Indecent Exposure*, 208–11.

123. Spector, *N-Town Play*, 2:436–37, 2:441–42, 2:446–47.

124. Gertsman, *Worlds Within*, 3.

125. Gail McMurray Gibson, *Theater of Devotion*, 215; Gertsman, *Worlds Within*, 2–3.

126. Gertsman, *Worlds Within*, 48; Gail McMurray Gibson, *Theater of Devotion*, 144. See also Martin Stevens, *Four Middle English Mystery Cycles: Textual, Contextual and Critical Interpretations* (Princeton, NJ: Princeton University Press, 1987), 244–47.

127. For a detailed description of this spectacle, see Gail McMurray Gibson, *Theater of Devotion*, 144–52.

128. N-Town 15.218–21, 15.246–53. See also Gail McMurray Gibson, "Scene and Obscene," 16.

129. Woolf, *English Mystery Plays*, 174; Muir, *Biblical Drama*, 96–97.

130. N-Town 14.86–87, 14.96–97, 14.166.

131. For more on the word *whore*, see Ruth Mazo Karras, *Common Women: Prostitution and Sexuality in Medieval England* (Oxford: Oxford University Press, 1998), 29–30.

132. For this particular stage direction, see Meredith and Kahrl, *N-Town Plays*, xxv, fol. 81v.

133. Arthur Percival Rossiter, *English Drama from Early Times to the Elizabethans: Its Background, Origins, and Developments* (London: Hutchinson's University Library, 1950), 71.

134. Decades after its publication, *The Play Called Corpus Christi* was named "the critical work most often assigned for supplementary reading" when teaching early English drama; Richard K. Emmerson, "Required and Recommended Readings for Students," in *Approaches to Teaching Medieval English Drama*, ed. Richard K. Emmerson (New York: Modern Language Association of America, 1990), 14–15. The recent celebration of the fiftieth anniversary of *The Play Called Corpus Christi* at the Folger Shakespeare Library (on December 5, 2016) only confirmed the book's continuing relevance and importance.

135. Kolve, *Play Called Corpus Christi*, 138–39.

136. Ibid., 139.

137. Ibid. For Gail McMurray Gibson's take on this passage, see "Scene and Obscene," 20.

138. Kolve, *Play Called Corpus Christi*, 139. Following Kolve, critics have tended to interpret N-Town's detractions of the Virgin as "crude," "misogynist," "carnal," "literal," "idolatrous," and "malicious" errors. It is argued that because, as David Bevington so aptly puts it, God gets "the last laugh" (that is, on Doomsday), the reader must anticipate this inevitability by resolving these errors as they unfold, even and especially when the text may appear to hesitate or fail to do so. David Bevington, "The Corpus Christi Cycle," in *Medieval Drama*, ed. David Bevington (Boston: Houghton Mifflin, 1975), 240. See, for example, Richard Moll, "Staging Disorder: Charivari in the *N-Town* Cycle," *Comparative Drama* 35, no. 2 (2001): 148; Matthew J. Kinservik, "The Struggle over Mary's Body: Theological and Dramatic Resolution in the N-Town Assumption Play," *Journal of English and Germanic Philology* 95, no. 2 (1996): 191; and William Fitzhenry, "The N-Town Plays and the Politics of Metatheater," *Studies in Philology* 100, no. 1

(2003): 34, 36. For an exception to this pattern, see Helen Cushman's brilliant "Handling Knowledge: Holy Bodies in the Middle English Mystery Plays," *Journal of Medieval and Early Modern Studies* 47, no. 2 (2017): 279–304, which interprets N-Town's apparent abuse of the Virgin as an integral part of a rigorous interrogation designed to provoke thought and deepen faith.

139. Waller, *Virgin Mary*, 19–20.

140. For a critique of this approach, see Theresa Coletti, "Reading REED: History and the Records of Early English Drama," in *Literary Practice and Social Change in Britain, 1380–1530*, ed. Lee Patterson (Berkeley: University of California Press, 1990), 248–284.

141. Even Waller, a rare advocate for a feminist, sex-positive interpretation of the Virgin, undercuts his own reading by admitting that he can find no implicit or explicit evidence from the Middle Ages to prove his point; instead, he relies on the feminist theology and psychoanalytic theory of the present. Waller, *Virgin Mary*, vii, 6, 41, 68.

142. I have been inspired by Coletti's suggestion that feminists should "study the diversity of roles and behaviors of the Virgin Mary" (or rather, as she later puts it, "Virgin Marys") in early English drama in order to historicize doctrines that seem "timeless and absolute"; "Feminist Approach," 86.

143. Steinberg, *Sexuality of Christ in Renaissance Art and in Modern Oblivion*, 3–5, 56.

144. My reading here builds on Kate Koppelman's studies of Mary's paradoxical and unstable meaning in the medieval period. See "Devotional Ambivalence: The Virgin Mary as 'Empresse of Helle,'" *Essays in Medieval Studies* 18, no. 1 (2001): 67–82; and "Becoming Her Man: Transcoding in Medieval Marian Literature," *Exemplaria* 22, no. 3 (2010): 203–4.

145. For more on the hermeneutics of early English drama, see Ruth Nisse's invaluable *Defining Acts: Drama and the Politics of Interpretation in Late Medieval England* (Notre Dame, IN: University of Notre Dame Press, 2005).

146. Giovanni Boccaccio, *Esposizioni sopra la Comedia di Dante*, ed. Giorgio Padoan, in *Tutte le opera di Giovanni Boccaccio*, ed. Vittore Branca (Verona: Arnoldo Mondadori, 1965), 6:1.2.18; Giovanni Boccaccio, *Boccaccio's Expositions on Dante's Comedy,* trans. Michael Papio (Toronto: University of Toronto Press, 2009), 82. My understanding of the ambiguity of medieval allegory is indebted to Noah Guynn's *Allegory and Sexual Ethics in the High Middle Ages* (New York: Palgrave Macmillan, 2007).

147. Diehl, *Staging Reform*, 170, 172–81.

148. See Jack T. Chick, *The Man in Black* (Ontario, CA: Chick, 2003); Jack T. Chick, *Why Is Mary Crying?* (Ontario, CA: Chick, 1987); Mark Kermode, *The Exorcist*, 2nd ed. (London: British Film Institute, 1998), 37; Randall Fallows, "*South Park* Heretics: Confronting Orthodoxy through the Theater of the Absurd," in *Taking South Park Seriously*, ed. Jeffrey Andrew Weinstock (Albany: State University of New York Press, 2008), 165–72; and "The Virgin Mary Defiled on *South Park*," *Catholic League for Religious and Civil Rights*, August 3, 2006.

149. See, for example, Marina Warner, *Alone of All Her Sex*, 35; and Ulrich Luz, *Matthew 1–7: A Commentary*, trans. James E. Crouch, Hermeneia (Minneapolis: Fortress, 2007), 100.

150. Peter Meredith, "Original-Staging Production of English Medieval Plays: Ideals, Evidence, and Practice," in *Popular Drama in Northern Europe in the Later Middle*

Ages: A Symposium, ed. Flemming G. Andersen et al. (Odense, Denmark: Odense University Press, 1988), 65–66.

151. John R. Elliott, *Playing God: Medieval Mysteries on the Modern Stage* (Toronto: University of Toronto Press, 1989), 44–47.

152. See Algernon Charles Swinburne, *Major Poems and Selected Prose*, ed. Jerome McGann and Charles L. Sligh (New Haven, CT: Yale University Press, 2004), 103; Karl Marx, *Marx: Early Political Writings*, ed. Joseph O'Malley (Cambridge: Cambridge University Press, 1994), 57–58; Rainer Maria Rilke, *The Life of the Virgin Mary*, trans. C. F. MacIntyre (Westport, CT: Greenwood, 1947), 30–31; and Colm Tóibín, *The Testament of Mary* (New York: Scribner, 2012), 58.

153. Elizabeth Cady Stanton, *The Woman's Bible*, 1895–98 (Boston: Northeastern University Press, 1993), 2:113–14; Simone de Beauvoir, *The Second Sex*, trans. Constance Borde and Sheila Malovany-Chevallier (New York: Knopf, 2010), 180. See also Mary Daly, *Beyond God the Father: Toward a Philosophy of Women's Liberation* (Boston: Beacon, 1973), esp. 149, 214; Kristeva, "Stabat Mater," 140–41; and Marina Warner, *Alone of All Her Sex*, xxi, 77–78.

154. Marina Warner, *Alone of All Her Sex*, 221–23.

155. Kristeva, "Stabat Mater," 139.

Chapter 1

1. Muir, *Biblical Drama*, 96–97.

2. Luz, *Matthew 1–7*, 93–94. In this chapter, my understanding of the Gospels of Matthew and Luke depends on the work of the New Testament scholars François Bovon, Bart Ehrman, Joseph A. Fitzmyer, Ulrich Luz, and, most of all, Jane Schaberg.

3. Elizabeth Baldwin, Lawrence M. Clopper, and David Mills, eds., *Cheshire Including Chester*, REED (Toronto: University of Toronto Press, 2007), 1.147.

4. N-Town 14.86–88, 14.205, 14.218.

5. Schaberg, *Illegitimacy of Jesus*, 43–44.

6. Bart D. Ehrman and Zlatko Pleše, eds., *The Apocryphal Gospels: Texts and Translations* (New York: Oxford University Press, 2012), 50–51. All subsequent references to the apocryphal Infancy Gospels of James and Pseudo-Matthew are taken from this source.

7. Schaberg, *Illegitimacy of Jesus*, 43; Bart D. Ehrman, *The New Testament: A Historical Introduction to the Early Christian Writings* (Oxford: Oxford University Press, 2004), 155–56.

8. "Ut tolleretur excusatio virginibus quae, propter incautelam suam, non vitant infamiam." Thomas Aquinas, *Summa Theologiae*, vol. 51, ed. Thomas R. Heath (London: Blackfriars, 1969), 58–61.

9. Matthew 12:46, 13:55–57; Luke 8:19–21; Mark 3:31; Galatians 1:19; Acts 1:14.

10. Tertullian, *De monogamia*, in *PL*, ed. J.-P Migne (Paris: Imprimerie Catholique, 1844), 2:939B; Tertullian, *Treatises on Marriage and Remarriage*, trans. William P. Le Saint, Ancient Christian Writers 13 (New York: Newman, 1951), 86.

11. For an introduction to the Gospel of James, see Ehrman and Pleše, *Apocryphal Gospels*, 31–38; Schaberg, *Illegitimacy of Jesus*, 164–66; and Glancy, *Corporal Knowledge*, 106–17.

12. Ehrman and Pleše, *Apocryphal Gospels*, 50–51, 88–93.

13. Ibid., 51.

14. Marina Warner, *Alone of All Her Sex*, 23, 33.

15. Italics mine. Luz, *Matthew 1–7*, 98; Jerome, *De perpetua virginitate B. Mariae adversus Helvidium*, in *PL*, ed. J.-P. Migne (Paris: Imprimerie Catholique, 1845), 23:193–216; Jerome, "On the Perpetual Virginity of the Virgin Mary against Helvidius," in *Jerome: Dogmatic and Polemic Works*, ed. John N. Hritzu, Fathers of the Church 53 (Washington, DC: Catholic University of America Press, 2010), 23–37.

16. "Si enim in virum sanctum fornicatio non cadit, et aliam eum uxorem habuisse non scribitur: Mariae autem quam putatus est habuisse, custos potius fuit, quam maritus: relinquitur, virginem eum mansisse cum Maria, qui pater Domini meruit appellari." Jerome, *Adversus Helvidium*, 213.

17. Dyan Elliott, *Spiritual Marriage: Sexual Abstinence in Medieval Wedlock* (Princeton, NJ: Princeton University Press, 1993), 3.

18. Frank Leslie Cross and Elizabeth A. Livingstone, eds., *The Oxford Dictionary of the Christian Church*, 3rd ed. (Oxford: Oxford University Press, 2005), 906.

19. Sara Lipton, *Images of Intolerance: Representations of Jews and Judaism in the Bible Moralisée* (Berkeley: University of California Press, 1999), 15–18.

20. Francesca Alberti, "'Divine Cuckolds': Joseph and Vulcan in Renaissance Art and Literature," in *Cuckoldry, Impotence and Adultery in Europe (15th–17th century)*, ed. Sara F. Matthews-Grieco (Burlington, VT: Ashgate, 2014), 153. See also this sixteenth-century Dutch stage direction, quoted by J. Vriend, which protests against the custom of dressing Joseph "like a buffoon or a vagabond"; J. Vriend, *The Blessed Virgin Mary in the Medieval Drama of England* (Pumerend, Holland: J. Muuusses, 1928), 61–62.

21. Heinz Schreckenberg, *The Jews in Christian Art: An Illustrated History* (New York: Continuum, 1996), 125 (fig. 1), 127 (fig. 6), 131 (fig. 13, 14), 135 (fig. 22), 136 (fig. 23), 139 (fig. 30); Steinberg, *Sexuality of Christ*, 48 (fig. 59), 72 (fig. 77), 79 (fig. 84), 132 (fig. 145), 156 (fig. 171). See also Kolve, *Play Called Corpus Christi*, 247–49.

22. My take on Joseph falls in line with the readings of Louise O. Vasvari, Francesca Alberti, and Anne Williams: Louise O. Vasvari, "Joseph on the Margin: The Mérode Tryptic and Medieval Spectacle," *Mediaevalia* 18 (1995): 163–89; Alberti, "'Divine Cuckolds'"; Anne Williams, "Satirizing the Sacred: Humor in Saint Joseph's Veneration and Early Modern Art," *Journal of Historians of Netherlandish Art* 10, no. 1 (2018), 1–45. For a more dignified representation of this saint, see Pamela Sheingorn, "Fragments of the Biography of Joseph the Carpenter," in *Framing the Family: Narrative and Representation in the Medieval and Early Modern Periods*, ed. Rosalynn Voaden and Diane Wolfthal (Tempe: Arizona Center for Medieval and Renaissance Studies, 2005), 161–80, esp. 161–62; Carolyn Wilson, *St. Joseph in Italian Renaissance Society and Art: New Directions and Interpretations* (Philadelphia: Saint Joseph's University Press, 2001); and Brian Patrick McGuire, *Jean Gerson and the Last Medieval Reformation* (University Park: Pennsylvania State University Press, 2005), 231–39.

23. Newman, *God and the Goddesses*, 284; Huizinga, *Autumn of the Middle Ages*, 193–96.

24. Plautus, *Amphitryon*, ed. and trans. Wolfgang de Melo, Loeb Classical Library 60 (Cambridge, MA: Harvard University Press, 2011), 14–133; Laura Kendrick, "Medieval

Vernacular Versions of Ancient Comedy," in *Ancient Comedy and Reception: Essays in Honor of Jeffrey Henderson*, ed. S. Douglas Olson (Berlin: de Gruyter, 2014), 377–96.

25. Kendrick, "Medieval Vernacular Versions of Ancient Comedy," 382. For an introduction to the fabliaux, see R. Howard Bloch, introduction to *The Fabliaux*, trans. Nathaniel E. Dubin (New York: Norton, 2013), xiii–xxv; John Hines, *The Fabliau in English* (New York: Longman, 1993).

26. See, for example, the Wife of Bath's triumph over Jankyn in Chaucer, "Wife of Bath's Prologue," *Canterbury Tales*, 595–825.

27. Alastair Matthews, "Performing Aristotle's Lessons," in *Aspects of the Performative in Medieval Culture*, ed. Manuele Gragnolati and Almut Suerbaum (Berlin: de Gruyter, 2010), 252–75.

28. Lesley Johnson, "Women on Top: Antifeminism in the Fabliaux," *Modern Language Review* 78, no. 2 (1983): 298–307.

29. See Herbert Friedmann, *The Symbolic Goldfinch: Its History and Significance in European Devotional Art* (New York: Pantheon Books, 1946), 7–35.

30. F. Vaz da Silva, "The Madonna and the Cuckoo: An Exploration in European Symbolic Conceptions," *Society for Comparative Study of Society and History* 46, no. 2 (2004): 273–99.

31. For more on cuckoos, see Nick Davies, *Cuckoo: Cheating by Nature* (London: Bloomsbury, 2015).

32. Alberti, "'Divine Cuckolds,'" 149–59.

33. Ibid., 177n25, 177n27.

34. Louise O. Vasvari, "Joseph on the Margin: The Mérode Tryptic and Medieval Spectacle," *Mediaevalia* 18 (1995): 168.

35. Williams, "Satirizing the Sacred," 22, reads "the elusive furry mouse" as a symbolic vagina, taking off from R. Howard Bloch's inclusion of *sorisete* (mouse) in his catalog of fabliau codes for female genitalia in "Modest Maidens and Modified Nouns: Obscenity in the Fabliaux," in *Obscenity: Social Control and Artistic Creation in the European Middle Ages*, ed. Jan M. Ziolkowski (Leiden: Brill, 1998), 301.

36. Augustine, *Sermones*, in *PL*, ed. J.-P. Migne (Paris: Imprimerie Catholique, 1841), 38:2.1210. See also Constas, *Proclus of Constantinople*, 301–2.

37. For a scholarly account of the infamous televised debate between Monty Python and the bishop of Southwark, see Richard A. Burridge, "The Church of England's Life of Python—Or 'What the Bishop Saw,'" in *Jesus and Brian: Exploring the Historical Jesus and His Times via Monty Python's "Life of Brian,"* ed. Joan E. Taylor (London: Bloomsbury, 2015), 19–42. For the debate between Celsus and Origen, see Origen, *Contra Celsum*, trans. Henry Chadwick (Cambridge: Cambridge University Press, 1953), 37–38.

38. Which in turn reworks the story of the blossoming of Aaron's rod from Numbers 17:1–8; for the association between Aaron's rod and the Nativity, see Albert C. Labriola and John W. Smeltz, eds., *The Bible of the Poor: A Facsimile and Edition of the British Library Blockbook C.9 d.2* (Pittsburg: Duquesne University Press, 1990), 146–47.

39. This and all subsequent references to the York plays are taken from Clifford Davidson, ed., *The York Corpus Christi Plays*, TEAMS Middle English Text Series (Kalamazoo, MI: Medieval Institute Publications, 2011), and Richard Beadle, ed., *The York*

Plays: A Critical Edition of the York Corpus Christi Play as Recorded in British Library Additional MS 35290, 2 vols., EETS (Oxford: Oxford University Press, 2009–13).

40. Ehrman and Pleše, *Apocryphal Gospels*, 50–51, 90–91; Charlton T. Lewis and Charles Short, eds., *A Latin Dictionary* (Oxford: Clarendon, 1879), s.v. "virga." This narrative is also included in York 13 and Towneley 10, but as flashbacks incorporated into monologues rather than as dramatic action.

41. Peter Brown, *The Body and Society: Men, Women, and Sexual Renunciation in Early Christianity*, 2nd ed. (New York: Columbia University Press, 2008), 17. See also Danielle Jacquart and Claude Alexandre Thomasset, *Sexuality and Medicine in the Middle Ages* (New York: Polity, 1988), 31, 79–81, 143, 169–73; Thomas Laqueur, *Making Sex: Body and Gender from the Greeks to Freud* (Cambridge, MA: Harvard University Press, 1990), 45.

42. Helen Rodnite Lemay, ed., *Women's Secrets: A Translation of Pseudo-Albertus Magnus' "De Secretis Mulierum" with Commentaries* (Albany: State University of New York Press, 1992), 137.

43. Frederick Millet Salter, *Mediaeval Drama in Chester* (Toronto: University of Toronto Press, 1955), 103–4.

44. For more on this sexual discourse of idolatry, see Sarah Stanbury, *The Visual Object of Desire in Late Medieval England* (Philadelphia: University of Pennsylvania Press, 2008), 30–32.

45. Gail McMurray Gibson, *Theatre of Devotion*, 152; Schreckenberg, *Jews in Christian Art*, 120 (fig. 2), 63 (fig. 20).

46. See Ehrman and Pleše, *Apocryphal Gospels*, 50–1, 90–1.

47. All references to Dunbar's *Tretis of the Tua Maritt Wemen and the Wedo* come from William Dunbar, *The Complete Works*, ed. John Conlee, TEAMS Middle English Texts (Kalamazoo, MI: Medieval Institute Publications, 2004). For more on Dunbar, see Sally Mapstone, ed., *William Dunbar, 'The Nobill Poyet': Essays in Honour of Priscilla Bawcutt* (East Linton, Scotland: Tuckwell Press, 2001).

48. This and all subsequent references to the Chester plays are taken from R. M. Lumiansky and David Mills, eds., *The Chester Mystery Cycle*, vol. 1, EETS (London: Oxford University Press, 1974).

49. For more on the fabliau convention of "the husband's unexpected return," see Baird and Baird, "Fabliau Form," 161.

50. The resemblance between *Amphitryon* and "Joseph's Doubt" was not lost on Johannes Burmeister (1576–1638), who combined the two in his Latin *Sacri Mater Virgo*, published in 1621. For more on this lost play, see Joannes Burmeister, *Aulularia and Other Inversions of Plautus*, ed. Michael Fontaine (Leuven: Leuven University Press, 2015), 203–37.

51. Jacquart and Thomasset, *Sexuality and Medicine*, 24; Lemay, *Women's Secrets*, 66.

52. Sugano, *N-Town Plays*, 375; Ambrose, *De institutione virginis*, in *PL*, ed. J.-P. Migne (Paris: Imprimerie Catholique, 1845), 16:320.

53. My reading here expands on Gail McMurray Gibson's interpretation of Joseph's entrance as a parody of the Incarnation; see *Theater of Devotion*, 152–54, and "'Porta haec clausa erit': Comedy, Conception, and Ezekiel's Closed Door in the *Ludus Coventriae* Play of 'Joseph's Return,'" *Journal of Medieval and Renaissance Studies* 8 (1978): 137–57, esp. 142, 152.

54. Madeline H. Caviness, *Visualizing Women in the Middle Ages: Sight, Spectacle, and Scopic Economy* (Philadelphia: University of Pennsylvania Press, 2001), 8; Gail McMurray Gibson, "Scene and Obscene," 17; Gertsman, *Worlds Within*, 16–18.

55. Anthony Bale, *The Jew in the Medieval Book: English Antisemitisms, 1350–1500* (Cambridge: Cambridge University Press, 2006), 67–68.

56. Gertsman, *Worlds Within*, 46–47.

57. *MED*, s.v. "speren."

58. N-Town 12.38, 12.64, 12.219.

59. *MED*, s.v. "japen."

60. Woolf, *English Mystery Plays*, 170.

61. Here I use Luz's translation of Matthew; see Luz, *Matthew 1–7*, 89.

62. François Bovon, *Luke 1: A Commentary*, trans. Christine M. Thomas, Hermeneia (Minneapolis: Fortress, 2002), 52; Joseph A. Fitzmyer, ed., *The Gospel According to Luke*, Anchor Bible (New York: Doubleday, 1981), 337–38, 350; Luz, *Matthew 1–7*, 95.

63. Schaberg, *Illegitimacy of Jesus*, 96–103.

64. See Robin M. Jensen, *Baptismal Imagery in Early Christianity* (Grand Rapids, MI: BakerAcademic, 2012), 118–20.

65. Marina Warner, *Alone of All Her Sex*, 34–36. See also Glenn Holland, "Celibacy and the Early Christian Church," in *Celibacy and Religious Traditions*, ed. Carl Olson (Oxford: Oxford University Press, 2007), 65–84.

66. Celsus, *On the True Doctrine: A Discourse against Christians*, trans. R. Joseph Hoffman (Oxford: Oxford University Press, 1987), 57; see also Origen, *Contra Celsum*, 36–37. See also Justin Martyr, *Dialogue with Trypho*, ed. Michael Slusser, trans. T. B. Falls (Washington, DC: Christian Heritage, 2003), 103.

67. Origen, *Contra Celsum*, 37.

68. Ibid., 36–37, 321.

69. Plutarch, *Moralia*, vol. 9, ed. and trans. Edwin L. Minar Jr., F. H. Sandbach, and W. C. Helmbold, Loeb Classical Library 425 (Cambridge, MA: Harvard University Press, 1961), 9.114–15; Diogenes Laertius, *Lives of Eminent Philosophers*, ed. and trans. R. D. Hicks, Loeb Classical Library 184 (Cambridge, MA: Harvard University Press, 1925), 1:276–77. See also Robert M. Grant, *Miracle and Natural Law in Graeco-Roman and Early Christian Thought* (Amsterdam: North-Holland, 1952), 173.

70. Justin Martyr, *Dialogue with Trypho*, 107–8.

71. For a comparative study of Mary's virginity in late antiquity, see Mary F. Foskett, *A Virgin Conceived: Mary and Classical Representations of Virginity* (Bloomington: Indiana University Press, 2002), esp. 157–64.

72. Graef, *Mary*, 67; Ambrose, *De institutione virginis*, 16:327.

73. Bernard of Clairvaux, *Sermones in Cantica Canticorum*, in *PL*, ed. J.-P. Migne (Paris: Imprimerie Catholique, 1854), 183:932–33; Parker, *Aesthetics of Antichrist*, 49–55. For more on the commentary on the Song of Songs by Honorius Augustodunensis, Rupert of Deutz, and Philip of Harvengt, see Rachel Fulton Brown, *From Judgment to Passion: Devotion to Christ and the Virgin Mary, 800–1200* (New York: Columbia University Press, 2002), 244–404.

74. Marina Warner, *Alone of All Her Sex*, 126; Bernard of Clairvaux, *Sermones in assumptione beatae Mariae Virginis*, in *PL*, ed. J.-P. Migne (Paris: Imprimerie Catholique, 1854), 183:996.

75. Graef, *Mary*, 249; Aelred of Rievaulx, *In Assumptione beatae Mariae*, in *PL*, ed. J.-P. Migne (Paris: Imprimerie Catholique, 1855), 195:254A. See also Marina Warner, *Alone of All Her Sex*, 130; Rubin, *Mother of God*, 212.

76. Godfrey of Admont, *Homiliae dominicales*, in *PL*, ed. J.-P. Migne (Paris: Imprimerie Catholique, 1854), 174:1025.

77. Newman, *God and the Goddesses*, 247–52; Steinberg, *Sexuality of Christ*, 3–5.

78. For more on the N-Town Assumption, see Seeta Chaganti, *The Medieval Poetics of the Reliquary: Enshrinement, Inscription, Performance* (New York: Palgrave Macmillan, 2008), 73–94.

79. For more on representations of the three-personed Trinity, see Robert Mills, "Jesus as Monster," in *The Monstrous Middle Ages*, ed. Bettina Bildhauer and Robert Mills (Toronto: University of Toronto Press, 2003), 38–43.

80. Gail McMurray Gibson, *Theater of Devotion*, 168.

81. Steinberg, *Sexuality of Christ*, 238–9; Caviness, *Visualizing Women*, 2; Waller, *Virgin Mary*, 34.

82. For more on the female orgasm in medieval letters, see Lochrie, *Heterosyncracies*, 76–102.

83. *MED*, s.v. "blisse."

84. Sugano, *N-Town Plays*, 110; Gail McMurray Gibson, *Theater of Devotion*, 144; Peter Meredith, "Carved and Spoken Words: The Angelic Salutation, the Mary Play and South Walsham Church, Norfolk," *Leeds Studies in English* 32 (2001): 380–81. See also Gertsman, *Worlds Within*, 57–59.

85. For an introduction to Scholastic debate, see Alex J. Novikoff, *The Medieval Culture of Disputation: Pedagogy, Practice, and Performance* (Philadelphia: University of Pennsylvania Press, 2013).

86. See, for example, Rupert of Deutz, *Commentaria in Cantica Canticorum*, in *Corpus Christianorum Continuatio Mediaevalis*, vol. 26, ed. Hrabanus Haacke (Turnhout: Brepols, 1972), 10; Graef, *Mary*, 192. For more on Rupert of Deutz's commentary on the Virgin, see Fulton Brown, *From Judgment to Passion*, 309–50.

87. Aristotle, *Generation of Animals*, ed. and trans. A. L. Peck, Loeb Classical Library 366 (Cambridge, MA: Harvard University Press, 1943), 97–10.

88. Hippocrates, *Generation*, ed. and trans. Paul Potter, Loeb Classical Library 520 (Cambridge, MA: Harvard University Press, 2012), 10.12–15.

89. Galen, *On the Usefulness of the Parts of the Body*, ed. and trans. Margaret Tallmadge May (Ithaca, NY: Cornell University Press, 1968), 633.

90. Ibid., 644–45.

91. Jacquart and Thomasset, *Sexuality and Medicine*, 69–70.

92. Origen, *Contra Celsum*, 36; Plutarch, *Moralia*, vol. 4, ed. and trans. Frank Cole Babbitt, Loeb Classical Library 305 (Cambridge, MA: Harvard University Press, 1936), 141. See also Richard Barber, ed., *Bestiary: Bodleian Library, Oxford MS Bodley 764* (Woodbridge, UK: Boydell, 1992), 126.

93. Michael J. Curley, ed. and trans., *Physiologus: A Medieval Book of Nature Lore* (Chicago: University of Chicago Press, 1979), 34–35; Marina Warner, *Alone of All Her Sex*, 36–37.

94. John Lydgate, *A Critical Edition of John Lydgate's Life of Our Lady*, ed. J. A. Lauritis, R. A. Klinefelter, and V. F. Gallagher (Pittsburg, Pennsylvania: Duquesne University Press, 1961), 357–75, esp. 359, 373–74.

95. Thomas Aquinas, *Summa Theologiae*, vol. 52, ed. Roland Potter (London: Blackfriars, 1972), 24–29; Aristotle, *Generation of Animals*, 193.

96. Benjamin H. Dunning, *Specters of Paul: Sexual Difference in Early Christian Thought* (Philadelphia: University of Pennsylvania Press, 2011), 97–123.

97. Aquinas, *Summa* 52:26–27.

98. Ibid., 52:54–55.

99. Love, *Love's Mirror*, 26; Newman, *Sister of Wisdom*, 175.

100. Graef, *Mary*, 192; Amadeus of Lausanne, "Homily 3," in *PL*, ed. J.-P. Migne (Paris: Imprimerie Catholique, 1855), 188:1313–19.

101. Hugh of Saint Victor, *On the Sacraments of the Christian Faith*, trans. Roy J. Deferrari (Cambridge, MA: Mediaeval Academy of America, 1951), 229; Hugh of Saint Victor, *De sacramentis Christianae fidei*, in *PL*, ed. J.-P. Migne (Paris: Imprimerie Catholique, 1854), 176:391–93. See also Newman, *Sister of Wisdom*, 136–37.

102. Hugh of Saint Victor, *De sacramentis Christianae fidei*, 393.

103. Graef, *Mary*, 200; Philip of Harvengt, *Commentaria in Cantica canticorum*, in *PL*, ed. J.-P. Migne (Paris: Imprimerie Catholique, 1855), 203:271A. For more on Philip of Harvengt's writing on the Virgin, see Fulton Brown, *From Judgment to Passion*, 351–404.

104. Hugh of Saint Victor, *De sacramentis Christianae fidei*, 393. "Non ergo libido carnis conceptionem in virgine operata est, quæ nec de carne viri semen accepit, nec de sua carne per amorem viri concepit, sed per amorem et operationem Spiritus sancti."

105. Newman, *Sister of Wisdom*, 175.

106. Ibid., 175–76; Hildegard of Bingen, "Ein unveroffentlichtes Hildegard-Fragment," ed. Heinrich Schipperges, *Slldhoffs Arclziv fiir Geschichte der Medizin* 40 (1956): 68.

107. Aristotle, *On Generation*, 102–3.

108. Hildegard, "Ein unveroffentlichtes Hildegard-Fragment," 68.

109. See also Newman, *Sister of Wisdom*, 175.

110. Hippocrates, *On Generation*, 12–13.

111. See N-Town 8.191, 8.204, 9.256–57.

112. Chaucer, "Wife of Bath's Prologue," *Canterbury Tales*, 614.

113. This and all subsequent quotations from the Towneley plays are taken from Martin Stevens and A. C. Cawley, eds., *The Towneley Plays*, 2 vols., EETS (Oxford: Oxford University Press, 1994).

114. See Genesis 6:2–4; Bill T. Arnold, *Genesis*, New Cambridge Bible Commentary (Cambridge: Cambridge University Press, 2008), 89–91; and Ronald Hendel, "The Nephilim Were on the Earth: Genesis 6:1–4 and Its Ancient Near-Eastern Context," in *The Fall of the Angels*, ed. Christoph Auffarth and Loren T. Stuckenbruck (Leiden: Brill, 2004), 17–22.

115. Constas, *Proclus of Constantinople*, 277, 286–87.

116. Ehrman and Pleše, *Apocryphal Gospels*, 54–57.

117. Lewis and Short, *Latin Dictionary*, s.v. "turbo."

118. Ehrman and Pleše, *Apocryphal Gospels*, 48–49, 86–87.

119. Spector, *N-Town Play*, 2:458.

120. Ehrman and Pleše, *Apocryphal Gospels*, 92–93.

121. Chaucer, "Wife of Bath's Prologue," *Canterbury Tales*, 304; Chaucer, "Miller's Tale," *Canterbury Tales*, 3315.

122. Shirley Neilsen Blum, "Hans Memling's Annunciation with Angelic Attendants," *Metropolitan Museum Journal* 27 (1992): 45 (fig. 1), 47 (fig. 2), 51 (fig. 6).

123. Ambrose, *Expositio in Lucam*, in *PL*, ed. J.-P. Migne (Paris: Imprimerie Catholique, 1887), 15:1636A. "Trepidare virginum est, et ad omnes ingressus viri pavere, omnes viri affatus vereri."

124. Blum, "Hans Memling's Annunciation," 43.

125. For more on Mary's body as bower, see Gertsman, *Worlds Within*, 47–48; Gail McMurray Gibson, *Theater of Devotion*, 142.

126. Love, *Love's Mirror*, 34.

127. Blum, "Hans Memling's Annunciation," 44, 46, 48.

128. Andreas Cappelanus, *The Art of Courtly Love*, ed. and trans. John Jay Parry (New York: Columbia University Press, 1990), 29.

129. Aelred of Rievaulx, *In Assumptione beatae Mariae*, 254A; Graef, *Mary*, 249.

130. Laura Kendrick, *Chaucerian Play: Comedy and Control in the Canterbury Tales* (Berkeley: University of California Press, 1988), 16.

131. Chaucer, "Miller's Tale," *Canterbury Tales*, 3199–3200. See also John B. Friedman, "Nicholas's 'Angelus Ad Virginem' and the Mocking of Noah," *Yearbook of English Studies* 22 (1992): 162–80.

132. Donald Queller, *The Office of Ambassador in the Middle Ages* (Princeton, NJ: Princeton University Press, 1967), 85–109; *MED*, s.v. "procuratour."

133. Constas, *Proclus of Constantinople*, 273–75; Barber, *Bestiary*, 110. See also Maurizio Bettini, *Women and Weasels: Mythologies of Birth in Ancient Greece and Rome* (Chicago: University of Chicago Press, 2013).

134. Marina Warner, *Alone of All Her Sex*, 37; Constas, *Proclus of Constantinople*, 297–99.

135. On the former, see Gertsman, *Worlds Within*, 59; on the latter, see Michael P. Carroll, *Catholic Cults and Devotions: A Psychological Inquiry* (Montreal: McGill-Queen's University Press, 1989), 35, and Gail McMurray Gibson, *Theater of Devotion*, 151.

136. Karen Saupe, ed., *Middle English Marian Lyrics*, TEAMS (Kalamazoo, MI: Medieval Institute Publications, 1997), p. 87, lines 2–3.

137. Italics mine.

138. Aulen, *Christus Victor*, 63–71; Parker, *Aesthetics of Antichrist*, 169–78.

139. Constas, *Proclus of Constantinople*, 302–3.

140. Ehrman and Pleše, *Apocryphal Gospels*, 94.

141. Ibid., 95.

142. I depart here from Kolve's maxim that the text "never laughs" at Mary; *Play Called Corpus Christi*, 139.

143. See also Martin Stevens and Cawley, *Towneley Plays*, 10.293–98.

144. Lorris and Meun, *Romance of the Rose*, 227.

145. Friedman, "Nicholas's 'Angelus Ad Virginem,'" 164–65.

146. This and all subsequent references to *Decameron* are taken from Giovanni Boccaccio, *Decameron*, 8th ed., ed. Vittore Branca (Milan: Arnoldo Mondadori, 2001), and Giovanni Boccaccio, *The Decameron*, trans. Wayne A. Rebhorn (New York: Norton, 2013).

147. Boccaccio, *Decameron*, ed. Branca, 351; Boccaccio, *Decameron*, trans. Rebhorn, 322.

148. Boccaccio, *Decameron*, ed. Branca, 353; Boccaccio, *Decameron*, trans. Rebhorn, 323.

149. Boccaccio, *Decameron*, ed. Branca, 354; Boccaccio, *Decameron*, trans. Rebhorn, 323–24.

150. See also Martin Stevens and Cawley, *Towneley Plays*, 10.291, 10.295.

151. Baird and Baird, "Fabliau Form," 163–64.

152. Boccaccio, *Decameron*, trans. Rebhorn, 518–19, 526–30.

153. Chaucer, "Wife of Bath's Prologue," *Canterbury Tales*, 231–34.

154. Lorris and Meun, *Romance of the Rose*, 219–21.

155. Ibid., 208.

Chapter 2

1. Davidson, *York Corpus Christi Plays*, 13.65; Martin Stevens and Cawley, *Towneley Plays*, 10.298.

2. Raymond E. Brown, "The Problem of the Virginal Conception of Jesus," *Theological Studies* 33, no. 1 (1972): 4–34; Raymond E. Brown, *The Birth of the Messiah: A Commentary on the Infancy Narratives in the Gospels of Matthew and Luke* (Garden City, NY: Doubleday, 1977); Fitzmyer, *Gospel According to Luke*, 338; Schaberg, *Illegitimacy of Jesus*, 73–77, 125–29.

3. Matthew 1:19–24.

4. Luz, *Matthew 1–7*, 96–98; Fitzmyer, *Gospel According to Luke*, 343; Bovon, *Luke 1*, 49; Schaberg, *Illegitimacy of Jesus*, 49–68, 69–73; Parker, *Aesthetics of Antichrist*, 180.

5. Frank Reilly, "Jane Schaberg, Raymond E. Brown, and the Problem of the Illegitimacy of Jesus," *Journal of Feminist Studies in Religion* 21 (2005): 58.

6. Raymond E. Brown, "Problem of the Virginal Conception," 33.

7. Monika Hellwig, "The Dogmatic Implications of the Birth of the Messiah," *Emmanuel* 84 (1978): 21–24; Reilly, "Jane Schaberg"; Jane Schaberg, "Feminist Interpretations of the Infancy Narrative of Matthew," in Schaberg, *Illegitimacy of Jesus*, 231–57.

8. Schaberg, *Illegitimacy of Jesus*, 169, 135–36.

9. Matthew 1:1–16; Schaberg, *Illegitimacy of Jesus*, 32–41.

10. Schaberg, *Illegitimacy of Jesus*, 172.

11. Ibid., 169.

12. Italics mine. Ernst Haenchen, *John 2: A Commentary on the Gospel of John, Chapters 7–21*, trans. Robert W. Funk, Hermeneia (Philadelphia: Fortress, 1984), 25, 29.

13. Schaberg, *Illegitimacy of Jesus*, 142.

14. Ibid., 149; Peter Schäfer, *Jesus in the Talmud* (Princeton, NJ: Princeton University Press, 2009), 7–9, 54–62.

15. Schaberg, *Illegitimacy of Jesus*, 152–53; Robert E. Van Voorst, *Jesus outside the New Testament: An Introduction to the Ancient Evidence* (Grand Rapids, MI: Wm. B. Eerdmans, 2000), 122–29; Schäfer, *Jesus in the Talmud*, 2–7. See also the forthcoming scholarly edition of the *Toledot Yeshu* edited by Peter Schäfer and Michael Meerson.

16. Cuffel, *Gendering Disgust*, 55–57; Schaberg, *Illegitimacy of Jesus*, 150; Glancy, *Corporal Knowledge*, 111–12. See also Kathleen O'Grady, "The Semantics of Taboo: Menstrual Prohibitions in the Hebrew Bible," in *Wholly Woman, Holy Blood: A Feminist Critique of Purity and Impurity*, ed. Kristin De Troyer, Judith A. Herbert, Judith Ann Johnson, and Anne-Marie Korte (Harrisburg, PA: Trinity Press International, 2003), 15–17.

17. Ehrman and Pleše, *Apocryphal Gospels*, 31–35. See also Bart Ehrman, *Forgery and Counter-forgery: The Use of Literary Deceit in Early Christian Polemics* (Oxford: Oxford University Press, 2013), 485–88.

18. Ehrman and Pleše, *Apocryphal Gospels*, 56–59, 94–99. Here and throughout the book, my readings of the apocryphal Infancy Gospels depend on the work of Bart Ehrman, Jane Schaberg, and Jennifer Glancy.

19. Kelly, *Performing Virginity*, 63–64.

20. Sarolta A. Takács, *Vestal Virgins, Sibyls, and Matrons: Women in Roman Religion* (Austin: University of Texas Press, 2008), 89.

21. Margaret H. Kerr, Richard D. Forsyth, and Michael J. Plyley, "Cold Water and Hot Iron: Trial by Ordeal in England," *Journal of Interdisciplinary History* 22, no. 4 (1992): 582–83, 588. For more on the medieval trial by ordeal, see Robert Bartlett, *Trial by Fire and Water: The Medieval Judicial Ordeal* (Oxford: Clarendon, 1986), and James Brundage, *Law, Sex, and Christian Society in Medieval Europe* (Chicago: University of Chicago Press, 1987).

22. Ehrman and Pleše, *Apocryphal Gospels*, 58–59.

23. For more on this episode, see Foskett, *Virgin Conceived*, 141–64; George Themolis Zervos, "Christmas with Salome," in *A Feminist Companion to Mariology*, ed. Amy-Jill Levine with Maria Mayo Robbins (London: Continuum, 2005), 79–95; and Glancy, *Corporal Knowledge*, 106–18.

24. Ehrman and Pleše, *Apocryphal Gospels*, 62–63.

25. For more on this transmission, see Rita Beyers, "The Transmission of Marian Apocrypha in the Latin Middle Ages," *Apocrypha* 23 (2012): 117–40; Mary Clayton, *The Apocryphal Gospels of Mary in Anglo-Saxon England* (Cambridge: Cambridge University Press, 1998); and Maureen Barry McCann Boulton, *Sacred Fictions of Medieval France: Narrative Theology in the Lives of Christ and the Virgin, 1150–1500* (Rochester, NY: D. S. Brewer, 2015).

26. Graef, *Mary*, 29; Marina Warner, *Alone of All Her Sex*, 29. These trials include the miracle of the blooming rod, Joseph's doubt, the trial of Mary and Joseph, the miracle of the cherry tree (or date palm), the doubting midwife (or midwives), Simeon's doubt at the purification of the Virgin, Jephonias's (also called Athonios, Reuben, and

Fergus) doubt at the funeral or dormition of the Virgin, and Thomas's doubt at the Assumption of the Virgin.

27. The incident that I refer to here is Simeon's doubt at the purification (based on Luke 2:25–35), which involves the miraculous and spectacular reappearance of the word *virgin* in a prop book of Isaiah; Lumiansky and Mills, *Chester Mystery Cycle* (1974), 11.25–103. For more on the Chester purification, see Parker, *Aesthetics of Antichrist*, 178–82; and Cushman, "Handling Knowledge," 298–300. For more on the association between scripture and Mary's body, see Gertsman, *Worlds Within*, 44–46.

28. For more on the apocryphal legends of Mary's life after Jesus's death, see Stephen J. Shoemarker, *Ancient Traditions of the Virgin Mary's Dormition and Assumption* (Oxford: Oxford University Press, 2003).

29. See also N-Town, 41.64, 41.68–74.

30. Ibid., 41.83–85.

31. Jacobus de Voragine, *The Golden Legend: Readings on the Saints*, trans. William Granger Ryan, 2 vols. (Princeton, NJ: Princeton University Press, 1993), 2:81.

32. "The Greek Narrative: The Discourse of St John the Divine concerning the Falling Asleep of the Holy Mother of God," in *The Apocryphal New Testament*, ed. J. K. Elliott (Oxford: Clarendon, 1993), 707; M. D. Anderson, *Drama and Imagery in English Medieval Churches* (Cambridge: Cambridge University Press, 1963), 138–39; N-Town, 41.3–4.

33. See Kinservik, "Struggle over Mary's Body," 190–92; Merrall Llewelyn Price, "Re-membering the Jews," 443–44.

34. N-Town, 41.475–89.

35. "Narrative by Joseph of Arimathea," in J. K. Elliott, *Apocryphal New Testament*, 715; Voragine, *Golden Legend*, 2:82; Davidson, *York Corpus Christi Plays*, 45.124–26.

36. Davidson, *York Corpus Christi Plays*, 45.166–69; Marina Warner, *Alone of All Her Sex*, 278–79; Ruth Evans, "When a Body Meets a Body: Fergus and Mary in the York Cycle," *New Medieval Literatures* 1 (1997): 210.

37. Ehrman, *Forgery and Counter-forgery*, 488–93.

38. Ulrich Luz, *Matthew 8–20: A Commentary*, trans. James E. Crouch, Hermeneia (Minneapolis: Fortress, 2001), 216–17. See also Matthew 12:38; Mark 8:11–12; Matthew 16:1–4; Luke 11:29–30.

39. Ignatius of Antioch, "Letter to the Ephesians 19," in *The New Testament and Other Early Christian Writings: A Reader*, 2nd ed., ed. Bart Ehrman (Oxford: Oxford University Press, 2004), 328.

40. Paula Fredriksen and Oded Irshai, "Christian Anti-Judaism: Polemics and Policies," in *The Cambridge History of Judaism*, vol. 4, *The Late Roman-Rabbinic Period*, ed. Steven T. Katz (Cambridge: Cambridge University Press, 2006), 977–1034.

41. Ehrman and Pleše, *Apocryphal Gospels*, 56–57; Merrall Llewelyn Price, "Re-membering the Jews," 444–45.

42. Ehrman and Pleše, *Apocryphal Gospels*, 100–101; N-Town, 15.184–85. Joseph assumes that the midwives will refuse to assist Mary if they see her smiling, which implies that they demand the performance of sorrow and suffering from their patients, presumably as penitence for Eve's crime.

43. "Narrative by Joseph of Arimathea," in J. K. Elliott, *Apocryphal New Testament*, 715; Voragine, *Golden Legend*, 2.81.

44. Justin Martyr, *Dialog with Trypho*, 103; Origen, *Contra Celsum*, 28–32; Jerome, *Adversus Helvidium*, 213. See also Parker, *Aesthetics of Antichrist*, 23–24.

45. Schaberg, *Illegitimacy of Jesus*, 145–49; Michael Frede, "Origen's Treatise *Against Celsus*," in *Apologetics in the Roman Empire: Pagans, Jews, and Christians*, ed. Mark J. Edwards, Martin Goodman, Simon Price, and Chris Rowland (Oxford: Oxford University Press, 1999), 131–56.

46. Celsus, *On the True Doctrine*, 57.

47. For more on Tertullian's paradoxical style, see Glancy, *Corporal Knowledge*, 117–21.

48. Ehrman and Pleše, *Apocryphal Gospels*, 40–53.

49. Ehrman, *Forgery and Counter-forgery*, 490. See also Spector, *N-Town Play*, 2:470 note 15/49–52.

50. Origen, *Contra Celsum*, 28.

51. Ibid., 29.

52. Ibid., 28.

53. Ibid., 32.

54. Ibid., 33.

55. Much illuminating work has been done in recent years on the intimate association between anti-Judaism and Mariology in the Middle Ages. See Kati Ihnat, *Mother of Mercy, Bane of the Jews: Devotion to the Virgin Mary in Anglo-Norman England* (Princeton, NJ: Princeton University Press, 2016); Lampert, *Gender and Jewish Difference*; Anthony Bale, *Jew in the Medieval Book*, 67–72; Miri Rubin, *Gentile Tales: The Narrative Assault on Late Medieval Jews* (Philadelphia: University of Pennsylvania Press, 2004), 7–29; Rubin, *Mother of God*, 161–88, 228–42.

56. Rubin, *Mother of God*, 43–45, 75, 161.

57. John V. Tolan, *Saracens: Islam in the Medieval European Imagination* (New York: Columbia University Press, 2002), 93–94. See also Glancy, *Corporal Knowledge*, 133–34.

58. Hyam Maccoby, *Judaism on Trial: Jewish-Christian Disputations in the Middle Ages* (Rutherford, NJ: Fairleigh Dickinson University Press, 1982), 19–38, 156–57, 165; Robert Chazan, *The Trial of the Talmud: Paris, 1240* (Toronto: Pontifical Institute of Medieval Studies, 2012), 68–69.

59. Maccoby, *Judaism on Trial*, 164.

60. McSheffrey, *Gender and Heresy*, 68, 154. See also John F. Davis, "Trials of Thomas Bylney," 779.

61. Lydgate, *Life of Our Lady*, 375–77. See also *MED*, s.v. "goundi"; and *OED*, s.v. "goundy."

62. See, for example, Marina Warner, *Alone of All Her Sex*, 35; and Luz, *Matthew 1–7*, 100.

63. Criticism has tended to emphasize God's punishments of Mary's detractors and doubt's resolution. See, for example, Woolf, *English Mystery Plays*, 178; Kolve, *Play Called Corpus Christi*, 138–39; Merrall Llewelyn Price, "Re-membering the Jews," 441–42; and Lampert, *Gender and Jewish Difference*, 126–27. By contrast, I (like Helen Cushman in her recent "Handling Knowledge") expand on Gail Gibson's thesis that N-Town "invite[s] the continued probing of Mary's—and God's—privy secrets"; Gibson, "Scene and Obscene," 20; Cushman, "Handling Knowledge," 280–81.

64. N-Town, 14.364–69, 15.254–94, 41.471–89.

65. Ibid., 10.276–84.

66. Ibid., 12.95–97.

67. Ibid., 15.37–39.

68. Ibid., 12.87–88, 15.53.

69. Readers of N-Town, too, have found Joseph strangely endearing. See, for example, Kolve, *Play Called Corpus Christi*, 251–52.

70. William Shakespeare, *Othello*, ed. E. A. J. Honigmann, Arden Shakespeare (London: Thomson, 2006), 4.1.16; Kelly, *Performing Virginity*, 122.

71. Sheila Delany, *Impolitic Bodies: Poetry, Saints, and Society in Fifteenth-Century England: The Work of Obsern Bokenham* (Oxford: Oxford University Press, 1998), 71–4; Peggy McCracken, *The Curse of Eve, the Wound of the Hero: Blood, Gender, and Medieval Literature* (Philadelphia: University of Pennsylvania Press, 2003), 4–5.

72. Marie H. Loughlin, *Hymeneutics: Interpreting Virginity on the Early Modern Stage* (Cranbury, NJ: Bucknell University Press, 1997), 45.

73. Moll, "Staging Disorder," 151; Emma Lipton, "Language on Trial: Performing the Law in the N-Town Trial Play," in *The Letter of the Law: Legal Practice and Literary Production in Medieval England*, ed. Emily Steiner and Candace Barrington (Ithaca, NY: Cornell University Press, 2002), 116.

74. By contrast, in "Re-membering the Jews," Merrall Llewelyn Price reads Raise-Slander and Back-Biter as being "identifiably Jewish" (445). See also Anthony Bale, *Feeling Persecuted: Christians, Jews and Images of Violence in the Middle Ages* (London: Reaktion Books, 2010), 102. And yet the traits that mark these Vices as Jewish to Price and Bale (literalism and skepticism) also function as allegorical mirrors of Christian error. For more on medieval Christianity's double use of these signs of Jewishness, see Jeremy Cohen, *Living Letters of the Law: Ideas of the Jew in Medieval Christianity* (Tel Aviv: Tel Aviv University Press, 1999); and Sara Lipton, *Dark Mirror: The Medieval Origins of Anti-Jewish Iconography* (New York: Metropolitan Books, 2014).

75. Ian Forrest, "The Summoner," in *Historians on Chaucer: The "General Prologue" to the Canterbury Tales*, ed. Stephen Rigby (Oxford: Oxford University Press, 2014), 421–42.

76. Colin Fewer, "The 'Fygure' of the Market: The N-Town Cycle and East Anglian Lay Piety," *Philological Quarterly* 77, no. 2 (1998): 130.

77. Forrest, "Summoner," 430–31.

78. Joseph Allen Bryant Jr., "The Function of *Ludus Coventriae* 14," *Journal of English and Germanic Philology* 52 (1953): 341.

79. Moll, "Staging Disorder," 155. As has often been noted, many of the names on the summoner's list also appear in Lydgate's *Disguising at Hertford* and Skelton's "The Tunnyng of Elynour Rummynge." See John Lydgate, *Disguising at Hertford*, in *Mummings and Entertainments*, ed. Claire Sponsler, TEAMS Middle English Texts (Kalamazoo, MI: Medieval Institute Publications, 2010), 44, 79, 93, 101, 115, 125; and John Skelton, "The Tunnyng of Elynour Rummynge," in *The Complete English Poems of John Skelton*, ed. John Scattergood (Liverpool: Liverpool University Press, 2015), 186–200.

80. Alan J. Fletcher, "Line 30 of the Man of Law's Tale and the Medieval Malkyn," *English Language Notes* 24, no. 2 (1986): 18; Malcolm Jones, *The Secret Middle Ages: Discovering the Real Medieval World* (London: Praeger, 2003), 167.

81. Ehrman and Pleše, *Apocryphal Gospels*, 54–55.

82. Douglas W. Hayes, "Backbiter and the Rhetoric of Detraction," *Comparative Drama* 34, no. 1 (2000): 53–78; Emma Lipton, "Language on Trial," 119–20.

83. N-Town 10.324–30.

84. Dyan Elliott, *Spiritual Marriage*, 9–10, 139–41, 272–73; Moll, "Staging Disorder," 149–50.

85. Staley, *Book of Margery Kempe*, 1.2.76.

86. Alison Hunt, "Maculating Mary: The Detractors of the N-Town Cycle's 'Trial of Mary and Joseph,'" *Philological Quarterly* 73, no. 1 (1994): 13; Emma Lipton, "Language on Trial," 119–21.

87. Ehrman and Pleše, *Apocryphal Gospels*, 56–57.

88. Ibid., 96–97.

89. Kolve, *Play Called Corpus Christi*, 139.

90. Moll, "Staging Disorder," 152–53.

91. Thomas Aquinas, *Summa Theologiae*, vol. 40, ed. Thomas Franklin O'Meara and Michael John Duffy (London: Blackfriars, 1968), 69.

92. Lydgate, *Life of Our Lady*, 373–74; Carol Falvo Heffernan, "The Old English Phoenix: A Reconsideration," *Neuphilologische Mitteilungen* 83, no. 3 (1982): 239–40.

93. For more on this episode from the book of Numbers, see Schaberg, *Illegitimacy of Christ*, 56; B. D. H. Miller, "'She Who Hath Drunk Any Potion . . . ,'" *Medium Aevum* 31 (1962): 188–93; Baruch A. Levine, *Numbers 1–20*, Anchor Bible (New York: Doubleday, 1993), 192–212; and Jacob Milgrom, *Numbers: The JPS Torah Commentary* (Philadelphia: Jewish Publication Society, 1990), 37–43, 346–54.

94. Ehrman and Pleše, *Apocryphal Gospels*, 58–59.

95. Ibid., 96–97.

96. *MED*, s.v. "shreuen"; *OED*, s.v. "beshrew." See also Chaucer, "Nuns' Priest's Tale," *Canterbury Tales*, 3425–27.

97. Valentin Groebner, "Losing Face, Saving Face: Noses and Honor in the Late Medieval Town," trans. Pamela Selwyn, *History Workshop Journal* 40 (1995): 1–15.

98. For more on Mary as stoic, see Glancy, *Corporal Knowledge*, 98.

99. N-Town 14.86–87, 14.166.

100. Augustine, *In Psalmum 98 Enarratio*, in *PL*, ed. J.-P. Migne (Paris: Imprimerie Catholique, 1865), 37:1264; Augustine, *Expositions of the Psalms, 73–98*, trans. Maria Boulding, ed. John E. Rotelle (Hyde Park, NY: New City, 2002), 474–75.

101. "Pascimur etiam et potamur carne et ejus sanguine in Filii sacramento: quia caro Christi et caro Mariae sicut matris et filii una caro est." Albertus Magnus, *De laudibus beatae Virginis*, in *B. Alberti Magni, Opera Omnia*, ed. Auguste Borgnet and Émile Borgnet (Paris: Louis Vivès, 1898), 36:83.

102. Bynum, *Holy Feast and Holy Fast*, 53–63; Beckwith, *Signifying God*, 114–17; Gertsman, *Worlds Within*, 67.

103. William Shakespeare, *Antony and Cleopatra*, ed. John Wilders, Arden Shakespeare (London: Thomson, 1995), 2.2.247–48. For a comparison of Shakespeare's Cleopatra and the Virgin Mary, see Ruben Espinosa, *Masculinity and Marian Efficacy in Shakespeare's England: Women and Gender in the Early Modern World* (Farnham, UK: Ashgate 2011), 152–58.

104. Lydgate, *Life of Our Lady*, 422 (2.1577); Ehrman and Pleše, *Apocryphal Gospels*, 58–59, 98–99. For more on Lydgate and N-Town, see Gail McMurray Gibson, "Bury St. Edmunds," 56–90.

105. Moll, "Staging Disorder," 152.

106. Ehrman and Pleše, *Apocryphal Gospels*, 98–99.

107. Lydgate, *Life of Our Lady*, 422–23 (2.1586–91).

108. Meredith and Kahrl, *N-Town Plays*, xxv, fol. 81v.

109. Geary, *Furta Sacra*, 134–35. See also Geary, "Humiliation of Saints"; Little, *Benedictine Maledictions*, 26–30, 83–85, 133.

110. Véronique Plesch, "Graffiti and Ritualization: San Sebastiano at Arborio," in *Medieval and Early Modern Ritual: Formalized Behavior in Europe, China, and Japan*, ed. Joelle Rollo-Koster (Leiden: Brill, 2002), 140–41.

111. Amy Knight Powell, *Depositions: Scenes from the Late Medieval Church and the Modern Museum* (New York: Zone Books, 2012), 93; Natalie Zemon Davis, "The Rites of Violence: Religious Riot in Sixteenth-Century France," *Past & Present* 59 (1973): 77; Richard C. Trexler, "Florentine Religious Experience: The Sacred Image," *Studies in the Renaissance* 19 (1972): 24–25.

112. Parish, *Monks, Miracles and Magic*, esp. 76.

113. Parker, *Aesthetics of Antichrist*, 125–35; Steven Justice, "Eucharistic Miracle and Eucharistic Doubt," *Journal of Medieval and Early Modern Studies* 42, no. 2 (2012): 307–32.

114. Whitley Stokes, trans., *Beunans Meriasek* (London: Trübner, 1872), 208–15; Markham Harris, trans., *The Life of Meriasek: A Medieval Cornish Miracle Play* (Washington, DC: Catholic University of America Press, 1977), 90–105. See also John Mirk, *Mirk's Festial: A Collection of Homilies*, ed. Theodor Erbe, EETS (London: Trübner, 1905), 248.

115. Markham Harris, *Life of Meriasek*, 101; Whitley Stokes, *Beunans Meriasek*, 210–11.

116. Markham Harris, *Life of Meriasek*, 103; Whitley Stokes, *Beunans Meriasek*, 214–15.

117. Margaret Aston, *Lollards and Reformers: Images and Literacy in Late Medieval Religion* (London: Hambledon, 1984), 173–74.

118. Ibid., 174; R. Foreville, "Manifestation de lollardisme à Exeter en 1421 d'après une lettre extravagente de Henri Chichele," *Le Moyen Âge* 69 (1963): 691.

119. Aston, *Lollards and Reformers*, 167–79; Maureen Jurkowski, "Lollardy in Oxfordshire and Northhamptonshire: The Two Thomas Compworths," in *Lollards and Their Influence in Late Medieval England*, ed. Fiona Somerset, Jill C. Havens, and Derrick G. Pitard (Woodbridge, UK: Boydell, 2003), 73–95.

120. Still to this day, the Christmas season inevitably inspires the theft of statues of the baby Jesus from outdoor Nativity scenes. This crime has its own Wikipedia entry ("Baby Jesus Theft") and is seasonally reported in local and national news; see, for example, Elahe Izadi, "People Keep Stealing Baby Jesus from Nativity Scenes," *Washington Post*, December 26, 2014; and Tim Donnelly, "Churches on High Alert as Baby Jesus Thefts Spike," *New York Post*, December 5, 2015.

121. Aston, *Lollards and Reformers*, 174n135; F. D. Logan, *Excommunication and the Secular Arm of the Law in Medieval England* (Toronto: University of Toronto Press, 1968), 52.

122. See, for example, Kolve, *Play Called Corpus Christi*, 139. For more on audience response, see Sue Niebrzydowski, "Secular Women and Late-Medieval Marian Drama," *Yearbook of English Studies* 43 (2013): 121–39; and Njus, "Margery Kempe."

123. Johnston and Rogerson, *York*, 1:47–48, 2:732–33; Evans, "When a Body Meets a Body." Following Ann Eljenholm Nichols, I classify this episode as a trial of the Virgin; see "The Hierosphthitic Topos, or the Fate of Fergus: Notes on the N-Town Assumption," *Comparative Drama* 25, no. 1 (1991): 29–41. The apocryphal Proto-Gospels stress that Mary's body must not touch the ground during her infancy, and the legend of her funeral the same after her dormition; in both traditions, the impurity of unconsecrated earth threatens Mary's perfection during vulnerable periods of transition. In this particular episode, attackers seek to touch what has remained untouched and humiliate (in its literal sense of "make low") what is about to ascend, thereby disproving Mary's exceptionalism, perfection, and purity.

124. *Piers the Plowman's Crede*, in *Six Ecclesiastical Satires*, ed. James M. Dean, TEAMS Middle English Texts (Kalamazoo, MI: Medieval Institute Publications, 1991), 77–78.

125. Johnston and Rogerson, *York*, 2:732.

126. Evans, "When a Body Meets a Body," 203–5.

127. Chaucer, "Wife of Bath's Prologue," *Canterbury Tales*, 558, 102.

128. Frederick Millet Salter, "The Banns of the Chester Plays," *Review of English Studies* 16, no. 62 (1940): 144.

129. My take on this episode is indebted to the illuminating readings of Gail Gibson, Ruth Evans, Elina Gertsman, and Helen Cushman. See Gibson, "Scene and Obscene," 16–21; Evans, "Virginities," esp. 21–23; Gertsman, *Worlds Within*, esp. 144–45; and Cushman, "Handling Knowledge," 292–98.

130. "Tunc Salome tentabit tangere Mariam in sexu secreto, et stamin arescent manus eius, et Clamando dicat." Lumiansky and Mills, *Chester Mystery Cycle* (1974), 118; David Mills, ed., *The Chester Mystery Cycle* (East Lansing, MI: Colleagues Press, 1992), 118.

131. See also Paris, Robert, and Bonnardot, *Miracles de Nostre Dame*, 185–93; Muir, *Biblical Drama*, 101; Gail McMurray Gibson, "Scene and Obscene," 16; and Gertsman, *Worlds Within*, 143–45.

132. Gail McMurray Gibson, "Scene and Obscene," 17; Glancy, *Corporal Knowledge*, 82–87; Gerstman, *Worlds Within*, 143.

133. Gertsman, *Worlds Within*, 62. See also Gail McMurray Gibson, "Scene and Obscene," 20; Evans, "Virginities," 22; and Cushman, "Handling Knowledge."

134. Jerome, "On the Perpetual Virginity," 23.

135. *MED*, s.v. "tasten."

136. John Gower, *Confessio Amantis*, ed. Russell A. Peck, 3 vols., TEAMS Middle English Texts (Kalamazoo, MI: Medieval Institute Publications, 2004), 3:5.7792–93.

137. For a complication of this distinction, see Gertsman, *Worlds Within*, 109–12.

138. *MED*, s.v. "assaien" 5; Cushman, "Handling Knowledge," 294–96.

139. N-Town 14.211–13, 14.226–28.

140. Nahum M. Sarna, *The JPS Torah Commentary: Genesis* (Philadelphia: Jewish Publication Society, 1989), 23, 342.

141. *MED*, s.v. "cleven"; *OED*, s.v "cleave"; Cushman, "Handling Knowledge," 294–95.

142. *MED*, s.v. "ransaken"; *OED*, s.v. "ransack."

143. Stephen Atkinson, "'They . . . Toke Their Shyldys before Them and Drew Oute Their Swerdys . . .': Inflicting and Healing Wounds in Malory's *Morte Darthur*," in *Wounds and Wound Repair in Medieval Culture*, ed. Larissa Tracy and Kelly DeVries (Leiden: Brill, 2015), 536–37, 540–42.

144. *OED*, s.v. "cut" 2, "slit," "gash" 1; *MED*, s.v. "slitte," "garse."

145. For other representative uses of the word *clean* in N-Town, see 10.70, 10.72, 10.74, 10.328, 10.486, 12.155, 12.157, 14.172, 14.226, 14.337, 14.340.

146. John 20:27; Haenchen, *John 2*, 211. This is a well-established comparison; see Cushman, "Handling Knowledge," 287–92; Caviness, *Visualizing Women*, 158–62; Gertsman, *Worlds Within*, 50, 88–89; and Evans, "Virginities," 22.

147. N-Town 15.218, 15.225, 15.247, 15.251, 15.256.

148. Diane E. Booton, "Variation on a Limbourg Theme: Anastasia at the Nativity in a Getty Book of Hours and in French Medieval Literature," *Fifteenth-Century Studies* 29 (2004): 62–63; Nichols, "Hierosphthitic Topos," 30–32.

149. Late medieval iconography tends to conflate and confuse Salome the Doubting Midwife with Saint Anastasia, another legendary witness of the Nativity; see Jacqueline A. Morgan, "The Midwife in the *Holkham Bible Picture Book*," *Notes and Queries* 39, no. 1 (1992): 23; and Booton, "Variation on a Limbourg Theme," 61.

150. Karma Lochrie, "Mystical Acts, Queer Tendencies," in *Constructing Medieval Sexuality*, ed. Karma Lochrie, Peggy McCracken, and James A. Schulz (Minneapolis: University of Minnesota Press, 1997), 190–91; Mark Amsler, "Affective Literacy: Gestures of Reading in the Later Middle Ages," *Essays in Medieval Studies* 18, no. 1 (2001): 98.

151. Lochrie, "Mystical Acts, Queer Tendencies," 190.

152. Lumiansky and Mills, *Chester Mystery Cycle* (1974), 6.525–39. See also Mirk, *Mirk's Festial*, 23; Frances A. Foster, ed., *A Stanzaic Life of Christ Compiled from Higden's Polychronicon and the Legenda Aurea Edited from MS. Harley 3909*, EETS (London: Oxford University Press, 1862), 15–16.

153. See, for example, Woolf, *English Mystery Plays*, 178–79; Merrall Llewelyn Price, "Re-membering the Jews," 442; Lampert, *Gender and Jewish Difference*, 126–27.

154. Augustine, *City of God*, trans. Henry Bettenson (London: Penguin Classics, 2003), 22.8.

155. Chaucer, "Miller's Prologue," *Canterbury Tales*, 3163–64.

156. *MED*, s.v. "privite"; *OED*, s.v. "privity."

157. Chaucer, "Miller's Prologue," *Canterbury Tales*, 3152.

158. Ibid., 3162.

159. The Miller's advice resembles Pascal's: if you "cannot believe," the performance of faith "will make you believe quite naturally, and will make you more docile." Blaise Pascal, *Pensées*, trans. A. J. Krailsheimer. (New York: Penguin Classics, 1966), 124–25.

160. Waller, *Virgin Mary*, 36, 57.

161. Desiderius Erasmus, *Seven Dialogues Both Pithie and Profitable* (London, 1606), image 69, available on EEBO.

162. See Gregory H. Roscow, *Syntax and Style in Chaucer's Poetry* (Woodbridge, UK: D. S. Brewer, 1981), 103–6.

163. Kendrick, *Chaucerian Play*, 18.

164. Chaucer, "Miller's Prologue," *Canterbury Tales*, 3141–42.

165. "Natus est rex" from MS Royal 18 B.xxiii in *Middle English Sermons*, ed. Woodburn O. Ross, EETS (London: Oxford University Press, 1940), 221–22.

166. Ignatius of Antioch, "Letter to the Ephesians 19," 328. See also Luigi Gambero, *Mary and the Fathers of the Church: The Blessed Virgin Mary in Patristic Thought*, trans. Thomas Buffer (San Francisco: Ignatius, 1991), 28.

167. Thomas Aquinas, *Catena Aurea: St. Matthew*, trans. Mark Pattison and John Henry Newman (Oxford: John Henry Parker, 1841), 1.1.41; Gambero, *Mary and the Fathers*, 292–301.

168. Luz, *Matthew 1–7*, 99–100. See also John Chrysostom, *Homilies on the Gospel of Matthew*, ed. Philip Schaff (New York: Christian Literature, 1888), 22.

169. Ian Logan, *Reading Anselm's "Proslogion": The History of Anselm's Argument and Its Significance Today* (Burlington, VT: Ashgate, 2009), 19.

Chapter 3

1. For more on the importance of cunning in the N-Town Plays, see Kathleen Ashley, "'Wyt' and 'Wysdam' in the N-Town Cycle," *Philological Quarterly* 58, no. 2 (1979): 121–35.

2. Spector, *N-Town Play*, 2:420 note 2/156.

3. As, for example, in Michelle P. Brown, ed., *The Holkham Bible Picture Book: A Facsimile* (London: British Library, 2007), fig. 4. For more on medieval representations of this scene, see John Flood, *Representations of Eve in Antiquity and the English Middle Ages* (New York: Routledge, 2011), 72–74.

4. On lying in Genesis 3, see Dallas G. Denery, *The Devil Wins: A History of Lying from the Garden of Eden to the Enlightenment* (Princeton, NJ: Princeton University Press, 2015), 47–51.

5. Sarna, *JPS Torah Commentary*, 25; Claus Westermann, *Genesis 1–11: A Commentary* (Minneapolis: Augsburg, 1984), 182, 240–48.

6. Westermann, *Genesis 1–11*, 248–50.

7. See, for example, Kristen E. Kvam, Linda S. Schearing, and Valarie H. Ziegler, eds., *Eve and Adam: Jewish, Christian, and Muslim Readings on Genesis and Gender* (Indianapolis: Indiana University Press, 1999), 112–13. Essential feminist readings of patristic misogyny include Beauvoir, *Second Sex*, 11; and Daly, *Beyond God the Father*, 44–68.

8. Tertullian, *De cultu feminarum*, ed. M. Turcan, Sources Chrétiennes 173 (Paris: Éditions du Cerf, 1971), 42–44; Kvam, Schearing, and Ziegler, *Eve and Adam*, 132–33.

9. Chaucer, "Wife of Bath's Prologue," *Canterbury Tales*, 720.

10. Beauvoir, *Second Sex*, 189.

11. Glancy, *Corporal Knowledge*, 93–94.

12. Justin Martyr, *Dialogue with Trypho*, 102–3; Justin Martyr, *Dialogus cum Tryphone*, in *PG*, ed. J.-P. Migne (Paris: Imprimerie Catholique, 1857), 6:710–11.

13. Luke 1:28; Brian Reynolds, *Gateway to Heaven: Marian Doctrine and Devotion, Imagery and Typology in the Patristic and Medieval Periods* (New York: New City, 2012), 1:133.

14. Westermann, *Genesis 1–11*, 183.

15. Ibid., 260–61.

16. Graef, *Mary*, 31; Irenaeus, *Adversus haereses*, ed. W. Wigan Harvey (Cambridge: Cambridge University Press, 1857), 2:124.

17. Newman, *Sister of Wisdom*, 167–71; Peters, *Patterns of Piety*, 130–32.

18. Ingo F. Walther and Norbert Wolf, *Codices Illustres: The World's Most Famous Illuminated Manuscripts, 400–1600* (London: Taschen, 2001), 382–83.

19. For more on the equation of the tree of knowledge and the Cross, see Tamarah Kohanski and C. David Benson, eds., *The Book of John Mandeville*, TEAMS Middle English Texts (Kalamazoo, MI: Medieval Institute Publications, 2007), 135–48. See also Spector, *N-Town Play*, 2:434 note 7/61–64.

20. Parker, *Aesthetics of Antichrist*, 49–55.

21. Justin Martyr, *Dialogue with Trypho*, 102; Justin Martyr, *Dialogus cum Tryphone*, 710.

22. Labriola and Smeltz, *Bible of the Poor*, 15, 57, 99, 143–45. See also Peters, *Patterns of Piety*, 139–40.

23. *Eve Spinning*, fifteenth century, stained glass, St. Mary's, Martham, Norfolk, available on ARTstor.

24. Chaucer, "Second Nun's Prologue," *Canterbury Tales*, 41–43. For more on the idea that Mary wove Jesus's body, see Coletti, "Devotional Iconography," 25–26; Gail McMurray Gibson, *Theater of Devotion*, 156–66; Kathryn M. Rudy and Barbara Baert, eds., *Weaving, Veiling, and Dressing: Textiles and Their Metaphors in the Late Middle Ages* (Turnhout: Brepols, 2007), 2–3; Gertsman, *Worlds Within*, 56.

25. Glancy, *Corporal Knowledge*, 94; Constas, *Proclus of Constantinople*, 277, 286–87; Reynolds, *Gateway to Heaven*, 114.

26. "Crediderat Eva serpenti, credidit Maria Gabrieli." Tertullian, *De carne Christi*, in *PL*, ed. J.-P. Migne (Paris: Imprimerie Catholique, 1844), 2:782B.

27. Flood, *Representations of Eve*, 14; Reynolds, *Gateway to Heaven*, 114–15.

28. Graef, *Mary*, 234; Engelbert of Admont, *De gratis et virtutibus beatae et gloriosae semper virginis Mariae*, in *Thesaurus anecdotorum novissimus*, ed. Bernhard Pez (Vienna: Veith, 1721), 1.758D, 1.738B.

29. Italics mine. Graef, *Mary*, 198. "O Virgo virginum, ubi es? ut si ullo modo Trinitas illa quaternitatem externam admitteret, tu sola quaternitatem compleres." Peter of Celle, *Sermones*, in *PL*, ed. J.-P. Migne (Paris: Imprimerie Catholique, 1855), 202:675D.

30. Graef, *Mary*, 170; Eadmer, *Liber de excellentia Virginis Mariae*, 575C, 587A–B.

31. Anselm of Canterbury, *Orationes sive meditationes*, in *S. Anselmi opera omnia*, ed. F. S. Schmitt (Stuttgart: Fromann, 1946), 3:22. For more on the Re-creation, see Newman, *Sister of Wisdom*, 162–64; and Ritchey, *Holy Matter*, 13–15.

32. Graef, *Mary*, 167; Ritchey, *Holy Matter*, 13; Anselm, *Orationes*, 21. For more on Anselm's theology of the Virgin, see Fulton Brown, *From Judgment to Passion*, 170–92.

33. Anselm, *Orationes*, 21; Eadmer, *Liber de excellentia Virginis Mariae*, 587A.

34. Anselm writes, "He who was able to make everything from nothing refused to remake it by force, but first became the Son of Mary" (Qui potuit omnia de nihilo facere: noluit ea violata, nisi prius fieret MARIAE filius, reficere); Anselm, *Orationes*, 22. Likewise, Eadmer specifies that God made everything through his power (*Deus sua potentia parando cuncta*), whereas Mary remade everything through her merit (*Maria suis meritis cuncta reparando*); Eadmer, *Liber de excellentia Virginis Mariae*, 587A.

35. Ritchey, *Holy Matter*, 52.

36. Bernardino of Siena, *De superadmirabili gratia et gloria Matris Dei*, 376; Graef, *Mary*, 249.

37. Newman, *Sister of Wisdom*, 162.

38. Barber, *Bestiary*, 118–19.

39. Newman, *Sister of Wisdom*, 163–64, 273–74.

40. Bernardino of Siena, *De superadmirabili gratia et gloria Matris Dei*, 380; Graef, *Mary*, 250.

41. For an introduction to the concept of the *felix culpa*, see David L. Jeffrey, *A Dictionary of Biblical Tradition in English Literature* (Grand Rapids, MI: William B. Eerdmans, 1992), 274–75.

42. Maxwell S. Luria and Richard L. Hoffman, eds., *Middle English Lyrics*, Norton Critical Edition (New York: Norton, 1974), 147.

43. "Et si ea inobediret Deo, sed et haec suasa est obedire Deo, uti virginis Evae virgo Maria fieret advocata." Irenaeus, *Adversus haereses*, 2:376.

44. N-Town 10.49, 10.394, 15.19, 15.37.

45. *MED*, s.v. "wilde."

46. Ibid., 2c.

47. Lemay, *Women's Secrets*, 141–42.

48. Monica Green, ed., *The Trotula: A Medieval Compendium of Women's Medicine* (Philadelphia: University of Pennsylvania Press, 2001), 77.

49. *OED*, s.v. "pica." For more on pica (also known as *cissa*), see Monica H. Green, ed., *Women's Healthcare in the Medieval West: Texts and Contexts* (Aldershot, UK: Routledge, 2000), 53–88; Sera Young, *Craving Earth: Understanding Pica—The Urge to Eat Clay, Starch, Ice, and Chalk* (New York: Columbia University Press, 2011).

50. Aristotle, *Historia animalium: Books 7–10*, ed. and trans. D. M. Balme, Loeb Classical Library 439 (Cambridge, MA: Harvard University Press, 1991), 3.446–47.

51. Chaucer, "Wife of Bath's Prologue," *Canterbury Tales*, 466.

52. Sherwyn T. Carr, "The Middle English Nativity Cherry Tree: The Dissemination of a Popular Motif," *Modern Language Quarterly* 36 (1975): 133–34.

53. R. W. Lightbown, *Carlo Crivelli* (New Haven, CT: Yale University Press, 2004), 21.

54. Luria and Hoffman, *Middle English Lyrics*, 228–29.

55. *MED*, s.v. "cheri."

56. See also Eugene B. Cantelupe and Richard Griffith, "The Gifts of the Shepherds in the Wakefield 'Secunda Pastorum': An Iconographical Interpretation," *Mediaeval Studies* 28 (1966): 331, 333.

57. Steinberg, *Sexuality of Christ*, fig. 138; Gerard David (1460–1525), *Holy Family*, Flemish, oil on panel, Museum of Fine Arts, Boston.

58. See Mark 11:12–14, 11:20–25; and Matthew 21:18–22. For more on the commentary tradition, see Adela Yardbro Collins, *Mark: A Commentary*, ed. Harold W. Attridge, Hermeneia (Minneapolis: Fortress, 2007), 522–37. For more on the parable of the barren fig tree (Luke 13.6–9) and the parable of the budding fig tree (Mark 13.28–31), see Arland J. Hultgren, *The Parables of Jesus: A Commentary* (Grand Rapids, MI: W. B. Eerdmans, 2000), 241–47.

59. For more on cherries as symbols of virginity, see Bruce A. Rosenberg, "The Cherry Tree Carol and the *Merchant's Tale*," *Chaucer Review* 5, no. 4 (1971): 268; and Barre Toelken, "Riddles Wisely Expounded," *Western Folklore* 25, no. 1 (1966): 3.

60. Ehrman and Pleše, *Apocryphal Gospels*, 106–9; Spector, *N-Town Play*, 2:469–70.

61. "The Cherry Tree Carol," in *The English and Scottish Popular Ballads*, ed. Francis James Child (Mineola, NY: Dover, 1965), 2:1–6; William Studwell, *The Christmas Carol Reader* (New York: Routledge, 2011), 41–42.

62. Carr, "Middle English Nativity Cherry Tree," 133, 142–43.

63. See, for example, Rosenberg, "Cherry Tree Carol," 272. My reading, by contrast, expands on Waller's comparison: *Virgin Mary*, 71.

64. For more on N-Town's representations of the womb, see also Sara Petrosillo, "A Microhistory of the Womb from the N-Town Mary Plays to Gorboduc," *Journal of Medieval and Early Modern Studies* 47, no. 1 (2017): 128–32, 138–42.

65. Susan Karant-Nunn and Merry Wiesner-Hanks, eds., *Luther on Women: A Sourcebook* (Cambridge: Cambridge University Press, 2003), 46.

66. For more on the paradoxical nature of the medieval Virgin, see Helen Philips, "'Almighty and Al Merciable Queene': Marian Titles and Marian Lyrics," in *Medieval Women: Texts and Contexts in Late Medieval Britain: Essays for Felicity Riddy*, ed. Jocelyn Wogan-Browne et al. (Turnhout: Brepols, 2000), 83–99; Kay, *Courtly Contradictions*, 179–215; and Koppelman, "Devotional Ambivalence" and "Becoming Her Man," 203–4.

67. Graef, *Mary*, 249–50.

68. Bernardino of Siena, *De superadmirabili gratia et gloria Matris Dei*, 376.

69. My own translation. See also Rubin, *Mother of God*, 299; and Graef, *Mary*, 249.

70. Chaucer, "Prioress's Prologue," *Canterbury Tales*, 467–73.

71. For more on the medieval tradition of the "Mystic Hunt of the Unicorn," see Gertrud Schiller, *Iconography of Christian Art* (London: Lund Humphries, 1971), 1:52–55; Margaret B. Freeman, *The Unicorn Tapestries* (New York: Metropolitan Museum of Art, 1976); Odell Shepard, *The Lore of the Unicorn* (New York: Harper Colophon Books, 1979); Adolfo Salvatore Cavallo, *The Unicorn Tapestries in the Metropolitan Museum of Art* (New York: Metropolitan Museum of Art, 1998); and Christa Grössinger, "The Unicorn on English Misericords," in *Medieval Art: Recent Perspectives*, ed. Gale R. Owen-Crocker and Timothy Graham (Manchester: Manchester University Press, 1998), 142–58.

72. Curley, *Physiologus*, 51, 86–87. See also *OED*, s.v. "monoceros."

73. John Trevisa, trans., *De proprietatibus rerum* (Westminster, UK: Wynkyn de Worde, 1495), 18.90, available on EEBO.

74. Jeanette Beer, *Beasts of Love: Richard de Fournival's "Bestiaire d'amour" and a Woman's "Response"* (Toronto: University of Toronto Press, 2003), 60.

75. Shepard, *Lore of the Unicorn*, 50.

76. Beer, *Beasts of Love*, 60–61.

77. Margaret B. Freeman, *Unicorn Tapestries*, 23.

78. Beer, *Beasts of Love*, 60–61.

79. Curley, *Physiologus*, 51; Shepard, *Lore of the Unicorn*, 49.

80. Barber, *Bestiary*, 36; Hildegard of Bingen, *Physica*, in *PL*, ed. J.-P. Migne (Paris: Imprimerie Catholique, 1855), 197:7.5.1317–18.

81. Christian Heck and Rémy Cordonnier, *The Grand Medieval Bestiary: Animals in Illuminated Manuscripts* (New York: Abbeville, 2012), 414.

82. Margaret B. Freeman, *Unicorn Tapestries*, 112–14, 80, 125, 120–21, 84.

83. Cavallo, *Unicorn Tapestries*, 10.

84. Shepard, *Lore of the Unicorn*, 50; Cavallo, *Unicorn Tapestries*, 24.

85. Barber, *Bestiary*, 36–37; Cavallo, *Unicorn Tapestries*, 21–22.

86. Curley, *Physiologus*, 51.

87. Gregory the Great, *S. Gregorii Magni Moralia in Job*, ed. Marci Adriaen, 3 vols. (Turnhout: Brepols, 1979–85), 3:1572f.

88. "Marye, mayde mylde and fre," in Saupe, *Middle English Marian Lyrics*, p. 165, lines 61–62.

89. Ellington, *From Sacred Body*, 63–64.

90. Lydgate, *Life of Our Lady*, 332–35. For more on Lydgate and N-Town, see Gail McMurray Gibson, "Bury St. Edmunds."

91. Lydgate, *Life of Our Lady*, p. 334, lines 337–38.

92. Ibid., lines 341–42.

93. *MED*, s.v. "wrappen"; *OED*, s.v. "wrap."

94. Trevisa, *De proprietatibus rerum*, 18.90.

95. Leena Mari Peltomaa, *The Image of the Virgin Mary in the Akathistos Hymn* (Leiden: Brill, 2001), 104.

96. I am borrowing a phrase from the news: Nicole Puglise, "'Pussy Grabs Back' Becomes Rallying Cry for Female Rage against Trump," *Guardian*, October 10, 2016. Thanks to Masha Raskolnikov for making this connection.

97. Cavallo, *Unicorn Tapestries*, 22–24, 44–58; Shepard, *Lore of the Unicorn*, 58–59.

98. Margaret B. Freeman, *Unicorn Tapestries*, 26; Cavallo, *Unicorn Tapestries*, 45–48.

99. Cavallo, *Unicorn Tapestries*, 51.

100. Cavallo, *Unicorn Tapestries*, 38; Margaret B. Freeman, *Unicorn Tapestries*, 47; Grössinger, "Unicorn on English Misericords," 147–48.

101. Cavallo, *Unicorn Tapestries*, 27.

102. Newman, *God and the Goddesses*, 313.

103. Ibid., 313, 405.

104. David Freedberg, "Johannes Molanus on Provocative Paintings: *De Historia Sanctarum Imaginum et Picturarum*, Book II, Chapter 42," *Journal of the Warburg and Courtauld Institutes* 34 (1971): 239–45, and "The Hidden God: Image and Interdiction in the Netherlands in the Sixteenth Century," *Art History* 5 (1982): 133–53.

105. Cavallo, *Unicorn Tapestries*, 22–23, 47–51.

106. Ibid., 64–65; Margaret B. Freeman, *Unicorn Tapestries*, 102–4.

107. Margaret B. Freeman, *Unicorn Tapestries*, 23.

108. Schiller, *Iconography of Christian Art*, 1:52–53.

109. Spector, *N-Town Play*, 2:451–52. For more on the "Parliament of Heaven," see Hope Traver, *The Four Daughters of God: A Study of the Versions of This Allegory* (Philadelphia: John Winston, 1907); Samuel Chew, *The Virtues Reconciled: An Iconographic Study* (Toronto: University of Toronto Press, 1947); Hans-Jürgen Diller, "From Synthesis to Compromise: The Four Daughters of God in Early English Drama," *EDAM Review* 18 (1996): 88–103; and Paul Williamson, ed., *Object of Devotion: Medieval English Alabaster Sculpture from the Victoria and Albert Museum* (Alexandria, VA: Art Services International, 2010), 116.

110. For more on the number 4,604, see Spector, *N-Town Play*, 2:452–53.

111. Adapted from the Vulgate: "Et pax Dei quae exsuperat omnem sensum" (Philippians 4:7).

112. Sugano, *N-Town Plays*, 107, note 187–88.

113. Hugh of Saint Victor, *De arca Noe morali*, in *PL*, ed. J.-P. Migne (Paris: Imprimerie Catholique, 1854), 176:621–25; Bernard of Clairvaux, *In Festo Annunciationis Beatae Virginis*, in *PL*, ed. J.-P. Migne (Paris: Imprimerie Catholique, 1862), 183:383–90.

114. Bernard of Clairvaux, *In Festo Annunciationis Beatae Virginis*, 388; Traver, *Four Daughters of God*, 16.

115. Bernard of Clairvaux, *In Festo Annunciationis Beatae Virginis*, 388. See also Spector, *N-Town Play*, 2:456 note 11.138–68.

116. Bernard of Clairvaux, *In Festo Annunciationis Beatae Virginis*, 388; Traver, *Four Daughters of God*, 16.

117. Bernard of Clairvaux, *In Festo Annunciationis Beatae Virginis*, 389; Traver, *Four Daughters of God*, 17.

118. E. Ruth Harvey, ed., *The Court of Sapience* (Toronto: University of Toronto Press, 1984), 9–19.

119. *The Castle of Perseverance*, in *Medieval Drama*, ed. David Bevington (Boston: Houghton Mifflin, 1975), 3159–61. All subsequent citations of *The Castle of Perseverance* refer to this edition.

120. Lydgate, *Life of Our Lady*, pp. 313–14, lines 41, 46, 49–51.

121. William Langland, *The Vision of Piers Plowman,* ed. A. V. C. Schmidt (New York: J. M. Dent and E. P. Dutton, 1978), 18.142. The meaning of the word *waltrot* is unclear. Skeat associates *waltrot* with *trotwal*, which the *Middle English Dictionary* defines as "vain talk, idle tale-telling, a trifle"; see *MED*, s.v. "trotevāle." William Langland, *The Vision of Piers Plowman in Three Parallel Texts Together with Richard the Redeless*, ed. Walter Skeat, 2 vols. (Oxford: Clarendon, 1886), 2:254n146.

122. Langland, *Vision of Piers Plowman,* 18.187.

123. Lydgate, *Life of Our Lady*, p. 323, line 187.

124. Here, the text refers to Psalm 144:9 in the Vulgate: "Suavis Dominus universis; et miserationes ejus super omnia opera ejus" (The Lord is sweet to all: and his tender mercies are over all his works). See also Lydgate, *Life of Our Lady*, p. 318, lines 113–14; and Harvey, *Court of Sapience*, p. 9, line 204.

125. Lydgate, *Life of Our Lady*, p. 319, lines 120–21.

126. Harvey, *Court of Sapience*, p. 9, lines 204–9.

127. See N-Town 8.9, 9.8, 11.338, 41.119, and 41.526 for references to Mary as the Mother of Mercy.

128. See Fulton Brown, *From Judgment to Passion*, 246–47.

129. Eadmer, *Liber de excellentia Virginis Mariae*, 570B.

130. Ibid. "Invocato autem nominee Matris, etsi merita invocantis non merentur: merita tamen Matris intercedunt, ut exaudiatur."

131. Graef, *Mary*, 212; Albertus Magnus, *De laudibus beatae Virginis*, 344.

132. For more on Mary's role as mankind's lawyer, see Williams-Boyarin, *Miracles of the Virgin in Medieval England*, 32–33.

133. Decker and Walsh, *Mariken van Nieumeghen*, 94–95.

134. Ibid., 96–97.

135. Ibid., 102–3.

136. I am thinking in particular of Mary and Saturn from the altarpiece from Boeslunde Church in West Zealand, Denmark, made in Germany in the early fifteenth century; in Poul Grinder-Hansen, *Guides to the National Museum: Danish Middle Ages and Renaissance* (Copenhagen: National Museum, 2002), 91.

137. Thomas Aquinas, *Summa Theologiae*, vol. 25, ed. John Fearon (London: Blackfriars, 1969), 109–14.

138. Augustine, *The Trinity*, trans. Stephen McKenna (Washington, DC: Catholic University of America Press, 1963), 360; Aquinas, *Summa* 25:108–9.

139. Chaucer, "Parson's Tale," *Canterbury Tales*, 330–31; Aquinas, *Summa* 25:108–9.

140. N-Town 21.115–32; Love, *Love's Mirror*, 19; Harvey, *Court of Sapience*, 146.

141. N-Town 11.177–84; Spector, *N-Town Play*, 2:457 note 11/183.

142. Robert Hasenfratz, ed., *Ancrene Wisse*, TEAMS Middle English Texts (Kalamazoo, MI: Medieval Institute Publications, 2000), 83–86.

143. Boccaccio, *Il Filostrato*, 172–73.

144. For more on the relationship between Venus and the Virgin, see Camille, *Gothic Idol*, 220–41.

145. See D. W. Robertson, "The Doctrine of Charity in Medieval Literary Gardens," *Speculum* 26 (1951): 43–45; Kenneth A. Bleeth, "The Image of Paradise in the *Merchant's Tale*," in *The Learned and the Lewed: Studies in Chaucer and Medieval Literature*, ed. Larry D. Benson (Cambridge, MA: Harvard University Press, 1974), 45–60; Rosenberg, "Cherry Tree Carol"; Mike Rodman Jones, "January's Genesis: Biblical Exegesis and Chaucer's *Merchant's Tale*," *Leeds Studies in English* 39 (2008): 53–87; and Chad Schrock, "The Ends of Reading in the *Merchant's Tale*," *Philological Quarterly* 91, no. 4 (2012): 591–609.

146. Chaucer, "Merchant's Tale," *Canterbury Tales*, 2335.

147. Rosenberg, "Cherry Tree Carol," 266.

148. Chaucer, "Merchant's Tale," *Canterbury Tales*, 2333.

149. Bleeth, "Image of Paradise," 53.

150. See Samantha Katz Seal, "Pregnant Desire: Eyes and Appetites in the *Merchant's Tale*," *Chaucer Review* 48, no. 3 (2014): 284–306; Carol A. Everest, "Pears and Pregnancy in Chaucer's 'Merchant's Tale,'" in *Food in the Middle Ages: A Book of Essays*, ed. Melitta Weiss Adamson (New York: Garland, 1995), 161–75; Carol Falvo Heffernan,

"Contraception and the Pear Tree Episode of Chaucer's 'Merchant's Tale,'" *Journal of English and German Philology* 94 (1995): 31–41.

151. Chaucer, "Merchant's Tale," *Canterbury Tales*, 2334.

152. Ibid., 1598.

153. Ibid., 1461–63; Rosenberg, "Cherry Tree Carol," 267–68.

154. D. W. Robertson, "Doctrine of Charity," 44.

155. Chaucer, "Merchant's Tale," *Canterbury Tales*, 2238–39.

156. Ibid., 2242, 2247–48, 2250–51. See also Ecclesiastes 7:27–29 in the Vulgate.

157. Chaucer, "Merchant's Tale," *Canterbury Tales*, 2252.

158. Ibid., 2057–68; Tory Vandeventer Pearman, "O Sweete Venym Queynte!': Pregnancy and the Disabled Female Body in the *Merchant's Tale*" in *Disability in the Middle Ages: Reconsiderations and Reverberations*, ed. Joshua R. Eyler (Burlington: Ashgate, 2010), 32–4.

159. Chaucer, "Merchant's Tale," *Canterbury Tales*, 2277, 2298.

160. Ibid., 2287–90.

161. Ibid., 2305–10.

162. Ibid., 2311–12.

163. Ibid., 2266–67.

164. Ibid., 2268–70.

165. Ibid., 2271.

166. See Leviticus 20:10.

167. See, for example, Chaucer, "Miller's Tale," *Canterbury Tales*, 3294–96.

168. *MED*, s.v. "swiven."

169. Chaucer, "Merchant's Tale," *Canterbury Tales*, 2408–10.

170. N-Town 14.306–9; "The Snow Drop," in *Gallic Salt: Eighteen Fabliaux*, trans. Robert Harrison (Berkeley: University of California Press, 1974), 380–89.

171. Chaucer, "Merchant's Tale," *Canterbury Tales*, 2418.

Chapter 4

1. For more on the importance of purgation and purity in N-Town's Mary plays, see Kathleen Ashley, "Image and Ideology: Saint Anne in Late Medieval Drama and Narrative," in *Interpreting Cultural Symbols: Saint Anne in Late Medieval Society*, ed. Kathleen Ashley and Pamela Sheingorn (Athens: University of Georgia Press, 1990), 115–21; Coletti, "Purity and Danger." See also Glancy, *Corporal Knowledge*, 106–17; and Lily C. Vuong, *Gender and Purity in the Protevangelium of James* (Tübingen, Germany: Mohr Siebeck, 2013).

2. Ehrman and Pleše, *Apocryphal Gospels*, 46–47.

3. Ibid., 46–47, 84–85; N-Town 9.45.

4. Ehrman and Pleše, *Apocryphal Gospels*, 48–49; N-Town 9.194, 9.207, 9.250.

5. Ehrman and Pleše, *Apocryphal Gospels*, 48–49, 86–87; N-Town 9.246–50. See also Spector, *N-Town Play*, 2:445.

6. N-Town 9.248. See also Pieter W. Van Der Horst, "Sex, Birth, Purity and Asceticism in the Protevangelium Jacobi," in *A Feminist Companion to Mariology*, ed. Amy-Jill

Levine and Maria Mayo Robbins (New York: Continuum, 2005), 65–66; Susan Signe Morrison, *Excrement in the Late Middle Ages: Sacred Filth and Chaucer's Fecopoetics* (New York: Palgrave Macmillan, 2008), 53–54; Cuffel, *Gendering Disgust*, 150–51; and Glancy, *Corporal Knowledge*, 111–12.

7. For the phrase *inventrix virginitatis*, see Hrotsvitha of Gandersheim, *The Non-dramatic Works of Hrosvitha*, ed. and trans. Maria Gonsalva Wiegand (Saint Louis, MI: Saint Louis University, 1936), pp. 174–75, line 290.

8. For more on the *consecratio virginum*, see Rabia Gregory, *Marrying Jesus in Medieval and Early Modern Northern Europe: Popular Culture and Religious Reform* (New York: Routledge, 2016), esp. 175.

9. Ehrman and Pleše, *Apocryphal Gospels*, 48–49. See also Charles T. Wood, "The Doctor's Dilemma: Sin, Salvation, and the Menstrual Cycle in Medieval Thought," *Speculum* 56, no. 4 (1981): 717–22; Gertsman, *Worlds Within*, 96–97; and Glancy, *Corporal Knowledge*, 111–12.

10. N-Town 10.10–11.

11. See Emma Lipton, *Affections of the Mind*, 101–2.

12. N-Town 10.93–94. See Augustine, *Expositions of the Psalms, 73–98*, 73–109.

13. N-Town 10.108–19.

14. Ibid., 10.120–32, 10.257–67.

15. Ibid., 8.196.

16. Sarna, *JPS Torah Commentary*, 13.

17. See Jeremy Cohen, *Be Fertile and Increase, Fill the Earth and Master It: The Ancient and Medieval Career of a Biblical Text* (Ithaca, NY: Cornell University Press, 1989), 76–82; Calum Carmichael, *Sex and Religion in the Bible* (New Haven, CT: Yale University Press, 2010), 1–5. For an exception to the rule, see Daniel Boyarin, *Carnal Israel: Reading Sex in Talmudic Culture* (Berkeley: University of California Press, 1993), 3.

18. For complications of this characterization of Jesus, see Peter Brown, *Body and Society*, 41; and Karen L. King's controversial "'Jesus Said to Them, 'My Wife . . .': A New Coptic Papyrus Fragment," *Harvard Theological Review* 107, no. 2 (2014): 131–59.

19. For more on clerical celibacy, see Helen Parish, *Clerical Celibacy in the West, c. 1100–1700* (Burlington, VT: Ashgate, 2010).

20. Peter Brown, *Body and Society*, 44–57.

21. See Stephen J. Stein, *The Shaker Experience in America: A History of the United Society of Believers* (New Haven, CT: Yale University Press, 1992); and Jeff Bach, *Voices of the Turtledoves: The Sacred World of Ephrata* (University Park: Pennsylvania State University Press, 2003).

22. Jerome, *Dialogue against Jovinianus*, in *Letters and Select Works*, trans. W. H. Fremantle, Nicene and Post-Nicene Fathers 6 (London: Parker, 1893), 360; Jerome, *Adversus Jovinianum*, in *PL*, ed. J.-P. Migne (Paris: Imprimerie Catholique, 1883), 23:246C. See also David G. Hunter, *Marriage, Celibacy, and Heresy in Ancient Christianity: The Jovinianist Controversy* (Oxford: Oxford University Press, 2007).

23. N-Town 9.172, 9.174, 9.178–82, 9.185, 9.217. See also Sugano, *N-Town Plays*, 357, note 172–85.

24. Kathleen Ashley and Pamela Sheingorn, introduction to *Interpreting Cultural Symbols*, ed. Ashley and Sheingorn, 27–32.

25. Dyan Elliott, *Spiritual Marriage*, 43–45.

26. Marina Warner, *Alone of All Her Sex*, xxi, 365.

27. Much has been written about the Virgin as a misogynist mechanism of sexual shame; see, for a representative example, Miryam Clough, *Shame, the Church and the Regulation of Female Sexuality* (New York: Routledge, 2017), 127–28.

28. For more on the Virgin as both exemplar and exception, see Marina Warner, *Alone of All Her Sex*, 79–80; Penny Schine Gold, *The Lady and the Virgin: Image, Attitude, and Experience in Twelfth-Century France* (Chicago: University of Chicago Press, 1985), 68–75; Joan Young Gregg, *Devils, Women, and Jews: Reflections of the Other in Medieval Sermon Stories* (New York: State University of New York Press, 1997), 105–6; and Alcuin Blamires, *The Case for Women in Medieval Culture* (Oxford: Clarendon, 1997), 120–21.

29. "Dicet aliquis: Cur exemplum attulisti Mariæ, quasi reperiri queat matrem Domini quæ possit iinitari?" Ambrose, *De virginibus*, in *PL*, ed. J.-P. Migne (Paris: Imprimerie Catholique, 1845), 16:212B.

30. Alcuin Blamires, ed., *Woman Defamed and Woman Defended: An Anthology of Medieval Texts* (Oxford: Clarendon, 1992), 13–14, 172; Giovanni Boccaccio, *The Corbaccio*, ed. and trans. Anthony K. Cassell (Urbana: University of Illinois Press, 1975), 32–34.

31. Ashley, "Image and Ideology," 120.

32. Bernard of Clairvaux, *Letters*, 292; Bernard of Clairvaux, "Epistola 174," 332D–333A.

33. Camille Chabaneau, ed., *Le romanz de Saint Fanuel et de Sainte Anne et de Nostre Dame et de Nostre Segnor et de ses Apostres* (Paris: Charles Leclerc, 1889), 11. See also Boulton, *Sacred Fictions of Medieval France*, 36–38.

34. Francesca Sautman, "Saint Anne in Folk Tradition: Late Medieval France," in Ashley and Sheingorn, *Interpreting Cultural Symbols*, 70–71.

35. See "Hayle, luminary and benigne lantern," in Saupe, *Middle English Marian Lyrics*, 51.23.

36. Morrison, *Excrement*, 25, 167.

37. Cuffel, *Gendering Disgust*, 60.

38. Merrall Llewelyn Price, "Re-membering the Jews," 447. For more on *The Book of Nestor the Priest*, see Ryan Szpiech, *Conversion and Narrative: Reading and Religious Authority in Medieval Polemic* (Philadelphia: University of Pennsylvania Press, 2012), 108–10.

39. Cuffel, *Gendering Disgust*, 58–66. For a more nuanced take on Tertullian's method of response in particular, see Glancy, *Corporal Knowledge*, 117–27.

40. Ehrman and Pleše, *Apocryphal Gospels*, 62–65.

41. Dyan Elliott, *Fallen Bodies*, 107–12.

42. Graef, *Mary*, 165–69.

43. Boccaccio, *Corbaccio*, 32–33. See also N-Town 14.340.

44. Anselm of Canterbury, *Cur Deus Homo*, in *PL*, ed. J.-P. Migne (Paris: Imprimerie Catholique, 1864), 158:419B.

45. Graef, *Mary*, 169–73; Eadmer, *De conceptione Beatae Mariae Virginis*, in *PL*, ed. J.-P. Migne (Paris: Imprimerie Catholique, 1854), 159:303C.

46. Graef, *Mary*, 172; Eadmer, *De conceptione*, 305C–D.

47. For more on this controversy, see Carlo Balic, "The Medieval Controversy over the Immaculate Conception up to the Death of Scotus," in *The Dogma of the Immaculate Conception: History and Significance*, ed. Edward Dennis O'Connor (South Bend, IN: University of Notre Dame Press, 1958), 161–212; Mayberry, "Controversy over the Immaculate Conception"; and Marielle Lamy, *L'Immaculée Conception: Étapes et enjeux d'une controverse au Moyen Âge: XIIe-XVe siècles* (Paris: Institut d'Études Augustiniennes, 2000).

48. Aristotle, *Historia animalium*, 434–35.

49. Virginia Nixon, *Mary's Mother: Saint Anne in Late Medieval Europe* (University Park: Pennsylvania State University Press, 2004), 14, 167.

50. "Aut certe peccatum quomodo non fuit, ubi libido non defuit?" Bernard of Clairvaux, "Epistola 174," 335C; Bernard of Clairvaux, *Letters*, 292.

51. Aquinas, *Summa* 51:14–15.

52. Dyan Elliott, *Fallen Bodies*, 112; Mayberry, "Controversy over the Immaculate Conception," 207–8; Marina Warner, *Alone of All Her Sex*, 239–40.

53. Bernard of Clairvaux, "Epistola 174," 335C; Bernard of Clairvaux, *Letters*, 292.

54. Boss, *Empress and Handmaid*, 123–55.

55. Marina Warner, *Alone of All Her Sex*, 236–38; Kristeva, "Stabat Mater," 139.

56. Mayberry, "Controversy over the Immaculate Conception," 208–9.

57. I would like to thank Mary Dzon for sharing her insights into this matter. See Bernard of Clairvaux, "Epistola 174," 335C; Bernard of Clairvaux, *Letters*, 292–93; and Gérard Blangez, ed., *Ci nous dit: Recueil d'exemples moraux*, 2 vols. (Paris: Publications de la Société des anciens textes français, 1979), 1:45–46.

58. Sautman, "Saint Anne in Folk Tradition," 70–72, 74.

59. Bernard of Clairvaux, "Epistola 174," 335D; Bernard of Clairvaux, *Letters*, 293.

60. Bernard of Clairvaux, "Epistola 174," 336C; Bernard of Clairvaux, *Letters*, 293.

61. Mayberry, "Controversy over the Immaculate Conception," 216; Nixon, *Mary's Mother*, 71–72.

62. Boss, *Empress and Handmaid*, 132–33; Ton Brandenbarg, "Saint Anne: A Holy Grandmother and Her Children," in *Sanctity and Motherhood: Essays on Holy Mothers in the Middle Ages*, ed. Anneke B. Mulder-Bakker (New York: Garland, 1995), 44–45, 47–50.

63. E. W. McDonnell, *The Beguines and Beghars in Medieval Culture* (New Brunswick, NJ: Rutgers University Press, 1954), 498–500; John Mahoney, "Alice of Bath: Her 'Secte' and 'Gentil Text,'" *Criticism* 6, no. 2 (1964): 144–55, esp. 151; Robert E. Lerner, *The Heresy of the Free Spirit in the Later Middle Ages* (Berkeley: University of California Press, 1972), 395–97; Carolyn Dinshaw, *Getting Medieval: Sexualities and Communities, Pre- and Postmodern* (Durham, NC: Duke University Press, 1999), 143–82, esp. 145–46.

64. Roger Ellis, ed., *The Liber Celestis of St Bridget of Sweden*, EETS (Oxford: Oxford University Press, 1987), 1:438.

65. Muir, *Biblical Drama*, 90.

66. Staley, *Book of Margery Kempe*, 1.1.405. See also Mayberry, "Controversy over the Immaculate Conception," 211–12.

67. Staley, *Book of Margery Kempe*, 1.1.406.

68. Ibid., 1.1.1115, 1.1.1118–19.

69. Ibid., 1.1.1111–12. See also Nixon, *Mary's Mother*, 13–16.

70. Ellis, *Liber Celestis*, 1:467; Brandenbarg, "Saint Anne," 54.

71. Chaucer, "Wife of Bath's Prologue," *Canterbury Tales*, 127.

72. Anneke Mulder-Bakker, "Introduction," in *Sanctity and Motherhood*, ed. Mulder-Bakker, 4, 27; Pierre Delooz, *Sociologie et canonisations* (Liège, Belgium: Faculté de droit, 1969), 330–33; Donald Weinstein and Rudolph M. Bell, *Saints and Society: The Two Worlds of Western Christendom* (Chicago: University of Chicago Press, 1982), 121–37.

73. For more on Elizabeth of Hungary, see Voragine, *Golden Legend*, 2:302–17; and Dyan Elliott, *Proving Woman*, 85–118. For more on Bridget of Sweden, see Marguerite Tjader Harris, ed., *Birgitta of Sweden: Life and Selected Revelations*, trans. Albert Ryle Kezel (New York: Paulist, 1991), 69–98; and Ellis, *Liber Celestis*, 1:1–5.

74. Voragine, *Golden Legend*, 2:304.

75. Ibid., 2:304–5; Dyan Elliott, *Proving Woman*, 94–95.

76. Marguerite Tjader Harris, *Birgitta of Sweden*, 75; Ellis, *Liber Celestis*, 1:1.

77. Nixon, *Mary's Mother*, 71–72; Brandenbarg, "Saint Anne," 45–54.

78. See Genesis 16:1–3, 25:26, 30:1–24; and 1 Samuel 1:1–20. See also N-Town 8.181–88.

79. Ehrman and Pleše, *Apocryphal Gospels*, 40–41.

80. Osbern Bokenham, *Life of St. Anne*, in *Middle English Legends of Women Saints*, ed. Sherry L. Reames, TEAMS Middle English Texts (Kalamazoo, MI: Medieval Institute Publications, 2003), 229, 244, 233–36, 239.

81. Chaucer, "Miller's Tale," *Canterbury Tales*, 3228.

82. Judith R. Baskin, *Midrashic Women: Formations of the Feminine in Rabbinic Literature* (Hanover, NH: Brandeis University Press, 2002), 126–28.

83. Schaberg, *Illegitimacy of Jesus*, 164; Emma Lipton, *Affections of the Mind*, 101–2.

84. Bokenham, *Life of St. Anne*, 259–60.

85. Ibid., 432, 442, 448.

86. Ibid., 444.

87. Matthew 1:1–16; Schaberg, *Illegitimacy of Jesus*, 32–43.

88. Ehrman and Pleše, *Apocryphal Gospels*, 40–45.

89. N-Town 8.89, 8.92, 8.124, 8.132, 8.153.

90. Ibid., 8.66, 8.78.

91. Ibid., 8.123–24. See also Ehrman and Pleše, *Apocryphal Gospels*, 42–43.

92. See N-Town 10.49–52, 10.394, 15.19, 15.37.

93. Mayberry, "Controversy over the Immaculate Conception," 213, 221–22; Ellington, *From Sacred Body*, 63–64.

94. N-Town 8.197, 10.63.

95. *MED*, s.v. "sinken."

96. Mayberry, "Controversy over the Immaculate Conception," 211; Boss, *Empress and Handmaid*, 141.

97. Nixon, *Mary's Mother*, 71–72.

98. Chaucer, "Wife of Bath's Prologue," *Canterbury Tales*, 102–3, 113–14, 149.

99. Brandenbarg, "Saint Anne," 54–56.

100. Maurice Vloberg, "Iconography of the Immaculate Conception," in *The Dogma of the Immaculate Conception: History and Significance*, ed. Edward Dennis O'Connor (Notre Dame, IN: University of Notre Dame Press, 1958), 465–66.

101. Voragine, *Golden Legend*, 2:307–9; Dyan Elliott, *Proving Woman*, 90; Marguerite Tjader Harris, *Birgitta of Sweden*, 85–86.

102. Dyan Elliott, *Spiritual Marriage*, 44.

103. Chaucer, "Wife of Bath's Prologue," *Canterbury Tales*, 28–29.

104. Luz, *Matthew 1–7*, 98; Jerome, *Adversus Helvidium*, 193–216; Jerome, "On the Perpetual Virginity," 23–37.

105. Ashley and Sheingorn, introduction, 11–12; Nixon, *Mary's Mother*, 16. For greater detail, see Jennifer Welsh, *The Cult of Saint Anne in Medieval and Early Modern Europe* (London: Routledge, 2017), 71–72.

106. Meredith and Kahrl, *N-Town Plays*, xxiii. See also Bokenham, *Life of St. Anne*, 108–10.

107. Pamela Sheingorn, "Appropriating the Holy Kinship: Gender and Family History," in Ashley and Sheingorn, *Interpreting Cultural Symbols*, 169–98, esp. 174, 186, 191.

108. Fulbert of Chartres, "In ortu almae virginis Mariae inviolatea," in *PL*, ed. J.-P. Migne (Paris: Imprimerie Catholique, 1854), 141:326D; Thomas Aquinas, *Commentary on Saint Paul's Epistle to the Galatians*, trans. M. L. Lamb (Albany, NY: Magi Books, 1966), 1.5; G. Albert, J. M. Parent, and A. Guillemette, "La légende des trois mariages de Sainte-Anne: Un texte nouveau," in *Études d'histoire littéraire et doctrinale du XIIIᵉ siècle* (Paris: Librairie Philosophique J. Vrin, 1932), 165–84; Brandenbarg, "Saint Anne," 44, 51–54.

109. Ashley, "Image and Ideology," 119; Elisabeth Lopez, *Colette of Corbie (1381–1447): Learning and Holiness*, trans. JoAnne Waller (New York: Franciscan Institute Publications, 2011), 113.

110. Brandenbarg, "Saint Anne," 51.

111. For complications to this narrative, see Welsh, *The Cult of Saint Anne*, 132–33 and 160–77.

112. Nixon, *Mary's Mother*, 38–39.

113. Ashley and Sheingorn, introduction, 47–48.

114. Ibid., 47; Charlene Villaseñor Black, "St. Anne Imagery and Maternal Archetypes in Spain and Mexico," in *Colonial Saints: Discovering the Holy in the Americas, 1500–1800*, ed. Allan Greer and Jodi Bilinkoff (New York: Routledge, 2003), 7–11; Johannes Molanus, *De Historia Sanctarum Imaginum et Picturarum*, in *Traité des saintes images*, ed. Francois Boespflug, Olivier Christin, and Benoit Tassel, 2 vols. (Paris: Editions du Cerf, 1996), 1:412–14. See also Welsh, *The Cult of Saint Anne*, 160–1.

115. Alexandre de Laborde, ed., *La Bible moralisée illustrée conservée à Oxford, Paris et Londres* (Paris: Société française de reproductions de manuscrits à peintures, 1911), vol. 1, plate 17.

116. Spector, *N-Town Play*, 2:424; Muir, *Biblical Drama*, 73–74. As Christina M. Fitzgerald argues, "Because of their figural association with the Virgin, female characters receive greater and more positive characterization in N-Town" than in its dramatic analogues; *The Drama of Masculinity and Medieval English Guild Culture* (New York:

Palgrave Macmillan, 2007), 5. For more on this distinction between N-Town and its analogues, see Coletti, "Feminist Approach," 88–89.

117. See Anna Jean Mill, "Noah's Wife Again," *PMLA* 56, no. 3 (1941): 613–26; V. A. Kolve, *Chaucer and the Imagery of Narrative: The First Five Canterbury Tales* (Stanford, CA: Stanford University Press, 1984), 198–205; and Alfred David, "Noah's Wife's Flood" in *The Performance of Middle English Culture: Essays on Chaucer and the Drama in Honor of Martin Stevens*, ed. James J. Paxson, Lawrence M. Clopper, and Sylvia Tomasch (Cambridge, UK: D.S. Brewer, 1998), 97–109.

118. Chaucer, "Miller's Tale," *Canterbury Tales*, 3538–40.

119. Woolf, *English Mystery Plays*, 138.

120. Kolve, *Play Called Corpus Christi*, 147.

121. On the limitations of this typology, see Katie Normington, *Gender and Medieval Drama* (Cambridge, UK: D. S. Brewer, 2004), 121–31.

122. See Birger A. Pearson, *Gnosticism, Judaism, and Egyptian Christianity* (Philadelphia: Fortress, 1990), 84–94; and Sergey Minov, "Noah and the Flood in Gnosticism," in *Noah and His Book(s)*, ed. Michael E. Stone, Aryeh Amihay, and Vered Hillel (Atlanta, GA: Society of Biblical Literature, 2010), 215–36.

123. Minov, "Noah and the Flood," 229.

124. See "The Nature of the Rulers" in *The Nag Hammadi Scriptures*, ed. Marvin W. Meyer (New York: Harper One, 2007), 194–95; and Gerard P. Luttikhuizen, *Gnostic Revisions of Genesis Stories and Early Jesus Traditions* (Leiden: Brill, 2006), 97–107.

125. Kolve, *Chaucer*, 201–3; George Warner, *Queen Mary's Psalter: Miniatures and Drawings by an English Artist of the 14th Century, Reproduced from Royal MS. 2 B. VII in the British Museum* (London: British Museum, 1912); Adelaide Bennett, "Noah's Recalcitrant Wife in the Ramsey Abbey Psalter," *Notes in the History of Art* 2, no. 1 (1982): 2–5; "Newcastle Play," in *Non-cycle Plays and Fragments*, ed. Norman Davis, EETS (London: Oxford University Press, 1970), 19–31.

126. "Newcastle Play," 112.

127. Kolve, *Chaucer*, 202; George Warner, *Queen Mary's Psalter*, 57.

128. For more on this moment, see Katie Normington, "'Have Her a Drink Full Good': A Comparative Analysis of Staging Temptation in the Newcastle Noah Play," *Staging Scripture: Biblical Drama, 1350–1600*, ed. Peter Happe and Wim Husken (Leiden: Brill, 2016), 166–81.

129. George Warner, *Queen Mary's Psalter*, plate 10a.

130. Sarah Stanbury, "Houses, Halls, and Roofed Chambers: The Ark as Playhouse" (paper presented at the Twentieth Biennial Congress of the New Chaucer Society, London, July 12, 2016).

131. "Newcastle Play," 136.

132. Ibid., 136–39; Kolve, *Chaucer*, 205, fig. 95.

133. For more on Noah's wife in Towneley, see Ruth Evans, "Feminist Re-enactments: Gender and the Towneley Uxor Noe," in *A Wyf Ther Was: Essays in Honour of Paule Mertens-Fonck*, ed. Juliette Dor (Liège, Belgium: Liège Language and Literature, 1992), 141–54; Sidhu, *Indecent Exposure*, 192–97.

134. Chaucer, "Wife of Bath's Prologue," *Canterbury Tales*, 489–90, and "Merchant's Tale," *Canterbury Tales*, 1670–73; Newman, *From Virile Woman to WomanChrist*, 115–16.

135. Martin Stevens and Cawley, *Towneley Plays*, 3.280–86.

136. Ibid., 3.560–72, 3.573–80. See also the Coventry Weavers' *Presentation and Disputation in the Temple*, in Norman Davis, *Non-cycle Plays and Fragments*, 472–74.

137. See Eve Salisbury, Georgiana Donavin, Merrall Llewelyn Price, eds., *Domestic Violence in Medieval Texts* (Gainesville: University of Florida Press, 2002); Sara Margaret Butler, *The Language of Abuse: Marital Violence in Later Medieval England* (Leiden: Brill, 2007); and Lillian Randall, *Images in the Margins of Gothic Manuscripts* (Berkeley: University of California Press, 1966), 157 and figs. 394, 576, 708–10.

138. Kolve, *Chaucer*, 205. For more on domestic violence in the Towneley Noah pageant, see Sidhu, *Indecent Exposure*, 197–98.

139. Chaucer, "Wife of Bath's Tale," *Canterbury Tales*, 503–24, 788–93.

140. Martin Stevens and Cawley, *Towneley Plays*, 3.328–31.

141. See, for example, Woolf, *English Mystery Plays*, 144–45; Kolve, *Chaucer*, 445; and David, "Noah's Wife's Flood," 97.

142. N-Town 10.206–7.

143. See, for example, Anderson, *Drama and Imagery*, 107; Woolf, *English Mystery Plays*, 190; and Waller, *Virgin Mary*, 75.

144. Martin Stevens and Cawley, *Towneley Plays*, 15.144–50.

145. See, for example, Jean-Claude Frère, *Early Flemish Painting* (Paris: Terrail, 2007), 14–21; Michelle P. Brown, *Holkham Bible Picture Book*, 48–49, fol. 14; John Plummer, ed., *The Hours of Catherine of Cleves* (New York: Braziller, 1966), fig. 13; and Martial Rose, *Stories in Stone: The Medieval Roof Carvings of Norwich Cathedral* (New York: Thames and Hudson, 1997), 118.

146. Albrecht Dürer, "The Flight into Egypt," in *Albrecht Dürer: His Art in Context*, ed. Jochen Sander (Munich: Prestel, 2013), 235–38.

147. C. M. Armstrong, *The Moralizing Prints of Cornelis Anthonisz* (Princeton, NJ: Princeton University Press, 1990), 37–44 and fig. 28; Malcolm Jones, *Secret Middle Ages*, 30–31.

148. Armstrong, *Moralizing Prints of Cornelis Anthonisz*, 37, 41; Ryan D. Giles, *The Laughter of the Saints: Parodies of Holiness in Late Medieval and Renaissance Spain* (Toronto: University of Toronto Press, 2009), 6–7; Martha Bayless, *Parody in the Middle Ages* (Ann Arbor: University of Michigan Press, 1996), 57–86. See also Dolan, *Whores of Babylon*, 110–15.

149. Dirk Bax, *Hieronymus Bosch: His Picture-Writing Deciphered* (Rotterdam: Balkema, 1979), 113.

150. Woolf, *English Mystery Plays*, 190.

151. See Meg Twycross, "'Transvestism' in the Mystery Plays," *Medieval English Theatre* 5, no. 2 (1983): 124, 126, 130; and James Stokes, "The Ongoing Exploration of Women and Performance in Early Modern England: Evidences, Issues, and Questions," *Shakespeare Bulletin* 33, no. 1 (2015): 9–31. See also R. W. Ingram, ed., *Coventry*, REED (Toronto: University of Toronto Press, 1981), 122; James M. Gibson, ed., *Kent, Diocese of Canterbury*, 2 vols., REED (Toronto: University of Toronto Press, 2002), 2:782; and Jean Robertson and D. J. Gordon, eds., *The Calendar of Dramatic Records in the Books of the Livery Companies of London* (Oxford: Oxford University Press, 1954), 14–15, 24.

152. Voragine, *Golden Legend*, 1:197. See also Twycross, "'Tranvestism,'" 132–35; Normington, *Gender and Medieval Drama*, 85–88; Jody Enders, *Death by Drama and Other Medieval Urban Legends* (Chicago: University of Chicago Press, 2002), 29–42; and Robert A. L. Clark and Claire M. Sponsler, "Queer Play: The Cultural Work of Cross-Dressing in Medieval Drama," *New Literary History* 28 (1997): 319–44.

153. Twycross, "'Tranvestism,'" 128.

154. Sidney J. H. Herrtage, ed., *Catholicon Anglicum, an English-Latin Wordbook Dated 1483*, EETS (London: Trübner, 1881), 175. See also Chaucer, "Pardoner's Tale," *Canterbury Tales*, 447.

155. Allardyce Nicoll, *Masks, Mimes, and Miracles: Studies in the Popular Theatre* (New York: Cooper Square, 1963), 92–99.

156. N-Town 11.178; Gertsman, *Worlds Within*, 83–85.

157. Twycross, "'Tranvestism,'" 129–30.

158. L. Petit de Julleville, *Les mystères* (Paris: Libraire Hachette, 1880), 2:127.

159. Peter Meredith and John E. Tailby, eds., *The Staging of Religious Drama in Europe in the Later Middle Ages: Texts and Documents in English Translation* (Kalamazoo, MI: Medieval Institute Publications, 1983), 209.

160. Ibid., 57, 144–45.

161. T. E. Bridgett, *Our Lady's Dowry: Or, How England Gained and Lost that Title* (London: Burns and Oates, 1875), 269; James Raine, ed., "The Will of William Brokshaw of East Retford," in *Testamenta Eboracensia: A Selection of Wills from the Registry at York* (Edinburgh: Surtees Society, 1869), 4:164.

162. Meredith and Tailby, *Staging of Religious Drama*, 57.

163. Marina Warner, *Alone of All Her Sex*, p. 114 and plate 15.

164. Mayberry, "Controversy over the Immaculate Conception," 216.

165. John King, *Tudor Royal Iconography: Literature and Art in an Age of Religious Crisis* (Princeton, NJ: Princeton University Press, 1989), 196–97; Eric Ives, *The Life and Death of Anne Boleyn* (Oxford: Blackwell, 2004), 220–24.

166. James P. Carley, *The Books of King Henry VIII and His Wives* (London: British Library, 2004), plates 93–94.

167. Rubin, *Mother of God*, 310; Rose-Marie Hagen and Rainer Hagen, *What Great Paintings Say* (New York: Taschen, 2003), 2:52–57. For yet another such legend (about Pope Alexander VI and Giulia Farnese), see Waller, *Virgin Mary*, 38.

168. Thomas Beard, *Antichrist the Pope of Rome: or, the Pope of Rome is Antichrist Proved in Two Treatises* (London, 1625), available on EEBO, 365.

169. Wallace H. Johnson, "The Origin of the *Second Shepherds' Play*: A New Theory," *Quarterly Journal of Speech* 52, no. 1 (1966): 53–54; Normington, *Gender and Medieval Drama*, 12.

170. Perhaps not coincidentally, Noah calls his wife Gill in the Towneley pageant of Noah's Flood; Martin Stevens and Cawley, *Towneley Plays*, 3.318.

171. For more on the typological structure of this pageant, see William M. Manly, "Shepherds and Prophets: Religious Unity in the Towneley *Secunda Pastorum*," *PMLA* 78, no. 3 (1963): 151–55; and Lawrence J. Ross, "Symbol and Structure in the *Secunda Pastorum*," *Comparative Drama* 1, no. 2 (1967): 122–49.

172. *The Second Shepherds' Play*, in *Medieval Drama*, ed. David Bevington (Boston: Houghton Mifflin, 1975), 392, line 246.

173. Martin Stevens and Cawley, *Towneley Plays*, 13.566.

174. Ibid., 13.718, 13.723.

175. *The Second Shepherds' Play*, in *Medieval Drama*, ed. Bevington, 403, line 587.

176. *MED*, s.v. "queint"; Chaucer, "Miller's Tale," *Canterbury Tales*, 3276, 3605.

177. *The Second Shepherds' Play*, in *Medieval Drama*, ed. Bevington, 395, line 342.

178. Ehrman, *Forgery and Counter-forgery*, 542–46.

179. Martin Stevens and Cawley, *Towneley Plays*, 2.511; Timothy Fry, "The Unity of the *Ludus Coventriae*," *Studies in Philology* 68 (1951): 527–70.

Chapter 5

1. Luz, *Matthew 1–7*, 89.

2. Lydgate, *Life of Our Lady*, p. 398, lines 1238–39.

3. Scholars agree that this law was not kept in practice; see Hermann L. Strack and Paul Billerbeck, *Kommentar zum Neuen Testament aus Talmud und Midrash*, 6 vols. (Munich: C. H. Beck, 1922–61), 1.51–52.

4. William Foxwell Albright and Cristopher Stephen Mann, *Matthew*, Anchor Bible (New Haven, CT: Yale University Press, 1971), 8.

5. See Franco Sottocornola, "Tradition and the Doubt of St. Joseph Concerning Mary's Virginity," *Marianum* 19 (1957): 127–41; and Thomas Aquinas, *Catena Aurea: A Commentary on the Four Gospels*, trans. John Henry Newman (Oxford: John Henry Parker, 1841), 45–47.

6. Jerome, *Commentaire sur Saint Matthieu*, ed. E. Bonnard, Sources Chrétiennes 242 (Paris: Les Éditions du Cerf, 1977), 78; Jerome, *Commentary on Matthew*, trans. Thomas P. Scheck (Washington, DC: Catholic University of America Press, 2008), 63.

7. John Chrysostom, *Homiliae in Matthaeum*, in *PG*, ed. J.-P. Migne (Paris: Imprimerie Catholique, 1862), 58:47–8; John Chrysostom, *The Homilies of Saint John Chrysostom on the Gospel of Matthew*, trans. George Prevost, 2 vols. (Oxford: J. H. Parker, 1843–44), 1:49–52.

8. Jerome, *Commentaire sur Saint Matthieu*, 78; Jerome, *Commentary on Matthew*, 63.

9. Deuteronomy 9:10; Matthew 5:27.

10. Jerome, *Commentaire sur Saint Matthieu*, 78; Jerome, *Commentary on Matthew*, 63.

11. See Haenchen, *John 2*, 21–22.

12. Augustine, *In Evangelium Joannis Tractatus CXXIV*, in *PL*, ed. J.-P. Migne (Paris: Imprimerie Catholique, 1864), 35:1648–49; Augustine, *Tractates on the Gospel of John 28–54*, trans. John W. Rettig, Fathers of the Church 88 (Washington, DC: Catholic University of America Press, 1993), 53–55.

13. Ambrose, *De Apologia Prophetae David*, ed. Carolus Schenkl (Milan: Bibliotheca Ambrosiana, 1981), 144.

14. Jennifer Knust, "'Taking Away From': Patristic Evidence and the Omission of the *Pericope Adulterae* from John's Gospel," in *The Pericope of the Adulteress in Con-

temporary Research, ed. David Alan Black and Jacob N. Cerone (London: Bloomsbury, 2016), 66.

15. Augustine, *De coniugis adulteriis*, in *PL*, ed. J.-P. Migne (Paris: Imprimerie Catholique, 1863), 40:474; Augustine, "Adulterous Marriages," in *Treatises on Marriage and Other Subjects*, ed. Roy Joseph Deferrari, trans. Charles T. Huegelmeyer, Fathers of the Church 27 (Washington, DC: Catholic University of America Press, 1955), 107. See also David Alan Black and Cerone, *Pericope of the Adulteress*.

16. "Quid est, Domine? Faves ergo peccatis?" Augustine, *In Evangelium Joannis Tractatus CXXIV*, 1650; Augustine, *Tractates on the Gospel*, 56–57.

17. See also Matthew 9:20–21; and Luke 13:10–17.

18. James A. Brundage, "Prostitution in the Medieval Canon Law," *Signs* 1, no. 4 (1976): 827–28.

19. Blamires, *Woman Defamed and Woman Defended*, 101.

20. See Luke 7:36–52, 8:1–3, 23:49; and Mark 16:1. For more on the role of women in early Christianity, see Nicola Denzey, *The Bone Gatherers: The Lost Worlds of Early Christian Women* (Boston: Beacon Press, 2007).

21. For an introduction to the history of Mary Magdalene, see Katherine Ludwig Jansen, *The Making of the Magdalen: Preaching and Popular Devotion in the Later Middle Ages* (Princeton, NJ: Princeton University Press, 2000); Jane Schaberg, *Resurrection of Mary Magdalene: Legends, Apocrypha, and the Christian Testament* (New York: Continuum, 2002); and Peter Loewen and Robin Waugh, eds., *Mary Magdalene in Medieval Culture: Conflicted Roles* (New York: Routledge, 2014).

22. The passage in full: "Christ was an adulterer for the first time with the woman at the well, for it was said, 'Nobody knows what he's doing with her' [John 4:27]. Again with Magdalene, and still again with the adulterous woman in John 8[:2–11], whom he let off so easily. So the good Christ had to become an adulterer before he died." Martin Luther, *Table Talk*, ed. Theodore G. Tappert, Luther's Works 54 (Philadelphia: Fortress, 1967), 154.

23. Ernst Robert Curtius, *European Literature and the Latin Middle Ages*, trans. Willard R. Trask (Princeton, NJ: Princeton University Press, 1953), 357–58.

24. See A. J. Minnis and A. B. Scott, eds., *Medieval Literary Theory and Criticism c. 1100–c. 1375: The Commentary Tradition* (Oxford: Clarendon, 1988), 460–61.

25. Horace, *Ars Poetica*, in *Horace for Students of Literature: The "Ars Poetica" and Its Tradition*, ed. O. B. Hardison and Leon Golden (Tampa: University of Florida Press, 1995), 10; Dante, *De Vulgari Eloquentia*, ed. Marianne Shapiro (Lincoln: University of Nebraska Press, 1990), 74. See also Leon Golden, "Aristotle on Comedy," *Journal of Aesthetics and Art Criticism* 42, no. 3 (1984): 283–90.

26. Auerbach, *Mimesis*, 151.

27. Chaucer, "General Prologue," *Canterbury Tales*, 739–40.

28. See K. M. Coleman, "Fatal Charades: Roman Executions Staged as Mythological Enactments," *Journal of Roman Studies* 80 (1990): 44–73.

29. Bernard of Clairvaux, *Sermo in ascensione Domini*, in *PL*, ed. J.-P. Migne (Paris: Imprimerie Catholique, 1862), 183:304.

30. Jerome, *Commentaire sur Saint Matthieu*, 72; Jerome, *Commentary on Matthew*, 59. My reading of Jesus's foremothers derives from Schaberg; see *Illegitimacy of Jesus*, 32–43, and "Feminist Interpretations." See also Gaventa, *Mary*, 33–40.

31. Melissa Jackson, *Comedy and Feminist Interpretation*, 55–58. For more on Tamar, see Genesis 38; Stephen A. Barney, "*Ordo paginis*: The Gloss on Genesis 38," *South Atlantic Quarterly* 91 (1992), 929–43; Esther Marie Menn, *Judah and Tamar (Genesis 38) in Ancient Jewish Exegesis: Studies in Literary Exegesis* (Leiden: Brill, 1997); Stefan Reif, "Early Rabbinic Exegesis of Genesis 38," in *The Exegetical Encounter Between Jews and Christians in Late Antiquity*, ed. Emmanouela Grypeou and Helen Spurling (Leiden: Brill, 2009), 221–44; and Schaberg, *Illegitimacy of Jesus*, 34–35.

32. For more on Rahab, see Joshua 2; Jeffrey S. Shoulson, *Fictions of Conversion: Jews, Christians, and Cultures of Change in Early Modern England* (Philadelphia: University of Pennsylvania Press, 2013), 58–64; and Schaberg, *Illegitimacy of Jesus*, 35–37.

33. For more on Ruth, see Ruth 3:7–15; Lesley Janette Smith, *Medieval Exegesis in Translation: Commentaries on the Book of Ruth* (Kalamazoo, MI: Medieval Institute Publications, 1996); and Schaberg, *Illegitimacy of Jesus*, 37–39.

34. For more on Bathsheba, see 2 Samuel 11; David Lyle Jeffrey, "Bathsheba in the Eye of the Beholder: Artistic Depiction from the Late Middle Ages to Rembrandt," in *Sacred and Profane in Chaucer and Late Medieval Literature: Essays in Honour of John V. Fleming*, ed. Robert William Epstein (Toronto: University of Toronto Press, 2010), 30–45; and Schaberg, *Illegitimacy of Jesus*, 39–41.

35. For an overview of this reading, which stems from Jerome, see Gaventa, *Mary*, 37.

36. Schaberg, *Illegitimacy of Jesus*, 41–43; Gaventa, *Mary*, 38.

37. Lumiansky and Mills, *Chester Mystery Cycle* (1974), 12.217–80; Davidson, *York Corpus Christi Plays*, 24.1–98. Important studies of this pageant include Peter Meredith, "*Nolo Mortem* and the *Ludus Coventriae* Play of the Woman Taken in Adultery," *Medium Ævum* 38, no. 1 (1969): 38–54; Gail McMurray Gibson, "Writing before the Eye"; and Normington, *Gender and Medieval Drama*, 112–15.

38. Bevington, introduction to "The Woman Taken in Adultery," in *Medieval Drama*, 460; Woolf, *English Mystery Plays*, 225.

39. See *MED*, s.v. "scoute"; *OED*, s.v. "scout"; *MED*, s.v. "bi-smare"; *OED*, s.v "bismer"; *MED*, s.v. "quene"; and *OED*, s.v. "quean."

40. N-Town 24.69, 24.119, 24.149, 41.392.

41. Sugano, *N-Town Plays*, p. 402, note 69.

42. See Rosemary Woolf, "The Theme of Christ the Lover-Knight in Medieval English Literature," *Review of English Studies* 13, no. 49 (1962): 1–16; and Newman, *From Virile Woman to WomanChrist*, 137–67.

43. See *MED*, s.v. "daliaunce"; and *OED*, s.v. "dalliance."

44. See *MED*, s.v. "gai"; and *OED*, s.v. "gay."

45. See Robert Louis Wilken, *The Christians as the Romans Saw Them*, 2nd ed. (New Haven, CT: Yale University Press, 2003); and Jennifer Wright Knust, *Abandoned to Lust: Sexual Slander and Ancient Christianity* (New York: Columbia University Press, 2006).

46. Pliny the Younger, *Correspondence with Trajan from Bythinia (Epistles X)*, trans. Wynne Williams (Warminster, UK: Aris and Phillips, 1990), 10.96.2.

47. Origen, *Contra Celsum*, 343, 355.

48. Minucius Felix, *The Octavius of Marcus Minucius Felix*, trans. G. W. Clarke, Ancient Christian Writers 39 (New York: Paulist, 1974), 9.5–6.

49. Peter Brown, *Body and Society*, 60–61.

50. Epiphanius of Salamis, *The Panarion of Epiphanius of Salamis: Book I (Sects 1–46)*, 2nd ed., trans. Frank Williams (Leiden: Brill, 2009), 93–94. See also Stephen Benko, "The Libertine Gnostic Sect of the Phibionites According to Epiphanius," *Vigiliae Christianae* 21, no. 2 (1967): 103–19.

51. Augustine, *In Evangelium Joannis Tractatus CXXIV*, 1650; Augustine, *Tractates on the Gospel*, 56–57.

52. Bevington, *Medieval Drama*, 460.

53. For more on "the hermeneutic Jew," see Cohen, *Living Letters of the Law*, 4–6; and Sara Lipton, *Dark Mirror*, 165.

54. I depart here from Bevington's identification of lust as the foremost sin of the adulteress's persecutors; introduction to "The Woman Taken in Adultery," *Medieval Drama*, 460.

55. *Mary Magdalene*, in Bevington, *Medieval Drama*, pp. 708–9, lines 564–614. See also Katherine Steele Brokaw, *Staging Harmony: Music and Religious Change in Late Medieval and Early Modern English Drama* (Ithaca, NY: Cornell University Press, 2016), 29.

56. See also Davidson, *York Corpus Christi Plays*, 29.283, 29.304, 29.306, 30.208, 30.359, 30.380, 30.531, 31.121, 31.277, 33.135, 33.416.

57. Chaucer, "Parson's Tale," *Canterbury Tales*, 1.885; *MED*, s.v. "harlot"; *OED*, s.v "harlot."

58. L. R. Poos, "Sex, Lies, and the Church Courts of Pre-Reformation England," *Journal of Interdisciplinary History* 25, no. 4 (1995): 591–92.

59. See N-Town 18.73–74, 18.76–77, 26.170, 26.309–10. For more on early English drama's inversions of the word *heretic* in particular, see Ruth Nisse, "Staged Interpretations: Civic Rhetoric and Lollard Politics in the York Plays," *Journal of Medieval and Early Modern Studies* 28, no. 2 (1998): 427–52.

60. All subsequent references to this text derive from the following editions: Gottfried von Strassburg, *Tristan*, trans. A. T. Hatto (London: Penguin Classics, 1967); Gottfried von Strassburg, *Tristan*, ed. Karl Marold (Leipzig: Eduard Uvenarius, 1906). For more on this image, see Margarita Yanson, "'Christ as a Windblown Sleeve': The Ambiguity of Clothing as a Sign in Gottfried von Straßburg's *Tristan*," in *Encountering Medieval Textiles and Dress: Objects, Texts, Images*, ed. D. G. Koslin and Janet E. Snyder (New York: Palgrave Macmillan, 2002), 121–36.

61. Strassburg, *Tristan*, trans. Hatto, 240–48; Strassburg, *Tristan*, ed. Marold, 219–20.

62. Chaucer, *Troilus and Criseyde*, 5.1042–43. For more on Criseyde's sleeve, see Laura F. Hodges, *Chaucer and Array: Patterns of Costume and Fabric Rhetoric in the "Canterbury Tales," "Troilus and Criseyde" and Other Works* (Cambridge, UK: D. S. Brewer, 2014), 84.

63. Chaucer, "Merchant's Tale," *Canterbury Tales*, 2045–46, 2149, 2168–84.

64. See Sharon Moughtin-Mumby, *Sexual and Marital Metaphors in Hosea, Jeremiah, Isaiah, and Ezekiel* (Oxford: Oxford University Press, 2008); Catherine E. Winiarski, "Adultery, Idolatry, and the Subject of Monotheism," *Religion & Literature* 38, no. 3 (2006): 41–63; and John Parker, "Holy Adultery: Marriage in *The Comedy of Errors, The Merchant of Venice*, and *The Merry Wives of Windsor*," in *The Oxford Handbook of Shakespearean Comedy*, ed. Heather Hirschfeld (Oxford: Oxford University Press, 2018). See also Hosea 4–14, Jeremiah 2–4, and Ezekiel 16 and 23. On the parallelism of the

first and second tablets of the law, see Margaret Aston, *England's Iconoclasts: Laws against Images* (Oxford: Clarendon, 1988), 466–79.

65. C. S. Lewis, "What Chaucer Really Did to *Il Filostrato*," *Essays and Studies* 17 (1932): 66.

66. P. G. Walsh, ed., *Andreas Capellanus on Love* (London: Duckworth, 1982), 38–39.

67. Thomas Malory, *Le Morte Darthur*, ed. Stephen H. A. Shepherd (New York: Norton, 2004), 268–69.

68. Graef, *Mary*, 249; Bernardino of Siena, *De superadmirabili gratia et gloria Matris Dei*, 376.

69. See John 4:4–26; and Acts 8:26–40.

70. Winiarski, "Adultery, Idolatry," 52. See also Ambrose, *Apologia David altera*, in *Sancti Ambrosii Opera*, ed. Carolus Schenkl, Corpus Scriptorum Ecclesiasticorum Latinorum 32 (Prague: F. Tempsky, 1897), 393.

71. Jerome, Letter XXII, in *Select Letters of Saint Jerome*, trans. Jeffrey Henderson, Loeb Classical Library 262 (Cambridge, MA: Harvard University Press, 1954), 63; Jerome, *Epistola ad Eustochium de virginitate*, in *PL*, ed. J.-P. Migne (Paris: Imprimerie Catholique, 1845), 22:397–98. See also Neil Adkin, *Jerome on Virginity: A Commentary on the "Libellus de virginitate servanda"* (Cambridge: Cambridge University Press, 2003).

72. For more on "the crown of virginity," see Jerome, *Adversus Helvidium*, 213D–14A.

73. Augustine, "De Sancta Virginitate: On Holy Virginity," in *De bono coniugali and De sancta virginitate*, trans. P. G. Walsh (Oxford: Oxford University Press, 2001), 103.

74. Irven M. Resnick, "Peter Damian on the Restoration of Virginity: A Problem for Medieval Theology," *Journal of Theological Studies* 39, no. 1 (1988): 125–34; R. Gaskin, "Peter Damian on Divine Power and the Contingency of the Past," *British Journal for the History of Philosophy* 5 (1997): 229–47.

75. Thomas Aquinas, *Summa Theologiae*, vol. 43, ed. Thomas Gilby (London: Blackfriars, 1968), 178–81.

76. "Potuit Deus homo ex utero virginali, salva virginitate, procedere; non poterit violatae virginitatis dispendium reparare?" Resnick, "Peter Damian on the Restoration," 129.

77. Voragine, *Golden Legend*, 1:227, 2:234; Ruth Mazo Karras, "Holy Harlots: Prostitute Saints in Medieval Legend," *Journal of the History of Sexuality* 1, no. 1 (1990): 3–32; Jansen, *Making of the Magdalen*, 145–48.

78. Coletti, *Mary Magdalene*, 155–56.

79. Normington, *Gender and Medieval Drama*, 104.

80. My reading here builds on Theresa Coletti's comparison of the Virgin Mary and Mary Magdalene; see *Mary Magdalene*, 90–94, 151–53, 164–91.

81. Bernardino of Siena, *De superadmirabili gratia et gloria Matris Dei*, 376.

82. "Porta igitur Maria, per quam Christus intravit in hunc mundum, quando virginali fusus est partu, et genitalia virginitatis claustra non solvit." Ambrose, *De institutione virginis*, 320. For more on the *porta clausa*, see Gail McMurray Gibson, *Theater of Devotion*, 154; and Gertsman, *Worlds Within*, 16, 77.

83. *MED*, s.v. "wombe"; OED, s.v. "womb."

84. Isidore of Seville, *Liber etymologiarum XI*, in *PL*, ed. J.-P. Migne (Paris: Imprimerie Catholique, 1850), 82:414a; Sophia M. Connell, *Aristotle on Female Animals: A Study*

of the Generation of Animals (Cambridge: Cambridge University Press, 2016), 297; Jacquart and Thomasset, *Sexuality and Medicine*, 24; Lemay, *Women's Secrets*, 66; Gertsman, *Worlds Within*, 65–66, 107–9.

85. Luigi Gambero, *Mary in the Middle Ages: The Blessed Virgin Mary in the Thought of Medieval Latin Theologians*, trans. Thomas Buffer (San Francisco: Ignatius, 2005), 135. For an example of the image of the aqueduct, see Bernard of Clairvaux, *De acquaeductu*, in *PL*, ed. J.-P. Migne (Paris: Imprimerie Catholique, 1862), 183:440. For the neck, see Ellington, *From Sacred Body*, 129; and Gail McMurray Gibson, *Theater of Devotion*, 139.

86. Peltomaa, *Image of the Virgin Mary*, 192; Gambero, *Mary and the Fathers*, 314–15.

87. "Lefdy blisful, of muchel might," in Saupe, *Middle English Marian Lyrics*, 52.7–8. Much thanks to John Parker for drawing my attention to this lyric.

88. For Kristeva's reading of Mary as hole, see Julia Kristeva and Catherine Clément, *The Feminine and the Sacred*, trans. Jane Marie Todd (New York: Columbia University Press, 2001), 78.

89. Constas, *Proclus of Constantinople*, 283; Reynolds, *Gateway to Heaven*, 212–13; Donavin, *Scribit Mater*, 203.

90. Marina Warner, *Alone of All Her Sex*, 285–89; Rubin, *Mother of God*, 132–34.

91. Eadmer, *Liber de excellentia virginis Mariae*, 580B; Gambero, *Mary in the Middle Ages*, 121.

92. Millard Meiss, "An Early Altarpiece from the Cathedral of Florence," *Metropolitan Museum of Art Bulletin* 12, no. 10 (1954): 302–17; Catherine Oakes, *Ora Pro Nobis: The Virgin as Intercessor in Medieval Art and Devotion* (Turnhout: Brepols, 2008), pp. 85–86, fig. 33.

93. "Sicut enim, o beatissima, omnis a te aversus et a te despectus necesse est ut intereat: ita omnis ad te conversus et a te respectus impossibile est ut pereat." Anselm, *Orationes sive meditationes*, 22; Anselm of Canterbury, *The Prayers and Meditations of Saint Anselm*, trans. Benedicta Ward (London: Penguin, 1973), 121.

94. Guibert of Nogent, *De laude S. Mariae*, in *PL*, ed. J.-P. Migne (Paris: Imprimerie Catholique, 1853), 156:556B, 564A, 577A; Graef, *Mary*, 176–77. See also Albertus Magnus, *De laudibus beatae Virginis*, 55; and Graef, *Mary*, 212.

95. Williams-Boyarin, *Miracles of the Virgin in Medieval England*, 46–47; Graef, *Mary*, 176.

96. Clayton, *Cult of the Virgin Mary*, 114.

97. Graef, *Mary*, 227–28.

98. "Beata Virgo optimam sibi elegit, quia facta est regina misericordiae, et Filius eius remansit reae iustitiae; et melior misericordia quam iustitia." Bonaventure, *De assumptione B. Virginis Mariae* in *Opera Omnia*, vol. 9, ed. P. David Fleming (Florence: Quaracchi, 1901), 703.

99. See, for example, Stefan Lochner's *Last Judgment*, in Julien Chapuis, *Stefan Lochner: Image Making in Fifteenth-Century Cologne* (Turnhout: Brepols, 2004), p. 262, plate 2.

100. Bonaventure, *De assumptione B. Virginis Mariae*, 705; Graef, *Mary*, 228.

101. Graef, *Mary*, 176–77.

102. "Ante Mariam non fuit qui sic detinere Dominum auderet." Conrad of Saxony, *Speculum beatae Mariae virginis*, in *Bibliotheca franciscana ascetica medii aevi* (Florence: Quaracchi, 1904), 2:105; Graef, *Mary*, 228–29.

103. For the phrase "Modyr of Mercy," see N-Town 8.9, 9.8, 11.338, 41.119, 41.526. For more on the iconography of the Madonna della Misericordia, see Avraham Ronen, "Gozzoli's St. Sebastian Altarpiece in San Gimignano," *Mitteilungen Des Kunsthistorischen Institutes in Florenz* 32, no. 1/2 (1988): 77–126, esp. 89; Oakes, *Ora Pro Nobis*, p. 278, plate 6; Tommaso Castaldi, *La Madonna della Misericordia: L'iconografia della Madonna della Misericordia e della Madonna delle frecce nell'arte di Bologna e della Romagna nel Tre e Quattrocento* (Bologna: Editrice La Mandragola, 2011); Gertsman, *Worlds Within*, 91–94.

104. Ronen, "Gozzoli's St. Sebastian Altarpiece," 88–100; Louise Marshall, "Manipulating the Sacred: Image and Plague in Renaissance Italy," *Renaissance Quarterly* 47, no. 3 (1994): 512–27.

105. Eadmer, *De conceptione Beatae Mariae Virginis*, 316A–18D.

106. For one version of this joke, see Theresa Sanders, *Celluloid Saints: Images of Sanctity in Film* (Macon, GA: Mercer University Press, 2002), 182. I heard it from Christine Schott.

107. See "Saint Theophilus," in Williams-Boyarin, *Miracles of the Virgin in Middle English*, 17–33. See also Graef, *Mary*, 133–34; Marina Warner, *Alone of All Her Sex*, 331; Rubin, *Mother of God*, 232; Lynette Muir, *Love and Conflict in Medieval Drama: The Plays and Their Legacy* (New York: Cambridge University Press, 2007), 65–69; and Koppelman, "Becoming Her Man," 207–13.

108. Williams-Boyarin, *Miracles of the Virgin in Medieval England*, 47.

109. For more on this image, see Ellen Ettlinger, "Folklore in Oxfordshire Churches," *Folklore* 73, no. 3 (1962): 166–67; John Edwards, "A 'Fifteenth-Century' Wall Painting at South Leigh," *Oxoniensia* 48 (1983): 131–42; and Richard F. Johnson, *Saint Michael the Archangel in Medieval English Legend* (Woodbridge, UK: Boydell, 2005), 148.

110. For more on Mary's scale-tipping, see Voragine, *Golden Legend*, 2:87; "The Dialogue of the Soul and the Body," in *A Study of Three Welsh Religious Plays*, ed. Gwenan Jones (Aberystwyth, Wales: Bala, 1939), 250–51; Eamon Duffy, *The Stripping of the Altars: Traditional Religion in England, 1400–1580*, 2nd ed. (New Haven, CT: Yale University Press: 2005), 319; and Francis Cheetham, *English Medieval Alabasters: With a Catalogue of the Collection in the Victoria and Albert Museum*, 2nd ed. (Woodbridge, UK: Boydell, 2005), 134.

111. For more on the association between the lady of courtly love and the Virgin, see Eileen Power, *Medieval Women*, ed. M. M. Postan (Cambridge: Cambridge University Press, 1975), 11–13; Marina Warner, *Alone of All Her Sex*, 134–48; and Kay, *Courtly Contradictions*, 180.

112. Alfonso X, *Songs of Holy Mary*, 2.

113. Clarissa W. Atkinson, *The Oldest Vocation: Christian Motherhood in the Middle Ages* (Ithaca, NY: Cornell University Press, 1991), 158.

114. Southern, *Making of the Middle Ages*, 248.

115. Boyd, *Middle English Miracles*, 142; Mary McLeod Banks, ed., *An Alphabet of Tales*, EETS (London: Trübner, 1904), 319–20; Alfonso X, *Songs of Holy Mary*, 71–72, 118–19.

116. Banks, *Alphabet of Tales*, 320.

117. For the phrase "patroness of sinners," see Alfonso X, *Songs of Holy Mary*, 71. For more on "The Miracle of the Pregnant Abbess," see Banks, *Alphabet of Tales*, 11–12; and Alan E. Knight, "The Pregnant Abbesses of Paris and Lille" in Maddox and Sturm-Maddox, *Parisian Confraternity Drama*, 135–47. My reading builds on Ruth Mazo Karras's "The Virgin and the Pregnant Abbess: Miracles and Gender in the Middle Ages," *Medieval Perspectives* 3 (1988), 112–32, and departs from the conclusion drawn in Eric T. Metzler's "The Miracle of the Pregnant Abbess: Refractions of the Virgin Birth," *Research on Medieval and Renaissance Drama* 52–53 (2014): 199–203.

118. Metzler, "Miracle of the Pregnant Abbess," 197.

119. Banks, *Alphabet of Tales*, 12.

120. Gail McMurray Gibson, "Writing before the Eye," 402–6.

121. Meredith and Kahrl, *N-Town Plays*, pp. xiv–v, fol. 225v.

122. Sugano, *N-Town Plays*, p. 433, note on "42. Judgment Day." See also Block, *Ludus Coventriæ*, 377; Spector, *N-Town Play*, 2:535–36.

Chapter 6

1. For more on the Madonna in early modern English culture, see Ruth Vanita, "Mariological Memory in *The Winter's Tale* and *Henry VIII*," *SEL: Studies in English Literature 1500–1900* 40, no. 2 (2000): 311–37; Katharine Goodland, *Female Mourning and Tragedy in Medieval and Renaissance English Drama: From the Raising of Lazarus to King Lear* (Aldershot, UK: Ashgate, 2005); Regina Buccola and Lisa Hopkins, eds., *Marian Moments in Early Modern Drama* (Burlington, VT: Ashgate, 2007); Espinosa, *Masculinity and Marian Efficacy*; and Waller, *Virgin Mary*.

2. For more on this transition, see H. C. Gardiner, *Mysteries' End: An Investigation of the Last Days of the Medieval Religious Stage* (New Haven, CT: Yale University Press, 1946); Bing D. Bills, "The 'Suppression Theory' and the English Corpus Christi Play: A Re-examination," *Theatre Journal* 32, no. 2 (1980): 157–68; Paul Whitfield White, "Reforming Mysteries' End: A New Look at Protestant Intervention in English Provincial Drama," *Journal of Medieval and Early Modern Studies* 29, no. 1 (1999): 111–47; Lawrence M. Clopper, "English Drama: From Ungodly *Ludi* to Sacred Play," in *The Cambridge History of Medieval English Literature*, ed. David Wallace (Cambridge: Cambridge University Press, 1999), 739–66; Michael O'Connell, *The Idolatrous Eye: Iconoclasm and Theater in Early-Modern England* (Oxford: Oxford University Press, 2000), 20–27; and James Simpson, *Reform and Cultural Revolution*, vol. 2 of *The Oxford English Literary History* (Oxford: Oxford University Press, 2002), 528–39.

3. Glynne Wickham et al., eds., *English Professional Theatre, 1530–1660* (Cambridge: Cambridge University Press, 2000), 69.

4. Stephen Gosson, *Playes Confuted in Fiue Actions* (London, 1582), E5v–E6r, available on EEBO. See also O'Connell, *Idolatrous Eye*, 88.

5. Audrey Douglas and Peter Greenfield, eds., *Cumberland, Westmorland, Gloucestershire*, REED (Toronto: University of Toronto Press, 1986), 219.

6. Scott Cutler Shershow, *Puppets and "Popular" Culture* (Ithaca, NY: Cornell University Press, 1995), 40–42. For more the relationship between actors and images in medieval drama, see Jill Stevenson, *Performance, Cognitive Theory, and Devotional Culture: Sensual Piety in Late Medieval York* (New York: Palgrave Macmillan, 2010), 120–25; Philip Butterworth, *Staging Conventions in Medieval English Theatre* (Cambridge: Cambridge University Press, 2014), 113–20; Elina Gertsman, "Image and Performance: An Art Historian at the Crossroads," *ROMARD* 51 (2012): 53; and Gertsman, *Worlds Within*, 135–42.

7. Johnston and Rogerson, *York*, 1:291–92. See also Andrea R. Harbin, "Virgin's End: The Suppression of the York Marian Pageants," *Medieval Feminist Forum: A Journal of Gender and Sexuality* 50, no. 2 (2015): 33–63.

8. Johnston and Rogerson, *York*, 1:307; Martin Stevens, "The Missing Parts of the Towneley Cycle," *Speculum* 45 (1970): 263.

9. Stevens, "The Missing Parts of the Towneley Cycle," 258–261, 263. See also Theresa Coletti and Gail McMurray Gibson, "The Tudor Origins of Medieval Drama," in *A Companion to Tudor Literature*, ed. Kent Cartwright (Malden, MA: Wiley-Blackwell, 2010), 240–41.

10. R. M. Lumiansky and David Mills, *The Chester Mystery Cycle: Essays and Documents* (Chapel Hill: University of North Carolina Press, 1983), 190–91.

11. O'Connell, *Idolatrous Eye*, 23–24; David Mills, "'Some Precise Cittizins': Puritan Objections to Chester's Plays," *Leeds Studies in English* 29 (1999): 225–26.

12. O'Connell, *Idolatrous Eye*, 25.

13. Douglas and Greenfield, *Cumberland, Westmorland, Gloucestershire*, 17–19; Beatrice Groves, *Texts and Traditions: Religion in Shakespeare, 1592–1604* (Oxford: Clarendon, 2007), 34–36.

14. Coletti and Gibson, "Tudor Origins of Medieval Drama"; Gail McMurray Gibson, "Manuscript as Sacred Object."

15. Michael O'Connell, "Continuities between 'Medieval' and 'Early Modern' Drama," in *A Companion to English Renaissance Literature and Culture*, ed. Michael Hattaway (Oxford: Blackwell, 2000), 477–85.

16. For pigs' bladders, see Andrea Ria Stevens, *Inventions of the Skin: The Painted Body in Early English Drama, 1400–1642* (Edinburgh: Edinburgh University Press, 2013), 54; for the devil, see John D. Cox, *The Devil and the Sacred in English Drama, 1350–1642* (Cambridge: Cambridge University Press, 2000). For more on staging practices, see Kurt A. Schreyer, *Shakespeare's Medieval Craft: Remnants of the Mysteries on the London Stage* (Ithaca, NY: Cornell University Press, 2014).

17. Crashaw, *Iesuites Gospel*, 16–17, 36. See also Dolan, *Whores of Babylon*, 103.

18. John Bale, *The image of both churches after the moste wonderfull and hevenly Revelacion of Sainct John* (London, 1548), 4r, available on EEBO. See also William Thomas, *The Pilgrim: A Dialogue on the Life and Actions of King Henry the Eighth*, ed. J. A. Froude (London: Parker, Son, and Bourn, 1861), 37–38.

19. Waller, *Virgin Mary*, 12–17, esp. 14; Diehl, *Staging Reform*, 162–63.

20. John Foxe, *Christ Jesus Triumphant* (London, 1607), A4r, available on EEBO.

21. John Stow, *A Survey of London, 1603*, 2 vols., ed. Charles Lethbridge Kingsford (Oxford: Clarendon, 1971), 2:266–67.

22. Italics mine. Crashaw, *Iesuites Gospel*, 36.

23. *OED*, s.v. "avowtery."

24. McSheffrey, *Gender and Heresy*, 146–47. See also *OED*, s.v. "elf."

25. For more on the pox, see Margaret Healy, *Fictions of Disease in Early Modern England: Bodies, Plagues, and Politics* (New York: Palgrave Macmillan, 2001); and Byron Lee Grigsby, *Pestilence in Medieval and Early Modern English Literature* (London: Routledge, 2004).

26. William Roye and Jerome Barlowe, *Rede Me and Be Nott Wrothe*, ed. Douglas H. Parker (Toronto: University of Toronto Press, 1992), 139.

27. Leanne Groeneveld, "A Theatrical Miracle: The Boxley Rood of Grace as Puppet," *Early Theatre* 10, no. 2 (January 2007): 16–17.

28. Ibid., 17.

29. Thomas S. Freeman, "Offending God: John Foxe and English Protestant Reactions to the Cult of the Virgin Mary," in *The Church and Mary*, ed. R. N. Swanson (Rochester, NY: Boydell and Brewer, 2004), 233. See also Richard Sheldon, *A Survey of the Miracles of the Church of Rome* (London, 1616), 14, available on EEBO.

30. Parish, *Monks, Miracles and Magic*, 81; Robert Whiting, "Abominable Idols: Images and Image-Breaking under Henry VIII," *Journal of Ecclesiastical History* 33, no. 1 (1982): 41–42.

31. Aston, *England's Iconoclasts*, 173.

32. John Sommerville, *The Secularization of Early Modern England: From Religious Culture to Religious Faith* (Oxford: Oxford University Press, 1992), 24.

33. James Gairdner, ed., *Letters and Papers, Foreign and Domestic, Henry VIII*, vol. 14.1 (London: Eyre and Spottiswoode, 1894), vol. 14.1, p. 155, no. 402.

34. Craig R. Koester, *Revelation*, Anchor Bible (New Haven, CT: Yale University Press, 2014), 671.

35. Ibid., 29–47, 670–95.

36. Victoria Brownlee, "Imagining the Enemy: Protestant Readings of the Whore of Babylon in Early Modern England," in *Biblical Women in Early Modern Literary Culture, 1550–1700*, ed. Victoria Brownlee and Laura Gallagher (Manchester: Manchester University Press, 2015), 213–18.

37. Diehl, *Staging Reform*, 158–72; Dolan, *Whores of Babylon*, 102–18; Regina Buccola, "Virgin Fairies and Imperial Whores: The Unstable Ground of Religious Iconography in Thomas Dekker's *The Whore of Babylon*," in Buccola and Hopkins, *Marian Moments*, 141–60; Goodland, *Female Mourning*, 4.

38. James Gairdner, ed., *Letters and Papers, Foreign and Domestic, Henry VIII* (London: Eyre and Spottiswoode, 1892), vol. 13.1, p. 437, no. 1177. See also Charles Wriothsley, *A Chronicle of England during the Reigns of the Tudors*, ed. William Douglas Hamilton (London: Camden Society, 1975), 1:80.

39. J. R. Reinhard, "Burning at the Stake in Mediaeval Law and Literature," *Speculum* 16, no. 2 (1941): 186–209; Barbara Hanawalt, "The Female Felon in Fourteenth-Century England," *Viator* 5, no. 1 (1974): 265.

40. Waller, *Virgin Mary*, 1–2; Margaret Aston, *Faith and Fire: Popular and Unpopular Religion, 1350–1600* (London: Hambledon, 1993), 267.

41. Karant-Nunn and Wiesner-Hanks, *Luther on Women*, 46; Martin Luther, *D. Martin Luthers Werke: Kritische Gesamtausgabe*, vol. 1.7, Weimarer Ausgabe (Weimar: Hermann Bohlaus Nachfolger, 1897), 575.

42. Kreitzer, *Reforming Mary*, 41; Crashaw, *Iesuites Gospel*, 36; Thomas Price, preface to *The History of Our B. Lady of Loreto: Tra[n]slated out of Latyn, into English*, by Orazio Torsellino (Saint-Omer, France: English College Press, 1608), 4, available on EEBO.

43. Karant-Nunn and Wiesner-Hanks, *Luther on Women*, 40.

44. N-Town 11.261–92; Spector, *N-Town Play*, p. 458 note 11/261–82; Martin Luther, *D. Martin Luthers Werke: Kritische Gesamtausgabe*, vol. 9 (Weimar: Hermann Böhlaus Nachfolger, 1893), 573–74.

45. Karant-Nunn and Wiesner-Hanks, *Luther on Women*, 39–40, 45–46; Kreitzer, *Reforming Mary*, 42.

46. Hugh Latimer, *Sermons and Remains*, ed. George Elwes Corrie (Cambridge: Cambridge University Press, 1845), 227.

47. Crashaw, *Iesuites Gospel*, 34, 48.

48. William Fleetwood, *An Account of the Life and Death of the Blessed Virgin, According to Romish Writers* (London, 1687), D2V, available on EEBO.

49. John 2:4 (King James Bible, available on the Bible in English Database); Latimer, *Sermons and Remains*, 117. See also Matthew 12:46–50.

50. Parish, *Monks, Miracles and Magic*, 215–17; Kreitzer, *Reforming Mary*, 32–34; Rubin, *Mother of God*, 367–78.

51. Kreitzer, *Reforming Mary*, 122–31.

52. Latimer, *Sermons and Remains*, 227.

53. Crashaw, *Iesuites Gospel*, 16.

54. Diehl, *Staging Reform*, 170–72.

55. Edmund Spenser, *The Faerie Queene: Book 1*, ed. Carol V. Kaske (Indianapolis: Hackett, 2006), p. 24, 1.2.5.

56. John Donne, "Show me, dear Christ, thy spouse, so bright and clear," in *Divine Poems*, ed. Helen Gardner (Oxford: Clarendon, 1969), 15.

57. Susannah Brietz-Monta, *Martyrdom and Literature in Early Modern England* (Cambridge: Cambridge University Press, 2005), 202–12.

58. Edmund Spenser, *The Faerie Queene: Books Three and Four*, ed. Dorothy Stephens (Indianapolis: Hackett, 2006), p. 5, bk. 3, proem, stanza 5. For more on this doubling, see Claire McEachern, *Poetics of English Nationhood, 1590–1612* (Cambridge: Cambridge University Press, 1996), 39–50; Carole Levin, *The Heart and Stomach of a King: Elizabeth I and the Politics of Sex and Power*, 2nd ed. (Philadelphia: University of Pennsylvania Press, 2013), 65–90.

59. John Knox, *A Faithful Admonition to the Professors of God's Truth in England, 1554*, in *The Works of John Knox*, ed. David Laing (Edinburgh: Wodrow Society, 1854), 3:294; Louis Montrose, *The Subject of Elizabeth: Authority, Gender, and Representation* (Chicago: University of Chicago Press, 2006), 195. For more on the association between Elizabeth I and the Virgin Mary, see Roy Strong, *The Cult of Elizabeth: Elizabethan Portraiture and Pageantry* (London: Thames and Hudson, 1977); and Helen Hackett, *Virgin Mother, Maiden Queen: Elizabeth I and the Cult of the Virgin Mary* (New York: St. Martin's, 1995).

60. For more on horn madness, see Mark Breitenberg, *Anxious Masculinity in Early Modern England* (Cambridge: Cambridge University Press, 1996); Pamela Allen Brown, *Better a Shrew Than a Sheep: Women, Drama, and the Culture of Jest in Early Modern England* (Ithaca, NY: Cornell University Press, 2003), 52–55.

61. Diehl, *Staging Reform*, 170, 172–81.

62. Donne, "Show me, dear Christ, thy spouse, so bright and clear," 15.

63. For more on Shakespeare's slandered wives as types of the Virgin, see O'Connell, "Continuities," 484; Groves, *Texts and Traditions*, 43; Waller, *Virgin Mary*, 157–80.

64. This phrase comes from William Gray, "The Fantassie of Idolatrie," in *Gray of Reading: A Sixteenth-Century Controversialist and Ballad-Writer*, ed. Ernest W. Dormer (Reading, UK: Bradley and Sons, 1923), 74. See also Parish, *Monks, Miracles and Magic*, 77.

65. See, for example, the downfalls of Vittoria in John Webster's *White Devil*, Evadne in Francis Beaumont and John Fletcher's *Maid's Tragedy*, Beatrice in Thomas Middleton and William Rowley's *Changeling*, and Annabella in John Ford's *'Tis Pity She's a Whore*.

66. For an expression of these feelings of loss, see, for example, "The Ruins of Walsingham," in *The New Oxford Book of Sixteenth-Century Verse*, ed. Emrys Jones (Oxford: Oxford University Press, 2002), 550; and Waller, *Virgin Mary*, 124–26.

67. Whiting, "Abominable Idols," 40.

68. Duffy, *Stripping of the Altars*, 403.

69. James Gairdner, ed., *Letters and Papers, Foreign and Domestic, Henry VIII* (London: Eyre and Spottiswoode, 1891), vol. 12.2, p. 218, no. 587.

70. Ibid.

71. C. E. Moreton, "The Walsingham Conspiracy of 1537," *Bulletin of the Institute of Historical Research* 63 (1990): 39.

72. Stephen Orgel, *Imagining Shakespeare: A History of Texts and Visions* (New York: Palgrave Macmillan, 2003), 65–70, 82–83.

73. Groves, *Texts and Traditions*, 5; Tarnya Cooper, *Searching for Shakespeare* (New Haven, CT: Yale University Press, 2006), 72–75.

74. For more on whitewashing, see Robert Whiting, *The Reformation of the English Parish Church* (Cambridge: Cambridge University Press, 2010).

75. William Shakespeare, *Henry VIII*, in *The Norton Shakespeare*, 2nd ed., ed. Stephen Greenblatt (New York: Norton, 2008), 5.2.32; William Shakespeare, *King John*, in *The Norton Shakespeare*, 2nd ed., ed. Stephen Greenblatt (New York: Norton, 2008), 2.1.539.

76. All subsequent quotations from *1 Henry VI* refer to William Shakespeare, *Henry VI, Part One*, ed. Michael Taylor (Oxford: Oxford University Press, 2003).

77. Exceptions include Albert Tricomi, "Joan la Pucelle and the Inverted Saints Play in *1 Henry VI*," *Renaissance and Reformation* 25 (2001): 21–22; and Espinosa, *Masculinity and Marian Efficacy*, 33. For a broader comparison of Joan and Mary, see Gillian Woods, *Shakespeare's Unreformed Fictions* (Oxford: Oxford University Press, 2013), 36–38. Among Shakespeare's heroines, the Virgin is most often compared to Hermione. See, for example, Darryll Grantley, "*The Winter's Tale* and Early Religious Drama," *Comparative Drama* 20 (1986): 17–37; Vanita, "Mariological Memory," 320–21; Waller, *Virgin Mary*, 171–80; and Frances Dolan, "Hermione's Ghost: Catholicism, the Feminine, and

the Undead in Early Modern Studies," in *The Impact of Feminism in English Renaissance Studies*, ed. Dympna Callaghan (New York: Palgrave Macmillan, 2007), 228–29.

78. For example, Tricomi reads "Joseph's Trouble about Mary" as a "gently humorous" celebration of the Virgin as opposed to Shakespeare's "farcical and satiric" takedown of Joan; ultimately, he concludes that Joan is Mary's "precise opposite." See "Joan la Pucelle," 22.

79. See Michael Taylor, introduction to Shakespeare, *Henry VI, Part One*, 40; and Gabriele Bernhard Jackson, "Topical Ideology: Witches, Amazons, and Shakespeare's Joan of Arc," *English Literary Renaissance* 18 (1988): 44.

80. Shakespeare, *1 Henry VI*, 1.3.89, 1.6.85. See also Woods, *Shakespeare's Unreformed Fictions*, 30–31.

81. Shakespeare, *1 Henry VI*, 5.3.1–24.

82. For an overview of the attempt to absolve Shakespeare of this play, see Richard Hardin, "Chronicles and Mythmaking in Shakespeare's Joan of Arc," *Shakespeare Survey* 42 (1989): 25.

83. Dyan Elliott, *Proving Woman*, 165.

84. For more on Joan's early reception history, see Pierre Champion, *Le procès de condamnation de Jeanne d'Arc: Texte, traduction et notes*, vol. 1 (Paris: Librairie spéciale pour l'histoire de France, 1920); Daniel Hobbins, *The Trial of Joan of Arc* (Cambridge, MA: Harvard University Press, 2007); and Deborah A. Fraioli, *Joan of Arc: The Early Debate* (Woodbridge, UK: Boydell, 2000).

85. See Vicki L. Hamblin, ed., *Le mistere du siege d'Orleans*, Textes littéraires français (Geneva: Droz, 2002); P. Studer, ed., *Saint Joan of Orleans: Scenes from the Fifteenth-Century "Mystere du siege d'Orleans,"* trans. Joan Evans (Oxford: Clarendon, 1926); and Lynette Muir, "French Saint Plays," in *The Saint Play in Medieval Europe*, ed. Clifford Davidson (Kalamazoo, MI: Medieval Institute Publications, 1986), 123–80. See also Christine de Pizan, *Le Ditié de Jeanne d'Arc*, ed. Angus J. Kennedy and Kenneth Varty (Oxford: Society for the Study of Medieval Languages and Literature, 1977).

86. Edward Hall, *Hall's Chronicle; Containing the History of England, during the Reign of Henry the Fourth and the Succeeding Monarchs to the End of the Reign of Henry the Eighth in Which Are Particularly Described the Manners and Customs of Those Periods. Carefully Collated with the Editions of 1548 and 1550*, ed. Henry Ellis (London: J. Johnson, 1809), 157. See also Raphael Holinshed, *The firste volume of the Chronicles of England, Scotlande, and Irelande* (London, 1577), 2:1241, available on EEBO; and Raphael Holinshed, *The first and second volumes of Chronicles* (London, 1587), 3:604–5, available on EEBO. See also Anke Bernau, "'Saint, Witch, Man, Maid or Whore?': Joan of Arc and Writing History," in Bernau, Evans, and Salih, *Medieval Virginities*, 214–33.

87. For more on Joan's long cultural history, see Marina Warner, *Joan of Arc: The Image of Female Heroism* (Berkeley: University of California Press, 1981); and Deborah McGrady, "Joan of Arc and the Literary Imagination," in *Cambridge Companion to French Literature*, ed. John D. Lyons (Cambridge: Cambridge University Press, 2016), 18–33.

88. Holinshed, *First and second volumes*, 3:604–5. For more on the trial of Joan's virginity, see Françoise Meltzer, *For Fear of the Fire: Joan of Arc and the Limits of Subjectivity* (Chicago: University of Chicago Press, 2001), 92–95.

89. Holinshed, *First and second volumes*, 3:605. See also 2 Corinthians 11:14 and Parish, *Monks, Miracles and Magic*, 49.

90. See also Hall, *Hall's Chronicle*, 148.

91. Karant-Nunn and Wiesner-Hanks, *Luther on Women*, 88–170; Parish, *Clerical Celibacy in the West*, 145. For more on clerical marriage during the Reformation, see Helen L. Parish, *Clerical Marriage and the English Reformation: Precedent, Policy, and Practice* (Burlington, VT: Ashgate, 2000); Marjorie Elizabeth Plummer, *From Priest's Whore to Pastor's Wife: Clerical Marriage and the Process of Reform in the Early German Reformation* (Burlington, VT: Ashgate, 2012).

92. Karant-Nunn and Wiesner-Hanks, *Luther on Women*, 140.

93. Ibid., 169.

94. William Tyndale, *Tyndale's Answer to Sir Thomas More's Dialogue*, ed. Henry Walter (Cambridge: Cambridge University Press, 1851), 52.

95. Thomas Becon, *The Worckes of Thomas Becon*, vol. 1 (London, 1564), CCCCClxxiiV, CCCClxiii, available on EEBO.

96. Parish, *Monks, Miracles and Magic*, 86; John Bale, *The first two partes of the Actes, or unchaste examples of the English votaryes* (London, 1551), 1.A2r, available on EEBO.

97. Reginald Scot, *The Discouerie of Witchcraft* (London, 1584), 79–80, available on EEBO. For a version of Scot's source, see Dyan Elliott, *Proving Woman*, 59.

98. John Bale, *The Image of Bothe Churches*, in *Select Works of John Bale*, ed. Henry Christmas (Cambridge: Cambridge University Press, 1849), 497.

99. Karant-Nunn and Wiesner-Hanks, *Luther on Women*, 99.

100. Ibid., 91, 101.

101. Ibid., 108. For more on greensickness, see Laurinda Dixon, *Perilous Chastity: Women and Illness in Pre-Enlightenment Art and Medicine* (Ithaca, NY: Cornell University Press, 1995); Helen King, *The Disease of Virgins: Green Sickness, Chlorosis, and the Problems of Puberty* (London: Routledge, 2004); Gail Kern Paster, *Humoring the Body: Emotions and the Shakespearean Stage* (Chicago: University of Chicago Press, 2004), 77–134.

102. William Shakespeare, *All's Well That Ends Well*, ed. G. K. Hunter, Arden Shakespeare (London: Thomson, 2006), 1.1.139.

103. Gwendolyn B. Needham, "New Light on Maids 'Leading Apes in Hell,'" *Journal of American Folklore* 75 (1962): 112.

104. Gordon Williams, *Shakespeare's Sexual Language: A Glossary* (London: Continuum, 2006), 160.

105. Ibid., 252, 273.

106. Nathalie Vienne-Guerrin, *Shakespeare's Insults: A Pragmatic Dictionary*, Arden Shakespeare (London: Bloomsbury, 2016), 186–88; Gordon Williams, *Shakespeare's Sexual Language*, 123–24; *OED*, s.v. "fig." See also Shakespeare, *Othello*, 1.3.320.

107. For Luther's more nuanced position, see Karant-Nunn and Wiesner-Hanks, *Luther on Women*, 29.

108. See Shakespeare, *1 Henry VI*, 1.3.102.

109. Foxe, *Second Volume of the Ecclesiastical History*, 1774–77, available on EEBO.

110. Dolan, *Whores of Babylon*, 103. See also Woods, *Shakespeare's Unreformed Fictions*, 38.

111. Hobbins, *Trial of Joan of Arc*, 65–66; Espinosa, *Masculinity and Marian Efficacy*, 48.

112. See Paul H. Freedman, *Images of the Medieval Peasant* (Stanford, CA: Stanford University Press, 1999), 86–104; and David Mark Whitford, *The Curse of Ham in the Early Modern Era: The Bible and Justifications for Slavery* (Burlington, VT: Ashgate, 2009).

113. See, for example, John Webster, *The White Devil*, in *The Works of John Webster*, ed. David Gunby, David Carnegie, and Antony Hammond (Cambridge: Cambridge University Press, 1995); Thomas Adams, *The White Devil, or, The Hypocrite Uncased* (London, 1613), available on EEBO.

114. Woods, *Shakespeare's Unreformed Fictions*, 33–38.

115. Bernard of Clairvaux, *On the Song of Songs II*, trans. Kilian Walsh, Cistercian Fathers 7 (Kalamazoo, MI: Cistercian, 1976), 3.50–57; Bernard of Clairvaux, *Sermones super Cantica Canticorum 1–35*, ed. J. Leclercq, C. H. Talbot, and H. M. Rochais (Rome: Editiones Cistercienses, 1957), 164–65.

116. See Sujata Iyengar, *Shades of Difference: Mythologies of Skin Color in Early Modern England* (Philadelphia: University of Pennsylvania Press, 2005), 44–79.

117. David Luscombe, *The Letter Collection of Peter Abelard and Heloise* (Oxford: Clarendon, 2013), 5.182–85.

118. Lisa Hopkins, "'Black but Beautiful': *Othello* and the Cult of the Black Madonna," in Buccola and Hopkins, *Marian Moments*, 77–79.

119. See Kreitzer, *Reforming Mary*, 8, 124; and Hugh Latimer, *The Works of Hugh Latimer*, ed. George Elwes Corrie (Cambridge: Cambridge University Press, 1844), 1.383–84.

120. Crashaw, *Iesuites Gospel*, 44–45.

121. Crashaw exaggerates: the doctrine of the Immaculate Conception did not actually become an article of the faith until 1884.

122. Crashaw, *Iesuites Gospel*, 19.

123. Ibid., 26–27.

124. For more on Rhodopis, see Herodotus, *The Landmark Herodotus: The Histories*, trans. Andrea L. Purvis (New York: Anchor Books, 2009), 178–79.

125. For more on Lucifer and Venus, see Marvin A. Sweeney, "Isaiah 1–39," in *The Prophets: Fortress Commentary on the Bible*, ed. Gale A. Yee, Hugh R. Page Jr., and Matthew J. M. Coomber (Minneapolis: Fortress, 2016), 685.

126. See, for example, Shakespeare, *1 Henry VI*, 1.3.98, 1.3.102, 1.6.85, 1.7.5–6, 1.7.12, 1.7.21.

127. Ibid., 5.5.59–64; Bernau, "'Saint, Witch, Man, Maid or Whore?,'" 214; Carole Levin and John Watkins, *Shakespeare's Foreign Worlds: National and Transnational Identities in the Elizabethan Age* (Ithaca, NY: Cornell University Press, 2009), 31–32.

128. Levin and Watkins, *Shakespeare's Foreign Worlds*, 25–28.

129. Holinshed, *First and second volumes*, 3:604.

130. Waller, *Virgin Mary*, 14; Anne J. Cruz, "Vindicating the *Vulnerata*: Cádiz and the Circulation of Religious Imagery as Weapons of War," in *Material and Symbolic Circulation between Spain and England, 1554–1604*, ed. Anne J. Cruz (Aldershot, UK: Ashgate, 2008), 48–49.

131. Stow, *Survey of London*, 2:266–67.

132. *MED*, s.v. "fre"; *OED*, s.v. "free."

Bibliography

Primary Works

Adams, Thomas. *The White Devil, or, The Hypocrite Uncased*. London, 1613. Available on EEBO.

Aelred of Rievaulx. *In Assumptione beatae Mariae*. In *PL*, edited by J.-P. Migne, vol. 195. Paris: Imprimerie Catholique, 1855.

Albertus Magnus. *De laudibus beatae Virginis*. In *B. Alberti Magni, Opera Omnia*, edited by Auguste Borgnet and Émile Borgnet, vol. 36. Paris: Louis Vivès, 1898.

Alfonso X. *Songs of Holy Mary of Alfonso X, the Wise: A Translation of the Cantigas de Santa Maria*. Translated by Kathleen Kulp-Hill. Tempe: Arizona Center for Medieval and Renaissance Studies, 2000.

Amadeus of Lausanne. "Homily 3." In *PL*, edited by J.-P. Migne, vol. 188. Paris: Imprimerie Catholique, 1855.

Ambrose. *Apologia David altera*. In *Sancti Ambrosii Opera*, edited by Carolus Schenkl. Corpus Scriptorum Ecclesiasticorum Latinorum 32. Prague: F. Tempsky, 1897.

——. *De Apologia Prophetae David*. Edited by Carolus Schenkl. Milan: Bibliotheca Ambrosiana, 1981.

——. *De institutione virginis*. In *PL*, edited by J.-P. Migne, vol. 16. Paris: Imprimerie Catholique, 1845.

——. *De virginibus*. In *PL*, edited by J.-P. Migne, vol. 16. Paris: Imprimerie Catholique, 1845.

——. *Expositio in Lucam*. In *PL*, edited by J.-P. Migne, vol. 15. Paris: Imprimerie Catholique, 1887.

Anselm of Canterbury. *Cur Deus Homo*. In *PL*, edited by J.-P. Migne, vol. 158. Paris: Imprimerie Catholique, 1864.

——. *Orationes sive meditationes*. In *S. Anselmi opera omnia*, edited by F. S. Schmitt, vol. 3. Stuttgart: Fromann, 1946.

——. *The Prayers and Meditations of Saint Anselm*. Translated by Benedicta Ward. London: Penguin, 1973.

Aquinas, Thomas. *Catena Aurea: A Commentary on the Four Gospels*. Translated by John Henry Newman. Oxford: John Henry Parker, 1841.

——. *Catena Aurea: St. Matthew*. Translated by Mark Pattison and John Henry Newman. Oxford: John Henry Parker, 1841.

——. *Commentary on Saint Paul's Epistle to the Galatians*. Translated by M. L. Lamb. Albany, NY: Magi Books, 1966.

——. *Summa Theologiae*. Vol. 25. Edited by John Fearon. London: Blackfriars, 1969.

——. *Summa Theologiae*. Vol. 40. Edited by Thomas Franklin O'Meara and Michael John Duffy. London: Blackfriars, 1968.

——. *Summa Theologiae*. Vol. 43. Edited by Thomas Gilby. London: Blackfriars, 1968.

——. *Summa Theologiae*. Vol. 51. Edited by Thomas R. Heath. London: Blackfriars, 1969.

——. *Summa Theologiae*. Vol. 52. Edited by Roland Potter. London: Blackfriars, 1972.

Aristotle. *Generation of Animals*. Edited and translated by A. L. Peck. Loeb Classical Library 366. Cambridge, MA: Harvard University Press, 1943.

——. *Historia animalium: Books 7–10*. Edited and translated by D. M. Balme. Loeb Classical Library 439. Cambridge, MA: Harvard University Press, 1991.

Augustine. "Adulterous Marriages." In *Treatises on Marriage and Other Subjects*, edited by Roy Joseph Deferrari, translated by Charles T. Huegelmeyer, 61–132 Fathers of the Church 27. Washington, DC: Catholic University of America Press, 1955.

——. *City of God*. Translated by Henry Bettenson. London: Penguin Classics, 2003.

——. *De coniugis adulteriis*. In *PL*, edited by J.-P. Migne, vol. 40. Paris: Imprimerie Catholique, 1863.

——. "De Sancta Virginitate: On Holy Virginity." In *De bono coniugali and De sancta virginitate*, translated by P. G. Walsh, 2–64. Oxford: Oxford University Press, 2001.

——. *Expositions of the Psalms, 73–98*. Translated by Maria Boulding. Edited by John E. Rotelle. Hyde Park, NY: New City, 2002.

——. *In Evangelium Joannis Tractatus CXXIV*. In *PL*, edited by J.-P. Migne, vol. 35. Paris: Imprimerie Catholique, 1864.

——. *In Psalmum 98 Enarratio*. In *PL*, edited by J.-P. Migne, vol. 37. Paris: Imprimerie Catholique, 1865.

——. *Sermones*. In *PL*, edited by J.-P. Migne, vol. 38. Paris: Imprimerie Catholique, 1841.

——. *Tractates on the Gospel of John 28–54*. Translated by John W. Rettig. Fathers of the Church 88. Washington, DC: Catholic University of America Press, 1993.

———. *The Trinity*. Translated by Stephen McKenna. Washington, DC: Catholic University of America Press, 1963.

Bale, John. *The first two partes of the Actes, or unchaste examples of the English votaryes*. London, 1551. Available on EEBO.

———. *The image of both churches after the moste wonderfull and hevenly Revelacion of Sainct John*. London, 1548. Available on EEBO.

———. *The Image of Bothe Churches*. In *Select Works of John Bale*, edited by Henry Christmas. Cambridge: Cambridge University Press, 1849.

Banks, Mary McLeod, ed. *An Alphabet of Tales*. EETS. London: Trübner, 1904.

Barber, Richard, ed. *Bestiary: Bodleian Library, Oxford MS Bodley 764*. Woodbridge, UK: Boydell, 1992.

Beadle, Richard, ed. *The York Plays: A Critical Edition of the York Corpus Christi Play as Recorded in British Library Additional MS 35290*. 2 vols. EETS. Oxford: Oxford University Press, 2009–13.

Beard, Thomas. *Antichrist the Pope of Rome: or, the Pope of Rome is Antichrist Proved in Two Treatises*. London, 1625. Available on EEBO.

Becon, Thomas. *The Worckes of Thomas Becon*. Vol. 1. London, 1564. Available on EEBO.

Benson, Larry, ed. *The Riverside Chaucer*. 3rd ed. Oxford: Oxford University Press, 1987.

Bernardino of Siena. *De superadmirabili gratia et gloria Matris Dei*. In *S. Bernardino Senensis Opera Omnia*, vol. 2. Florence: Quaracchi, 1950.

Bernard of Clairvaux. *De acquaeductu*. In *PL*, edited by J.-P. Migne, 183:437–48. Paris: Imprimerie Catholique, 1862.

———. "Epistola 174: Ad Canonicos Lugdunensis, de conceptione S. Mariae." In *PL*, edited by J.-P. Migne, vol. 182. Paris: Imprimerie Catholique, 1859.

———. *In Festo Annunciationis Beatae Virginis*. In *PL*, edited by J.-P. Migne, vol. 183. Paris: Imprimerie Catholique, 1862.

———. *The Letters of Bernard of Clairvaux*. Translated by Bruno Scott James. Kalamazoo, MI: Cistercian, 1998.

———. *On the Song of Songs II*. Translated by Kilian Walsh. Cistercian Fathers 7. Kalamazoo, MI: Cistercian, 1976.

———. *Sermo in ascensione Domini*. In *PL*, edited by J.-P. Migne, vol. 183. Paris: Imprimerie Catholique, 1862.

———. *Sermones in Cantica Canticorum*. In *PL*, edited by J.-P. Migne, vol. 183. Paris: Imprimerie Catholique, 1854.

———. *Sermones super Cantica Canticorum 1–35*. Edited by J. Leclercq, C. H. Talbot, and H. M. Rochais. Rome: Editiones Cistercienses, 1957.

Bevington, David. *Medieval Drama*. Boston: Houghton Mifflin, 1975.

Blangez, Gérard, ed. *Ci nous dit: Recueil d'exemples moraux*. 2 vols. Paris: Publications de la Société des anciens textes français, 1979.

Block, K. S. *Ludus Coventriæ, or, The plaie called Corpus Christi: Cotton ms. Vespasian D. VIII*. EETS. London: Oxford University Press, 1922.

Boccaccio, Giovanni. *Boccaccio's Expositions on Dante's Comedy*. Translated by Michael Papio. Toronto: University of Toronto Press, 2009.

———. *The Corbaccio*. Edited and translated by Anthony K. Cassell. Urbana: University of Illinois Press, 1975.

——. *Decameron.* 8th ed. Edited by Vittore Branca. Milan: Arnoldo Mondadori, 2001.

——. *The Decameron.* Translated by Wayne A. Rebhorn. New York: Norton, 2013.

——. *Esposizioni sopra la Comedia di Dante.* Edited by Giorgio Padoan. In *Tutte le opera di Giovanni Boccaccio,* edited by Vittore Branca, vol. 6. Verona: Arnoldo Mondadori, 1965.

——. *Il Filostrato.* Translated by Robert P. Roberts and Anna Bruni Seldis. New York: Garland, 1986.

Bokenham, Osbern. *Life of St. Anne.* In *Middle English Legends of Women Saints,* edited by Sherry L. Reames. TEAMS Middle English Texts. Kalamazoo, MI: Medieval Institute Publications, 2003.

Bonaventure. *De assumptione B. Virginis Mariae.* In *Opera Omnia,* vol. 9, edited by P. David Fleming. Florence: Quaracchi, 1901.

Boyd, Beverly. *The Middle English Miracles of the Virgin.* San Marino, CA: Huntington Library Press, 1964.

Brown, Michelle P. *The Holkham Bible Picture Book: A Facsimile.* London: British Library, 2007.

Burmeister, Joannes. *Aulularia and Other Inversions of Plautus.* Edited and translated by Michael Fontaine. Leuven: Leuven University Press, 2015.

Byron, George Gordon. *Cain, A Mystery.* London: H. Gray, 1822.

Cappelanus, Andreas. *The Art of Courtly Love.* Edited and translated by John Jay Parry. New York: Columbia University Press, 1990.

The Castle of Perseverance. In *Medieval Drama,* edited by David Bevington. Boston: Houghton Mifflin, 1975.

Celsus. *On the True Doctrine: A Discourse against Christians.* Translated by R. Joseph Hoffman. Oxford: Oxford University Press, 1987.

Cennini, Cennino D'Andrea. *The Craftsman's Handbook "Il Libro dell' Arte."* Translated by Daniel V. Thompson Jr. New Haven, CT: Yale University Press, 1933.

Chabaneau, Camille, ed. *Le romanz de Saint Fanuel et de Sainte Anne et de Nostre Dame et de Nostre Segnor et de ses Apostres.* Paris: Charles Leclerc, 1889.

Champion, Pierre. *Le procès de condamnation de Jeanne d'Arc: Texte, traduction et notes.* Vol. 1. Paris: Librairie spéciale pour l'histoire de France, 1920.

Charter of the Abbey of the Holy Ghost. In *Yorkshire Writers,* edited by C. Horstman. London: S. Sonnenschein, 1895.

Chaucer, Geoffry. *The Riverside Chaucer.* 3rd ed. Edited by Larry D. Benson. Boston: Houghton Mifflin, 1987.

Child, Francis James, ed. *The English and Scottish Popular Ballads.* Vol. 2. Mineola, NY: Dover, 1965.

Christine de Pizan. *Le Ditié de Jeanne d'Arc.* Edited by Angus J. Kennedy and Kenneth Varty. Oxford: Society for the Study of Medieval Languages and Literature, 1977.

Chrysostom, John. *Homiliae in Matthaeum.* In *PL,* edited by J.-P. Migne, vol. 58. Paris: Imprimerie Catholique, 1862.

——. *The Homilies of Saint John Chrysostom on the Gospel of Matthew.* Translated by George Prevost. 2 vols. Oxford: J. H. Parker, 1843–44.

——. *Homilies on the Gospel of Matthew.* Edited by Philip Schaff. New York: Christian Literature, 1888.

Conrad of Saxony. *Speculum beatae Mariae virginis.* In *Bibliotheca franciscana ascetica medii aevi*, vol. 2. Florence: Quaracchi, 1904.

Crashaw, William. *The Iesuites Gospel.* London, 1610. Available on EEBO.

Curley, Michael J., ed. and trans. *Physiologus: A Medieval Book of Nature Lore.* Chicago: University of Chicago Press, 1979.

Dante. *De Vulgari Eloquentia.* Edited by Marianne Shapiro. Lincoln: University of Nebraska Press, 1990.

Davidson, Clifford, ed. *The York Corpus Christi Plays.* TEAMS Middle English Texts. Kalamazoo, MI: Medieval Institute Publications, 2011.

Davis, Norman, ed. *Non-cycle Plays and Fragments.* EETS. London: Oxford University Press, 1970.

Decker, Therese, and Martin W. Walsh, eds. *Mariken van Nieumeghen: A Bilingual Edition.* Columbia, SC: Camden House, 1994.

Diogenes Laertius. *Lives of Eminent Philosophers.* Vol. 1. Edited and translated by R. D. Hicks. Loeb Classical Library 184. Cambridge, MA: Harvard University Press, 1925.

Donne, John. *Divine Poems.* Edited by Helen Gardner. Oxford: Clarendon, 1969.

Dubin, Nathaniel E., trans. *The Fabliaux.* New York: Norton, 2013.

Dunbar, William. *The Complete Works.* Edited by John Conlee. TEAMS Middle English Texts. Kalamazoo, MI: Medieval Institute Publications, 2004.

Eadmer. *De conceptione Beatae Mariae Virginis.* In *PL*, edited by J.-P. Migne, vol. 159. Paris: Imprimerie Catholique, 1854.

——. *Liber de excellentia Virginis Mariae.* In *PL*, edited by J.-P. Migne, vol. 159. Paris: Imprimerie Catholique, 1854.

Elliott, J. K., ed. *The Apocryphal New Testament.* Oxford: Clarendon, 1993.

Ellis, Roger, ed. *The Liber Celestis of St Bridget of Sweden.* Vol. 1. EETS. Oxford: Oxford University Press, 1987.

Engelbert of Admont. *De gratis et virtutibus beatae et gloriosae semper virginis Mariae.* In *Thesaurus anecdotorum novissimus*, edited by Bernhard Pez. Vienna: Veith, 1721.

Epiphanius of Salamis. *The Panarion of Epiphanius of Salamis: Book I (Sects 1–46).* 2nd ed. Translated by Frank Williams. Leiden: Brill, 2009.

Fairholt, Frederick W., ed. *The Civic Garland: A Collection of Songs from London Pageants.* In *Early English Poetry, Ballads, and Popular Literature of the Middle Ages*, vol. 19. London: Percy Society, 1846.

Fleetwood, William. *An Account of the Life and Death of the Blessed Virgin, According to Romish Writers.* London, 1687. Available on EEBO.

Foster, Frances A., ed. *A Stanzaic Life of Christ Compiled from Higden's Polychronicon and the Legenda Aurea Edited from MS. Harley 3909.* EETS. London: Oxford University Press, 1862.

Foxe, John. *Christ Jesus Triumphant.* London, 1607. Available on EEBO.

——. *The First Volume of the Ecclesiastical History Containing the Acts and Monuments.* London: John Daye, 1576. Available on EEBO.

——. *The Second Volume of the Ecclesiastical History Containing the Acts and Monuments.* London: John Daye, 1570. Available on EEBO.

Fulbert of Chartres. "In ortu almae virginis Mariae inviolatea." In *PL*, edited by J.-P. Migne, vol. 141. Paris: Imprimerie Catholique, 1854.

Gairdner, James, ed. *Letters and Papers, Foreign and Domestic, Henry VIII*. Vol. 12.2. London: Eyre and Spottiswoode, 1891.

———. *Letters and Papers, Foreign and Domestic, Henry VIII*. Vol. 13.1. London: Eyre and Spottiswoode, 1892.

———. *Letters and Papers, Foreign and Domestic, Henry VIII*. Vol. 14.1. London: Eyre and Spottiswoode, 1894.

Galen. *On the Usefulness of the Parts of the Body*. Edited and translated by Margaret Tallmadge May. Ithaca, NY: Cornell University Press, 1968.

Gautier de Coinci. *Les miracles de Nostre Dame*. Edited by Frédéric Koenig. 4 vols. Geneva: Droz, 1955–70.

———. *Of the Tumbler of Our Lady & Other Miracles*. Translated by Alice Kemp-Welch. London: Chatto and Windus, 1908.

Gerson, Jean. "Sermo de nativitate Domini." In *Opera Omnia*, edited by L. Ellies du Pin, 3:932–60. Antwerp: Sumptibus Societatis, 1706.

Godfrey of Admont. *Homiliae dominicales*. In *PL*, edited by J.-P. Migne, vol. 174. Paris: Imprimerie Catholique, 1854.

Gosson, Stephen. *Playes Confuted in Fiue Actions*. London, 1582. Available on EEBO.

Gower, John. *Confessio Amantis*. Edited by Russell A. Peck. 3 vols. TEAMS Middle English Texts. Kalamazoo, MI: Medieval Institute Publications, 2004.

Gray, William. "The Fantassie of Idolatrie." In *Gray of Reading: A Sixteenth-Century Controversialist and Ballad-Writer*, edited by Ernest W. Dormer, 66–75. Reading, UK: Bradley and Sons, 1923.

Green, Monica, ed. *The Trotula: A Medieval Compendium of Women's Medicine*. Philadelphia: University of Pennsylvania Press, 2001.

Gregory the Great. *S. Gregorii Magni Moralia in Job*. Edited by Marci Adriaen. 3 vols. Turnhout: Brepols, 1979–85.

Guibert of Nogent. *De laude S. Mariae*. In *PL*, edited by J.-P. Migne, vol. 156. Paris: Imprimerie Catholique, 1853.

Hall, Edward. *Hall's Chronicle; Containing the History of England, during the Reign of Henry the Fourth and the Succeeding Monarchs to the End of the Reign of Henry the Eighth in Which Are Particularly Described the Manners and Customs of Those Periods. Carefully Collated with the Editions of 1548 and 1550*. Edited by Henry Ellis. London: J. Johnson, 1809.

Hamblin, Vicki L., ed. *Le mistere du siege d'Orleans*. Textes littéraires français. Geneva: Droz, 2002.

Harris, Marguerite Tjader, ed. *Birgitta of Sweden: Life and Selected Revelations*. Translated by Albert Ryle Kezel. New York: Paulist, 1991.

Harris, Markham, trans. *The Life of Meriasek: A Medieval Cornish Miracle Play*. Washington, DC: Catholic University of America Press, 1977.

Harrison, Robert, trans. *Gallic Salt: Eighteen Fabliaux*. Berkeley: University of California Press, 1974.

Harvey, E. Ruth, ed. *The Court of Sapience*. Toronto: University of Toronto Press, 1984.

Hasenfratz, Robert, ed. *Ancrene Wisse*. TEAMS Middle English Texts. Kalamazoo, MI: Medieval Institute Publications, 2000.

Herodotus. *The Landmark Herodotus: The Histories*. Translated by Andrea L. Purvis. New York: Anchor Books, 2009.

Herrtage, Sidney J. H., ed. *Catholicon Anglicum, an English-Latin Wordbook Dated 1483*. EETS. London: Trübner, 1881.

Hildegard of Bingen. "Ein unveroffentlichtes Hildegard-Fragment." Edited by Heinrich Schipperges. *Slldhoffs Arclziv fiir Geschichte der Medizin* 40 (1956): 41–77.

———. *Physica*. In *PL*, edited by J.-P. Migne, vol. 197. Paris: Imprimerie Catholique, 1855.

Hilton, Walter. *The Goad of Love*. Edited by Clare Kirchberger. London: Faber and Faber, 1952.

Hippocrates. *Generation*. Edited and translated by Paul Potter. Loeb Classical Library 520. Cambridge, MA: Harvard University Press, 2012.

Holinshed, Raphael. *The first and second volumes of Chronicles*. Vol. 3. London, 1587. Available on EEBO.

———. *The firste volume of the Chronicles of England, Scotlande, and Irelande*. Vol. 2. London, 1577. Available on EEBO.

Horace. *Ars Poetica*. In *Horace for Students of Literature: The "Ars Poetica" and Its Tradition*, edited by O. B. Hardison and Leon Golden. Tampa: University of Florida Press, 1995.

Hrotsvitha of Gandersheim. *The Non-dramatic Works of Hrosvitha*. Edited and translated by Maria Gonsalva Wiegand. Saint Louis, MI: Saint Louis University, 1936.

Hudson, Anne, ed. *Selections from Wycliffite Writings*. Medieval Academy Reprints for Teaching 38. Toronto: University of Toronto Press, 1997.

Hugh of Saint Victor. *De arca Noe morali*. In *PL*, edited by J.-P. Migne, vol. 176. Paris: Imprimerie Catholique, 1854.

———. *De sacramentis Christianae fidei*. In *PL*, edited by J.-P. Migne, vol. 176. Paris: Imprimerie Catholique, 1854.

———. *On the Sacraments of the Christian Faith*. Translated by Roy J. Deferrari. Cambridge, MA: Mediaeval Academy of America, 1951.

Hutchinson, Roger. *The Works of Roger Hutchingson*. Edited by John Bruce. Cambridge: Cambridge University Press, 1842.

Ignatius of Antioch. "Letter to the Ephesians." In *The New Testament and Other Early Christian Writings: A Reader*, 2nd ed., edited by Bart Ehrman, 227–31. Oxford: Oxford University Press, 2004.

Irenaeus. *Adversus haereses*. Edited by W. Wigan Harvey. 2 vols. Cambridge: Cambridge University Press, 1857.

Isidore of Seville. *Liber etymologiarum XI*. In *PL*, edited by J.-P. Migne, 82:397–424. Paris: Imprimerie Catholique, 1850.

Jerome. *Adversus Jovinianum*. In *PL*, edited by J.-P. Migne, vol. 23. Paris: Imprimerie Catholique, 1883.

———. *Commentaire sur Saint Matthieu*. Edited by E. Bonnard. Sources Chrétiennes 242. Paris: Les Éditions du Cerf, 1977.

———. *Commentary on Matthew*. Translated by Thomas P. Scheck. Washington, DC: Catholic University of America Press, 2008.

———. *De perpetua virginitate B. Mariae adversus Helvidium*. In *PL*, edited by J.-P. Migne, vol. 23. Paris: Imprimerie Catholique, 1845.

———. *Dialogue against Jovinianus*. In *Letters and Select Works*, translated by W. H. Fremantle. Nicene and Post-Nicene Fathers 6. London: Parker, 1893.

———. *Epistola ad Eustochium de virginitate*. In *PL*, edited by J.-P. Migne, vol. 22. Paris: Imprimerie Catholique, 1845.

———. "On the Perpetual Virginity of the Virgin Mary against Helvidius." In *Jerome: Dogmatic and Polemic Works*, edited by John N. Hritzu, 3–43. Fathers of the Church 53. Washington, DC: Catholic University of America Press, 2010.

———. *Select Letters of Saint Jerome*. Translated by Jeffrey Henderson. Loeb Classical Library 262. Cambridge, MA: Harvard University Press, 1954.

Julian of Norwich. *The Writings of Julian of Norwich*. Edited by Nicholas Watson and Jacqueline Jenkins. Philadelphia: Pennsylvania State University Press, 2005.

Justin Martyr. *Dialogue with Trypho*. Edited by Michael Slusser. Translated by T. B. Falls. Washington, DC: Christian Heritage, 2003.

———. *Dialogus cum Tryphone*. In *PG* edited by J.-P. Migne, vol. 6. Paris: Imprimerie Catholique, 1857. Irenaeus

Kane, Harold, ed. *The Prickynge of Love*. 2 vols. Salzburg: Institut für Anglistik und Amerikanistik der Universität Salzburg, 1983.

Knox, John. *A Faithful Admonition to the Professors of God's Truth in England, 1554*. In *The Works of John Knox*, vol. 3, edited by David Laing. Edinburgh: Wodrow Society, 1854.

Kohanski, Tamarah, and C. David Benson, eds. *The Book of John Mandeville*. TEAMS Middle English Texts. Kalamazoo, MI: Medieval Institute Publications, 2007.

Laborde, Alexandre de, ed. *La Bible moralisée illustrée conservée à Oxford, Paris et Londres*. Vol. 1. Paris: Société française de reproductions de manuscrits à peintures, 1911.

Labriola, Albert C., and John W. Smeltz, eds. *The Bible of the Poor: A Facsimile and Edition of the British Library Blockbook C.9 d.2*. Pittsburg: Duquesne University Press, 1990.

Langland, William. *The Vision of Piers Plowman in Three Parallel Texts Together with Richard the Redeless*. Edited by Walter Skeat. 2 vols. Oxford: Clarendon, 1886.

———. *The Vision of Piers Plowman*. Edited by A. V. C. Schmidt. Everyman's University Library. New York: J. M. Dent and E. P. Dutton, 1978.

Latimer, Hugh. *Sermons and Remains*. Edited by George Elwes Corrie. Cambridge: Cambridge University Press, 1845.

———. *The Works of Hugh Latimer*. Edited by George Elwes Corrie. Cambridge: Cambridge University Press, 1844.

Lemay, Helen Rodnite, ed. *Women's Secrets: A Translation of Pseudo-Albertus Magnus's "De Secretis Mulierum" with Commentaries*. Albany: State University of New York Press, 1992.

Lorris, Guillaume de, and Jean de Meun. *Le Roman de la Rose*. Edited by André Lanly. 2 vols. Paris: Librairie Honoré Champion, 1971–82.

———. *The Romance of the Rose*. Translated by Frances Hogan. Oxford: Oxford World's Classics, 2008.

Love, Nicholas. *Love's Mirror of the Blessed Life of Jesus Christ: A Critical Edition Based on Cambridge University Library Additional MSS 6578 and 6686*. Edited by Michael G. Sargent. New York: Garland, 1992.

Lumiansky, R. M., and David Mills, eds. *The Chester Mystery Cycle*. 2 vols. EETS. London: Oxford University Press, 1974.

Luria, Maxwell S., and Richard L. Hoffman, eds. *Middle English Lyrics*. Norton Critical Edition. New York: Norton, 1974.

Luther, Martin. *D. Martin Luthers Werke: Kritische Gesamtausgabe*. Vol. 1.7. Weimarer Ausgabe. Weimar: Hermann Bohlaus Nachfolger, 1897.

——. *D. Martin Luthers Werke: Kritische Gesamtausgabe*. Vol. 9. Weimar: Hermann Böhlaus Nachfolger, 1893.

——. *Table Talk*. Edited by Theodore G. Tappert. Luther's Works 54. Philadelphia: Fortress, 1967.

Lydgate, John. *A Critical Edition of John Lydgate's Life of Our Lady*. Edited by J. A. Lauritis, R. A. Klinefelter, and V. F. Gallagher. Pittsburg, Pennsylvania: Duquesne University Press, 1961.

——. *Disguising at Hertford*. In *Mummings and Entertainments*, edited by Claire Sponsler. TEAMS Middle English Texts. Kalamazoo, MI: Medieval Institute Publications, 2010.

Malory, Thomas. *Le Morte Darthur*. Edited by Stephen H. A. Shepherd. New York: Norton, 2004.

McDonald, Nicola, ed. *Medieval Obscenities*. Rochester, NY: Boydell for York Medieval Press, 2006.

Meredith, Peter, ed. *The Mary Play from the N. Town Manuscript*. London: Longman, 1987.

Meredith, Peter, and Stanley J. Kahrl, eds. *The N-Town Plays: A Facsimile of British Library MS Cotton Vespasian D VIII*. Leeds Texts and Monographs: Medieval Drama Facsimiles 4. Leeds: University of Leeds, 1977.

Meyer, Marvin W., ed. *The Nag Hammadi Scriptures*. New York: Harper One, 2007.

Minucius Felix. *The Octavius of Marcus Minucius Felix*. Translated by G. W. Clarke. Ancient Christian Writers 39. New York: Paulist, 1974.

Mirk, John. *Mirk's Festial: A Collection of Homilies*. Edited by Theodore Erbe. EETS. London: Trübner, 1905.

Molanus, Johannes. *De Historia Sanctarum Imaginum et Picturarum*. In *Traité des saintes images*, edited by Francois Boespflug, Olivier Christin, and Benoit Tassel. 2 vols. Paris: Editions du Cerf, 1996.

Origen. *Contra Celsum*. Translated by Henry Chadwick. Cambridge: Cambridge University Press, 1953.

Paris, Gaston Bruno Paulin, Ulysse Robert, and François Bonnardot, eds. *Miracles de Nostre Dame par personnages*. Paris: Firmin Didot et Cie, 1876.

Pascal, Blaise. *Pensées*. Translated by A. J. Krailsheimer. New York: Penguin Classics, 1966.

Peter of Celle. *Epistola 171*. In *PL*, edited by J.-P. Migne, 202:613–622. Paris: Imprimerie Catholique, 1855.

——. *Sermones*. In *PL*, edited by J.-P. Migne, vol. 202. Paris: Imprimerie Catholique, 1855.

Philip of Harvengt. *Commentaria in Cantica canticorum*. In *PL*, edited by J.-P. Migne, vol. 203. Paris: Imprimerie Catholique, 1855.

Piers the Plowman's Crede. In *Six Ecclesiastical Satires*, edited by James M. Dean. TEAMS Middle English Texts. Kalamazoo, MI: Medieval Institute Publications, 1991.

Plautus. *Amphitryon*. Edited and translated by Wolfgang de Melo. Loeb Classical Library 60. Cambridge, MA: Harvard University Press, 2011.

Pliny the Younger. *Correspondence with Trajan from Bythinia (Epistles X)*. Translated by Wynne Williams. Warminster, UK: Aris and Phillips, 1990.

Plummer, John, ed. *The Hours of Catherine of Cleves*. New York: Braziller, 1966.

Plutarch. *Moralia*. Vol. 4. Edited and translated by Frank Cole Babbitt. Loeb Classical Library 305. Cambridge, MA: Harvard University Press, 1936.

——. *Moralia*. Vol. 9. Edited and translated by Edwin L. Minar Jr., F. H. Sandbach, and W. C. Helmbold. Loeb Classical Library 425. Cambridge, MA: Harvard University Press, 1961.

Price, Thomas. Preface to *The History of Our B. Lady of Loreto: Tra[n]slated out of Latyn, into English*, by Orazio Torsellino. Saint-Omer, France: English College Press, 1608. Available on EEBO.

Raftery, Margaret M., ed. *Mary of Nemmegen*. Leiden: E. J. Brill, 1991.

Raine, James, ed. "The Will of William Brokshaw of East Retford." In *Testamenta Eboracensia: A Selection of Wills from the Registry at York*, 4:164. Edinburgh: Surtees Society, 1869.

Rilke, Rainer Maria. *The Life of the Virgin Mary*. Translated by C. F. MacIntyre. Westport, CT: Greenwood, 1947.

Ross, Woodburn O., ed. *Middle English Sermons*. EETS. London: Oxford University Press, 1940.

Roye, William, and Jerome Barlowe. *Rede Me and Be Nott Wrothe*. Edited by Douglas H. Parker. Toronto: University of Toronto Press, 1992.

Rupert of Deutz. *Commentaria in Cantica Canticorum*. In *Corpus Christianorum Continuatio Mediaevalis*, vol. 26, edited by Hrabanus Haacke. Turnhout: Brepols, 1972.

Saupe, Karen, ed. *Middle English Marian Lyrics*. TEAMS Middle English Texts. Kalamazoo, MI: Medieval Institute Publications, 1997.

Scot, Reginald. *The Discouerie of Witchcraft*. London, 1584. Available on EEBO.

The Second Shepherds' Play. In *Medieval Drama*, edited by David Bevington. Boston: Houghton Mifflin, 1975.

Shakespeare, William. *All's Well That Ends Well*. Edited by G. K. Hunter. Arden Shakespeare. London: Thomson, 2006.

——. *Antony and Cleopatra*. Edited by John Wilders. Arden Shakespeare. London: Thomson, 1995.

——. *Henry VI, Part One*. 3rd ed. Edited by Michael Taylor. Oxford: Oxford University Press, 2003.

——. *Henry VIII (All Is True)*. In *The Norton Shakespeare*, 2nd ed., edited by Stephen Greenblatt, 3119–3201. New York: Norton, 2008.

——. *The Life and Death of King John*. In *The Norton Shakespeare*, 2nd ed., edited by Stephen Greenblatt, 1045–1110. New York: Norton, 2008.

——. *Othello*. Edited by E. A. J. Honigmann. Arden Shakespeare. London: Thomson, 2006.

Sheldon, Richard. *A Survey of the Miracles of the Church of Rome*. London, 1616. Available on EEBO.

Skelton, John. "Elynour Rummynge." In *The Complete English Poems of John Skelton*, edited by John Scattergood, 186–200. Liverpool: Liverpool University Press, 2015.

Spector, Stephen, ed. *The N-Town Play: Cotton MS Vespasian D. 8*. 2 vols. EETS. Oxford: Oxford University Press, 1991.

Spenser, Edmundo. *The Faerie Queene: Book One*. Edited by Carol V. Kaske. Indianapolis: Hackett, 2006.

———. *The Faerie Queene: Books Three and Four*. Edited by Dorothy Stephens. Indianapolis: Hackett, 2006.

Staley, Lynne, ed. *The Book of Margery Kempe*. Kalamazoo, MI: Medieval Institute Publications, 1996.

Stevens, Martin, and A. C. Cawley, eds. *The Towneley Plays*. 2 vols. EETS. Oxford: Oxford University Press, 1994.

Stokes, James, ed. *Lincolnshire*. 2 vols. REED. Toronto: University of Toronto Press, 2009.

———. "The Ongoing Exploration of Women and Performance in Early Modern England: Evidences, Issues, and Questions," *Shakespeare Bulletin* 33, no. 1 (2015): 9–31.

Stokes, Whitley, trans. *Beunans Meriasek*. London: Trübner, 1872.

Stow, John. *A Survey of London, 1603*. 2 vols. Edited by Charles Lethbridge Kingsford. Oxford: Clarendon, 1971.

Strassburg, Gottfried von. *Tristan*. Edited by Karl Marold. Leipzig: Eduard Uvenarius, 1906.

———. *Tristan*. Translated by A. T. Hatto. London: Penguin Classics, 1967.

Studer, P., ed. *Saint Joan of Orleans: Scenes from the Fifteenth-Century "Mystere du siege d'Orleans."* Translated by Joan Evans. Oxford: Clarendon, 1926.

Sugano, Douglas, ed. *The N-Town Plays*. TEAMS Middle English Texts. Kalamazoo, MI: Medieval Institute Publications, 2007.

Swinburne, Algernon Charles. *Major Poems and Selected Prose*. Edited by Jerome McGann and Charles L. Sligh. New Haven, CT: Yale University Press, 2004.

Tertullian. *Contre Marcion*. Edited by René Braun. Sources Chrétiennes 399. Paris: Éditions du Cerf, 1994.

———. *De carne Christi*. In *PL*, edited by J.-P. Migne, vol. 2. Paris: Imprimerie Catholique, 1844.

———. *De cultu feminarum*. Edited by M. Turcan. Sources Chrétiennes 173. Paris: Éditions du Cerf, 1971.

———. *De monogamia*. In *PL*, edited by J.-P Migne, vol. 2. Paris: Imprimerie Catholique, 1844.

———. *Treatises on Marriage and Remarriage*. Translated by William P. Le Saint. Ancient Christian Writers 13. New York: Newman, 1951.

Thomas, William. *The Pilgrim: A Dialogue on the Life and Actions of King Henry the Eighth*. Edited by J. A. Froude. London: Parker, Son, and Bourn, 1861.

Thomson, R. M., and M. Winterbottom, eds. *William of Malmesbury: The Miracles of the Blessed Virgin Mary*. Rochester, NY: Boydell, 2015.

Tóibín, Colm. *The Testament of Mary*. New York: Scribner, 2012.

Trevisa, John, trans. *De proprietatibus rerum*. Westminster, UK: Wynkyn de Worde, 1495. Available on EEBO.

Tyndale, William. *Tyndale's Answer to Sir Thomas More's Dialogue.* Edited by Henry Walter. Cambridge: Cambridge University Press, 1851.

Vasari, Giorgio. *Le Vite de' più eccellenti pittori, scultori, e architettori da Cimabue insino a' tempi nostril.* 2 vols. Turin, Italy: Einaudi, 1986.

Voragine, Jacobus de. *The Golden Legend: Readings on the Saints.* Translated by William Granger Ryan. 2 vols. Princeton, NJ: Princeton University Press, 1993.

Warner, George. *Queen Mary's Psalter: Miniatures and Drawings by an English Artist of the 14th Century, Reproduced from Royal MS. 2 B. VII in the British Museum.* London: British Museum, 1912.

Webster, John. *The White Devil.* In *The Works of John Webster,* edited by David Gunby, David Carnegie, and Antony Hammond. Cambridge: Cambridge University Press, 1995.

Wright, James. *Historia Histrionica.* London: G. Croom, 1699.

Wriothsley, Charles. *A Chronicle of England during the Reigns of the Tudors.* Vol. 1. Edited by William Douglas Hamilton. London: Camden Society, 1975.

Secondary Works

Abrams, Floyd. *Speaking Freely: Trials of the First Amendment.* New York: Penguin, 2006.

Adams, Henry. *The Education of Henry Adams.* New York: Modern Library, 1931.

Adkin, Neil. *Jerome on Virginity: A Commentary on the "Libellus de virginitate servanda."* Cambridge: Cambridge University Press, 2003.

Albert, G., J. M. Parent, and A. Guillemette. "La légende des trois mariages de Sainte-Anne: Un texte nouveau." In *Études d'histoire littéraire et doctrinale du XIIIe siècle,* 165–84. Paris: Librairie Philosophique J. Vrin, 1932.

Alberti, Francesca. "'Divine Cuckolds': Joseph and Vulcan in Renaissance Art and Literature." In *Cuckoldry, Impotence and Adultery in Europe (15th–17th Century),* edited by Sara F. Matthews-Grieco, 149–80. Burlington, VT: Ashgate, 2014.

Albright, William Foxwell, and Cristopher Stephen Mann. *Matthew.* Anchor Bible. New Haven, CT: Yale University Press, 1971.

Amsler, Mark. "Affective Literacy: Gestures of Reading in the Later Middle Ages." *Essays in Medieval Studies* 18, no. 1 (2001): 83–110.

Anderson, M. D. *Drama and Imagery in English Medieval Churches.* Cambridge: Cambridge University Press, 1963.

Armstrong, C. M. *The Moralizing Prints of Cornelis Anthonisz.* Princeton, NJ: Princeton University Press, 1990.

Arnold, Bill. *Genesis.* New Cambridge Bible Commentary. Cambridge: Cambridge University Press, 2008.

Aronson-Lehavi, Sharon. *Street Scenes: Late Medieval Acting and Performance.* New York: Palgrave Macmillan, 2011.

Ashley, Kathleen. "Image and Ideology: Saint Anne in Late Medieval Drama and Narrative." In *Interpreting Cultural Symbols: Saint Anne in Late Medieval Society,* edited by Kathleen Ashley and Pamela Sheingorn, 111–30. Athens: University of Georgia Press, 1990.

———. "'Wyt' and 'Wysdam' in the N-Town Cycle." *Philological Quarterly* 58, no. 2 (1979): 121–35.

Ashley, Kathleen, and Pamela Sheingorn. Introduction to *Interpreting Cultural Symbols: Saint Anne in Late Medieval Society*, edited by Kathleen Ashley and Pamela Sheingorn, 1–68. Athens: University of Georgia Press, 1990.

Aston, Margaret. *England's Iconoclasts: Laws against Images*. Oxford: Clarendon, 1988.

———. *Faith and Fire: Popular and Unpopular Religion, 1350–1600*. London: Hambledon, 1993.

———. *Lollards and Reformers: Images and Literacy in Late Medieval Religion*. London: Hambledon, 1984.

Atkinson, Clarissa W. *The Oldest Vocation: Christian Motherhood in the Middle Ages*. Ithaca, NY: Cornell University Press, 1991.

Atkinson, Stephen. "'They . . . Toke Their Shyldys before Them and Drew Oute Their Swerdys . . .': Inflicting and Healing Wounds in Malory's *Morte Darthur*." In *Wounds and Wound Repair in Medieval Culture*, edited by Larissa Tracy and Kelly DeVries, 519–43. Leiden: Brill, 2015.

Auerbach, Erich. *Mimesis: The Representation of Reality in Western Literature*. Translated by Willard R. Trask. Princeton, NJ: Princeton University Press, 2003.

Aulen, Gustaf. *Christus Victor: An Historical Study of the Three Main Types of the Idea of Atonement*. London: SPCK, 1953.

Bach, Jeff. *Voices of the Turtledoves: The Sacred World of Ephrata*. University Park: Pennsylvania State University Press, 2003.

Baird, Joseph L., and Lorrayne Y. Baird. "Fabliau Form and the Hegge *Joseph's Return*." *Chaucer Review* 8, no. 2 (1973): 159–69.

Bakhtin, Mikhail. *Rabelais and His World*. Translated by Helene Iswolsky. Bloomington: Indiana University Press, 1984.

Baldwin, Elizabeth, Lawrence M. Clopper, and David Mills, eds. *Cheshire Including Chester*. REED. Toronto: University of Toronto Press, 2007.

Bale, Anthony. *Feeling Persecuted: Christians, Jews and Images of Violence in the Middle Ages*. London: Reaktion Books, 2010.

———. *The Jew in the Medieval Book: English Antisemitisms, 1350–1500*. Cambridge: Cambridge University Press, 2006.

Balic, Carlo. "The Medieval Controversy over the Immaculate Conception up to the Death of Scotus." In *The Dogma of the Immaculate Conception: History and Significance*, edited by Edward Dennis O'Connor, 161–212. South Bend, IN: University of Notre Dame Press, 1958.

Barney, Stephen A. "*Ordo paginis*: The Gloss on Genesis 38." *South Atlantic Quarterly* 91 (1992): 929–43.

Bartlett, Robert. *Trial by Fire and Water: The Medieval Judicial Ordeal*. Oxford: Clarendon, 1986.

Baskin, Judith R. *Midrashic Women: Formations of the Feminine in Rabbinic Literature*. Hanover, NH: Brandeis University Press, 2002.

Bax, Dirk. *Hieronymus Bosch: His Picture-Writing Deciphered*. Rotterdam: Balkema, 1979.

Bayless, Martha. *Parody in the Middle Ages*. Ann Arbor: University of Michigan Press, 1996.

Beadle, Richard. "Prolegomena to a Literary Geography of Later Medieval Norfolk." In *Regionalism in Late Medieval Manuscripts and Texts*, edited by Felicity Riddy, 89–108. Woodbridge, UK: Brewer, 1991.

Beadle, Richard, and Alan J. Fletcher, eds. *The Cambridge Companion to Medieval English Theatre*. 2nd ed. Cambridge: Cambridge University Press, 2008.

Beattie, Tina. *God's Mother, Eve's Advocate: A Marian Narrative of Women's Salvation.* New York: Continuum, 2002.

Beauvoir, Simone de. *The Second Sex*. Translated by Constance Borde and Sheila Malovany-Chevallier. New York: Knopf, 2010.

Becker, Carol. "Brooklyn Museum: Messing with the Sacred." In *Chris Ofili*, 78–84. New York: Skira Rizzoli, 2009.

Beckwith, Sarah. *Christ's Body: Identity, Culture and Society in Late Medieval Writings.* London: Routledge, 1996.

——. *Signifying God: Social Relation and Symbolic Act in the York Corpus Christi Plays.* Chicago: University of Chicago Press, 2001.

Beer, Jeanette. *Beasts of Love: Richard de Fournival's "Bestiaire d'amour" and a Woman's "Response."* Toronto: University of Toronto Press, 2003.

Begg, Ean. *The Cult of the Black Virgin*. 2nd ed. London: Arkana, 1996.

Benko, Stephen. "The Libertine Gnostic Sect of the Phibionites According to Epiphanius." *Vigiliae Christianae* 21, no. 2 (1967): 103–19.

Bennett, Adelaide. "Noah's Recalcitrant Wife in the Ramsey Abbey Psalter." *Notes in the History of Art* 2, no. 1 (1982): 2–5.

Bernau, Anke. "'Saint, Witch, Man, Maid or Whore?': Joan of Arc and Writing History." In *Medieval Virginities*, edited by Anke Bernau, Ruth Evans, and Sarah Salih, 214–33. Toronto: University of Toronto Press, 2003.

Bernau, Anke, Ruth Evans, and Sarah Salih, eds. *Medieval Virginities*. Toronto: University of Toronto Press, 2003.

Bettini, Maurizio. *Women and Weasels: Mythologies of Birth in Ancient Greece and Rome.* Chicago: University of Chicago Press, 2013.

Bevington, David. "The Corpus Christi Cycle." In *Medieval Drama*, edited by David Bevington, 225–41. Boston: Houghton Mifflin, 1975.

Beyers, Rita. "The Transmission of Marian Apocrypha in the Latin Middle Ages." *Apocrypha* 23 (2012): 117–40.

Bills, Bing D. "The 'Suppression Theory' and the English Corpus Christi Play: A Reexamination." *Theatre Journal* 32, no. 2 (1980): 157–68.

Birnbaum, Lucia Chiavola. *Black Madonnas: Feminism, Religion, and Politics in Italy.* Boston: Northeastern University Press, 1993.

Black, Charlene Villaseñor. "St. Anne Imagery and Maternal Archetypes in Spain and Mexico." In *Colonial Saints: Discovering the Holy in the Americas, 1500–1800*, edited by Allan Greer and Jodi Bilinkoff, 3–30. New York: Routledge, 2003.

Black, David Alan, and Jacob N. Cerone, eds. *The Pericope of the Adulteress in Contemporary Research*. London: Bloomsbury, 2016.

Black, Gregory D. *The Catholic Crusade against the Movies, 1940–1975*. Cambridge: Cambridge University Press, 1997.

Blamires, Alcuin. *The Case for Women in Medieval Culture*. Oxford: Clarendon, 1997.

——, ed. *Woman Defamed and Woman Defended: An Anthology of Medieval Texts.* Oxford: Clarendon, 1992.

Bleeth, Kenneth A. "The Image of Paradise in the *Merchant's Tale*." In *The Learned and the Lewed: Studies in Chaucer and Medieval Literature,* edited by Larry D. Benson, 45–60. Cambridge, MA: Harvard University Press, 1974.

Bloch, R. Howard. Introduction to *The Fabliaux,* translated by Nathaniel E. Dubin, xiii–xxv. New York: Norton, 2013.

——. "Modest Maidens and Modified Nouns: Obscenity in the Fabliaux." In *Obscenity: Social Control and Artistic Creation in the European Middle Ages,* edited by Jan M. Ziolkowski, 293–307. Leiden: Brill, 1998.

——. *The Scandal of the Fabliaux.* Chicago: University of Chicago Press, 1986.

Blum, Shirley Neilsen. "Hans Memling's Annunciation with Angelic Attendants." *Metropolitan Museum Journal* 27 (1992): 43–58.

Booton, Diane E. "Variation on a Limbourg Theme: Anastasia at the Nativity in a Getty Book of Hours and in French Medieval Literature." *Fifteenth-Century Studies* 29 (2004): 52–79.

Boss, Sarah Jane. *Empress and Handmaid: On Nature and Gender in the Cult of the Virgin Mary.* New York: Cassell, 2000.

Boulton, Maureen Barry McCann. *Sacred Fictions of Medieval France: Narrative Theology in the Lives of Christ and the Virgin, 1150–1500.* Rochester, NY: D. S. Brewer, 2015.

Bovon, François. *Luke 1: A Commentary.* Translated by Christine M. Thomas. Hermeneia. Minneapolis: Fortress, 2002.

Boyarin, Daniel. *Carnal Israel: Reading Sex in Talmudic Culture.* Berkeley: University of California Press, 1993.

Brandenbarg, Ton. "Saint Anne: A Holy Grandmother and Her Children." In *Sanctity and Motherhood: Essays on Holy Mothers in the Middle Ages,* edited by Anneke B. Mulder-Bakker, 31–65. New York: Garland, 1995.

Breitenberg, Mark. *Anxious Masculinity in Early Modern England.* Cambridge: Cambridge University Press, 1996.

Bridgett, T. E. *Our Lady's Dowry: Or, How England Gained and Lost that Title.* London: Burns and Oates, 1875.

Brietz-Monta, Susannah. *Martyrdom and Literature in Early Modern England.* Cambridge: Cambridge University Press, 2005.

Brokaw, Katherine Steele. *Staging Harmony: Music and Religious Change in Late Medieval and Early Modern English Drama.* Ithaca, NY: Cornell University Press, 2016.

Brown, Pamela Allen. *Better a Shrew Than a Sheep: Women, Drama, and the Culture of Jest in Early Modern England.* Ithaca, NY: Cornell University Press, 2003.

Brown, Peter. *The Body and Society: Men, Women, and Sexual Renunciation in Early Christianity.* 2nd ed. New York: Columbia University Press, 2008.

Brown, Raymond E. *The Birth of the Messiah: A Commentary on the Infancy Narratives in the Gospels of Matthew and Luke.* Garden City, NY: Doubleday, 1977.

——. "The Problem of the Virginal Conception of Jesus." *Theological Studies* 33, no. 1 (1972): 4–34.

Brown, Raymond E., Karl P. Donfried, Joseph A. Fitzmyer, and John Reumann, eds. *Mary in the New Testament.* Philadelphia: Fortress, 1978.

Brownlee, Victoria. "Imagining the Enemy: Protestant Readings of the Whore of Baby-lon in Early Modern England." In *Biblical Women in Early Modern Literary Culture, 1550–1700*, edited by Victoria Brownlee and Laura Gallagher, 213–33. Manchester: Manchester University Press, 2015.

Brundage, James A. *Law, Sex, and Christian Society in Medieval Europe*. Chicago: University of Chicago Press, 1987.

——. "Prostitution in the Medieval Canon Law." *Signs* 1, no. 4 (1976): 825–45.

Bryant, Joseph Allen, Jr. "The Function of *Ludus Coventriae* 14." *Journal of English and Germanic Philology* 52 (1953): 340–45.

Buccola, Regina, and Lisa Hopkins, eds. *Marian Moments in Early Modern Drama*. Burlington, VT: Ashgate, 2007.

——. "Virgin Fairies and Imperial Whores: The Unstable Ground of Religious Iconography in Thomas Dekker's *The Whore of Babylon*." In *Marian Moments in Early Modern Drama*, edited by Regina Buccola and Lisa Hopkins, 141–60. Burlington, VT: Ashgate, 2007.

Burridge, Richard A. "The Church of England's Life of Python—Or 'What the Bishop Saw.'" In *Jesus and Brian: Exploring the Historical Jesus and His Times via Monty Python's "Life of Brian,"* edited by Joan E. Taylor, 19–42. London: Bloomsbury, 2015.

Butler, Sara Margaret. *The Language of Abuse: Marital Violence in Later Medieval England*. Leiden: Brill, 2007.

Butterworth, Philip. *Staging Conventions in Medieval English Theatre*. Cambridge: Cambridge University Press, 2014.

Bynum, Caroline Walker. *Fragmentation and Redemption: Essays on Gender and the Human Body in Medieval Religion*. New York: Zone, 1991.

——. *Holy Feast and Holy Fast: The Religious Significance of Food to Medieval Women*. Berkeley: University of California Press, 1987.

——. *Jesus as Mother: Studies in the Spirituality of the High Middle Ages*. Berkeley: University of California Press, 1982.

Cameron, Kenneth M., and Stanley J. Kahrl. "Staging the N-Town Cycle." *Theatre Notebook* 21 (1967): 122–38, 152–65.

Camille, Michael. *The Gothic Idol: Ideology and Image-Making in Medieval Art*. New York: Cambridge University Press, 1989.

——. *Image on the Edge: The Margins of Medieval Art*. London: Reaktion Books, 1992.

Cantelupe, Eugene B., and Richard Griffith. "The Gifts of the Shepherds in the Wakefield 'Secunda Pastorum': An Iconographical Interpretation." *Mediaeval Studies* 28 (1966): 328–35.

Carley, James P. *The Books of King Henry VIII and His Wives*. London: British Library, 2004.

Carlson, Cindy L., and Angela Jane Weisl, eds. *Constructions of Widowhood and Virginity in the Middle Ages*. New York: St. Martin's, 1999.

——. "Like a Virgin: Mary and Her Doubters in the N-Town Cycle." In *Constructions of Widowhood and Virginity in the Middle Ages*, edited by Cindy L. Carlson and Angela Jane Weisl, 199–217. St Martin's, 1999.

Carmichael, Calum. *Sex and Religion in the Bible*. New Haven, CT: Yale University Press, 2010.

Carr, Sherwyn T. "The Middle English Nativity Cherry Tree: The Dissemination of a Popular Motif." *Modern Language Quarterly* 36 (1975): 133–47.

Carroll, Michael P. *Catholic Cults and Devotions: A Psychological Inquiry*. Montreal: McGill-Queen's University Press, 1989.

Castaldi, Tommaso. *La Madonna della Misericordia: L'iconografia della Madonna della Misericordia e della Madonna delle frecce nell'arte di Bologna e della Romagna nel Tre e Quattrocento*. Bologna: Editrice La Mandragola, 2011.

Cavallo, Adolfo Salvatore. *The Unicorn Tapestries in the Metropolitan Museum of Art*. New York: Metropolitan Museum of Art, 1998.

Caviness, Madeline H. *Visualizing Women in the Middle Ages: Sight, Spectacle, and Scopic Economy*. Philadelphia: University of Pennsylvania Press, 2001.

Chaganti, Seeta. *The Medieval Poetics of the Reliquary: Enshrinement, Inscription, Performance*. New York: Palgrave Macmillan, 2008.

Chambers, Edmund Kerchever. *The Mediaeval Stage*. 2 vols. Oxford: Oxford University Press, 1903.

Chapuis, Julien. *Stefan Lochner: Image Making in Fifteenth-Century Cologne*. Turnhout: Brepols, 2004.

Chazan, Robert. *The Trial of the Talmud: Paris, 1240*. Toronto: Pontifical Institute of Medieval Studies, 2012.

Cheetham, Francis. *English Medieval Alabasters: With a Catalogue of the Collection in the Victoria and Albert Museum*. 2nd ed. Woodbridge, UK: Boydell, 2005.

Chew, Samuel. *The Virtues Reconciled: An Iconographic Study*. Toronto: University of Toronto Press, 1947.

Clark, Robert A. L., and Claire M. Sponsler. "Queer Play: The Cultural Work of Cross-Dressing in Medieval Drama." *New Literary History* 28 (1997): 319–44.

Classen, Albrecht, ed. *Sexuality in the Middle Ages and Early Modern Times: New Approaches to a Fundamental Cultural-Historical and Literary-Anthropological Theme*. Berlin: Walter de Gruyter, 2008.

Clayton, Mary. *The Apocryphal Gospels of Mary in Anglo-Saxon England*. Cambridge: Cambridge University Press, 1998.

——. *The Cult of the Virgin Mary in Anglo-Saxon England*. Cambridge: Cambridge University Press, 1990.

Clopper, Lawrence M. *Drama, Play, and Game: English Festive Culture in the Medieval and Early Modern Period*. Chicago: University of Chicago Press, 2001.

——. "English Drama: From Ungodly *Ludi* to Sacred Play." In *The Cambridge History of Medieval English Literature*, edited by David Wallace, 739–66. Cambridge: Cambridge University Press, 1999.

Clough, Miryam. *Shame, the Church and the Regulation of Female Sexuality*. New York: Routledge, 2017.

Cohen, Jeremy. *Be Fertile and Increase, Fill the Earth and Master It: The Ancient and Medieval Career of a Biblical Text*. Ithaca, NY: Cornell University Press, 1989.

——. *Living Letters of the Law: Ideas of the Jew in Medieval Christianity*. Tel Aviv: Tel Aviv University Press, 1999.

Coleman, K. M. "Fatal Charades: Roman Executions Staged as Mythological Enactments." *Journal of Roman Studies* 80 (1990): 44–73.

Coletti, Theresa. "Devotional Iconography in the N-Town Marian Plays." *Comparative Drama* 11, no. 1 (1977): 22–44.

——. "A Feminist Approach to the Corpus Christi Cycles." In *Approaches to Teaching Medieval English Drama*, edited by Richard K. Emmerson, 78–89. New York: Modern Language Association of America, 1990.

——. *Mary Magdalene and the Drama of Saints: Theater, Gender, and Religion in Late Medieval England*. Philadelphia: University of Pennsylvania Press, 2004.

——. "N-Town Plays." In *Dictionary of Literary Biography: Old and Middle English Literature*, edited by Jeffrey Helterman and Jerome Mitchell, 146:405–14. Detroit: Gale Research, 1994.

——. "Purity and Danger: The Paradox of Mary's Body and En-gendering of the Infancy Narrative in the English Mystery Cycles." In *Feminist Approaches to the Body in Medieval Literature*, edited by Linda Lomperis and Sarah Stanbury, 65–95. Philadelphia: University of Pennsylvania Press, 1993.

——. "Reading REED: History and the Records of Early English Drama." In *Literary Practice and Social Change in Britain, 1380–1530*, edited by Lee Patterson, 248–284. Berkeley: University of California Press, 1990.

Coletti, Theresa, and Gail McMurray Gibson. "The Tudor Origins of Medieval Drama." In *A Companion to Tudor Literature*, edited by Kent Cartwright, 228–45. Malden, MA: Wiley-Blackwell, 2010.

Collins, Adela Yardbro. *Mark: A Commentary*. Edited by Harold W. Attridge. Hermeneia. Minneapolis: Fortress, 2007.

Connell, Sophia M. *Aristotle on Female Animals: A Study of the Generation of Animals*. Cambridge: Cambridge University Press, 2016.

Constas, Nicholas. *Proclus of Constantinople and the Cult of the Virgin in Late Antiquity*. Leiden: Brill, 2003.

Cooper, Tarnya. *Searching for Shakespeare*. New Haven, CT: Yale University Press, 2006.

Cox, John D. *The Devil and the Sacred in English Drama, 1350–1642*. Cambridge: Cambridge University Press, 2000.

Cruz, Anne J. "Vindicating the *Vulnerata*: Cádiz and the Circulation of Religious Imagery as Weapons of War." In *Material and Symbolic Circulation between Spain and England, 1554–1604*, edited by Anne J. Cruz, 39–60. Aldershot, UK: Ashgate, 2008.

Cuffel, Alexandra. *Gendering Disgust in Medieval Religious Polemic*. Notre Dame, IN: University of Notre Dame Press, 2007.

Curtius, Ernst Robert. *European Literature and the Latin Middle Ages*. Translated by Willard R. Trask. Princeton, NJ: Princeton University Press, 1953.

Cushman, Helen. "Handling Knowledge: Holy Bodies in the Middle English Mystery Plays." *Journal of Medieval and Early Modern Studies* 47, no. 2 (2017): 279–304.

Daly, Mary. *Beyond God the Father: Toward a Philosophy of Women's Liberation*. Boston: Beacon, 1973.

David, Alfred. "Noah's Wife's Flood." In *The Performance of Middle English Culture: Essays on Chaucer and the Drama in Honor of Martin Stevens*, edited by James J. Paxson, Lawrence M. Clopper, and Sylvia Tomasch, 97–109. Cambridge, UK: D. S. Brewer, 1998.

Davidson, Clifford. *Festivals and Plays in Late Medieval Britain*. Aldershot, UK: Ashgate, 2007.

Davies, Nick. *Cuckoo: Cheating by Nature*. London: Bloomsbury, 2015.

Davis, John F. "The Trials of Thomas Bylney and the English Reformation." *Historical Journal* 24, no. 4 (1981): 775–90.

Davis, Natalie Zemon. "The Rites of Violence: Religious Riot in Sixteenth-Century France." *Past & Present* 59 (1973): 51–91.

Delany, Sheila. *Impolitic Bodies: Poetry, Saints, and Society in Fifteenth-Century England: The Work of Obsern Bokenham*. Oxford: Oxford University Press, 1998.

Delooz, Pierre. *Sociologie et canonisations*. Liège, Belgium: Faculté de droit, 1969.

Denery, Dallas G. *The Devil Wins: A History of Lying from the Garden of Eden to the Enlightenment*. Princeton, NJ: Princeton University Press, 2015.

Denysenko, Nicholas. "An Appeal to Mary: An Analysis of Pussy Riot's Punk Performance in Moscow." *Journal of the American Academy of Religion* 81, no. 4 (2013): 1061–92.

Denzey, Nicola. *The Bone Gatherers: The Lost Worlds of Early Christian Women*. Boston: Beacon Press, 2007.

Diehl, Huston. *Staging Reform, Reforming the Stage: Protestantism and Popular Theater in Early Modern England*. Ithaca, NY: Cornell University Press, 1997.

Diller, Hans-Jürgen. "From Synthesis to Compromise: The Four Daughters of God in Early English Drama." *EDAM Review* 18 (1996): 88–103.

Dillon, Janette. *The Cambridge Introduction to Early English Theatre*. Cambridge: Cambridge University Press, 2006.

Dinshaw, Carolyn. *Chaucer's Sexual Poetics*. Madison, WI: University of Wisconsin Press, 1989.

——. *Getting Medieval: Sexualities and Communities, Pre- and Postmodern*. Durham, NC: Duke University Press, 1999.

Dixon, Laurinda. *Perilous Chastity: Women and Illness in Pre-Enlightenment Art and Medicine*. Ithaca, NY: Cornell University Press, 1995.

Dolan, Frances. "Hermione's Ghost: Catholicism, the Feminine, and the Undead in Early Modern Studies." In *The Impact of Feminism in English Renaissance Studies*, edited by Dympna Callaghan, 213–37. New York: Palgrave Macmillan, 2007.

——. *Whores of Babylon: Catholicism, Gender, and Seventeenth-Century Print Culture*. Ithaca, NY: Cornell University Press, 1999.

Donavin, Georgiana. *Scribit Mater: Mary and the Language Arts in the Literature of Medieval England*. Washington, DC: Catholic University of America Press, 2012.

Douglas, Audrey, and Peter Greenfield, eds. *Cumberland, Westmorland, Gloucestershire*. REED. Toronto: University of Toronto Press, 1986.

Duffy, Eamon. "A. G. Dickens and the Late Medieval Church." *Historical Research* 77 (2004): 98–110.

——. *The Stripping of the Altars: Traditional Religion in England, 1400–1580*. 2nd ed. New Haven, CT: Yale University Press, 2005.

Dunning, Benjamin H. *Specters of Paul: Sexual Difference in Early Christian Thought*. Philadelphia: University of Pennsylvania Press, 2011.

Edwards, John. "A 'Fifteenth-Century' Wall Painting at South Leigh." *Oxoniensia* 48 (1983): 131–42.

Ehrman, Bart D. *Forgery and Counter-forgery: The Use of Literary Deceit in Early Christian Polemics*. Oxford: Oxford University Press, 2013.

———. *The New Testament: A Historical Introduction to the Early Christian Writings*. Oxford: Oxford University Press, 2004.

Ehrman, Bart D., and Zlatko Pleše, eds. *The Apocryphal Gospels: Texts and Translations*. New York: Oxford University Press, 2012.

Ellington, Donna Spivey. *From Sacred Body to Angelic Soul: Understanding Mary in Late Medieval and Early Modern Europe*. Washington, DC: Catholic University of America Press, 2001.

Elliott, Dyan. *The Bride of Christ Goes to Hell: Metaphor and Embodiment in the Lives of Pious Women, 200–1500*. Philadelphia: University of Pennsylvania Press, 2012.

———. *Fallen Bodies: Pollution, Sexuality, and Demonology in the Middle Ages*. Philadelphia: University of Pennsylvania Press, 1999.

———. *Proving Woman: Female Spirituality and Inquisitional Culture in the Later Middle Ages*. Princeton, NJ: Princeton University Press, 2004.

———. *Spiritual Marriage: Sexual Abstinence in Medieval Wedlock*. Princeton, NJ: Princeton University Press, 1993.

Elliott, John R. *Playing God: Medieval Mysteries on the Modern Stage*. Toronto: University of Toronto Press, 1989.

Emmerson, Richard K. "Required and Recommended Readings for Students." In *Approaches to Teaching Medieval English Drama*, edited by Richard K. Emmerson, 13–15. New York: Modern Language Association of America, 1990.

Enders, Jody. *Death by Drama and Other Medieval Urban Legends*. Chicago: University of Chicago Press, 2002.

Erasmus, Desiderius. *Seven Dialogues Both Pithie and Profitable*. London, 1606.

Espinosa, Ruben. *Masculinity and Marian Efficacy in Shakespeare's England: Women and Gender in the Early Modern World*. Farnham, UK: Ashgate, 2011.

Ettlinger, Ellen. "Folklore in Oxfordshire Churches." *Folklore* 73, no. 3 (1962): 160–77.

Evans, Ruth. "Feminist Re-enactments: Gender and the Towneley Uxor Noe." In *A Wyf Ther Was: Essays in Honour of Paule Mertens-Fonck*, edited by Juliette Dor, 141–54. Liège, Belgium: Liège Language and Literature, 1992.

———. "Virginities." In *The Cambridge Companion to Medieval Women's Writing*, edited by Carolyn Dinshaw and David Wallace, 21–39. Cambridge: Cambridge University Press, 2003.

———. "When a Body Meets a Body: Fergus and Mary in the York Cycle." *New Medieval Literatures* 1 (1997): 193–212.

Everest, Carol A. "Pears and Pregnancy in Chaucer's 'Merchant's Tale.'" In *Food in the Middle Ages: A Book of Essays*, edited by Melitta Weiss Adamson, 161–75. New York: Garland, 1995.

Farnhill, Ken. *Guilds and the Parish Community in Late Medieval East Anglia, c. 1470–1550*. Rochester, NY: Boydell, 2001.

Fewer, Colin. "The 'Fygure' of the Market: The N-Town Cycle and East Anglian Lay Piety." *Philological Quarterly* 77, no. 2 (1998): 117–47.

Fitzgerald, Christina M. *The Drama of Masculinity and Medieval English Guild Culture.* New York: Palgrave Macmillan, 2007.

Fitzhenry, William. "The N-Town Plays and the Politics of Metatheater." *Studies in Philology* 100, no. 1 (2003): 22–43.

Fitzmyer, Joseph A., ed. *The Gospel According to Luke.* Anchor Bible. New York: Doubleday, 1981.

Fletcher, Alan J. "Line 30 of the Man of Law's Tale and the Medieval Malkyn." *English Language Notes* 24, no. 2 (1986): 15–20.

Flood, John. *Representations of Eve in Antiquity and the English Middle Ages.* New York: Routledge, 2011.

Foreville, R. "Manifestation de lollardisme à Exeter en 1421 d'après une lettre extravagente de Henri Chichele." *Le Moyen Âge* 69 (1963): 691–706.

Forrest, Ian. "The Summoner." In *Historians on Chaucer: The "General Prologue" to the Canterbury Tales,* edited by Stephen Rigby, 421–42. Oxford: Oxford University Press, 2014.

Fortnum, Rebecca. *Contemporary British Women Artists: In Their Own Words.* New York: Palgrave Macmillan, 2007.

Foskett, Mary F. *A Virgin Conceived: Mary and Classical Representations of Virginity.* Bloomington: Indiana University Press, 2002.

Fowler, Elizabeth. *Literary Character: The Human Figure in Early English Writing.* Ithaca, NY: Cornell University Press, 2003.

Fraioli, Deborah A. *Joan of Arc: The Early Debate.* Woodbridge, UK: Boydell, 2000.

France, James. "The Heritage of Saint Bernard in Medieval Art." In *A Companion to Bernard of Clairvaux,* edited by Brian Patrick McGuire, 305–36. Leiden: Brill, 2011.

Frede, Michael. "Origen's Treatise *Against Celsus.*" In *Apologetics in the Roman Empire: Pagans, Jews, and Christians,* edited by Mark J. Edwards, Martin Goodman, Simon Price, and Chris Rowland, 131–55. Oxford: Oxford University Press, 1999.

Fredriksen, Paula, and Oded Irshai. "Christian Anti-Judaism: Polemics and Policies." In *The Cambridge History of Judaism,* vol. 4, *The Late Roman-Rabbinic Period,* edited by Steven T. Katz, 977–1034. Cambridge: Cambridge University Press, 2006.

Freedberg, David. "The Hidden God: Image and Interdiction in the Netherlands in the Sixteenth Century." *Art History* 5 (1982): 133–53.

——. "Johannes Molanus on Provocative Paintings: *De Historia Sanctarum Imaginum et Picturarum,* Book II, Chapter 42." *Journal of the Warburg and Courtauld Institutes* 34 (1971): 229–45.

Freedman, Paul H. *Images of the Medieval Peasant.* Stanford, CA: Stanford University Press, 1999.

Freeman, Margaret B. *The Unicorn Tapestries.* New York: Metropolitan Museum of Art, 1976.

Freeman, Thomas S. "Offending God: John Foxe and English Protestant Reactions to the Cult of the Virgin Mary." In *The Church and Mary,* edited by R. N. Swanson, 228–38. Rochester, NY: Boydell and Brewer, 2004.

Frère, Jean-Claude. *Early Flemish Painting.* Paris: Terrail, 2007.

Friedman, John B. "Nicholas's 'Angelus Ad Virginem' and the Mocking of Noah." *Yearbook of English Studies* 22 (1992): 162–80.

Friedmann, Herbert. *The Symbolic Goldfinch: Its History and Significance in European Devotional Art*. New York: Pantheon Books, 1946.

Fry, Timothy. "The Unity of the *Ludus Coventriae*." *Studies in Philology* 68 (1951): 527–70.

Fulton Brown, Rachel. *From Judgment to Passion: Devotion to Christ and the Virgin Mary, 800–1200*. New York: Columbia University Press, 2002.

Gambero, Luigi. *Mary and the Fathers of the Church: The Blessed Virgin Mary in Patristic Thought*. Translated by Thomas Buffer. San Francisco: Ignatius, 1991.

——. *Mary in the Middle Ages: The Blessed Virgin Mary in the Thought of Medieval Latin Theologians*. Translated by Thomas Buffer. San Francisco: Ignatius, 2005.

Gardiner, H. C. *Mysteries' End: An Investigation of the Last Days of the Medieval Religious Stage*. New Haven, CT: Yale University Press, 1946.

Gaskin, R. "Peter Damian on Divine Power and the Contingency of the Past." *British Journal for the History of Philosophy* 5 (1997): 229–47.

Gauchet, Marcel. *The Disenchantment of the World: A Political History of Religion*. Translated by Oscar Burge. Princeton, NJ: Princeton University Press, 1999.

Gaventa, Beverly Roberts. *Mary: Glimpses of the Mother of Jesus*. Minneapolis: Fortress, 1999.

Geary, Patrick. *Furta Sacra: Thefts of Relics in the Central Middle Ages*. Princeton, NJ: Princeton University Press, 1978.

——. "Humiliation of Saints." In *Saints and Their Cults: Studies in Religious Sociology, Folklore, and History*, edited by Stephen Wilson, 123–40. Cambridge: Cambridge University Press, 1983.

Gertsman, Elina. "Image and Performance: An Art Historian at the Crossroads." *ROMARD* 51 (2012): 51–60.

——. *Worlds Within: Opening the Medieval Shrine Madonna*. University Park: Pennsylvania State University Press, 2015.

Gibson, Gail McMurray. "Bury St. Edmunds, Lydgate, and the N-Town Cycle." *Speculum* 56, no. 1 (1981): 56–90.

——. "The Images of Doubt and Belief: Visual Symbolism in the Middle English Plays of Joseph's Troubles about Mary." PhD diss., University of Virginia, 1975.

——. "Manuscript as Sacred Object: Robert Hegge's N-Town Plays." *Journal of Medieval and Early Modern Studies* 44, no. 3 (2014): 503–29.

——. "'Porta haec clausa erit': Comedy, Conception, and Ezekiel's Closed Door in the *Ludus Coventriae* Play of 'Joseph's Return.'" *Journal of Medieval and Renaissance Studies* 8 (1978): 137–57.

——. "Saint Anne and the Religion of Childbed: Some East Anglian Texts and Talismans." In *Interpreting Cultural Symbols: Saint Anne in Late Medieval Society*, edited by Kathleen Ashley and Pamela Sheingorn, 95–110. Athens: University of Georgia Press, 1990.

——. "Scene and Obscene: Seeing and Performing Late Medieval Childbirth." *Journal of Medieval and Early Modern Studies* 29, no. 1 (1999): 7–24.

——. *The Theater of Devotion: East Anglian Drama and Society in the Late Middle Ages*. Chicago: University of Chicago Press, 1989.

——. "Writing before the Eye: The N-Town 'Woman Taken in Adultery' and the Medieval Ministry Play." *Comparative Drama* 27, no. 4 (1993): 399–407.

Gibson, James M., ed. *Kent, Diocese of Canterbury.* 2 vols. REED. Toronto: University of Toronto Press, 2002.

Giles, Ryan D. *The Laughter of the Saints: Parodies of Holiness in Late Medieval and Renaissance Spain.* Toronto: University of Toronto Press, 2009.

Glancy, Jennifer. *Corporal Knowledge: Early Christian Bodies.* Oxford: Oxford University Press, 2010.

Gold, Penny Schine. *The Lady and the Virgin: Image, Attitude, and Experience in Twelfth-Century France.* Chicago: University of Chicago Press, 1985.

Golden, Leon. "Aristotle on Comedy." *Journal of Aesthetics and Art Criticism* 42, no. 3 (1984): 283–90.

Goodland, Katharine. *Female Mourning and Tragedy in Medieval and Renaissance English Drama: From the Raising of Lazarus to King Lear.* Aldershot, UK: Ashgate, 2005.

Gordon, Dillian. "The Wilton Diptych: An Introduction." In *The Regal Image of Richard II and the Wilton Diptych*, edited by Dillian Gordon, Lisa Monnas, and Caroline Elam, 19–27. Coventry, UK: Harvey Miller, 1997.

Graef, Hilda. *Mary: A History of Doctrine and Devotion.* 1963, 1965. Rev. ed., with a new chapter covering Vatican II and beyond by Thomas A. Thompson. Notre Dame, IN: Ave Maria, 2009.

Granger, Penny. *The N-Town Play: Drama and Liturgy in Medieval East Anglia.* Cambridge, UK: D. S. Brewer, 2009.

Grant, Robert M. *Miracle and Natural Law in Graeco-Roman and Early Christian Thought.* Amsterdam: North-Holland, 1952.

Grantley, Darryll. "*The Winter's Tale* and Early Religious Drama," *Comparative Drama* 20 (1986): 17–37.

Green, Monica H., ed. *Women's Healthcare in the Medieval West: Texts and Contexts.* Aldershot, UK: Routledge, 2000.

Greg, Walter Wilson. *Bibliographical and Textual Problems of the English Miracle Cycles.* London: Alexander Moring, 1914.

Gregg, Joan Young. *Devils, Women, and Jews: Reflections of the Other in Medieval Sermon Stories.* New York: State University of New York Press, 1997.

Gregory, Rabia. *Marrying Jesus in Medieval and Early Modern Northern Europe: Popular Culture and Religious Reform.* New York: Routledge, 2016.

Grigsby, Byron Lee. *Pestilence in Medieval and Early Modern English Literature.* London: Routledge, 2004.

Groebner, Valentin. "Losing Face, Saving Face: Noses and Honor in the Late Medieval Town." Translated by Pamela Selwyn. *History Workshop Journal* 40 (1995): 1–15.

Groeneveld, Leanne. "A Theatrical Miracle: The Boxley Rood of Grace as Puppet." *Early Theatre* 10, no. 2 (January 2007): 11–50.

Grössinger, Christa. "The Unicorn on English Misericords." In *Medieval Art: Recent Perspectives*, edited by Gale R. Owen-Crocker and Timothy Graham, 142–58. Manchester: Manchester University Press, 1998.

Groves, Beatrice. *Texts and Traditions: Religion in Shakespeare, 1592–1604.* Oxford: Clarendon, 2007.

Guynn, Noah. *Allegory and Sexual Ethics in the High Middle Ages.* New York: Palgrave Macmillan, 2007.

Hackett, Helen. *Virgin Mother, Maiden Queen: Elizabeth I and the Cult of the Virgin Mary.* New York: St. Martin's, 1995.

Haenchen, Ernst. *John 1: A Commentary on the Gospel of John, Chapters 1–6.* Translated by Robert W. Funk. Hermeneia. Philadelphia: Fortress, 1984.

——. *John 2: A Commentary on the Gospel of John, Chapters 7–21.* Translated by Robert W. Funk. Hermeneia. Philadelphia: Fortress, 1984.

Hagen, Rose-Marie, and Rainer Hagen. *What Great Paintings Say.* Vol. 2. New York: Taschen, 2003.

Hanawalt, Barbara. "The Female Felon in Fourteenth-Century England." *Viator* 5, no. 1 (1974): 253–68.

Harbin, Andrea R. "Virgin's End: The Suppression of the York Marian Pageants." *Medieval Feminist Forum: A Journal of Gender and Sexuality* 50, no. 2 (2015): 33–63.

Hardin, Richard. "Chronicles and Mythmaking in Shakespeare's Joan of Arc." *Shakespeare Survey* 42 (1989): 25–35.

Harris, Carissa. *Obscene Pedagogies: Transgressive Talk and Sexual Education in Late Medieval Britain.* Ithaca, NY: Cornell University Press, 2018.

Hayes, Douglas W. "Backbiter and the Rhetoric of Detraction." *Comparative Drama* 34, no. 1 (2000): 53–78.

Healy, Margaret. *Fictions of Disease in Early Modern England: Bodies, Plagues, and Politics.* New York: Palgrave Macmillan, 2001.

Heck, Christian, and Rémy Cordonnier. *The Grand Medieval Bestiary: Animals in Illuminated Manuscripts.* New York: Abbeville, 2012.

Heffernan, Carol Falvo. "Contraception and the Pear Tree Episode of Chaucer's 'Merchant's Tale.'" *Journal of English and German Philology* 94 (1995): 31–41.

——. "The Old English Phoenix: A Reconsideration." *Neuphilologische Mitteilungen* 83, no. 3 (1982): 239–54.

Hellwig, Monika. "The Dogmatic Implications of the Birth of the Messiah." *Emmanuel* 84 (1978): 21–24.

Hendel, Ronald. "The Nephilim Were on the Earth: Genesis 6:1–4 and Its Ancient Near-Eastern Context." In *The Fall of the Angels,* edited by Christoph Auffarth and Loren T. Stuckenbruck, 11–34. Leiden: Brill, 2004.

Hines, John. *The Fabliau in English.* New York: Longman, 1993.

Hobbins, Daniel. *The Trial of Joan of Arc.* Cambridge, MA: Harvard University Press, 2007.

Hodges, Laura F. *Chaucer and Array: Patterns of Costume and Fabric Rhetoric in the "Canterbury Tales," "Troilus and Criseyde" and Other Works.* Cambridge, UK: D. S. Brewer, 2014.

Holland, Glenn. "Celibacy and the Early Christian Church." In *Celibacy and Religious Traditions,* edited by Carl Olson, 65–84. Oxford: Oxford University Press, 2007.

Holsinger, Bruce. *Music, Body and Desire in Medieval Culture: Hildegard of Bingen to Chaucer.* Stanford, CA: Stanford University Press, 2001.

Hone, William. *Ancient Mysteries Described: English Miracle Plays Founded on Apocryphal New Testament Story.* London: printed for William Hone, 1823.

Hopkins, Lisa. "'Black but Beautiful': *Othello* and the Cult of the Black Madonna." In *Marian Moments in Early Modern Drama*, edited by Regina Buccola and Lisa Hopkins, 75–86. Burlington, VT: Ashgate, 2007.

Huizinga, Johan. *The Autumn of the Middle Ages.* Translated by Rodney J. Payton and Ulrich Mammitzsch. Chicago: University of Chicago Press, 1996.

Hultgren, Arland J. *The Parables of Jesus: A Commentary.* Grand Rapids, MI: W. B. Eerdmans, 2000.

Hunt, Alison. "Maculating Mary: The Detractors of the N-Town Cycle's 'Trial of Mary and Joseph.'" *Philological Quarterly* 73, no. 1 (1994): 11–29.

Hunter, David G. *Marriage, Celibacy, and Heresy in Ancient Christianity: The Jovinianist Controversy.* Oxford: Oxford University Press, 2007.

Hutchinson, Roger. *The Works of Roger Hutchinson.* Edited by John Bruce. Cambridge: Cambridge University Press, 1842.

Ihnat, Kati. *Mother of Mercy, Bane of the Jews: Devotion to the Virgin Mary in Anglo-Norman England.* Princeton, NJ: Princeton University Press, 2016.

Ingram, R. W., ed. *Coventry.* REED. Toronto: University of Toronto Press, 1981.

Ives, Eric. *The Life and Death of Anne Boleyn.* Oxford: Blackwell, 2004.

Iyengar, Sujata. *Shades of Difference: Mythologies of Skin Color in Early Modern England.* Philadelphia: University of Pennsylvania Press, 2005.

Jackson, Gabriele Bernhard. "Topical Ideology: Witches, Amazons, and Shakespeare's Joan of Arc." *English Literary Renaissance* 18 (1988): 40–65.

Jackson, Melissa. *Comedy and Feminist Interpretation of the Hebrew Bible: A Subversive Collaboration.* Oxford: Oxford University Press, 2012.

Jacquart, Danielle, and Claude Alexandre Thomasset. *Sexuality and Medicine in the Middle Ages.* New York: Polity, 1988.

Jakobsen, Janet R., and Ann Pellegrini, eds. *Secularisms.* Durham, NC: Duke University Press, 2008.

James, M. R., and E. W. Tristram. "The Wall Paintings in Eton College Chapel and in the Lady Chapel of Winchester Cathedral." *Volume of the Walpole Society* 17 (1928–29): 1–43.

Jansen, Katherine Ludwig. *The Making of the Magdalen: Preaching and Popular Devotion in the Later Middle Ages.* Princeton, NJ: Princeton University Press, 2000.

Jeffrey, David Lyle. "Bathsheba in the Eye of the Beholder: Artistic Depiction from the Late Middle Ages to Rembrandt." In *Sacred and Profane in Chaucer and Late Medieval Literature: Essays in Honour of John V. Fleming*, edited by Robert William Epstein, 30–45. Toronto: University of Toronto Press, 2010.

Johnson, Lesley. "Women on Top: Antifeminism in the Fabliaux." *Modern Language Review* 78, no. 2 (1983): 298–307.

Johnson, Richard F. *Saint Michael the Archangel in Medieval English Legend.* Woodbridge, UK: Boydell, 2005.

Johnson, Wallace H. "The Origin of the *Second Shepherds' Play*: A New Theory." *Quarterly Journal of Speech* 52, no. 1 (1966): 47–57.

Johnson, William Bruce. *Miracles and Sacrilege: Roberto Rossellini, the Church, and Film Censorship in Hollywood.* Toronto: University of Toronto Press, 2008.

Johnston, Alexandra F. "What If No Texts Survived? External Evidence for Early English Drama." In *Contexts for Early English Drama*, edited by Marianne G. Briscoe and John C. Coldewey, 1–19. Bloomington: Indiana University Press, 1989.

Johnston, Alexandra F., and Margaret Rogerson, eds. *York*. 2 vols. REED. Toronto: University of Toronto Press, 1979.

Jones, Gwenan, ed. *A Study of Three Welsh Religious Plays*. Aberystwyth, Wales: Bala, 1939.

Jones, Malcolm. *The Secret Middle Ages: Discovering the Real Medieval World*. London: Praeger, 2003.

Jones, Mike Rodman. "January's Genesis: Biblical Exegesis and Chaucer's *Merchant's Tale*." *Leeds Studies in English* 39 (2008): 53–87.

Julleville, L. Petit de. *Les mystères*. Vol. 2. Paris: Libraire Hachette, 1880.

Jurkowski, Maureen. "Lollardy in Oxfordshire and Northamptonshire: The Two Thomas Compworths." In *Lollards and Their Influence in Late Medieval England*, edited by Fiona Somerset, Jill C. Havens, and Derrick G. Pitard, 73–95. Woodbridge, UK: Boydell, 2003.

Justice, Steven. "Eucharistic Miracle and Eucharistic Doubt." *Journal of Medieval and Early Modern Studies* 42, no. 2 (2012): 307–32.

Karant-Nunn, Susan, and Merry Wiesner-Hanks, eds. *Luther on Women: A Sourcebook*. Cambridge: Cambridge University Press, 2003.

Karras, Ruth Mazo. *Common Women: Prostitution and Sexuality in Medieval England*. Oxford: Oxford University Press, 1998.

——. "Holy Harlots: Prostitute Saints in Medieval Legend." *Journal of the History of Sexuality* 1, no. 1 (1990): 3–32.

——. "The Virgin and the Pregnant Abbess: Miracles and Gender in the Middle Ages." *Medieval Perspectives* 3 (1988): 112–32.

Kay, Sarah. *Courtly Contradictions: The Emergence of the Literary Object in the Twelfth Century*. Stanford, CA: Stanford University Press, 2002.

Kean, Margaret, ed. *John Milton's "Paradise Lost": A Sourcebook*. London: Routledge, 2005.

Kearns, Cleo McNelly. *The Virgin Mary, Monotheism and Sacrifice*. Cambridge: Cambridge University Press, 2008.

Kelly, Kathleen Coyne. *Performing Virginity and Testing Chastity in the Middle Ages*. New York: Routledge, 2000.

Kelly, Kathleen Coyne, and Marina Leslie, eds. *Menacing Virgins: Representing Virginity in the Middle Ages and Renaissance*. Newark: University of Delaware Press, 1999.

Kendrick, Laura. *Chaucerian Play: Comedy and Control in the Canterbury Tales*. Berkeley: University of California Press, 1988.

——. "Medieval Vernacular Versions of Ancient Comedy." In *Ancient Comedy and Reception: Essays in Honor of Jeffrey Henderson*, edited by S. Douglas Olson, 377–96. Berlin: de Gruyter, 2014.

Kerr, Margaret H., Richard D. Forsyth, and Michael J. Plyley. "Cold Water and Hot Iron: Trial by Ordeal in England." *Journal of Interdisciplinary History* 22, no. 4 (1992): 573–95.

King, Helen. *The Disease of Virgins: Green Sickness, Chlorosis, and the Problems of Puberty*. London: Routledge, 2004.

King, John. *Tudor Royal Iconography: Literature and Art in an Age of Religious Crisis.* Princeton, NJ: Princeton University Press, 1989.

King, Karen L. "'Jesus Said to Them, 'My Wife . . .': A New Coptic Papyrus Fragment." *Harvard Theological Review* 107, no. 2 (2014): 131–59.

Kinservik, Matthew. "The Struggle over Mary's Body: Theological and Dramatic Resolution in the N-Town Assumption Play." *Journal of English and Germanic Philology* 95, no. 2 (1996): 190–203.

Knight, Alan E. "The Pregnant Abbesses of Paris and Lille." In *Parisian Confraternity Drama of the Fourteenth Century,* edited by Donald Maddox and Sara Sturm-Maddox, 135–47. Turnhout: Brepols, 2008.

Knust, Jennifer Wright. *Abandoned to Lust: Sexual Slander and Ancient Christianity.* New York: Columbia University Press, 2006.

——. "'Taking Away From': Patristic Evidence and the Omission of the *Pericope Adulterae* from John's Gospel." In *The Pericope of the Adulteress in Contemporary Research,* edited by David Alan Black and Jacob N. Cerone, 65–88. London: Bloomsbury, 2016.

Koester, Craig R. *Revelation.* Anchor Bible. New Haven, CT: Yale University Press, 2014.

Koldeweij, Jos. "'Shameless and Naked Images': Obscene Badges as Parodies of Popular Devotion." In *Art and Architecture of Late Medieval Pilgrimage in Northern Europe and the British Isles,* edited by Sarah Blick and Rita Tekippe, 1:493–510. Leiden: Brill, 2004.

Kolve, V. A. *Chaucer and the Imagery of Narrative: The First Five Canterbury Tales.* Stanford, CA: Stanford University Press, 1984.

——. *The Play Called Corpus Christi.* Stanford, CA: Stanford University Press, 1966.

Koppelman, Kate. "Becoming Her Man: Transcoding in Medieval Marian Literature." *Exemplaria* 22, no. 3 (2010): 200–222.

——. "Devotional Ambivalence: The Virgin Mary as 'Empresse of Helle.'" *Essays in Medieval Studies* 18, no. 1 (2001): 67–82.

Krause, Kathy M., and Alison Stones, eds. *Gautier de Coinci: Miracles, Music, and Manuscripts.* Turnhout: Brepols, 2006.

Kreitzer, Beth. *Reforming Mary: Changing Images of the Virgin Mary in Lutheran Sermons of the Sixteenth Century.* Oxford: Oxford University Press, 2004.

Kristeva, Julia. "Stabat Mater." Translated by Arthur Goldhammer. *Poetics Today* 6, no. 1/2 (1985): 133–52.

Kristeva, Julia, and Catherine Clément. *The Feminine and the Sacred.* Translated by Jane Marie Todd. New York: Columbia University Press, 2001.

Kvam, Kristen E., Linda S. Schearing, and Valarie H. Ziegler, eds. *Eve and Adam: Jewish, Christian, and Muslim Readings on Genesis and Gender.* Indianapolis: Indiana University Press, 1999.

Lampert, Lisa. *Gender and Jewish Difference from Paul to Shakespeare.* Philadelphia: University of Pennsylvania Press, 2004.

Lamy, Marielle. *L'Immaculée Conception: Étapes et enjeux d'une controverse au Moyen Âge, XXIe-XVe siècles.* Paris: Institut d'Études Augustiniennes, 2000.

Laqueur, Thomas. *Making Sex: Body and Gender from the Greeks to Freud.* Cambridge, MA: Harvard University Press, 1990.

Lea, Henry Charles. *A History of the Inquisition of the Middle Ages*. 3 vols. New York: Macmillan, 1906.

Lerner, Robert E. *The Heresy of the Free Spirit in the Later Middle Ages*. Berkeley: University of California Press, 1972.

Levin, Carole. *The Heart and Stomach of a King: Elizabeth I and the Politics of Sex and Power*. 2nd ed. Philadelphia: University of Pennsylvania Press, 2013.

Levin, Carole, and John Watkins. *Shakespeare's Foreign Worlds: National and Transnational Identities in the Elizabethan Age*. Ithaca, NY: Cornell University Press, 2009.

Levine, Baruch A. *Numbers 1–20*. Anchor Bible. New York: Doubleday, 1993.

Lewis, C. S. "What Chaucer Really Did to *Il Filostrato*." *Essays and Studies* 17 (1932): 56–75.

Lightbown, R. W. *Carlo Crivelli*. New Haven, CT: Yale University Press, 2004.

Lipton, Emma. *Affections of the Mind: The Politics of Sacramental Marriage in Late Medieval English Literature*. Notre Dame, IN: University of Notre Dame Press, 2007.

——. "Language on Trial: Performing the Law in the N-Town Trial Play." In *The Letter of the Law: Legal Practice and Literary Production in Medieval England*, edited by Emily Steiner and Candace Barrington, 115–35. Ithaca, NY: Cornell University Press, 2002.

Lipton, Sara. *Dark Mirror: The Medieval Origins of Anti-Jewish Iconography*. New York: Metropolitan Books, 2014.

——. *Images of Intolerance: Representations of Jews and Judaism in the Bible Moralisée*. Berkeley: University of California Press, 1999.

Little, Lester. *Benedictine Maledictions: Liturgical Cursing in Romanesque France*. Ithaca, NY: Cornell University Press, 1996.

Lochrie, Karma. *Heterosyncrasies: Female Sexuality When Normal Wasn't*. Minneapolis: University of Minnesota Press, 2005.

——. "Mystical Acts, Queer Tendencies." In *Constructing Medieval Sexuality*, edited by Karma Lochrie, Peggy McCracken, and James A. Schulz, 180–200. Minneapolis: University of Minnesota Press, 1997.

Loewen, Peter, and Robin Waugh, eds. *Mary Magdalene in Medieval Culture: Conflicted Roles*. New York: Routledge, 2014.

Logan, F. D. *Excommunication and the Secular Arm of the Law in Medieval England*. Toronto: University of Toronto Press, 1968.

Logan, Ian. *Reading Anselm's "Proslogion": The History of Anselm's Argument and Its Significance Today*. Burlington, VT: Ashgate, 2009.

Lopez, Elisabeth. *Colette of Corbie (1381–1447): Learning and Holiness*. Translated by JoAnne Waller. New York: Franciscan Institute Publications, 2011.

Loughlin, Marie H. *Hymeneutics: Interpreting Virginity on the Early Modern Stage*. Cranbury, NJ: Bucknell University Press, 1997.

Lumiansky, R. M., and David Mills. *The Chester Mystery Cycle: Essays and Documents*. Chapel Hill: University of North Carolina Press, 1983.

Luscombe, David. *The Letter Collection of Peter Abelard and Heloise*. Oxford: Clarendon, 2013.

Luttikhuizen, Gerard P. *Gnostic Revisions of Genesis Stories and Early Jesus Traditions*. Leiden: Brill, 2006.

Luz, Ulrich. *Matthew 1–7: A Commentary*. Translated by James E. Crouch. Hermeneia. Minneapolis: Fortress, 2007.

———. *Matthew 8–20: A Commentary*. Translated by James E. Crouch. Hermeneia. Minneapolis: Fortress, 2001.

Maccoby, Hyam. *Judaism on Trial: Jewish-Christian Disputations in the Middle Ages*. Rutherford, NJ: Fairleigh Dickinson University Press, 1982.

Maddox, Donald, and Sara Sturm-Maddox, eds. *Parisian Confraternity Drama of the Fourteenth Century: The Miracles de Nostre Dame par personnages*. Turnhout: Brepols, 2008.

Mahoney, John. "Alice of Bath: Her 'Secte' and 'Gentil Text.'" *Criticism* 6, no. 2 (1964): 144–55.

Manly, William M. "Shepherds and Prophets: Religious Unity in the Towneley *Secunda Pastorum*." *PMLA* 78, no. 3 (1963): 151–55.

Mapstone, Sally, ed. *William Dunbar, 'The Nobill Poyet': Essays in Honour of Priscilla Bawcutt*. East Linton, Scotland: Tuckwell Press, 2001.

Marshall, Louise. "Manipulating the Sacred: Image and Plague in Renaissance Italy." *Renaissance Quarterly* 47, no. 3 (1994): 512–27.

Marx, Karl. *Marx: Early Political Writings*. Edited by Joseph O'Malley. Cambridge: Cambridge University Press, 1994.

Matthews, Alastair. "Performing Aristotle's Lessons." In *Aspects of the Performative in Medieval Culture*, edited by Manuele Gragnolati and Almut Suerbaum, 245–76. Berlin: de Gruyter, 2010.

Mayberry, Nancy. "The Controversy over the Immaculate Conception in Medieval and Renaissance Art, Literature, and Society." *Journal of Medieval and Renaissance Studies* 21, no. 2 (1991): 207–24.

McCracken, Peggy. *The Curse of Eve, the Wound of the Hero: Blood, Gender, and Medieval Literature*. Philadelphia: University of Pennsylvania Press, 2003.

McDonnell, E. W. *The Beguines and Beghars in Medieval Culture*. New Brunswick, NJ: Rutgers University Press, 1954.

McEachern, Claire. *Poetics of English Nationhood, 1590–1612*. Cambridge: Cambridge University Press, 1996.

McGrady, Deborah. "Joan of Arc and the Literary Imagination." In *Cambridge Companion to French Literature*, edited by John D. Lyons, 18–33. Cambridge: Cambridge University Press, 2016.

McGuire, Brian Patrick. *Jean Gerson and the Last Medieval Reformation*. University Park: Pennsylvania State University Press, 2005.

McSheffrey, Shannon. *Gender and Heresy: Women and Men in Lollard Communities, 1420–1530*. Philadelphia: University of Pennsylvania Press, 1995.

Meiss, Millard. "An Early Altarpiece from the Cathedral of Florence." *Metropolitan Museum of Art Bulletin* 12, no. 10 (1954): 302–17.

Meltzer, Françoise. *For Fear of the Fire: Joan of Arc and the Limits of Subjectivity*. Chicago: University of Chicago Press, 2001.

Menn, Esther Marie. *Judah and Tamar (Genesis 38) in Ancient Jewish Exegesis: Studies in Literary Exegesis*. Leiden: Brill, 1997.

Meredith, Peter. "Carved and Spoken Words: The Angelic Salutation, the Mary Play and South Walsham Church, Norfolk." *Leeds Studies in English* 32 (2001): 369–98.

———. "*Nolo Mortem* and the *Ludus Coventriae* Play of the Woman Taken in Adultery." *Medium Ævum* 38, no. 1 (1969): 38–54.

———. "Original-Staging Production of English Medieval Plays: Ideals, Evidence, and Practice." In *Popular Drama in Northern Europe in the Later Middle Ages: A Symposium*, edited by Flemming G. Andersen, Julia McGrew, Tom Pettitt, and Reinhold Schroder, 65–100. Odense, Denmark: Odense University Press, 1988.

Meredith, Peter, and John E. Tailby, eds. *The Staging of Religious Drama in Europe in the Later Middle Ages: Texts and Documents in English Translation*. Kalamazoo, MI: Medieval Institute Publications, 1983.

Metzler, Eric T. "The Miracle of the Pregnant Abbess: Refractions of the Virgin Birth." *Research on Medieval and Renaissance Drama* 52–53 (2014): 195–206.

Milgrom, Jacob. *Numbers: The JPS Torah Commentary*. Philadelphia: Jewish Publication Society, 1990.

Mill, Anna Jean. "Noah's Wife Again." *PMLA* 56, no. 3 (1941): 613–26.

Miller, B. D. H. "'She Who Hath Drunk Any Potion . . .'" *Medium Ævum* 31 (1962): 188–93.

Miller, Jeremy, and Philip Hoare. *Tania Kovats*. Oxford: Ruskin School of Drawing and Fine Art, 2010.

Miller, Sarah Alison. *Medieval Monstrosity and the Female Body*. New York: Routledge, 2010.

Mills, David. "'Some Precise Cittizins': Puritan Objections to Chester's Plays." *Leeds Studies in English* 29 (1999): 219–33.

Mills, Robert. "Ecco Homo." In *Gender and Holiness: Men, Women and Saints in Late Medieval Europe*, edited by Samantha J. E. Riches and Sarah Salih, 152–73. London: Routledge, 2002.

———. "Jesus as Monster." In *The Monstrous Middle Ages*, edited by Bettina Bildhauer and Robert Mills, 28–54. Toronto: University of Toronto Press, 2003.

Minnis, A. J., and A. B. Scott, eds. *Medieval Literary Theory and Criticism c. 1100–c. 1375: The Commentary Tradition*. Oxford: Clarendon, 1988.

Minov, Sergey. "Noah and the Flood in Gnosticism." In *Noah and His Book(s)*, edited by Michael E. Stone, Aryeh Amihay, and Vered Hillel, 215–36. Atlanta, GA: Society of Biblical Literature, 2010.

Moll, Richard. "Staging Disorder: Charivari in the *N-Town* Cycle." *Comparative Drama* 35, no. 2 (2001): 145–61.

Montrose, Louis. *The Subject of Elizabeth: Authority, Gender, and Representation*. Chicago: University of Chicago Press, 2006.

Moreton, C. E. "The Walsingham Conspiracy of 1537." *Bulletin of the Institute of Historical Research* 63 (1990): 29–43.

Morgan, Jacqueline A. "The Midwife in the *Holkham Bible Picture Book*." *Notes and Queries* 39, no. 1 (1992): 22–24.

Morrison, Susan Signe. *Excrement in the Late Middle Ages: Sacred Filth and Chaucer's Fecopoetics*. New York: Palgrave Macmillan, 2008.

———. *Women Pilgrims in Late Medieval England: Private Piety as Public Performance*. London: Routledge, 2000.

Mortensen, Reid. "Art, Expression, and the Offended Believer." In *Law and Religion*, edited by Rex J. Ahdar, 181–97. Burlington, VT: Ashgate, 2000.

Moughtin-Mumby, Sharon. *Sexual and Marital Metaphors in Hosea, Jeremiah, Isaiah, and Ezekiel*. Oxford: Oxford University Press, 2008.

Muir, Lynette. *The Biblical Drama of Medieval Europe*. Cambridge: Cambridge University Press, 1995.

———. "French Saint Plays." In *The Saint Play in Medieval Europe*, edited by Clifford Davidson, 123–80. Kalamazoo, MI: Medieval Institute Publications, 1986.

———. *Love and Conflict in Medieval Drama: The Plays and Their Legacy*. New York: Cambridge University Press, 2007.

Mulder-Bakker, Anneke. "Introduction." In *Sanctity and Motherhood: Essays on Holy Mothers in the Middle Ages*, edited by Anneke Mulder-Bakker, 3–30. New York: Garland, 1995.

Needham, Gwendolyn B. "New Light on Maids 'Leading Apes in Hell.'" *Journal of American Folklore* 75 (1962): 106–19.

Nelson, Alan H. *The Medieval English Stage: Corpus Christi Pageants and Plays*. Chicago: University of Chicago Press, 1974.

Newman, Barbara. *From Virile Woman to WomanChrist: Studies in Medieval Religion and Literature*. Philadelphia: University of Pennsylvania Press, 1995.

———. *God and the Goddesses: Vision, Poetry, and Belief in the Middle Ages*. Philadelphia: University of Pennsylvania Press, 2003.

———. *Sister of Wisdom: St. Hildegard's Theology of the Feminine*. Berkeley: University of California Press, 1997.

Nichols, Ann Eljenholm. "The Hierosphthitic Topos, or the Fate of Fergus: Notes on the N-Town Assumption." *Comparative Drama* 25, no. 1 (1991): 29–41.

Nicoll, Allardyce. *Masks, Mimes, and Miracles: Studies in the Popular Theatre*. New York: Cooper Square, 1963.

Niebrzydowski, Sue. *Bonoure and Buxum: A Study of Wives in Late Medieval English Literature*. Oxford: Peter Lang, 2006.

———. "Marian Literature." In *The History of British Women's Writing*, edited by L. McAvoy and D. Watt, 1:112–120. Basingstoke, UK: Palgrave Macmillan, 2011.

———. "Secular Women and Late-Medieval Marian Drama." *Yearbook of English Studies* 43 (2013): 121–39.

Nisse, Ruth. *Defining Acts: Drama and the Politics of Interpretation in Late Medieval England*. Notre Dame, IN: University of Notre Dame Press, 2005.

———. "Staged Interpretations: Civic Rhetoric and Lollard Politics in the York Plays." *Journal of Medieval and Early Modern Studies* 28, no. 2 (1998): 427–52.

Nixon, Virginia. *Mary's Mother: Saint Anne in Late Medieval Europe*. University Park: Pennsylvania State University Press, 2004.

Njus, Jesse. "Margery Kempe and the Spectatorship of Medieval Drama." *Fifteenth-Century Studies* 38 (2013): 123–52.

Nolan, Mary Lee, and Sidney Nolan. *Christian Pilgrimage in Modern Western Europe*. Chapel Hill: University of North Carolina Press, 1989.

Normington, Katie. "'Faming of the Shrews': Medieval Drama and Feminist Approaches." *Yearbook of English Studies* 43 (2013): 105–20.

——. *Gender and Medieval Drama*. Cambridge, UK: D. S. Brewer, 2004.

——. "'Have Her a Drink Full Good': A Comparative Analysis of Staging Temptation in the Newcastle Noah Play." In *Staging Scripture: Biblical Drama, 1350–1600*, edited by Peter Happe and Wim Husken, 166–81. Leiden: Brill, 2016.

Novikoff, Alex J. *The Medieval Culture of Disputation: Pedagogy, Practice, and Performance*. Philadelphia: University of Pennsylvania Press, 2013.

Oakes, Catherine. *Ora Pro Nobis: The Virgin as Intercessor in Medieval Art and Devotion*. Turnhout: Brepols, 2008.

O'Connell, Michael. "Continuities between 'Medieval' and 'Early Modern' Drama." In *A Companion to English Renaissance Literature and Culture*, edited by Michael Hattaway, 477–85. Oxford: Blackwell, 2000.

——. *The Idolatrous Eye: Iconoclasm and Theater in Early-Modern England*. Oxford: Oxford University Press, 2000.

O'Grady, Kathleen. "The Semantics of Taboo: Menstrual Prohibitions in the Hebrew Bible." In *Wholly Woman, Holy Blood: A Feminist Critique of Purity and Impurity*, edited by Kristin De Troyer, Judith A. Herbert, Judith Ann Johnson, and Anne-Marie Korte, 1–28. Harrisburg, PA: Trinity Press International, 2003.

Oleszkiewicz-Peralba, Malgorzata. *The Black Madonna in Latin America and Europe: Tradition and Transformation*. Albuquerque: University of New Mexico Press, 2007.

O'Malley, John. *Trent and All That: Renaming Catholicism in the Early Modern Era*. Cambridge, MA: Harvard University Press, 2002.

Orgel, Stephen. *Imagining Shakespeare: A History of Texts and Visions*. New York: Palgrave Macmillan, 2003.

Parish, Helen L. *Clerical Celibacy in the West, c. 1100–1700*. Burlington, VT: Ashgate, 2010.

——. *Clerical Marriage and the English Reformation: Precedent, Policy, and Practice*. Burlington, VT: Ashgate, 2000.

——. *Monks, Miracles and Magic: Reformation Representations of the Medieval Church*. London: Routledge, 2005.

Parker, John. *The Aesthetics of Antichrist*. Ithaca, NY: Cornell University Press, 2007.

——. "Holy Adultery: Marriage in *The Comedy of Errors*, *The Merchant of Venice*, and *The Merry Wives of Windsor*." In *The Oxford Handbook of Shakespearean Comedy*, edited by Heather Hirschfeld. Oxford: Oxford University Press, 2018.

——. "Valhalla is Burning: Theory, The Middle Ages, and Secularization." *PMLA* 130.3 (2015): 787–98.

——. "Who's Afraid of Darwin? Revisiting Chambers and Hardison . . . and Nietzsche," *Journal of Medieval and Early Modern Studies* 40, no. 1 (2010): 7–35.

Paster, Gail Kern. *Humoring the Body: Emotions and the Shakespearean Stage*. Chicago: University of Chicago Press, 2004.

Pastoureau, Michel. *Blue: The History of a Color*. Princeton, NJ: Princeton University Press, 2001.

Pearman, Tory Vandeventer. "'O Sweete Venym Queynte!': Pregnancy and the Disabled Female Body in the *Merchant's Tale*." In *Disability in the Middle Ages: Reconsiderations and Reverberations*, edited by Joshua R. Eyler, 25–37. Burlington, VT: Ashgate, 2010.

Pearson, Birger A. *Gnosticism, Judaism, and Egyptian Christianity*. Philadelphia: Fortress, 1990.

Peltomaa, Leena Mari. *The Image of the Virgin Mary in the Akathistos Hymn*. Leiden: Brill, 2001.

Peters, Christine. *Patterns of Piety: Women, Gender, and Religion in Late Medieval and Reformation England*. Cambridge: Cambridge University Press, 2003.

Petrosillo, Sara. "A Microhistory of the Womb from the N-Town Mary Plays to Gorboduc." *Journal of Medieval and Early Modern Studies* 47, no. 1 (2017): 121–46.

Philips, Helen. "'Almighty and Al Merciable Queene': Marian Titles and Marian Lyrics." In *Medieval Women: Texts and Contexts in Late Medieval Britain: Essays for Felicity Riddy*, edited by Jocelyn Wogan-Browne, R. Voaden, A. Diamond, A. M. Hutchison, C. Meale, and L. Johnson, 83–99. Turnhout: Brepols, 2000.

Plesch, Véronique. "Graffiti and Ritualization: San Sebastiano at Arborio." In *Medieval and Early Modern Ritual: Formalized Behavior in Europe, China, and Japan*, edited by Joelle Rollo-Koster, 127–46. Leiden: Brill, 2002.

Plummer, Marjorie Elizabeth. *From Priest's Whore to Pastor's Wife: Clerical Marriage and the Process of Reform in the Early German Reformation*. Burlington, VT: Ashgate, 2012.

Pollard, Anthony James. *Imagining Robin Hood: The Late-Medieval Stories in Historical Context*. London: Routledge, 2004.

Poos, L. R. "Sex, Lies, and the Church Courts of Pre-Reformation England." *Journal of Interdisciplinary History* 25, no. 4 (1995): 585–607.

Powell, Amy Knight. *Depositions: Scenes from the Late Medieval Church and the Modern Museum*. New York: Zone Books, 2012.

Power, Eileen. *Medieval Women*. Edited by M. M. Postan. Cambridge: Cambridge University Press, 1975.

Price, Merrall Llewelyn. "Re-membering the Jews: Theatrical Violence in the N-Town Marian Plays." *Comparative Drama* 41, no. 4 (2007–8): 439–63.

Prosser, Eleanor. *Drama and Religion in the English Mystery Plays: A Re-evaluation*. Stanford, CA: Stanford University Press, 1961.

Queller, Donald. *The Office of Ambassador in the Middle Ages*. Princeton, NJ: Princeton University Press, 1967.

Randall, Lillian. *Images in the Margins of Gothic Manuscripts*. Berkeley: University of California Press, 1966.

Reif, Stefan. "Early Rabbinic Exegesis of Genesis 38." In *The Exegetical Encounter between Jews and Christians in Late Antiquity*, edited by Emmanouela Grypeou and Helen Spurling, 221–44. Leiden: Brill, 2009.

Reilly, Frank. "Jane Schaberg, Raymond E. Brown, and the Problem of the Illegitimacy of Jesus." *Journal of Feminist Studies in Religion* 21 (2005): 57–80.

Reinhard, J. R. "Burning at the Stake in Mediaeval Law and Literature." *Speculum* 16, no. 2 (1941): 186–209.

Resnick, Irven M. "Peter Damian on the Restoration of Virginity: A Problem for Medieval Theology." *Journal of Theological Studies* 39, no. 1 (1988): 125–34.

Reynolds, Brian. *Gateway to Heaven: Marian Doctrine and Devotion, Imagery and Typology in the Patristic and Medieval Periods*. Vol. 1. New York: New City, 2012.

Rice, Nicole R., and Margaret Aziza Pappano. *The Civic Cycles: Artisan Drama and Identity in Premodern England*. ReFormations: Medieval and Early Modern. Notre Dame, IN: University of Notre Dame Press, 2015.

Ritchey, Sara. *Holy Matter: Changing Perceptions of the Material World in Late Medieval Christianity*. Ithaca, NY: Cornell University Press, 2014.

Ritson, Alicia. "Between Heaven and Hell: *The Holy Virgin Mary* at the Brooklyn Museum." In *Chris Ofili: Night and Day*, edited by Massimiliano Gioni, 163–81. New York: Skira Rizzoli, 2014.

Robertson, D. W. "The Doctrine of Charity in Medieval Literary Gardens." *Speculum* 26 (1951): 24–49.

Robertson, Jean, and D. J. Gordon, eds. *The Calendar of Dramatic Records in the Books of the Livery Companies of London*. Oxford: Oxford University Press, 1954.

Rogerson, Margaret. "Audience Responses and the York Corpus Christi Play." In *Staging Scripture: Biblical Drama, 1350–1600*, edited by Peter Happé and Wim Hüsken, 360–83. Leiden: Brill, 2016.

Ronen, Avraham. "Gozzoli's St. Sebastian Altarpiece in San Gimignano." *Mitteilungen Des Kunsthistorischen Institutes in Florenz* 32, no. 1/2 (1988): 77–126.

Roscow, Gregory H. *Syntax and Style in Chaucer's Poetry*. Woodbridge, UK: D. S. Brewer, 1981.

Rose, Martial. *Stories in Stone: The Medieval Roof Carvings of Norwich Cathedral*. New York: Thames and Hudson, 1997.

Rosenberg, Bruce A. "The Cherry Tree Carol and the *Merchant's Tale*." *Chaucer Review* 5, no. 4 (1971): 264–76.

Ross, Lawrence J. "Symbol and Structure in the *Secunda Pastorum*." *Comparative Drama* 1, no. 2 (1967): 122–49.

Rossiter, Arthur Percival. *English Drama from Early Times to the Elizabethans: Its Background, Origins, and Developments*. London: Hutchinson's University Library, 1950.

Rubin, Miri. *Corpus Christi: The Eucharist in Late Medieval Culture*. Cambridge: Cambridge University Press, 1991.

———. *Gentile Tales: The Narrative Assault on Late Medieval Jews*. Philadelphia: University of Pennsylvania Press, 2004.

———. *Mother of God: A History of the Virgin Mary*. New Haven, CT: Yale University Press, 2009.

Rudy, Kathryn M., and Barbara Baert, eds. *Weaving, Veiling, and Dressing: Textiles and Their Metaphors in the Late Middle Ages*. Turnhout: Brepols, 2007.

Salih, Sarah. *Versions of Virginity in Late Medieval England*. Cambridge, UK: D. S. Brewer, 2001.

Salisbury, Eve, Georgiana Donavin, and Merrall Llewelyn Price, eds. *Domestic Violence in Medieval Texts*. Gainesville: University of Florida Press, 2002.

Salter, Frederick Millet. "The Banns of the Chester Plays." *Review of English Studies* 16, no. 62 (1940): 137–48.

———. *Mediaeval Drama in Chester*. Toronto: University of Toronto Press, 1955.

Sander, Jochen, ed. *Albrecht Dürer: His Art in Context*. Munich: Prestel, 2013.

Sarna, Nahum M. *The JPS Torah Commentary: Genesis*. Philadelphia: Jewish Publication Society, 1989.

Sautman, Francesca. "Saint Anne in Folk Tradition: Late Medieval France." In *Interpreting Cultural Symbols: Saint Anne in Late Medieval Society*, edited by Kathleen Ashley and Pamela Sheingorn, 69–94. Athens: University of Georgia Press, 1990.

Schaberg, Jane. *The Illegitimacy of Jesus: A Feminist Theological Interpretation of the Infancy Narratives*. 2nd ed. Sheffield, UK: Sheffield Phoenix, 2006.

———. *Resurrection of Mary Magdalene: Legends, Apocrypha, and the Christian Testament*. New York: Continuum, 2002.

Schäfer, Peter. *Jesus in the Talmud*. Princeton, NJ: Princeton University Press, 2009.

Scheer, Monique. "From Majesty to Mystery: Change in the Meanings of Black Madonnas from the Sixteenth to Nineteenth Centuries." *American Historical Review* 107, no. 5 (2002): 1412–40.

Scherb, Victor. *Staging Faith: East Anglian Drama in the Later Middle Ages*. Madison, NJ: Fairleigh Dickinson University Press, 2001.

Schiller, Gertrud. *Iconography of Christian Art*. 2 vols. London: Lund Humphries, 1971.

Schmitt, Jean-Claude. *The Holy Greyhound: Guinefort, Healer of Children since the Thirteenth Century*. Translated by Martin Thom. Cambridge: Cambridge University Press, 1983.

Schreckenberg, Heinz. *The Jews in Christian Art: An Illustrated History*. New York: Continuum, 1996.

Schreyer, Kurt A. *Shakespeare's Medieval Craft: Remnants of the Mysteries on the London Stage*. Ithaca, NY: Cornell University Press, 2014.

Schrock, Chad. "The Ends of Reading in the *Merchant's Tale*." *Philological Quarterly* 91, no. 4 (2012): 591–609.

Schwarz, Kathryn. "The Wrong Question: Thinking through Virginity." *differences: A Journal of Feminist Cultural Studies* 13, no. 2 (2002): 1–34.

Seal, Samantha Katz. "Pregnant Desire: Eyes and Appetites in the *Merchant's Tale*." *Chaucer Review* 48, no. 3 (2014): 284–306.

Sergi, Matthew. "Beyond Theatrical Marketing: Play Banns in the Records of Kent, Sussex, and Lincolnshire." *Medieval English Theatre* 36 (2014): 3–23.

Sheingorn, Pamela. "Appropriating the Holy Kinship: Gender and Family History." In *Interpreting Cultural Symbols: Saint Anne in Late Medieval Society*, edited by Kathleen Ashley and Pamela Sheingorn, 169–98. Athens: University of Georgia Press, 1990.

———. "Fragments of the Biography of Joseph the Carpenter." In *Framing the Family: Narrative and Representation in the Medieval and Early Modern Periods*, edited by Rosalynn Voaden and Diane Wolfthal, 161–80. Tempe: Arizona Center for Medieval and Renaissance Studies, 2005.

Shepard, Odell. *The Lore of the Unicorn*. New York: Harper Colophon Books, 1979.

Shershow, Scott Cutler. *Puppets and "Popular" Culture*. Ithaca, NY: Cornell University Press, 1995.

Shoemarker, Stephen J. *Ancient Traditions of the Virgin Mary's Dormition and Assumption*. Oxford: Oxford University Press, 2003.

Shoulson, Jeffrey S. *Fictions of Conversion: Jews, Christians, and Cultures of Change in Early Modern England*. Philadelphia: University of Pennsylvania Press, 2013.

Sidhu, Nicole Nolan. *Indecent Exposure: Gender, Politics, and Obscene Comedy in Middle English Literature*. Philadelphia: University of Pennsylvania Press, 2016.

Silva, F. Vaz de. "The Madonna and the Cuckoo: An Exploration in European Symbolic Conceptions." *Society for Comparative Study of Society and History* 46, no. 2 (2004): 273–99.

Simeonova, Kristina. "The Aesthetic Function of the Carnivalesque in Medieval Drama." In *Bakhtin, Carnival and Other Subjects*, edited by David Shepherd, 70–79. Atlanta: Rodopi, 1993.

Simpson, James. *Reform and Cultural Revolution*. Vol. 2 of *The Oxford English Literary History*. Oxford: Oxford University Press, 2002.

———. *Under the Hammer: Iconoclasm in the Anglo-American Tradition*. Oxford: Oxford University Press, 2010.

Sissa, Giula. "Maidenhood without Maidenhead: The Female Body in Ancient Greece." In *Before Sexuality: The Construction of Erotic Experience in the Ancient Greek World*, edited by David M. Halperin, John J. Winkler, and Froma I. Zeitlin, 339–64. Princeton, NJ: Princeton University Press, 1990.

Smith, Lesley Janette. *Medieval Exegesis in Translation: Commentaries on the Book of Ruth*. Kalamazoo, MI: Medieval Institute Publications, 1996.

Sommerville, John. *The Secularization of Early Modern England: From Religious Culture to Religious Faith*. Oxford: Oxford University Press, 1992.

Sottocornola, Franco. "Tradition and the Doubt of St. Joseph Concerning Mary's Virginity." *Marianum* 19 (1957): 127–41.

Southern, R. W. *The Making of the Middle Ages*. New Haven, CT: Yale University Press, 1953.

Stanbury, Sarah. *The Visual Object of Desire in Late Medieval England*. Philadelphia: University of Pennsylvania Press, 2008.

Stanton, Elizabeth Cady. *The Woman's Bible*. 1895–98. 2 vols. Boston: Northeastern University Press, 1993.

Stein, Stephen J. *The Shaker Experience in America: A History of the United Society of Believers*. New Haven, CT: Yale University Press, 1992.

Steinberg, Leo. *The Sexuality of Christ in Renaissance Art and in Modern Oblivion*. 2nd edition. Chicago: University of Chicago Press, 1996.

Stevens, Andrea Ria. *Inventions of the Skin: The Painted Body in Early English Drama, 1400–1642*. Edinburgh: Edinburgh University Press, 2013.

Stevens, Martin. *Four Middle English Mystery Cycles: Textual, Contextual and Critical Interpretations*. Princeton, NJ: Princeton University Press, 1987.

———. "The Missing Parts of the Towneley Cycle." *Speculum* 45 (1970): 254–65.

Stevenson, Jill. *Performance, Cognitive Theory, and Devotional Culture: Sensual Piety in Late Medieval York*. New York: Palgrave Macmillan, 2010.

Stokes, James. "The Ongoing Exploration of Women and Performance in Early Modern England: Evidences, Issues, and Questions." *Shakespeare Bulletin* 33, no. 1 (2015): 9–31.

Strack, Hermann L., and Paul Billerbeck. *Kommentar zum Neuen Testament aus Talmud und Midrash*. 6 vols. Munich: C. H. Beck, 1922–61.

Strong, Roy. *The Cult of Elizabeth: Elizabethan Portraiture and Pageantry*. London: Thames and Hudson, 1977.

Studwell, William. *The Christmas Carol Reader*. New York: Routledge, 2011.

Sugano, Douglas. "'This Game Wel Pleyd in Good A-ray': The N-Town Playbooks and East Anglian Games." *Comparative Drama* 28, no. 2 (1994): 221–34.

Sweeney, Marvin A. "Isaiah 1–39." In *The Prophets: Fortress Commentary on the Bible*, edited by Gale A. Yee, Hugh R. Page Jr., and Matthew J. M. Coomber, 673–97. Minneapolis: Fortress, 2016.

Symes, Carol. *A Common Stage: Theater and Public Life in Medieval Arras.* Ithaca, NY: Cornell University Press, 2007.

Szpiech, Ryan. *Conversion and Narrative: Reading and Religious Authority in Medieval Polemic.* Philadelphia: University of Pennsylvania Press, 2012.

Takács, Sarolta A. *Vestal Virgins, Sibyls, and Matrons: Women in Roman Religion.* Austin: University of Texas Press, 2008.

Taylor, Charles. *A Secular Age.* Cambridge, MA: Harvard University Press, 2007.

Temperman, Jeroen. "'Mother of God, Drive Putin Away': On Blasphemy and Activist Art in the Jurisprudence of the European Court of Human Rights." In *Blasphemy and Freedom of Expression: Comparative, Theoretical and Historical Reflections after the Charlie Hebdo Massacre*, edited by Jeroen Temperman and András Koltay, 294–316. Cambridge: Cambridge University Press, 2017.

Toelken, Barre. "Riddles Wisely Expounded." *Western Folklore* 25, no. 1 (1966): 1–16.

Tolan, John V. *Saracens: Islam in the Medieval European Imagination.* New York: Columbia University Press, 2002.

Traver, Hope. *The Four Daughters of God: A Study of the Versions of This Allegory.* Philadelphia: John Winston, 1907.

Trexler, Richard C. "Florentine Religious Experience: The Sacred Image." *Studies in the Renaissance* 19 (1972): 7–41.

Tricomi, Albert. "Joan la Pucelle and the Inverted Saints Play in *1 Henry VI*." *Renaissance and Reformation* 25 (2001): 5–31.

Twycross, Meg. "'Transvestism' in the Mystery Plays." *Medieval English Theatre* 5, no. 2 (1983): 123–80.

Van Der Horst, Pieter W. "Sex, Birth, Purity and Asceticism in the Protevangelium Jacobi." In *A Feminist Companion to Mariology*, edited by Amy-Jill Levine and Maria Mayo Robbins, 55–66. New York: Continuum, 2005.

Vanita, Ruth. "Mariological Memory in *The Winter's Tale* and *Henry VIII*." *SEL: Studies in English Literature 1500–1900* 40, no. 2 (2000): 311–37.

Van Voorst, Robert E. *Jesus outside the New Testament: An Introduction to the Ancient Evidence.* Grand Rapids, MI: Wm. B. Eerdmans, 2000.

Vasvari, Louise O. "Joseph on the Margin: The Mérode Tryptic and Medieval Spectacle." *Mediaevalia* 18 (1995): 163–89.

Vienne-Guerrin, Nathalie. *Shakespeare's Insults: A Pragmatic Dictionary.* Arden Shakespeare. London: Bloomsbury, 2016.

Vloberg, Maurice. "Iconography of the Immaculate Conception." In *The Dogma of the Immaculate Conception: History and Significance*, edited by Edward Dennis O'Connor, 463–502. Notre Dame, IN: University of Notre Dame Press, 1958.

Vriend, J. *The Blessed Virgin Mary in the Medieval Drama of England.* Pumerend, Holland: J. Muuusses, 1928.

Vuong, Lily C. *Gender and Purity in the Protevangelium of James.* Tübingen, Germany: Mohr Siebeck, 2013.

Waller, Gary. *The Virgin Mary in Late Medieval and Early Modern English Literature and Popular Culture.* Cambridge: Cambridge University Press, 2011.

——. "The Virgin's 'Pryvytes': Walsingham and the Late Medieval Sexualization of the Virgin." In *Walsingham in Literature and Culture from the Middle Ages to Modernity,* edited by Dominic Janes and Gary Waller, 113–30. Farnham, UK: Ashgate, 2010.

Walsh, P. G., ed. *Andreas Capellanus on Love.* London: Duckworth, 1982.

Walter, Katie L. "The Child before the Mother: Mary and the Excremental in *The Prickynge of Love.*" In *Words and Matter: The Virgin Mary in Late Medieval and Early Modern Parish Life,* edited by Jonas Carlquist and Virginia Langum, 149–63. Stockholm: Sällskapet Runica et Mediævalia, 2015.

Walther, Ingo F., and Norbert Wolf. *Codices Illustres: The World's Most Famous Illuminated Manuscripts, 400–1600.* London: Taschen, 2001.

Warner, Marina. *Alone of All Her Sex: The Myth and Cult of the Virgin Mary.* New York: Knopf, 1976.

——. *Joan of Arc: The Image of Female Heroism.* Berkeley: University of California Press, 1981.

Warton, Thomas. *The History of English Poetry, from the Close of the Eleventh to the Commencement of the Eighteenth Century.* 3 vols. London, 1778.

Waters, Claire. *Translating "Clergie": Status, Education, and Salvation in Thirteenth-Century Vernacular Texts.* Philadelphia: University of Pennsylvania Press, 2016.

Waterton, Edmund. *Pietas Mariana Britannica: A History of English Devotion to the Most Blessed Virgin Marye Mother of God.* London: St. Joseph's Catholic Library, 1879.

Watson, Nicholas. "Censorship and Cultural Change: Vernacular Theology, the Oxford Translation Debate, and Arundel's Constitutions of 1409." *Speculum* 70, no. 4 (1995): 822–64.

Weber, Max. *The Protestant Ethic and the Spirit of Capitalism.* Translated by Talcott Parsons. New York: Routledge Classics, 2001.

Weinstein, Donald, and Rudolph M. Bell. *Saints and Society: The Two Worlds of Western Christendom.* Chicago: University of Chicago Press, 1982.

Welsh, Jennifer. *The Cult of Saint Anne in Medieval and Early Modern Europe.* London: Routledge, 2017.

Wessel, Susan. *Cyril of Alexandria and the Nestorian Controversy: The Making of a Saint and of a Heretic.* Oxford: Oxford University Press, 2004.

Westermann, Claus. *Genesis 1–11: A Commentary.* Minneapolis: Augsburg, 1984.

White, Paul Whitfield. "Reforming Mysteries' End: A New Look at Protestant Intervention in English Provincial Drama." *Journal of Medieval and Early Modern Studies* 29, no. 1 (1999): 111–47.

Whitford, David Mark. *The Curse of Ham in the Early Modern Era: The Bible and Justifications for Slavery.* Burlington, VT: Ashgate, 2009.

Whiting, Robert. "Abominable Idols: Images and Image-Breaking under Henry VIII." *Journal of Ecclesiastical History* 33, no. 1 (1982): 30–47.

——. *The Reformation of the English Parish Church.* Cambridge: Cambridge University Press, 2010.

Wickham, Glynne, Herbert Berry, and William Ingram, eds. *English Professional Theatre, 1530–1660*. Cambridge: Cambridge University Press, 2000.

Wilken, Robert Louis. *The Christians as the Romans Saw Them*. 2nd ed. New Haven, CT: Yale University Press, 2003.

Williams, Anne. "Satirizing the Sacred: Humor in Saint Joseph's Veneration and Early Modern Art." *Journal of Historians of Netherlandish Art* 10, no. 1 (2018): 1–45.

Williams, Gordon. *Shakespeare's Sexual Language: A Glossary*. London: Continuum, 2006.

Williams-Boyarin, Adrienne. *Miracles of the Virgin in Medieval England: Law and Jewishness in Marian Legends*. Cambridge, UK: D. S. Brewer, 2010.

——, ed. *Miracles of the Virgin in Middle English*. Peterborough, ON: Broadview, 2015.

Williamson, Paul, ed. *Object of Devotion: Medieval English Alabaster Sculpture from the Victoria and Albert Museum*. Alexandria, VA: Art Services International, 2010.

Wilson, Carolyn. *St. Joseph in Italian Renaissance Society and Art: New Directions and Interpretations*. Philadelphia: Saint Joseph's University Press, 2001.

Winiarski, Catherine E. "Adultery, Idolatry, and the Subject of Monotheism." *Religion & Literature* 38, no. 3 (2006): 41–63.

Winstead, Karen. *Virgin Martyrs: Legends of Sainthood in Late Medieval England*. Ithaca, NY: Cornell University Press, 1997.

Witt, Elizabeth A. *Contrary Marys in Medieval English and French Drama*. New York: Peter Lang, 1995.

Wittern-Keller, Laura, and Raymond J. Habersku. *The Miracle Case: Film Censorship and the Supreme Court*. Lawrence: University Press of Kansas, 2008.

Wogan-Browne, Jocelyn. *Saints' Lives and Women's Literary Culture, 1150–1300: Virginity and Its Authorizations*. Oxford: Oxford University Press, 2001.

Wood, Charles T. "The Doctor's Dilemma: Sin, Salvation, and the Menstrual Cycle in Medieval Thought." *Speculum* 56, no. 4 (1981): 710–27.

Woods, Gillian. *Shakespeare's Unreformed Fictions*. Oxford: Oxford University Press, 2013.

Woolf, Rosemary. *The English Mystery Plays*. Berkeley: University of California Press, 1972.

——. "The Theme of Christ the Lover-Knight in Medieval English Literature." *Review of English Studies* 13, no. 49 (1962): 1–16.

Yanson, Margarita. "'Christ as a Windblown Sleeve': The Ambiguity of Clothing as a Sign in Gottfried von Straßburg's *Tristan*." In *Encountering Medieval Textiles and Dress: Objects, Texts, Images*, edited by D. G. Koslin and Janet E. Snyder, 121–36. New York: Palgrave Macmillan, 2002.

Young, Sera. *Craving Earth: Understanding Pica—The Urge to Eat Clay, Starch, Ice, and Chalk*. New York: Columbia University Press, 2011.

Zervos, George Themolis. "Christmas with Salome." In *A Feminist Companion to Mariology*, edited by Amy-Jill Levine with Maria Mayo Robbins, 77–100. London: Continuum, 2005.

Ziolkowski, Jan. "Juggling the Middle Ages: The Reception of *Our Lady's Tumbler* and *Le Jongleur de Notre-Dame*." *Studies in Medievalism* 15 (2006): 157–197.

Index

CPSIA information can be obtained
at www.ICGtesting.com
Printed in the USA
LVHW031819271218
601925LV00004B/16/P